What's up with...

GABY VARGAS
YORDI ROSADO

What's up with...!

- YOUR BODY
- GUYS
- YOUR LOOKS
- DRUGS
- INTERNET
- SEX
- AND EVERYTHING ELSE...

AGUILAR

What's up with...

INDEX

Chapter 1
What's up with... my body

Chapter 2
What's up with... my relationships

Chapter 3
What's up with... my looks

Chapter 4
What's up with... my sexuality

Chapter 5
What's up with... my mind

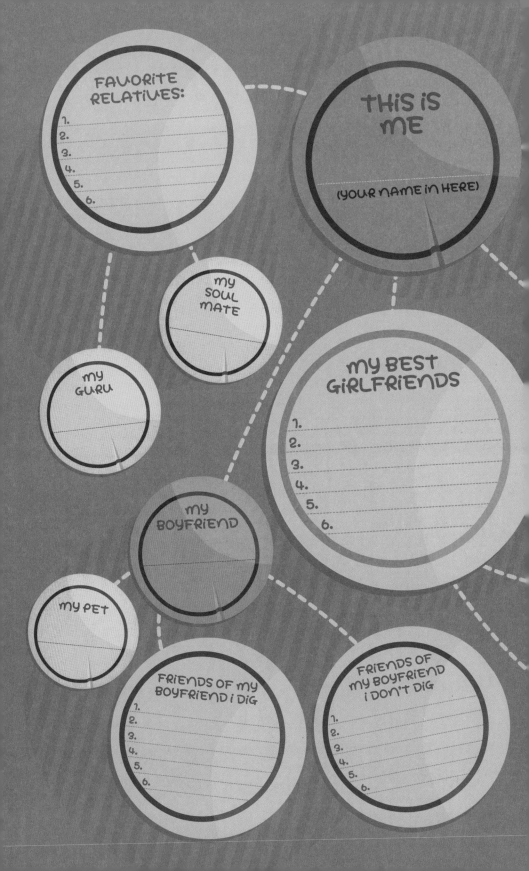

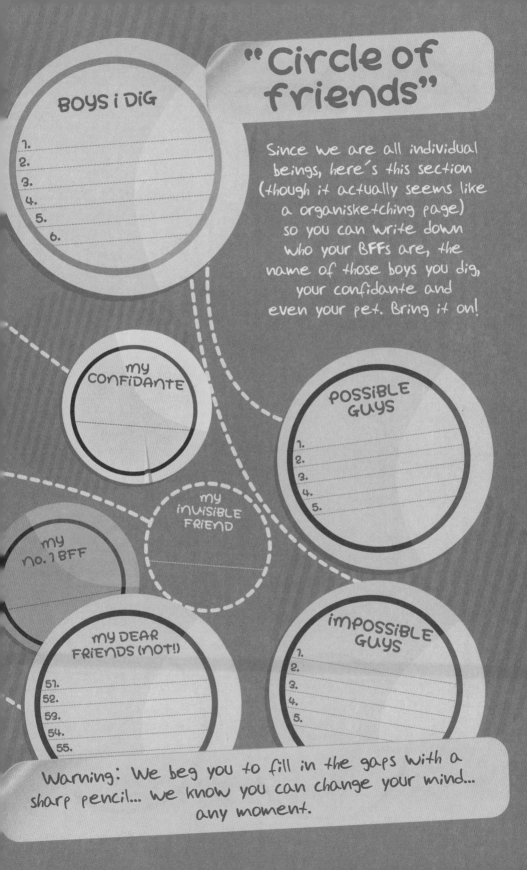

Foreword

What's up with...
welcome

Hello!!! In the pages of *What's Up With...* we'd like to provide you with all the information you need in order to find out what's going on with you, what to expect, as well as those things that you've been waiting for. Of course, we'll try to do this in a fun, cool and, at the same time, informative way.

We know that you probably freak out every now and then. Well, take it easy! The things that we talk about in this book are not only happening to you! Actually, many girls—probably every single one—are going through the same. The difference, you'll see, is in the way you face and solve these situations.

What's Up With... is divided into five general topics: your body, your relationships, your looks, your sexuality and your mind. The book has been designed in such a way that you can read it however you wish: from the very first page to the end or in sections. It depends entirely on how you want to do it.

Both of us had a great time writing this book. We also learned a lot. Perhaps the combination of Gaby and Yordi seems a bit odd, and maybe you're even asking yourself: "Why did these two get together to write this book?" Well, we did it because we believe that the difference in our ages, genders and ways of thinking actually compliment the book—making it even more interesting.

The idea popped up while we were jogging on the gym's treadmills. As soon as we realized that neither of us would ever become Olympic medalists, we ran... but in another direction.

We went on to interview girls who could help us to understand their worries and concerns, and we consulted specialists from diverse backgrounds and fields of study to make sure that you are provided with the most accurate and trustworthy information.

Naturally, we sometimes argued about lexicon and language, the way to approach certain issues and even about the jokes that were to be included. The mission of the book always remained clear, though: to *inform you in the most objective and neutral possible way so that you would have the necessary tools to make your own choices when dealing with the issues of adolescence.*

You are going to love this book's Interactive Zone. You'll be able to do cool stuff, like writing the name of your ex boyfriends in a cemetery, a yearbook so you can classify your school's groups of people, a lab full of toads so you can keep track of how many you've had to kiss before meeting your prince... and so on.

We'd want this book to be like a diary as well. Keep it with you always, so when you become an adult you can live this stage of life again. This way you'll be able to recall your concerns, your preferences, your friends, and even your ex boyfriends.

We really hope you enjoy reading the book as much as we enjoyed putting it together. We'll definitely feel that our work has been worthwhile if *What's Up With...* helps you in even the slightest way.

GABY Y YORDI

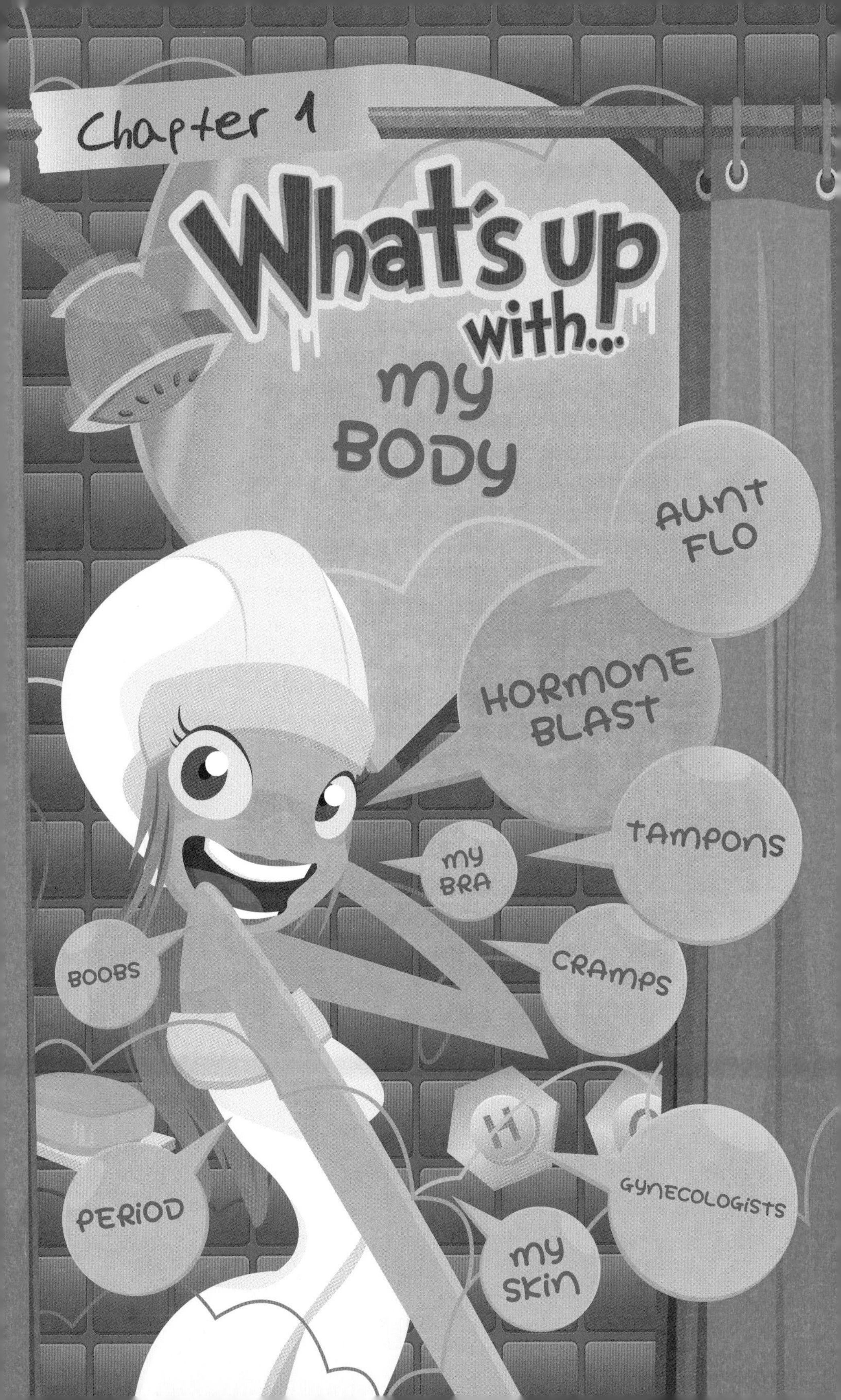
Chapter 1
What's up with...
my BODY
AUNT FLO
HORMONE BLAST
TAMPONS
my BRA
BOOBS
CRAMPS
PERIOD
GYNECOLOGISTS
my SKIN

Between ages nine and 13, it seems that pretty much every day is your birthday. You wake up and there's always something new… but on your body! And just like on your birthdays, though you can get some awesome stuff, you can also get the type of things that make you think: "What?!" And unlike birthdays, none of these presents can be taken back to the shop.

The revolution that your body is going through can seem unbelievable. When you notice the first changes, you start saying things like: "Jeez! My boobs are getting bigger." Then, you either get all excited about it and get yourself a hot t-shirt to show off nature's blessings… or you simply refuse to accept the changes and hide them as much as you can.

It's quite funny, actually: first you feel ashamed, but then you kind of feel happy about them. If your boobs really do get as big as those of a *big* top model—without her face or legs —you're likely to turn a bit shy again.

And then, it hits you:

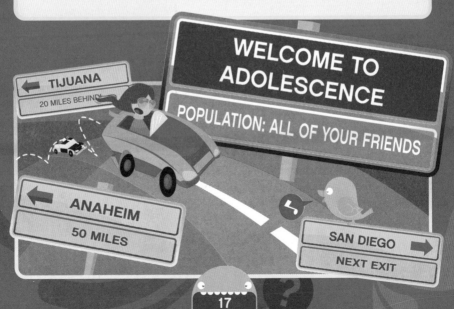

TIJUANA
20 MILES BEHIND!

WELCOME TO
ADOLESCENCE

POPULATION: ALL OF YOUR FRIENDS

ANAHEIM
50 MILES

SAN DIEGO
NEXT EXIT

Adolescence is also known in the adult world as:

the awkward age

the time when i don't give a damn, and if my folks don't like it, i couldn't care less. The kids are having a pubefest.

The teen-loathe-age or The abhorrent teens

it's the "Rite of passage".

Adolescence is an awesome stage. It's fun and cool, but it can also get way complicated.

It's not only about changes in the body. You'll start to notice that the way you interact with your friends and family will change as well. Have you noticed the variations in the way you think and feel yet?

The games you used to play as a young girl can be dangerous now. If you start playing doctor with your boyfriend (you know, the shots and stuff), you might end up playing mom and dad—in real life. And the story won't end there, but that... that's another story that we're going to get to later on.

The thing is, you're entering one of life's most marvelous stages. Throughout this chapter we're going to talk about the changes your body will experience. But before going on, try answering the following test to find out how much of an adolescent you are:

Abhorrence test

IMA

INSTITUTE OF ABHORRENCE AUTOTEST Nº 1
PROMOTING SOCIETIES WITH HAPPY TEENAGERS

	AUTO TEST NO. 1
RESULTS	THE BEGINNING OF ABHORRENCE

Our test's been designed by a select team of specialists. Please read carefully before answering. Avoid copying or any other method that may be classified as cheating.

YES NO You don't feel understood and you sense more pressures.

YES NO You are in a really bad mood, Grinchlike.

YES NO Your level of tolerance used to be 100%, and now it's more like 35%.

YES NO Being with your friends is the best thing in the world.

YES NO You're very concerned about your looks.

YES NO You question every single word that comes from your parents: the way you're supposed to dress and talk, permissions to go out…

YES NO You're hypersensitive.

YES NO Your group of friends is a treasure for you.

YES NO It's been over two years since you last played with your Barbie dolls.

YES NO You're happy one moment, but then you feel like crying!

YES NO You answer back at your parents all the time –even if they actually didn't formulate a question.

YES NO You don't even understand yourself.

· WHAT'S UP WITH… THE TEST ·

HB 2

19

YES NO You've got thousands of problems with your parents. You don't want them to get involved in your life, and every time you get scolded you simply pretend they don't exist.

YES NO That guy that used to be cute is now soooo hot. Moreover, you want to kiss him all day long. Even his braces seem sexy now.

YES NO The way you view things has changed: now you look at your boobs more often than you read your books.

YES NO The things you did for fun now seem lame.

YES NO You have super unstable self-esteem.

YES NO You used to agree wiith everything your parents said; now their suggestions don't seem that cool.

YES NO Planet Earth's got four elements: earth, fire, wind and water. You've got your own as well: parties, clothing, friends and music.

If you answered YES 1 – 3 times, you're an adolescent.
If you answered YES 4 – 10 times, you're a complete adolescent.
If you answered YES 11 – 19 times, your degree of adolescence is so high that your picture should be included in the Encyclopedia of Adolescence.

Boobs

People refer to breasts with lots of words: jugs, titties, boobs, knockers, melons, knobs, a rack... Boobs are pretty much the pinnacle of female sexuality, although some men actually have breasts too (check out the professional wrestlers on TV! They usually chart in at size 38B).

Plenty of girls feel frankly embarrassed about their boobs. Some prefer walking humpbacked to try to minimize the sight of them; others wear Winnie the Pooh sweatshirts hoping people will mistake their breasts for the bear's yellow cheeks (Poor Pooh! You'll make him gain 15 pounds in a go!).

And without any doubt, there are also girls who just can't wait to see their timid little hills turn into the Colorado Rockies.

Breasts grow thanks to estrogens.

Estro… what?

Estrogens are hormones that stimulate the growth of the mammary glands. They convince your body to build up fatty tissue around the glands as a protective measure since your body is also creating a network of milk ducts to be used later on for breastfeeding.

What type of boobs do you have?

Once you welcome your boobs into your life, you'll start spotting boobs absolutely everywhere! (Yep, just like boys do, although guys will keep doing it till the end of time.) Big ones, small ones, the divorcees (they go differents ways), the friendly (always sticking together), the dreamers (always looking to the sky) or the depressed ones (looking always down)… you'll find there's all types of them.

Smaller! Bigger! Can they both at least be the same size?

When it comes to the size and shape of boobs, there are no established rules. But it's super important to keep in mind that all of them are absolutely normal.

Perhaps you think your own boobs are bigger or smaller than those of the rest of the girls in your class. They're either medium-sized grapefruits or small-looking lemons. Don't sweat it! The truth is that no girl is ever completely happy with her own set—always wanting them smaller, bigger, more even or more rounded or pointier. Asymmetric breasts are quite common as well, but it doesn't matter whether one boob is bigger than the other one, nor does it matter if they seem a little cross-eyed. They are absolutely normal. With time, almost all breasts achieve balance—so relax!

The size of your boobs will be changing constantly. As you approach your period—and while it lasts—you will find them slightly bigger and more sensitive. During that time of the month it will seem they've been pumped up but... they'll deflate afterwards, so don't call victory till the last whistle.

Every woman develops in a different way. Boobs can reach their full potential in either three months of growth, or it may take them 10 years. Seriously.

However, if your 55 year old aunt is flat chested yet still hopeful, you will have to give her the bad news: "Hey, sit down, we need to have a talk."

Giant pumpkins

tiny peas

Huge watermelons

Perfect apples

juicy oranges

Round melons

And how are yours, girl?

Nipples

Available in all sizes and colors. Especially sensitive to temperature changes. Really! They contract themselves when it gets chilly, just like they do with sexual arousal. So if you're just cold, wear a thicker bra; you could also try a couple of skin-colored patches, the kind especially made for these situations. No patches? Try band-aids—thought they're the pirated version, they'll work perfectly fine.

If that isn't enough, put on a ski jacket or a thicker sweater. People will barely see your face.

In cases like these, all men tend to behave like little boys. Trust us: they'll feel equally embarrassed if they realize that you've noticed them looking at your boobs, so feel free to look right back at them.

LEFT   RIGHT

As we mentioned, there's a wide variety of nipples. Some of them are inverted—usually turned just slightly inwards cause they're afraid to come out! Inverted nipples are also absolutely normal and they tend to loosen up closer to age 18.

Hair may grow around your nipples. If you don't want to look like a werewolf, try getting rid of them with a pair of scissors or tweezers. Just be careful.

It is also normal to have one nipple harder or larger than the other one. If there's an odd change, though, don't hesitate to go to the doctor for a check-up.

Boobs should be protected. They also need to be kept in their comfort zone to avoid unnecessary bouncing. Boobs need somewhere cushy to remain stable amidst this world's uncertainties. So let us introduce you to...

Your Royal Highness: the bra!

Chronicle of a bra foretold

The very first time your mom buys you a bra, a bodice, or any sort of little top that shows everyone your navel, you will obviously feel immensely embarrassed.

First, because moms just love to introduce daughters to the wonderful world of womanhood. Don't let them get obsessed with it, least of all in front of all your friends. It's bad enough, but you're going to make it through.

The usual comments from your mom's part of the world will be: "I bought Pauline her very first little bra. It's adorable and just so teeny tiny." What's the deal with informing Aunt Anne and Cousin Tricia that your boobs are developing anyway? Well your mom is just happy to see you grow and she won't mind broadcasting it.

When you both arrive to the boutique she'll likely ask—quite loudly—like 20 times, to the store clerk: "Which size, do you think, would suit my little girl?" If someone in the store hasn't noticed that she's getting you your very first bra, it's your mom's job to point it out to them. And, to top it all off, the guy you like the most will have been dragged by his mom into the same boutique that very same day. Moms try to embarrass their kids all at once, so as to save energy.

Then your mom will actually come into the fitting room to provide special assistance so you can learn the difficult art of fastening up your first bra. Later on, you'll find out by yourself if it fits you better with clips or some special knitted adjustable device.

Just pray to Saint Bra that your mom doesn't go further adjusting the straps of your brand new bra in front of everyone. That would be quite awful.

On the other hand, you could also be the sort of girl who's dying to wear a bra because all of your friends already have one... and are showing it off! Some might even think about emailing a pic: "My boobs' first hammock."

Either way, keep in mind that your mother is just trying to help. She probably doesn't notice that these things can actually be embarrassing. Talk to her; she'll get it, without a doubt.

I want to change shoes, hairdo... and boobs!

There's a wide range of things you can do to change your boobs. You can try padded bras, socks, tissue paper, the shoulder pads of one of your mom's old jackets and even makeup. You can be like a TV star sometimes or just be yourself and, whichever way you try, you're going to come out perfectly normal.

The important thing is that you realize that no woman needs to change her breasts in order to improve herself. A pair of breasts cannot define your self-esteem, personality or the way you appreciate life. Don't forget: you are much—MUCH—more than a pair of boobs.

The bigger ones can cause problems like chronic backaches, painful shoulders, and some pretty hardcore neck problems (in the worst case scenario, your boyfriend will start using them as pillows). In these cases, some women go through breast-reduction surgery. They do feel much better, but this kind of treatment is relatively radical and not the kind of thing you can do on your own until you're at least 18. And it's only rarely that the breasts of someone under 18 develop to such an extent that medical intervention is necessary—so please, don't get yourself too worked up yet.

It seems that talking about breast implants and similar enhancements like plastic surgery is absolutely normal nowadays. Don't forget that having your boobs done is a serious personal decision and there are a lot of implications. Despite recent technological advances, implants can still cause complications in some women and they are not the sort of thing one does on a whim. There are cases, however, in which implants work perfectly fine.

Breast enlargement or enhancement is positively discouraged before you are age 18 and with good reason. Your breasts are still developing—and so is your mind. Even though some women may feel more secure with a new set of boobs, these will never—ever—make you a better or worse person.

Genitals!

The hormone blast

YES!

Rounder hips

Body change!

If all of a sudden you feel that your body is undergoing a revolution, don't worry. That's also totally and absolutely normal: a massive army of hormones has taken over your insides.

Your hips will be their first target. They'll turn rounder while your waistline accentuates. Soon, your external genitals will start growing hair, a bit darker than the hair in the rest of your body and your internal genitals will be changing too. Now, if you were daydreaming during your Sex Ed sessions and they seem even weirder than an A+ in Math, you should definitely check this out.

You do know what we're talking about, don't you?

Some parts of your genitals are outside you body (although that doesn't necessarily mean that they're clearly visible). Some others are inside. Knowing what is going on down there is very, very important.

On the blackboard:

1. pubis
2. vulva
3. labia
4. clitoris
5. urethra

Pubis

The genital zone starts here. The pubis is an elevated area, slightly above the pubic bone, that grows hair during puberty.

Vulva

It includes the labia majora (exterior lips) and the clitoris. Exploring this area sounds like a great idea, but you'll definitely need to be a professional contortionist to peep properly. A small mirror may come in handy. Just put it between your legs and feel free to check yourself out.

Labia

The first set of labia is on the outside of your body. Their mission is to protect the rest of your sexual organs—that's why they get covered up with pubic hair. The second set of labia (labia minora), however, is the door to your vagina. They're smaller, hairless and mega-sensitive. And of course, this little door has no bell to ring.

Clitoris

Thousands of men have tried to find the clitoris throughout their lives only to sadly give up. If you look towards the upper part of your genitals, you will see something like a small button. This button, however, is formed by thousands of supersensitive nerve endings. It gets stimulated when it's touched, and the tissue expands when sexual arousal occurs or during sex.

The sole mission of the clitoris is to generate sexual pleasure. All fun and no work! Once an orgasm is over or sexual arousal has passed, this tiny button rests and goes back to its normal, smaller size.

Urethra

Your system gets rid of urine through this tiny tube. It's right in the middle of the clitoris and the vagina, and it's not a sexual organ.

The hidden ones

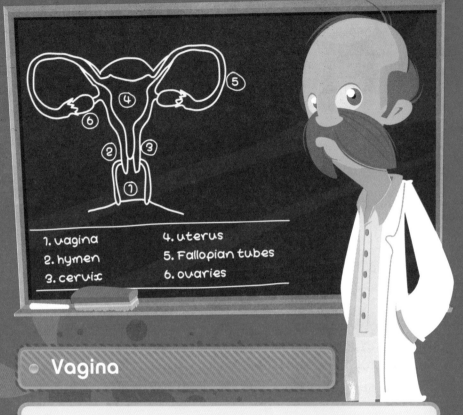

1. vagina
2. hymen
3. cervix
4. uterus
5. Fallopian tubes
6. ovaries

Vagina

The vagina is a muscular canal that goes all the way from the uterus to the vulva. The vagina is in charge of letting out menstrual blood and letting in your partner's penis during sex. It is also the last stretch that a baby must cross before it's born—and that's why the walls are so elastic and will stretch considerably.

The internal walls are rarely dry, and the degree of moisture varies depending on the stage of your menstrual cycle. As your period comes closer, you'll notice that your vagina is drier.

The moistest days happen when you're about to ovulate (between 10 to 15 days prior to your period).

When something in a magazine or on TV turns you on, a few glands immediately receive the following message from your brain: "Lubricate and get ready for penetration!" But what's even more amazing about this organ is that it shelters the vaginal flora: its own defense system against infections.

The germs of the vaginal flora keep the walls just as acidic as needed and fight off most—but not all—invading bacteria.

Every time your period starts, the cells in both the uterus and the vagina either transform or die—physiological hygiene at its best. So you don't need to worry too much about the inner part, just do keep your outside clean!

Hymen

Without any doubt, the hymen is a celebrity in the world of virginity fantasy. In reality, for ages people have been concerned about this super thin and permeable (microperforated) membrane located at the entrance of the vagina. At times, the tissue can break or tear apart due to just brusque movements. Some women bleed during their first sex encounter—or slightly afterwards. P.S. No normal man can tell whether the hymen is present or not.

Cervix

It's more or less the entrance to the canal that leads to the uterus. When a pregnant woman is about to give birth, the uterus gets so big that the cervix practically disappears. Baby coming through. Ouch!

Uterus

With the exception of pregnant women, this organ is the size and shape of an inverted pear. Its walls are thick, muscular and also very elastic—this is important when you're trying to fit in one or more babies. Also, the uterus (or womb) has a special lining called endometrium, a mucus that's in charge of holding fast to a fecundated ovum (egg) and starting the process of nurturing it. If no egg is present, the endometrial lining will shed, month after month, with tissue and blood that has formed in the uterus. And actually, this is exactly what provokes your menstrual period.

Fallopian tubes

These two flexible tubes have the monthly mission of transporting one ovum towards the uterus, right after ovulation. They are attached to the upper part of the womb, each leading to a different ovary. If by chance a sperm met an ovum here, the tube would then bring the egg down and attach it to the endometrium.

Ovaries

Shaped and sized like almonds. It doesn't matter much if you don't know what almonds look like—they're just like ovaries!

Seriously, these two have the responsibility of keeping around 300,000 (yes! Three hundred thousand) ovum—eggs—inside tiny sacks called follicles. You'll be liberating each and every one of them between puberty and menopause!

The entire process of liberating one of these eggs is known as ovulation. Basically, what happens is that the pituitary gland (sound's funny, but that is his name) produces a series of hormones that travel along your bloodstream to ask the ovarian follicles to liberate a ready-to-cook ovum. Some women actually feel a small cramp in the lower part of their abdomen—a signal of possible oncoming sensitivity and fertility.

What is amazing, though, is that each of these tiny ovaries contains your entire genetic information or DNA: the color of your eyes, hair, and the shape of your body… etc.

Get out of here! The mysterious stain

Have you ever freaked out after seeing a yellowish or whitish mucus-like stain in your panties? Again, relax! It's completely normal.

Vaginal discharge, as it's known, is your vagina's natural cleaning system. Most girls usually notice its debut one or two years before their first period. There are two types:

NORMAL

Moist, transparent, whitish and itch-free. It might turn a bit yellow in your underwear once it dries up but, all in all, it's nothing to be too concerned about. In fact, it's one good reason to wear underwear in the first place.

The amount of discharge varies depending on your hormone levels. Sexual arousal will increase its production.

ABNORMAL

If discharge is thick and sticky and makes your genitalia itchy, you should then visit your doctor. You've probably got an infection, and it is super important to take care of it ASAP. Treatment is simple, standard and usually pretty fast.

Write down your Gynecologist's telephone number.

My period

AKA The Crimson Wave

"I'd like to congratulate Maggie, who opens her petals to become a beautiful flower."

Is he drunk?

Who cares? He talks so good

There are many ways to call it: your period, menstruation, kool aid, the periodical, the rag, the menstrual cycle, the red river, Aunt Flo... Your mom's friends will simply say: "Welcome aboard!"

Getting your first period represents one of the most important and significant changes in your body. To start off, it means that you've entered a stage of life in which you can get pregnant —so watch out. There's no rush at all! It's the change that some people call "the passing from girlhood to womanhood". And if that sounds a bit melodramatic, well, that's because it actually is. You'll be becoming a woman through a lot of changes—both public and private—and these physical processes are just some of the most obvious.

Month after month—as we've mentioned already—the hypophysis produces hormones in order to make an ovum grow, mature and head towards the fallopian tubes (by the way, Fallopian is NOT the name of an elephant). Once it gets there, the ovum may get fertilized in the next 12 to 24 hours if it meets sperm within.

The thing is that, just as all of this is happening, the endometrial lining builds up in the uterus in order to welcome the fertilized ovum (egg, at this stage). It's sort of a cushion, so that the egg has an easy landing. And if the ovum doesn't get fertilized, the lining sheds and produces a bleeding called… menstruation! You'll be ragging it! And of course, we're talking about the feared and scary "period."

nine

interesting facts that every woman should know. (Or in other words, 9 points men don't really give a darn about.)

nine basics

1. It takes two to three years for your period to become "regular".

2. It is totally normal that the duration of your period differs from that of your friends. It can be anything between two and eight days (four to six on average). The important thing is that it does become regular and steady within the first two to three years.

3. Normally, the whole cycle lasts around one month —between 21 and 35 days. On average, the cycle takes 28 days.

4. Cycles can be altered due to changes in climate, nutrition, stress (during exams at school, for instance), age, traveling and loss or gain of weight. Being in love can also disrupt the cycle, as well as being pregnant —although this one will actually stop your period! So lots of factors can affect the process.

5. You're going to be getting your period for about the next 40 years—pregnancies and nursing periods excluded. That's 400 to 500 periods in your lifetime! Take a deep breath and, more importantly, take it easy. A few tantrums are totally understandable.

6. Your first bleeding may be brown—not red. This is also completely normal.

7. You may find brown spots in your underwear as your period begins or comes to an end. Another way of knowing your period is on its way is if you start arguing with everyone at home for no reason.

8. The best way to find out when your first period will arrive is by asking your mom or your sisters or your grandmother when they got their own first period. Much of this stuff is genetic, so chances are yours is going to be similar.

9. If you're 17 years old and still haven't had your first period, you need to visit your doctor to find out what's going on.

Ouch! My first period!

Oh, cramp!

Your first period can make you feel very uncomfortable. After all, it's your own blood you're looking at. Anxiety can rise as well, mainly due to the fact that you don't really know when it's going to show up!

Before anything, we'd like to say that your period demonstrates that you're actually braver than boys—just as you probably are in many other ways. Can you picture one of your male-friends menstruating for his first time? He'd go

through a nervous breakdown at the first cramp and then...
you'd find out that you've lost him.

You're going to have a terrible time if you actually believe
that everyone's staring at you just because you're going
through your first period. "Look at her! She's menstruating
for the first time!" Relax! Nobody's thinking like that. Nobody
can really even tell and no one really even cares.

Tell me the type of period you have and I'll tell you who you are

the mother in law:
You love her when she's gone and you despise her when she's back.

Brother:
Literally bothering you all day long.

the pizza:
You can't wait for it to arrive!

the total Knockout:
Throws you in bed before you knew what hit you.

Halley's Comet:
You never know when it'll pass.

the pimple:
Annoying even before it shows up.

the nos-

the Weekender:
Gone before you could even enjoy it.

the String on your Finger:
Reminds you throughout the day that it's there.

37

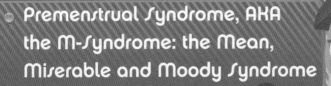

Premenstrual Syndrome, AKA the M-Syndrome: the Mean, Miserable and Moody Syndrome

As you reach the third week of your cycle, your body starts getting hormonally ready so that the endometrial lining sheds via menstruation. Some changes may appear, such as:

- Headaches
- Depression
- Irritability
- Sensitivity
- Acne
- Cramps
- Boob pain
- Tiredness
- Swollen belly
- Body water retention

The M-Syndrome tends to make women miserable, moody and even mean. At times you can't even stand yourself. Don't worry too much, though, you can forgive yourself anytime! So go ahead and cry or throw a tantrum as much as you want to. Everyone does it.

Since you are, in fact, more sensitive at this time of the month, some people say that creativity will actually develop during that specific time. Make an effort and try to write, paint, listen to music, meditate... or you can even write a note to your boyfriend!

Even though your friends may understand you, it's not easy to know EXACTLY what's going on. (After all, you don't wear a t-shirt announcing to everyone "I'M HAVING MY PERIOD" do you?) Some of your peers might freak out a bit, but just let your confidantes know that you've got the M-Syndrome. Remember: boys have never felt it, so you'll need to explain it to them carefully and in such a way that they understand properly—we promise this will save a lot of troubles.

Cramps

It will be one of your longest standing enemies, possibly for the next 40 years.

Menstrual cramps are sudden spasms that provoke lower abdominal pain, sometimes extending even to the lower back. The twinge can get pretty hardcore in some women but it is now easier to control than ever before in history. In order to get rid of menstrual flow, your uterus' muscles are actually contracting. These twinges may also occur during ovulation, about 10 to 15 days after having your period—but it's never any fun.

Some extraordinarily lucky women go through their period, month after month, without having any of the aforementioned symptoms. But there are less fortunate gals that start with a light pain… and are then almost knocked out and sent to bed by fierce, intense pains.

Hi, my name is TWINGE

And my second name is ALL DAY LONG

Treating the pain (twinges) and discomfort of cramps

There are finally some great pills out there. Advil, Midol and Premsyn take care of most, if not all, of the pain for some girls. But don't forget to consult your mom and/or your physician before taking ANY medicine—you might be allergic to it and not even know it. (Talk to your physician before taking any medicine.)

You can also try putting a hot water bottle on your belly. Rub your hands and, once they're warm, massage the aching area. There are also neat sticky heat patches that you put into your underwear and… voila! Pain-relieving warmth for up to 12 hours. These are available at drugstores everywhere.

- Try Termo Panti. Attached to the panty you'll find a sealed pack of gel that warms up automatically once it's activated.

- Lifting heavy things at this time is strictly prohibited. Also you should avoid standing in place for long durations of time.

- And most doctors recommend that you stay away from greasy and spicy foods as well as red meat.

- Work out! It improves your blood circulation.

- Cut back on salt, sugar and caffeine. Stay away from booze —you do know it's illegal till you turn 21, right?

- Eat more veggies and carbs.

- Take two drops of "Tolerit"… tolerate it! For sure, the cheapest method—and for many the least helpful too.

Help yourself!

During "that time of the month" you might feel your boobs are slightly bigger and more sensitive. To avoid any additional pain, keep away from clumsy people: Murphy's law states that the uncoordinated will bump into your boobs every two seconds—and a half-hearted "Sorry!" will definitely not take the pain away.

Other PMS symptoms are wicked headaches and backaches, as well as fatigue. All of these will make you feel dreadful, but don't worry too much about them being anything more serious. As time goes by, you'll start to figure out what needs to be done to control pain and you'll be able to make yourself feel better.

Visiting the doctor after your first period is a must. Keep track of your cycle; write down on a calendar the dates of menstruation, the duration as well as the number and intensity of cramps. Don't lose it! This information is really important for your doctor in order to know if you have a 24, 28 or 30-day cycle—or if it's still irregular.

Protection: Tampons vs. Pads

Most girls prefer using pads, although many other girls like tampons—or a combination of both. It's simply a question of your own comfort and preferences.

How many do I need?

You'll want to use the whole package in the beginning, but as time passes you'll figure out the proper amount depending on your menstrual flow. As we mentioned, be sure to change those pads every three to four hours to stay fresh, clean and free of odors.

Tampons freak me out!

A tampon is sort of a plug made out of cotton. Women put them in their vagina to get internal protection. They come with a string so one can pull them out afterwards, so don't panic. Picturing the procedure in your head sucks big time, but it isn't as bad as you might think.

Chapter 2

What's up with...

my relationships

PLAYING CUPID

UGH, GUYS STUFF

THE BREAK-UP

MY CRUSHES

MY (REAL) BOYFRIEND

FRIENDS WITH BENEFITS

MY FRIENDS

HOOKING UP

MY BRAIN AND HIS BRAIN

Men

The first things men see in women

AKA: Spotted you

When a guy you've just met promises you the moon and the stars, he starts saying stuff like:

He: Your eyes were the first thing I saw.

You (think): Right… 150 feet away?

[You "think" because even though you perfectly know that this is not true, it feels nicer to remain in doubt.]

Or, it's summertime and you're at the beach. You're wearing the hottest swimsuit in the world and your suntan is absolutely gorgeous. Then, he comes close and says: "Hi there! You've got the nicest nose ever." Are you kidding me? He might as well have said: "Hi there! That shoulder blade of yours is so pretty."

This is also so typical:

—Hi! You are so pretty!

—Thanks.

—So… what's your friend's name over there? (What? Get lost, you sleazy snail.)

The thing is that only a guy who's spotted you before (maybe at school, maybe in the mall) can come close enough and say things like these. Don't worry! These are just the least fortunate comments— and they're not necessarily typical.

A group of researchers from Georgetown University in Washington D.C. did a very interesting study: "What do we see in people in the blink of an eye?" These were the results:

WHAT MEN SPOT FIRST IN OTHER WOMEN

BODY
43%
I SAW HER BOOBS
WHOA, DID YOU SEE HER ABS?
AND HER BUTT?

FACE
31%
I LIKE HER EYES
KISSABLE LIPS

THE WAY SHE DRESSES
26%
WHAT A SKIRT!

WHAT WOMEN SPOT FIRST IN OTHER WOMEN

THE WAY SHE DRESSES
43%

I SAW THAT DRESS FIRST

THOSE JEANS MAKE HER SO, UGH!

I HATE HER, SHE LOOKS GREAT!

FACE
28%

WOW! NO FACIAL HAIR AT ALL

AS SMOOTH AS A BABY'S BUTT

HAIR
29%

WHERE DID YOU GET YOUR HAIR DONE?

WHAT'S UP WITH HER HAIR DO

47

WHAT WOMEN SPOT FIRST IN MEN

THE WAY HE DRESSES

30%

FACE (SMILE)

EYES

BODY

21%

25%

I LOVE HIS FILTHY LOOKS

24%

HE KNOCKED ME OUT

THOSE ARE HYPNOEYES

HE'S SO HOT IN THAT OUTFIT

CUT CHUBBY CHUBB

OH, BABYFACE!

I LOVE DEEP BLUE

CHANGE THOSE PANTS ONCE IN A WHILE, WILL YOU?

I DON'T LIKE HIM SO BUILT

48

As you can see, men put their eyes first on the body whereas women generally check the outfit first.

The way you dress is constantly showing who you are, your personality, the mood you're in, your tastes... And in some cases, it even shows if you use bleach to do the laundry.

If any of the following points makes you feel uncomfortable, relax! This book is intended to help you improve your situation. And remember: "There isn't a second chance to make a good first impression."

What's flirting all about?

When two people are hitting on each other, what they're really doing is negotiating an endless list of petitions that both request—and both may give into. We're talking about a guy and a girl who simply succumb to the roaring avalanche of their own hormonal activity.

Flirting is fun. As a matter of fact, it could be an international competition in the Olympics. Now, that would be a lot more interesting than archery, right?

The thing is that sometimes, when meeting a boy, you send out signals that are rejected. And then, you feel that you need a prayer and a miracle to get some positive feedback... If that doesn't happen, well, don't worry too much! Check out the 5 stages, the processes that everyone must go through. Pay attention! If you read this chapter carefully, you'll succeed in the blink of an eye—just like an expert.

Stages

Understanding these stages is really important so you can track down the entire "state of affairs." Also, it may let you see how the innocent-looking girly-girl next door morphs into the most accomplished of flirts.

Now, if the interaction of these signs is working well but you still feel like running to the nearest emergency exit when a boy says: "Hi there! What's your name?" you're not freaking out—you're just frightened to death! Calm down. The more you learn about this, the sooner you will become a star.

• *Stage one:* **Attracting attention**

Before anything, keep in mind that both men and women mark their territory—yep, just like dogs! Well, not exactly that way. Whether it's in a club or at a party, guys and girls tend to mark their presence at a table, a chair or on a wall. (It's quite odd but science has never been able to determine why men love leaning on walls.)

If you look closely, you'll notice the type of things that go on when someone's checking out another person:

They stretch, they stand up straight and throw their shoulders back, they suck in their stomachs, they laugh out loud, they exaggerate their body movements.

Guys

They emphasize the movement of their hips, they use their fingers to twiddle with their hair, they turn red, they lift up their eyebrows, they smile.

Girls

• *Stage two:* **Acknowledgement**

Eye contact can determine the future of the whole thing. The observed person may react in three different ways:

○ Smiling or confirming eye contact. Most women apply the "cute puppy" technique, that is, a timid smile while tilting the head, slightly. If the guy's close enough to you, he'll try to start a conversation; if he's far away, he'll spin his whole body towards you so the distance between the two of you is reduced. The game with the eyes may go on until the time to actually talk, although the spin-around is a great message already! In some cases, frightened guys will go home as if nothing had occurred. No big deal. This guy is either super shy or way too insecure about himself. Either way: boring!

- Looking away. If you feel intimidated when he looks back, you'll automatically perform the "displacement gesture". That means you're playing the game but prefer concentrating your eyes on something else. You then start twiddling your hair, your purse, your sunglasses, your cell phone, your ears… Check him out; if you don't like him, simply turn around or leave. This is known as the "get lost" gesture.

- Strategy. If you're sure that the guy's looking at you (and not at the top model sitting next to you), you'll have to work out a plot in order to get closer—avoid extravagance and try something casual! (For more details, check out Plan B on page 66.)

Stage three: Talking

This stage usually starts with a silly phrase or a soft compliment: "Hey, what's up?", "Who did you come here with?" "What's happening?", "Cool party, huh?", "You have nice eyes!" (Those who are crazy for you will say it even if a pair of sunglasses is actually covering your eyes), "Do you know this guy? I think he's a sophomore at your school…" (this is, for sure, the dorkiest of all questions, yet it works). The objective of this approach is to get verbal feedback from you and begin to talk.

Unlike during other conversations, he may start talking with a great deal of rhythm. His voice can become smooth and its tone may very well increase—an important thing to remember.

The contrast is so big. It's like that friend of yours who's discussing important issues on her cell phone with another girl: "No way, mach, I'm not going out together with that sleazy..." But when she puts in on hold to answer her boy-friend's call, she goes: "Hi honey, I love you so much."

Astonishingly, our voice reveals a great deal of informa-tion: intentions, background, upbringing and even the num-ber of drinks you've had[1]—assuming you've been drinking secretly.[2]

---

[1] Drinking age nationwide is 21.
[2] For further information regarding alcohol, jump to page 241.

Squeak Warning

One's voice may immediately attract or repel the guy flirting with you. Avoid squeaking! It can happen—it's all part of being terrifically nervous. You should try to enjoy it.

Fase 4. Touching

Physical contact begins here. The first moment is known as "codes of intention," and it occurs when we get physically closer to the person we're flirting with. If you look closely you'll see how we extend our legs or arms to get closer.

Touching may seem an insignificant action, but let the truth be told: your guts tremble whenever it happens. It would seem that both of you have keen sensors that store every single physical contact in your brain's hard drive. When there's a higher level of trust, you may even slap the guy on the shoulder and say, in a flirtatious way: "Stop it!"

The more adventurous of you may dare touching his knee, as if you were simply leaning on it. On the other hand, men seldom dare to touch a girl (even thought they're dying to do it); so they grab your shoulders and start directing you through traffic. It doesn't matter if the final destination is just two steps ahead, the important thing is to have some sort of physical contact.

Most of these contacts happen so quickly that they're almost invisible to our eyes. However, they are important: even though he might pretend that nothing's happened, of course he's noticed every move! Now, if the other person smiles back, leans forward or begins to have more physical contact (in a cool way, of course)... then you're ready for stage five!

If, however, he responds to the gesture by throwing himself upon you, watch it! You might be hitting on a guy who is way too excited... Or a professional wrestler. You can, and should, stay in control.

Stage five: **Total body synchronicity**

AKA: "Love being a copycat?"

This stage is funny! Once the interaction has reached a higher level, both guy and girl start to make the same body movements—for real.

First, they align themselves in such a way that their shoulders end up facing each other's—this can happen before or during the conversation. Believe it or not, this does occur;

it's just a question of paying close attention to what's going on. Once the mimicking process begins, it'll become endless: if he grabs a glass, you'll grab one as well; if one crosses a leg, the other person will do exactly the same; if you tilt towards your right, he'll do the same thing. It's like you're dancing together, although there's no soundtrack being played!

Despite the fact that love is way more complex and even profound, the flirting issue is the first step. If it isn't handled properly, you could lose your potential boyfriend in... just 5 simple stages.

The He-likes-me-NOT Acute illness

AKA Cannot-flirt syndrome

SYMPTOMS

ONE

You feel that you somehow screw up every time you go near that guy.

TWO

You suspect your Best Female Friend's boyfriend is not well "supplied". Because he should have been supplied to you!

THREE

You think your qualities define you as a superhero —"The Invisible Woman."

FOUR

Instead of feeling pretty, you're pretty sure that you are totally freaking ugly.

FIVE

You're soooo popular… With the grossest dudes in your class.

SIX

The more you put makeup on and fix your hair, the more you feel like an absolute clown.

If you've been unsuccessful hitherto... Loosen up! You've been diagnosed with Acute "He-likes-me-NOT" Syndrome, and we will prescribe just the medicine you need.

It's quite common to feel that nobody is interested in you. Despite the fact that you may feel lonely in the middle of a rumbling storm, there are lots of other girls that have the same issue—in fact, maybe most of them do—so sit back and relax. Perhaps you haven't realized it yet but that's because no one goes around screaming: "I have 'Accute He-likes-me-not!' Get Robert Pattinson here now!"

If it's been a while since the last time a guy showed any interest, you've probably reached the phase in which you wished guys were for rent in tuxedo shops. Taking one home wouldn't be a bad idea at all: you'd feel better, you could prove to yourself that things aren't that bad... and you wouldn't mind being seen with such a hunk, would you?

Well, as you go through a phase like this, you might feel stupid when talking to a guy or worse, you might end up being more sexually cooperative—just so he doesn't lose interest. At times, you might analyze or over-analyze a 90 second conversation you had recently, word by word, just to find out how you messed it up.

The point is that all of this stuff makes you feel sad and confused. Just as you ask yourself what is it that men want that you lack, a deep sense of nagging emptiness develops in your belly. Moreover, if you see the guy you die for talking to another girl, you could go wild and start hating everyone and everything. It is a hodgepodge of anger, sadness, desperation and emptiness, right?

Never forget that the value of a person is not solely defined by the looks. It is true; some girls seem to have received all of the goodies and look perfect—but they aren't. Perhaps they seem fine, but they've got other issues on their own minds.

The important thing is to bear in mind that none of the following are reasons why guys don't approach certain girls: being chubby, not being all that pretty, having pimples, having a big nose.

What truly makes a person repel another person is lack of security and love, as well as respect for oneself. No question about it. In other words, it's all in the degree of self-confidence you personally possess.

Unconsciously, men are able to gauge self-confidence and, without a doubt, they prefer keeping away from girls with low self-confidence and low self esteem. It is quite common to hear that someone who didn't have a girlfriend or a boyfriend begins to be overwhelmed by tons of admirers as soon as he or she finally gets involved in a relationship. This is absolutely true! When someone finally gets a boyfriend or a girlfriend, their level of personal security increases due to the sense of satisfaction. There's no need to look for someone. After perceiving this unconsciously, the rest of the crowd will frequently come calling.

True security rests inside of you, and you must search for it there whenever you're feeling down. The true value of people is defined by who they are, not by how they look, much less by how well they flirt. That's why you can find not-so-pretty girls dating the hottest guys in school. They know who they are, what their virtues are and what they're worth.

We interviewed a bunch of guys in order to find out what aspect of girls drives them crazy. Here are the results:

ONE	TWO	THREE
Self-confidence	Authenticity	She ain't easy, but she's not unreachable either.

So, stop panicking and become aware of what you're worth. That special one you've been waiting for is still to come. You know what's the secret? It's having many friends (romance-free), hanging out with them, becoming their true friend... Moreover, it's also about having a blast every single day of your life—or at least most of them.

Once you start embracing life—as opposed to being weary all the time because you don't have a boyfriend—you'll start to notice the amount of guys who'd give everything to be with a girl like you.

Some signs are so obvious, right? Like the guy who literally drools when he bumps into you—again. It's really easy to identify this type: always leaving traces of saliva everywhere you've been to! Afterwards, he becomes your secret admirer, leaving chocolates and flowers on your desk. What about those who aren't so obvious, though? To be honest, men are quite predictable when it comes to flirting, and identifying their CM (Cupid Moves) will be a piece of cake.

CM at school

The Annoyer

At school, it is very—very—common that the guy who likes you actually ends up bugging you. We're talking about the type of dude who slightly pulls your hair and then plays dumb, as though he had nothing to do with it... Duh! What he really wants, however, is to attract your attention: "I'm here! Look at me!" He'll also pretend to be mean and stick his foot in your way. He'll bump into you and even try to mimic you. This is all fine early on but let's face it: it gets truly annoying! The point is that he'll do everything within his power to annoy you and pretend to be a jerk, but remember: he digs you; he simply doesn't have the guts to tell you.

the Bodyguard

The type of guy who's near at all times even though he shares no classes with you. He's always there, "accidentally," at lunch time, outside the bathrooms, around the places where you usually hang out. It's like having a personal bodyguard! He does it because he really enjoys looking at you and, believe it or not, he sometimes counts the minutes before he rushes out to "bump into you." He's so obvious that his friends will inevitably push him towards you when you're passing close.

the team-player

Another trick that boys use is homework. For real. He'll call you or text you every once in a while to find out about school stuff. Teamwork is the best chance he's got: as soon as the teacher makes the magical statement "Get yourself a partner and do some research about…" he'll start praying so you don't find a workmate before he approaches. Then, he'll "casually" ask you if you want to work together, as if there wasn't a hidden agenda.

cm at parties

When you are a bit older, either you or the guy will simply get close and start a conversation. If you're just getting started though, all of these situations can be hilarious!

The Hesitant

Once you're alone, he'll think "Go! Go! Go!" but when he finally decides to make his move, the mission is abruptly aborted—your friend has just come back. The same thing will happen again and again throughout the party because he's incapable of getting closer to you. But the story doesn't end there: he'll manage to get your phone number and text you a month later... For real! He'll try to be the coolest dude on earth, but the truth is that his hands will be shaking as he writes "Hi! Remember me? I was wearing a yellow t-shirt that night." Give him a break. Really nervous guys can be cute.

The Distractor

This is the type of guy who approaches a group of girls and begins to make open questions: "What are your names?", "How old are you, guys?", "What type of music are you girls into?" Despite being nice to everyone, his real intention is to find out more about you. Pay close attention: in a while, you'll be the only girl he's calling by her name. His mission has been to learn but one word all the way.

Cruise-Control

One can also find the guy who's hanging out miles away from you, pretending to be cool and carefree, and in one startling moment, he's right next to you! A few minutes will pass before he starts talking to you, like: "How did I end up here? Isn't that funny?"

Identified a CM yet? If you like the guy, analyze the situation and give him a hand. Men get so scared that they can go on like this for ages! Then, when you meet this fellow six years later, he'll confess: "You won't believe me, but I used to be crazy for you."

Secrets that will make him go crazy for you

How come some chicks have gazillions of guys drooling over them, and at the same time there are girls who believe that there are no available men on this planet? And why are some women treated like stars when other nicer, cuter ones get dissed over and over again? Why do men lose interest in a woman as time passes by?

There are girls who act in such a way that they simply become totally irresistible to a lot of guys. You might wonder "Oh my god! How does she do it?" Well, we'll share some of the secrets right here.

Let's get started. Many men love challenges, conquests and hard-to-achieve goals—regardless of whether they are publicly acceptable. That's why many of them are into sports, extreme hobbies, games and similar activities where they have a chance to show off and play the victor.

Having this in mind, the worst strategy any girl could choose is nagging:

- Calling a guy day after day, using silly excuses.
- Making up stories just to be with him.
- Saying yes to sexual come-ons.

Besides giving away all your secrets, you're destroying the natural sense of conquest that guys may look for and even really want. Boring.

On the other hand… if you project yourself as the "unreachable" girl, the type who's too hard to get, their wish for success and conquest will awaken lightning fast. Simultaneously, it will make them show some appreciation for you, and—for sure—you will feel awesome about the whole thing.

Perhaps what we've just said seems old-fashioned, a bit outdated for the 21st century, but believe us, though: the following advice does work! Try it even if it sounds like the stuff your grandma's granny might say.

1. Feel like you're *THE* girl

Picture yourself like the woman that everyone's dying for. We're not talking just about looks, either. It's a question of attitude, a state of mind. Feel great! Feel proud of yourself! Think, act, and walk like a top model.

2. Put him to work

Dating is like a waltz, so let him lead. Avoid being the one who talks first or paying for movie tickets, and don't stare at him as if you were planning the honeymoon already. Try not to talk too much and don't get into intimate, deep or philosophical issues (boring!). In contrast, you've got to be intelligent, interesting and mysterious. At this stage, pass up things like: "I have a blast next to you", or "My friends want to meet you already! I've told them so much about you!" Relax, take it easy and don't add any pressure.

3. Hang tough

Be nice if he calls to ask you out, but tell him that you've got other plans. It doesn't matter if you have nothing to do and you're actually staying in to watch old reruns on TV. He's got to realize that you're so busy that you won't be able to fit him into your tight schedule that easily (like, "I need to be booked in advance, all right?"). Especially reject last-minute invitations: someone else has probably blown him off already, and you definitely don't want to be the second option.

4. Say good-bye before he does

Even if you're the kind of girl who can be on the phone for ages and narrate the day's highlights in minute detail, hold your tongue. If necessary, count the time with a chronometer and shut up! Put an end to the conversation by saying something like "I've got to go now," or "Sorry, but I've got to

get some things done." After this, he'll want to talk more, and will start wondering: "Is she seeing someone else? Why did she hang up so quickly? Am I that boring?"

5. Be sweet
Be nice to him and laugh at his jokes but don't get too excited. Don't feel obligated to say anything when there is a moment of silence. You love being treated properly, don't you? Well, let him do his work, like opening the car door or pulling out a chair. Always say "please" and "thanks" to this type of gestures, and never criticize the place, the food, the service or whatever—even if it sucked big time. Look for the bright side of everything.

6. Limit your dates
Men fall in love quicker than women, but they fall *out* of love faster too. That's why you have to go out with them from time to time, even if instinct or the desire to see them more often is making you nuts. If he asks, "What are you doing tomorrow?" before he says good-bye, bite your tongue and answer: "I'm going to be so busy." If this task proves impossible and you give in, you'll see how quickly he loses interest in you.

7. Don't lose your dignity
It is crucial that you keep your dignity and don't turn into a stalker. Don't pay attention to him every once in a while. Men dig this and enjoy the hype of it! If you're after them all day long, you'll become dull and boring—not to mention that they'll feel so secure that they won't take you seriously. And then you'll be doomed to being simply "friend with benefits," or maybe just someone with a reputation for being obsessive.

What if things are so bad that you can't even catch a cold?

If you've performed well in all the previous tasks and he still doesn't make a move, you either lack time to flirt or you have developed the "absent body syndrome"—it's like being invisible to him. Everybody is—at some time or another—a victim of this syndrome. Actually, it happens to 10 out of every 11 girls.

> You can't do too much because he might think you're kinda slutty.

> You can't do too little because you could lose him to another girl.

Extreme cases: Plan B

- Laugh a lot. You want to look like the coolest girl on Earth. (Just don't laugh TOO much, if you know what we mean.)
- If you're dancing at a party or a club, seize him with your eyes and discretely point at him with your fingers (rhythmically!), like: "You! Yes, you!" Now, if a song that suits the moment is being played, fantastic!
- Bumping into him is not a bad option—that is, if you have a really good line to connect with him. Play the "what a coincidence" game, you know?

- Speak a bit louder so you're heard but don't be TOO LOUD.
- Freshen up, look hot, and attract his attention. Avoid mini-skirts, hardcore cleavages or any extreme makeup—excess can distort reality and, instead of being an attractive young woman, you can end up just looking extremely insecure.
- Whether you're at a club, at a party or even at school, roam the place a couple of times so you're able to spot the guys and make sure they see you too. Guys usually bump into you and apologize—a great opportunity to start flirting. Smile at him the next time you meet. Try not to wander around too much because, again, you just come off as insecure and even lost. No luck in the reconnaissance mission? Flirt candidates arrive when you least expect them. So enjoy yourself and concentrate on having a good time.
- Without being obvious, find a seat next to him and be cool.
- Use every woman's secret weapon: your eyes. Look at him… stop looking at him! Look at him again… and then pretend he's invisible. Now, if he doesn't get the message, he's just a Flirtard.
- If the eye game goes well, go to the bathroom (with a friend). If he's keen on meeting you, he'll likely stand up and try to bump into you and start a conversation.
- Warning: go to the bathroom with just one friend. Guys tend to be insecure and they'll get scared if you go with a bunch of girls. The idea of being dissed in front of a lot of people is scary, if not outright humiliating.
- Play the game even if the grossest dude of the bunch starts hitting on you. He may end up being the passport

to the guy you like. Remember: the end justifies the means... Even though the means may be kind of uncool.

A guy digs knowing that someone's got a crush on him, but don't be too obvious. Maybe he's never noticed a girl's existence, but as soon as he finds out that this girl likes him... he begins to weigh the possibilities and says stuff like: "She isn't bad-looking at all," "You know what? She's pretty cool", "I kinda like her, too," or "I've liked her for ages, but lost hope months ago". However, if your BFF tells him that you like him in any obvious way, there is still a chance that he'll reply by saying: "Whatever!"

What NOT to do under any circumstance

Don't get drunk in order to attract his attention or anyone else's. You'll only look stupid, unattractive and unworthy.

Never ask "Hey, what are you doing?" The question does not invite any sort of reply. He might as well answer: "Hum... holding a glass? Duh!"

The style you apply when dressing up doesn't matter as much as you may think. Men may like girly, hippie, classy, good, rocker, preppy, exuberant or even cheesy girls. However, scruffy chicks or girls who don't fix their hair are going to have a bad time. Bad breath, stained shirts and bitten nails are hated as much as radical makeup and hooker like outfits.

- Swear as little as possible. Guys don't like women who talk like truckers. There's no problem if you use the softer words every once in a while but be classy.
- Never, ever, ask for a phone number. Even if you're on the verge of a nervous breakdown and he's about to say good-bye. Chill! If you ask for it, he'll feel so sure about the situation that you guys will end up being cute friends —and that's it. If he doesn't ask for it, don't sweat it! There will be other opportunities.
- If you've reached the stage in which you talk or text everyday, do not give him a buzz every five minutes to ask "What's up?" You run the risk of getting an unwanted answer: "Nothing, just thinking how terrible it would be if you and I were together."
- Now, in the end, if the dude you're head over heels for does not notice your existence… throw your shoe at him, run away and pray he's seen Cinderella!

Relationships are like that: it's a give-and-take game that involves pushing and pulling. Put as much effort into it, but please don't spend all the time taking just a little and giving lots of yourself away.

Types of Guys

It's impossible to label all men. At some level, though, they do seem to do everything possible to be catalogued in one of the following types.

We put together a group of girls (a rather large group, by the way) to see if we could find out what they think about the different types of men, their characteristics, where you can find them, and which have powers and weapons that need to be conquered. As a result, we found out the real cons when it comes to sex appeal, meaning, which ones are so dangerous you shouldn't even kiss them (levels 1 to 5). Here's what they told us:

TYPE OF GUY:

THE CORNBALL

CHARACTERISTICS:

Intense, driven, very loving, and more tender than the truly corny. He forgets his life to "help" you live yours. And he's so focused on the details that you need to be a database technician to sort through all the stuff he keeps in his head —much of it about you.

WHERE TO FIND HIM:

The gift wrap section at a Hallmark store.

COSTUME:

He dresses just as you want him to, no style of his own.

SAMPLE PHRASE:

"So where do you want to go?... No, you tell me."

POWERS:

Has learned more than 70 ways to fold little love notes.

PROS:

You get the final say... on everything; and he will cry with you at the movies.

CONS:

Sometimes you might find it hard to breathe. Could be very dangerous if he discovers that there are gummy candies shaped like hearts.

WEAPONS:

Puppy dog face whenever you say no to something.

KNOWN ENEMY:

Any guy who treats you badly, especially if you still talk to them.

LEVEL OF SEX APPEAL:

But in the end we had to drop him another .5, because he was bugging us for a kiss during the tallying. 2.5 Final.

From me to you

SUSPECTS:

AGENTS NOTES:

FRIENDS WHO ARE LIKE THIS:

TYPE OF GUY:

THE COMEDIAN

CHARACTERISTICS:

Safe, light-hearted, but if you ask questions like "Is he cute?", you'll get answer's like, "Well, he's super funny"... He is the soul of the party, and if people have to pay to get in to his party, well, many of them will.

WHERE TO FIND HIM:

In the center of everything, telling a joke.

COSTUME:

Boxers with all sorts of whacky characters, shirts with similar characters or symbols. If he is a little hefty, he's not afraid to wear the shirt a little tight–even if he looks somehow ridiculous.

SAMPLE PHRASE:

"What? You actually believed me?"

POWERS:

Everybody wants him. (Except teachers, principals and emos.)

PROS:

He's not afraid of ridicule. (Unfortunately you may be.)

CONS:

Can be difficult to talk seriously with him.

WEAPONS:

Makes you laugh and you may start to like it.

KNOWN ENEMY:

Anywhere where he can't talk (church, funerals, tests, etc.).

LEVEL OF SEX APPEAL:

1 2 3 **4** 5

SUSPECTS:

AGENTS NOTES:

FRIENDS WHO ARE LIKE THIS:

TYPE OF GUY:
THE ALTERNA-ROCKER

CHARACTERISTICS:

Life is short. He's educated, light-hearted, intelligent and can speak profoundly about a glass of water—if he feels like it. He loves some garage rock, but really hates lots of other music. Cannot stand superficial people and boasts that his friends are hippies (the dirtier, the better). Has never danced to the Macarena or to any other "popular music."

WHERE TO FIND HIM:

Bookstores, music festivals, art exhibits, the movies, bars with live music, funkier clubs, near any disc jockey or strange smelling cloud of smoke.

COSTUME:

Torn jeans worn well below the waist, t-shirts with whatever music band on them, Converse, Vans or any kind of sneakers, jewelry with marijuana leaves that he's worn for 2 years (though, truth be told, he's forgotten where it came from).

SAMPLE PHRASE:

"What's happening?" (articulated slowly)

SUSPECTS:

POWERS:

He's always relaxed and easy going.

PROS:

Never fights over anything beneath him and has zero personal insecurity.

AGENTS NOTES:

CONS:

He's not romantic, or detail oriented and is really too lazy to socialize.

WEAPONS:

His backpack (which is full of cables to hook up his various devices).

KNOWN ENEMY:

Any fashionable yuppies, particularly the color coordinated ones.

LEVEL OF SEX APPEAL:

1 **2** 3 4 5

FRIENDS WHO ARE LIKE THIS:

THE MASTER FLIRT

CHARACTERISTICS:

Everybody is dying for this guy (sigh). Quality control is low though, i.e.; watch out for all the people throwing themselves at him. Lots of ladies fall for him, but seriously, actually going anywhere with him is a death wish. This guy is for / after fun, only.

WHERE TO FIND HIM:

Any place fashionable or trendy, or wherever the ladies are.

COSTUME:

As he never fails to pull a seductive face, just about any rag can look good on him.

SAMPLE PHRASE:

"You're the best looking one here, seriously. Can you spare 20 dollars?"

POWERS:

You both know he's full of it, but he's so well enough aware that it's almost acceptable, at least for the moment.

PROS:

Well, he is fun... And can be a very effective way to increase jealousy in an existing boyfriend.

CONS:

If he asks for your phone number, say your prayers... nothing good can come from that.

SUSPECTS:

AGENTS NOTES:

WEAPONS:

We're positive he has a masters degree in making out.

KNOWN ENEMY:

Any master lover, that is, older guys who play the same game... a little bit better.

LEVEL OF SEX APPEAL:

4.5 but it could raise, depending on your mood.

FRIENDS WHO ARE LIKE THIS:

TYPE OF GUY:
THE GEEK

CHARACTERISTICS:

Will plan for 10,000 variables before saying a word to you, and then, when he opens his mouth, well, just a squeak will come out. He'll apologize for that. He's very good at school and only gets angry when everyone wants to copy his notes.

WHERE TO FIND HIM:

The lab, leaning over a Bunsen burner.

COSTUME:

Pants way up, belt, jeans—frequently ironed—hiking shoes, although he doesn't go off the beaten path much.

SAMPLE PHRASE:

"Hi, Hi, Sorry, How are you?"

POWERS:

He's trustworthy—yes, you read that right... Utterly faithful.

PROS:

Able to identify flowering plants and cryptogams; might even fix your computer.

CONS:

Extreme nervousness can be grating.

WEAPONS:

His vast knowledge impresses even your parents.

KNOWN ENEMY:

Breaks from school.

LEVEL OF SEX APPEAL:

He's waited so long, when he touches a woman for the first time it can cause second degree burns.

SUSPECTS:

AGENTS NOTES:

FRIENDS WHO ARE LIKE THIS:

TYPE OF GUY:

THE TOTALLY COOL GUY

CHARACTERISTICS:

Totally acceptable, agreeable guy. Nothing wrong with him at all. Makes room for everyone, especially you.

WHERE TO FIND HIM:

He could very well be hanging out with your ex-boyfriend, he's totally forgiving and has no problem hanging out with anyone.

COSTUME:

He always looks good, but no one really notices what he's wearing.

SAMPLE PHRASE:

"Don't worry, I can help."

POWERS:

He listens. It seems impossible, but he's the real deal.

PROS:

You'll feel respected, even loved and all your friends love him too.

CONS:

Your friends all love him.

WEAPONS:

Even your parents love his super good vibes. What's with this guy?

KNOWN ENEMY:

Girls who only see his physical attributes.

LEVEL OF SEX APPEAL:

1 2 3 4 5 *none*

SUSPECTS:

AGENTS NOTES:

FRIENDS WHO ARE LIKE THIS:

TYPE OF GUY:

THE JERK

CHARACTERISTICS:

Keeps no promises. You already knew that. He's skillful with words and even if you believe none of them at least he keeps you busy. He's a bit of a cross between a couple of cute guy types, but in the end he's got no pedigree.

WHERE TO FIND HIM:

He's usually somewhere close, eyeing your cleavage along with that of any woman within a hundred yards in any direction.

COSTUME:

Tends toward loudish party shirts–unbuttoned to some fairly obnoxious level or the classic V-neck T, a couple sizes too small.

SAMPLE PHRASE:

"Can I call you a cab?"

POWERS:

Makes a lot of promises, tends to speak with his hands. Watch them!

PROS:

You could become popular—for being one of his five girlfriends.

CONS:

He tends to pick up new dates, while you step away to the ladies room.

WEAPONS:

Dances well, and tends to say exactly what you like hearing.

KNOWN ENEMY:

Girls who don't take him up. Most guys.

LEVEL OF SEX APPEAL:

SUSPECTS:

AGENTS NOTES:

FRIENDS WHO ARE LIKE THIS:

TYPE OF GUY:

THE SOUL MATE

CHARACTERISTICS:

He is, but he's not. He hates both the word girlfriend, and the phrase "I want you to meet my parents." Zero commitments, but 1000% chemically compatible.

WHERE TO FIND HIM:

In your planner with 5 stars, but with the phone number crossed out six times. (You can still almost read it.)

COSTUME:

Really, it's the last thing he worries about. He knows you guys are perfect together.

SAMPLE PHRASE:

"But I don't want to compromise our 'friendship.'"

POWERS:

He's magical. Today you see him—tomorrow you don't.

PROS:

You have a great time together. And with no obligations and no fighting. But as with any chemistry experiment, well, you're never sure how it's going to turn out.

CONS:

You can fall desperately in love, and obviously he's not having any of that.

WEAPONS:

He knows everything that you like and dislike, in guys. (All of them.)

KNOWN ENEMY:

All the poor guys who seriously want you.

LEVEL OF SEX APPEAL:

1 2 3 4 **5**

SUSPECTS:

AGENTS NOTES:

FRIENDS WHO ARE LIKE THIS:

TYPE OF GUY:
THE BEST FRIEND

CHARACTERISTICS:

There are two possible options: either he is secretly in love with you, or he is secretly, totally, in love with you.

WHERE TO FIND HIM:

Dinner at your grandmother's, your school play, the vet —when your hamster is ill, etc.

COSTUME:

He plays cool and would dress exactly like you, except he is a guy, so you have to decide some of it for him.

SAMPLE PHRASE:

"You deserve better."

POWERS:

He's always comforting you.

PROS:

You really like him.

CONS:

Your best friend really wants you... to kiss him.

WEAPONS:

Uses information you told him about everything you hated in your ex—to do exactly the opposite.

KNOWN ENEMY:

Any man that you like though he only pretends to be rooting for them.

LEVEL OF SEX APPEAL:

Varies between 0 (brother-like) and 6 (on a scale of 1 to 5)

SUSPECTS:

AGENTS NOTES:

FRIENDS WHO ARE LIKE THIS:

TYPE OF GUY:
THE UN-ATTAINABLE GUY

CHARACTERISTICS:

Colgate smile, soooo cute, there's not a single girl who doesn't know all about this guy. Indeed, even his individual body parts are famous (pecs, arms, etc.). When you run into him there is even a good chance that he won't even turn to look.

WHERE TO FIND HIM:

His photos are inside lockers and the yearbook gave him an extra fold out section.

COSTUME:

Sort of a Prince Charming—or at worst, that guy in Pocahontas.

SAMPLE PHRASE:

" _____ " (He only talks to his friends).

POWERS:

Everybody wants him, but he doesn't want everybody.

PROS:

If you walk in with him, you have something to tell your grandchildren about.

CONS:

No matter how many times you've met him, he always says, "Nice to meet you." If you go out with him, you can forget your own name. You'll simply be known as *his girlfriend*.

WEAPONS:

He knows that everybody wants him.

KNOWN ENEMY:

The teachers who despise him because everybody wants him.

LEVEL OF SEX APPEAL:

1 **2** 3 4 5

SUSPECTS:

AGENTS NOTES:

FRIENDS WHO ARE LIKE THIS:

Bobby! You look so cute! Quack like a duck... 4 times

Quack, quack, quack, quack

Things you can't tell a guy—ever

Picture this in your head: there's this really tough guy who's about 6' 3" tall. He weighs about 220 lbs., and he doesn't have such a friendly face. He's the kind of guy that everyone's scared of, but when his girlfriend asks him to quack like a duckling, he gives in—yep, despite his 220 lbs.

   That this massive and fearful guy may be seen quacking like a tender little duckling at times, doesn't mean he's a loser. It means that both guys and girls have very sensitive fibers that might be seen in public under certain conditions.

Just as men make an effort to constrain their mouths in order not to hurt you (you've got to grant it to them, at least they try), you should try doing the same. Don't offend a guy in front of his friends and family.

Despite the existence of secure men and women who don't give a darn about things like these, don't mind us for giving you some advice:

If your BF is still a bit insecure, you'll infuriate him by saying silly things like how handsome the guy next door is. Avoid saying anything like this out loud, but don't stop checking out guys!

Do not make him feel bad about material stuff that other guys may have, but that he can't afford.

Don't brag about someone else's job or compare him to another guy's performance at school or work, unless you're aiming his wellbeing.

You'll be better off if you don't criticize his family (giving advice is very different from being critical). He might forget the issue, but his family won't… ever!

Do not use curse words when arguing and avoid any kind of aggression. Once the line of respect is crossed, it's really hard to go back to normal.

Don't minimize the things he likes or say that they're meaningless.

Bringing up your ex-boyfriend's cute gestures is not a good idea at all. Don't do it!

If you're a family-oriented type of girl, don't tell him how much your parents liked your ex-boyfriend and don't pressure him to get involved in the family dynamics. Take it easy, go with the flow.

Don't pressure him to take you to the trendiest and coolest places. He might not have cash and is a bit shy to tell you about it. If that's case, it wouldn't be a bad idea taking him out, would it?

We don't want to say that this sort of comments will destroy your relationship, but by avoiding them you'll save yourself unwanted troubles. Besides, he'll feel good about himself and about your relationship.

CHECK THIS OUT!

How to tell if your boyfriend is cheating

No matter how you call it: two-timing, double-dipping, dual front—whatever. You will feel like crap. If you thought you cried too much when your parents poured alcohol on your skinned knee, well, that was nothing.

The truth is that some men—if you can call them that—actually love two-timing. And when you least imagine it, their flirting eyes are all over the playing field.

The specimen, *Infidelius Stupiduz*, attacks your peace of mind. And this sort of boyfriend is constantly distracted by the rest of the herd. Below are just a few signs that you may be dating an *Infidelius Stupiduz*.

♥ His Cellphone is always locked. The records are freshly erased. He knows that his cellphone is a jealous girlfriend's best friend. You will see him being very careful with every call and text he sends or receives, especially if you're the prying type. So if he is going to cheat well, he probably knows he needs a totally separate cell phone.

- 💔 Facebook, Facebook, Facebook, ah, and Twitter. Tell me who tagged and I tell you where is he.
- 💔 He freaks out when he opens his social networks in front of you and never, never, he allow you surf the web.
- 💔 He has a best friend that you never see, meet or hear about from anyone else. Is his best friend Victor? Or Victoria!
- 💔 Whenever you're together for a long time, he'll start looking for ways to separate from you under any excuse, to make a call, to check something outside, you know this story…
- 💔 Though he used to insist on lots of kisses or some sort of making-out, suddenly he is distracted and has lots of other stuff to do.
- 💔 He is suddenly going to a lot of places where his cell phone has no signal or is out of range. If he is not working in the Mohabi Desert, don't buy it.
- 💔 His pet-name for you has suddenly changed from something attractive and even sexy, to something more appropriate for one of the guys. So, "Precious" is now being treated as "Bubba?"
- 💔 He forgot his cellphone at your house, and then drove, at 60 mph, through your front yard to get it back?
- 💔 That cellphone just keeps turning up lost, battery is dying all the time, etc., etc., etc.
- 💔 When you want to go to the movies it suddenly turns out that he already saw the movie you've been talking about for weeks. Hmm, when? With whom?
- 💔 Party X or Disco 2000 is suddenly, unexpectedly, inexplicably off limits to him? He doesn't like that music since when? And there's nothing you can do to convince him to go?
- 💔 Certain phone calls make him super nervous, testy—even angry—and he keeps the phone smashed up against his ear. Is the name plugged into the phone a mysteri-

ous looking man's name, like Jack Eagle? A cheap trick he learned from a James Bond movie.

- ♥ Or he's suddenly hanging up again—right before meeting you.
- ♥ Christmas or other gifts suddenly become beyond his "budget?"
- ♥ Returns from one of his unknown "missions" and is now super nice, overly loving and affectionate.
- ♥ Even his mother is wrapped up in it, lying about where he is when she thinks you're not listening. Who is she talking to?
- ♥ Songs about infidelity or "Your cheating heart" cause him to suddenly switch the radio station or turn the TV off.
- ♥ Avoids eye contact with you. Gazes off. Acts tortured or heartbroken. Big red flag.

If your boyfriend meets one or two of the conditions above, just relax. You don't need to become the panicked, searching, clawing girlfriend yet—much less a spy looking into every corner of his life. One or two points is probably nothing.

But is your heart-throb clocking in with yes on 5 or more of the points above? Chances are you're kidding yourself.

If this is your case, what you do is totally up to you. But don't kid yourself and don't stay with someone who's not respecting you. Sometimes it's not so easy to realize this, and other times it is just as obvious as the nose on his face.

If that's the story of your relationship, it's better to let go and to take this relationship as a learning experience. Someone who cheats on you once will almost certainly cheat on you twice. But the good news is that investing time in finding a faithful man can be both a positive challenge and a way to strengthen your own self-steem. Besides, let us tell you that faithful men do actually exist!

That said, there are also guys who will make mistakes and forgiving them is not out of the question. Look at how methodical was he. Was he setting it up to be a long-term thing or was it just a one-time mistake? Has there been a series of one-time mistakes? If that's the case, then he is a serial mistake maker and your forgiveness is what fuels him. Not worth it.

Give yourself the opportunity to love someone who truly loves (only) you back.

Dating and hanging out

Mom! Dad! This is my boyfriend, Lennon, and we're getting married in a month.

Dating is awesome and, for sure, it's way more than flirting. It's sort of an official caring relationship that involves all sorts of emotions: love, fun, illusion and commitment. However, it's got a tough side to it too since confusion, anger, break ups and jealousy can also emerge. It all comes in the same box.

So don't worry if one day you feel like flying to the moon and the next you feel like disappearing into the depths of the Earth. Congratulations! You have a relationship—and all of its extremes.

TYPES OF RELATIONSHIPS

Lunchtime relationship: it lasts about that long.

Siamese relationship: You're so close all the time, you seem to be one person, not two

Paparazzi relationship: You keep hiding from everyone.

Low proficiency relationship: You keep failing.

Karate relationship: You're together, but you can't stop kicking each other

Titanic relationship: Love till you die.

Gangster relationship: it's all about betrayal.

Greenpeace relationship: You're only perpetuating the species. Meaning: dating your BFF brother.

Speaking of the "love birds" condition, have you ever felt that your boyfriend and you think too differently? You really, really like him but it worries you that he might not feel the same? One day you love him and the next one you hate him? Well, this is also absolutely normal.

At this stage of life, feelings change all the time, just like that. Things can get more difficult if there are wide gaps in ages, culture, education, values or customs, but even if you're from similar backgrounds, things can change quickly.

You know what, though? Differences are also cool because they make you guys compliment each other. When love is big enough in a relationship, it can really conquer all.

Relationship advice: Basics

> Relationships have highs and lows. Try to enjoy them both.
> Respect each other's space. Being stuck together all day long can be a pain.
> Don't be controlling or absorbing. Men despise that! (You probably do too.)
> Don't think about bugging him all day long with stuff like: "Do you love me?" or "You never tell me you like me, or that I'm hot"… Boring! Men can be shy at times, and in some cases, come-ons like that are simply not part of their repertoire.
> Talk to him about the stuff you dig and the things you hate.
> Constant fights weaken love. Arguing every once in a while is fine, though never let verbal or physical aggression be part of it.
> Average jealousy is all right. Hardcore jealousy is just the reaction of a super insecure person.
> Never let him make you do things you don't want to.
> If there's cheating going on, it's better to stop the whole thing, quickly.
> Did you feel like dying after breaking up with your boyfriend? Calm down, without a doubt you won't die. Even though it's terrible, you always get over it and fall in love again. Read carefully: Always!

Relationships grow when you're with the right person. It won't only be about having fun or hanging out for a while. You'll want to be with him for the rest of your life.

My girlfriends

Having a good friend BFF

Having a BFF is so important! Nobody except her will ever understand what's going on with your life, your concerns as well as your feelings. Why? In broad terms, it's because she's going through the same things you are.

You can cry in front of her free of shame, or tell her how depressed you feel about this or that situation. You girls just need to meet each other's eyes to figure out what's going on and burst into laughter.

There are no two alike

Some girl friends are definitely ephemeral, you know? The ones that come and go like the girl you hang out with when you're out of town during the summer but you never get to see again. There are other friends that share a random class with you, or a hobby or a sport, though you could also find the recyclable friends, you know which kind, right? The ones you used to love but then had an argument and later became sort of friends again. True friends, however, are something totally different. We're talking about the group of people with whom you feel totally identified and you really care for.

Even though there might be a nice friendship between a guy and a girl, there are still certain things that you can only trust to a woman, you know what we mean?

Friends are just like the seats in a movie theater. The friends in your VIP group (usually composed of two or three ladies) have the same values as you do and share the way you view life. You can open up your heart to them without fear of being criticized afterwards. In a theater, you'd definitely seat them right in the middle, so they can have the best view.

There's also a broader group, the bunch of friends you hang out with. Take care of them and seat them right behind the VIP group. Note that there's another group of girls you'd put in the middle on the aisles—but just because you were in a good mood.

The rest of the people would be seated either way up or way down, although there's also the annoying and mean girls who you'd simply refuse to let in: "Sorry, sold out!"

Just as in all relationships, open and honest communication is the key to success. By doing this, your friendships will last for years and endure the conflicts that inevitably arise. But if you're crabby all the time and you're being shady with the rest of the ladies... Watch it! They might end up throwing *you* out of the movie theater.

"I suck at making friends"

"I haven't been able to make friends since I entered Middle School about two months ago. I don't know anyone—just moved into town—and I spend most of my time on my own 'cause I suck at making friends. I'm by myself at lunchtime while everyone else is having fun, you know what I mean? It is pretty depressing. I'm a bit shy and quiet, and I sometimes feel that people think I'm a freak... Who knows?" This was Liz's comment.

It's true: not everyone in the world can make friends easily. It's basically a question of temperament, something you are born with and won't be able to change. But you can be more accessible.

iF YOU'RE AN INTROVERT

Just like Liz, introverts can sometimes actually feel like freaks. They generally share little information about themselves and, when they do, it is usually about their thoughts—not their feelings. Introverts are the type of people who enjoy reaching the essence of things and reflecting about them. They're great observers and listeners, and their patience makes them excellent friends.

Lunchtime usually makes introverts feel even more awkward! Since they don't have anyone to talk to, they're either reading a book or making sure their homework is totally perfect—just to kill some time. Is this your case? Chill out! You're not alone, it happens to a lot of people. It can be tough, but you can start making friends by approaching someone just to ask a few questions.

Ask her about the lesson taught in class or about sports or a cool TV show. Even better—ask where she gets her hair cut or where she bought her shoes... Little by little you'll start talking about all sorts of things. And all of a sudden, you'll be having lunch together and the friendship will begin.

Bear in mind that sometimes people associate shyness with being cocky. That's why we'd recommend you to put a big smile on your face and try to keep an open mind so you're not misunderstood. We'd also strongly suggest that you don't go after her food the very first day you have lunch together.

iF YOU'RE RATHER AN EXTROVERT

Extroverts have the capacity to talk about their entire lives right after you've just met. They love being busy all the time and enjoy going out. Extroverts are always happy to meet different people as well as to experiment a bunch of things at the same time.

An extrovert can be a real chatterbox and some are terrible listeners. These girls usually screw up or get into trouble because they talk without thinking.

If you're an extrovert, making friends will be a piece of cake for you. Just be sure to look after your friends and try to show interest in them. By the way, consider closing your mouth every once in a while! At least you'd like to know the basic stuff, you know, like their names.

Conflicts and complications

There will always be situations (internal or external) that challenge the friendship between two or more girls. Some days you love your BFF and think: "Oh my god! What would I do without her?" Some other days you hate her and think: "Gee! What am I going to do with her?"

It's inevitable. In order to fix up any situation, it is necessary to talk things over and show patience and trust.

Feelings in a friendship

> Admiration: "My friend Jenny is gorgeous! There are so many guys who are nuts about her. Besides, she's the smartest girl in class and best friends with everyone."

> Possession: "What! You're going to the movies with Veronica? We were going to study together, remember?" Yep. A few inches from calling her an idiot.

> Annoyance: "You are such a copycat. You're always wearing the same things that I'm wearing. Don't even think about taking that purple shirt to the party. I'm wearing mine!"

> Envy: "Maria is going to the concert and my Dad won't let me go! And she's going with Joe! Grrrr! I hope the singer gets sick and cancels the whole gig."

> Competition: "Christy is one of my best friends, but still, I have to get better grades than she does. If not that, then at

least I want to look hotter than her on the day we get our grades back. Tee hee."

> Jealousy: "Ever since you got a boyfriend it's like I don't exist" or "My best friend's cool and everything, and all the guys in class are after her. Why wouldn't they be? She's tall, skinny, she has fabulous hair... She's perfect. I hate her! But then again, if I was a guy, I'd definitely want to go out with her."

> Solidarity: "Relax! I'll come home with you and show you how to solve the math problems. It's super easy, you'll see. Of course you can!"

> Deception: "My best friend flirted around with Joe and didn't mean anything. But it's irritating because I like him so much! She apologized several times, but I'm not sure she's being sincere."

> Affinity: "I have a blast with my friends! We love walking around the mall on Fridays and then going to the movies."

> Unconditional love: "Melissa has so many problems at home. Even though she's not that pretty, I try to give her a hand. I love her to death."

> Treason: "And now, my friend hangs out with Michelle cause she smokes and I don't. It pisses me off so bad!" or "Denise told the whole school my secret." And it can get even worse: "Ann stole my man and dumped him the next day."

For real! All of these things can happen in a friendship—and the list goes on and on. It is all absolutely normal! The important thing is to find out for yourself whether these feelings are temporary nonsense or not. It could turn out that this girl you've been having trouble with is not a real friend after all.

If you're not OK with something, speak up! Talk things through so nothing is misunderstood. Good friendships should affect and enrich your life in many ways—but they need to be nurtured.

Friends can last forever, especially those you make at this stage of life, and that's the best thing that can happen to you. Just don't forget that friendships are like a two-way road: you give and you take—that's the rule of this game.

Be THE BFF

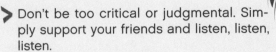

> Don't be too critical or judgmental. Simply support your friends and listen, listen, listen.
> Dare to talk about stuff that other girls keep to themselves. Be sincere.
> If a friend of yours is talking about her concerns, pay close attention to her.
> If someone else is picking on your friend, don't be ashamed to stand up for her.
> Keep suggestions to yourself unless you're asked for your own point of view.
> Secrets must always be kept that way: secret.
> Don't try to change your friends. Let them be who they are.
> "The only way to have a friend is to be one." –R.W. Emerson.

CHECK THIS OUT

They bring me down... Bullying

I hate going to school. Two girls there will not stop bothering me. Whenever I'm anywhere near them, they say terrible things about me—including my name and then they laugh. They push me, they hide my things and they throw spit balls at me.

One day they wrote, "you're a bitch" on my backpack and when I tried to tell on them I found out they were recording me. They pretty much died of laughter and then jumped to put the whole thing on the Internet. It was probably the worst day of my life. I thought about taking some of my mother's pills and just never going back to school.

First it was just two girls, and then it became almost my whole class. I hate them, but I can't say anything. I really don't know what to do!

Susana, 14 years old

It never fails. Everyone, at some point in life, gets made fun of and has to bear the brunt of cruel and really mean taunts, jokes and insults. It's called "bullying" and unfortunately it seems to have increased in frequency for as long as there have been schools. We want you to know that this happens in all schools and absolutely everyone gets knocked on the head. How you face it makes all the difference between a miserable school experience and one you can live perfectly well with.

Unfortunately, parents sometimes don't pay nearly enough attention to this problem either. Sometimes they think this type of harassment is typical but, in fact, it's a problem that has grown dramatically. This situation has come to affect thousands of guys and girls everywhere. Furthermore, the psychological damage inflicted can be tremendous and can last for years—long into adulthood.

We asked some experts how young girls can face bullying. We thought you might like hearing their answers.

what makes one kid more likely to be bullied than others?

The bully attacks anything and everything that is different. The way someone dresses, if they're ugly, fat, dirty, talk differently, or smell different. People get picked on for their hair, the color of their skin, for their grades, for being shy or strange and for much more significant reasons. Basically anyone who is different or vulnerable in any way, is fair game for a bully.

How widespread is the problem of bullying?

Bullying is very common, especially between middle school and junior high. In part it can be explained by the fact that some over-protective parents don't teach children to defend themselves. That same child can become unable to adjust, and having developed a tolerance for abuse, an extremely low self-esteem and no means of defense, is likely to become prey of those who turn on others—or to believe that she's actually stupid or lazy. There are also children or teenagers who simply want to have power over others. This allows them to express their anger and frustration and thus to gain some control over their own lives.

What can a young person do if they find themselves being victimized by a bully?

Below are some suggestions that we picked up from young people, experts on youth problems and a variety of other sources.

- Pretend that you simply don't mind, even if you feel like dying inside.
- Do not give them power. If you're sad or they see you suffering, then they've achieved their objective and it can get worse. It's best to team up with a friend or friends and make it clear that you're not afraid—even if you are scared to death.
- If you acknowledge that you're upset and angry and that the whole thing is bringing you down, then you can really start to fight back. It may be the only way to gain a bully's respect. We all have flaws, and telling the bully on his own is one route you can try to take. In the beginning the bully will pretend as if nothing's wrong, but he or she will be feeling really bad. If everyone sees and makes fun of the bully he or she will need to control him or herself, but remember, a bully is a very insecure person and is disturbing you just to cover that up. Bringing the faults of the bully out into the open can do some good but don't become a bully yourself.
- Talk to your parents or teacher. But ask for advice, don't accuse the bullies. Just remember: bullying is hardly a situation you can handle on your own. You need a helping hand.

- Talk in private with the bully even though it sounds like bullycide. It can help a lot. First of all, it takes a lot of courage to face the bully (and he or she knows it), and second because it is likely that the bully's been "brought down" in the past via harassment as well.
- Talk to anyone else being bullied. Although this might sound strange or suicidal, it can really help a lot. First, it takes courage and they may very well notice it, and second, as they are also suffering, you may be able to come up with a strategy to fight the bully off.
- Body language is very important. Stand up tall and proud and avoid walking hunched over, and looking down as if you don't exist, even if you really feel like disappearing. Walking like you're wounded is really going to fuel further attacks.
- You can change things like your hairstyle and the way you dress. And you may open yourself up to some initial mockery—but a change for the better is always going to bring you more pride, dignity and self-worth. Don't go backwards—not even one step.
- Make a big long list of your qualities—all the good things about you, and accept your "differences" with pride. Do not be belittled and don't miss school.
- Claim your rights. And, more than anything, construct an image of yourself that you're sure commands respect— and live up to it. That is, live your own image of yourself.

When I was in fourth grade, there was this very pretty girl, named Sofia. One day she began to annoy me in front of everybody, telling me that my dad was very dark. The others began to laugh at me and at that age it all hit me very hard. She continued doing it for several weeks, until I decided I had to do something.

One evening after school, it occurred to me to begin to call her "salami" (give me a break! I was in fourth grade!). I asked a friend to help me by saying the same thing. The next day, I arrived at school and said: "Hello Salami." Obviously, at first, no one understood. But every time we were near Sofia, we said: "Smells like salami, doesn't it?" And we joked all day about that funny little word. And eventually the rest of the class started in on the joke too.

The thing is that by the end of the day Sofia was in tears and begging me to stop. I did, and she stopped bothering me. I never imagined that something so silly would help me to solve a problem which I found so overwhelming at the time.

Indeed, it works. The important thing is to use it for self-defense only. **And you must never become one of them.**

Yordi

Another really important thing to remember is that the world is like a mirror. People see you as you see yourself. The label you put on yourself will be the one that others use to decide about you. And above all, pay attention: "People treat you like you let them do it." Good luck!

NOTE:

If you are a bully—someone who feels superior, or someone who, just for fun, or to get attention needs to bring other people down well, think of the damage you can cause. In some cases it is irreversible.

Put yourself in other peoples' shoes for a change and ask yourself if you'd like all of that done to you. Remember that everything you do in life sooner or later will backfire to you, just like a boomerang.

If you see your friend picking on someone and you don't like it, just get away. People who pick on other people do it—almost exclusively—to demonstrate their own power. Make an effort and try to convince them to stop.

The need to feel that you belong to something is a pretty serious matter that touches the deep fibers of human essence. During adolescence, belonging or not belonging to a group of friends might seem like a matter of life or death. But it isn't—even if it really seems that way. However, group pressure can affect just about every other aspect of your life.

Most girls between ages 12 and 19 do what they do because "everybody's doing it." It doesn't matter if it's lying, drinking, buying fancy clothes, smoking, skipping class, having sex… Everything is justified by the same "everybody else is doing it" motto.

Feeling that you don't belong anywhere can be so totally distressing that you'd sell your brother just to get some attention in return. That's why we'd better talk about this stuff.

"My friends at school blacklisted me just because I'm nice to a girl who everyone else seems to hate. I pity her and I wouldn't like to be treated like that, but my friends don't seem to get it. I don't know what to do," Allie said.

Getting over a situation in which you're completely blown off by other people can be very difficult. It doesn't matter if the reasons are silly or complicated. The fact is that you're put into a super vulnerable position—and the girls you hang out with know this well or can at least sense it. This is when a group puts a member to test: the privilege of "belonging" is earned through merits or some kind of initiation.

This pressure can get pretty hardcore if not totally frustrating. It may make you do things that you would never do willingly under normal circumstances. If you've been through this situation it's important to know how humans respond to these kinds of tests.

Peer Pressure

Without a doubt, you'll meet people down the road who think you've got to be somebody else or behave in a certain way. As if that's not enough, these people will seriously try to influence you and force you to change. This can be quite confusing, especially when a) it comes from someone you otherwise appreciate, like a good friend or a guy you like, or b) you may still not know who you really are.

And don't forget, suggestions and advice can be helpful sometimes. You can get access to new ideas and maybe figure things out differently when you consider an issue or problem from different points of view. But if people are taking you in a direction that makes you feel uncomfortable —even if it's just a bit—be careful.

Pay attention to your intuition and do not do it!

Allie also said: "If you don't do what everyone else is doing, your friends make you feel like crap. They make fun of you, they criticize you, and they make you feel bad or they simply exclude you."

Why do we tend to give in to peer pressure?

Because rejection, on one hand, is deeply intertwined with our greatest fears: being abandoned, being humiliated or being embarrassed (we are truly scared of making a fool of ourselves, aren't we?). The idea of screwing things up and being singled out is just scary, don't you think? It's an awful feeling, without a doubt! Failure and rejection are powerful motivating factors no matter what. And that's why some-things can be so hard to get out of or be opposed to and why it can be difficult to stand up for yourself.

How to face it?

- Learn how to say no. Say it convincingly, strong and out loud. Maybe your friends will reject you in the beginning, but they'll definitely show you more respect afterwards.
- Don't believe that everybody is actually "doing it." It's a total fallacy: not everyone gets hammered, not everyone smokes pot, not everyone cried when watching whatever movie, not everyone has sex and not everyone lies to their parents, friends and teachers. Hundreds buy into this phrase and end up doing silly stuff.
- Beware of "Just once" as well. It's the type of thing that sounds easy to do and instantly convinces: "Just once! Nothing's going to happen. C'mon! It's no big deal." Watch out! You can really screw yourself up with this kind of things. That little burst of false-confidence might also lead you to events you won't be able to stop later on. Pushing pedal to the metal, drugs, shop-lifting, or random (and unsafe) sex... just because you heard that some of that stuff is "cool" or trendy.
- Don't fool yourself with the "That won't happen to me" idea. Why not? Take five minutes to talk to somebody who ended up in a wheelchair after a car accident. It can happen to anyone—and, in fact, it happens to someone every day.
- Pay close attention to your body's reactions. Your body is very wise. It will let you know when you're not acting well or when something smells fishy—besides, the reaction is lightning fast. Your body has loads of good self-preservation mechanisms. As matter of fact, there are serious studies that have confirmed that in certain cases your intuition is more accurate that your reason. So get used to trusting it!
- Establish alliances. Look for somebody who feels the same way you do. It's much easier to deal with peer

pressure when you feel supported and let's face it—you never have to be totally alone.

Finally, just remember that you are the only person with the ability to build your own life. Nobody else can do it for you. True friends are those who accept you just as you are without demonstrating anything at all. So say NO to peer pressure, and… say no to global warming! (It has nothing to do with the topic, but it kind of just popped up in our heads).

INSTRUCTIONS

Groups exist in every single school. In order to complete your school's mental yearbook follow these instructions:
- Wander around at school.
- Look closely at hidden corners of the athletics track.
- Spot and identify your school's groups. (The loud group of people right in the middle of the cafeteria, are usually known as the attention seekers).
- Find something to munch out on. This has nothing to do with filling in the yearbook, but it seems like a good idea. Identify the members of your group. Maybe you can even
- draw their pic.

Even though people socialize in groups of affinity by nature, it's super important that you keep in mind that no group or person is better than the other.

We each have different interests and preferences, and that is what makes us feel comfortable with ourselves. Respecting others is super important.

Remember: every person is an individual, and that's what makes us so special. Just imagine: what if we were all the same? Boring!

My Family

You were born there

You might be able to choose your friends, your boyfriend and the sports you play. What you can't choose is your family.

You were born here. You belong here. In the best of cases, a family is a source of love, support and consolation. But lots of families can also be a source of pain, frustration and distress. In most cases it's a combination of both situations.

It's funny, but it's quite common to see your parents as perfect human beings when you're a small kid. You believe that all parents are alike and share the same concerns regarding your education, the values taught at home, the way they treat you and your siblings as well as the way they interact as a couple.

But when you grow up and become a little bit more independent, you start seeing your parents and your family from a different perspective (Whoa! What happened to my folks?). Suddenly you find out that they're just like other people—with positive and negative aspects.

At the same time, you get to see how other families interact. All these contrasts allow you to identify and appreciate your family. You'll see that your family has an influence on what you fancy—what you're OK with—and what you're definitely not ok with, as well as all the things you'd like to change. Just remember that no matter how much you'd sometimes like to, you cannot change your siblings nor your parents.

Relationships: highs and lows

Regardless of which family we're talking about, there will always be things you'd like to change. Maybe it's stuff that hurts, or maybe it's stuff that bothers you, but there's no other option except to learn to live with it.

Fights, love and hatred between kids can occur in every family. The processes of change that you're all going through will affect your relationship with your parents, your brothers and your sisters. It may have several stages, as well as many highs and lows. But it's all normal, everybody's got them.

It's also common that after loving and admiring your parents for such a long time, all of a sudden you want to strangle them in front of your friends! Sometimes you feel really proud of them but some other times you don't even want to acknowledge them as your folks.

It's like when you run into this huge crush of yours or your coolest friends, and your parents are looking terrible. The question is always: "Are those your parents?" And your reply is something like, "Who? Them? No, no, I don't even know them. They must work here. Poor guys, they look so tired." Or how about when your mother brings out the old photo album with pictures of you in the nude or when dad is singing a super retro song in the car—packed with your friends, of course.

The truth is, parents can be truly embarrassing.

Types of parents

Before getting into the depths of parenthood, we must realize that there are different sorts of homes: with both parents, with mom or dad only, those that include grandma or grandpa, or maybe your father's or mother's new partner. So when we talk about parents, we'd like to refer to those special people in your life, the people with whom you share the good and the bad, your highs and your lows.

What is wrong with them?

Like we've said, when adolescence arrives, your body sends out signals: hair here, cramps, pimple there… EVERYWHERE. The thing is that your changes affect your parents as well. The issue is that they can't tell what's going on. Just think, in the least expected moment, their little daughter is not interested in the dolls they used to buy for her, but rather she is after REAL guys she chooses for herself.

And so, all sudden the past solutions for past problems stop working.

Going against… everything

Suddenly, you want to go against… everything. You know why? When we're kids, our parents are our role models: we want to be like them. And we really do behave like them.

First of all, it's genetics (character and abilities, even those Dumbo ears you have), and second, it's about the way they've managed your upbringing.

The thing is that adolescence provokes your own search for individuality. Your instinct is asking you to be just who you are, and boom! You realize that you've just wanted to be like your parents for such a long time. Unconsciously, you chose to go against them in just about everything because you just need to stop being like them—and start being like you really are.

The whole problem starts there. Even if they say: "The sky is blue", you answer back saying: "Well, I see it pink. Period." So they ground you, and that pink you saw everywhere might turn to brown.

Let's face it: neither you nor your parents are guilty. It's just a stage in life that neither of you chooses, and both parts must learn to live with it and manage it.

There are no perfect parents

There are divorces, second marriages, problems, arguments, absent parents, single parents, half brothers and step-sisters…

However, parents love their kids and will look after them like no one else will—even though sometimes it doesn't seem like it.

The parent-child relationship can be conflictive at any age, but things get more extreme during adolescence. The changes you're going through, and the way you and your parents regard independence, tend to make things more difficult. On one hand, your parents feel that they're losing control over you; that you're totally out of whack. And on the other hand, you're striving to be in control of your own life. But they love you to death and the idea of something bad happening to you totally petrifies them. That's why they get so grumpy at times.

Ok, Dad, i'm going to jenny's place and then to the movies. Oh, right: i'll be back in a month. See you then!

The source of most troubles

The origin of almost every conflict is the lack of information. If you demonstrate to your parents that you're trustworthy, the quicker they'll realize that you're capable of being responsible and looking after yourself.

If you keep your parents posted on what you do, where you're off to and whom you get along with, their fears will definitely cool down. Easy tasks like saying the truth will calm them down. Trust between you guys will develop to the point that you'll be able to talk about things you know are not OK: "I skipped class." Instead of scolding you, in most cases they will actually appreciate your honesty and understand that, every once in a while, things like these are absolutely normal.

But if you deny them information, everything is going to be upside down. Fear is going to make them want to find out more and more about you and will actually keep them from letting you go on your own. Then you get angry, they ground you, you lock yourself up in your room, and you stop talking to each other. Of course, the relationship deteriorates and wears out completely. Everybody loses, especially you.

My parents are so embarrassing... they don't even speak English!

It's awful, We know, but the truth is that many girls go through this—not all of them, of course. We spoke to several girls who shared with us some of their thoughts:

- ✖ I feel embarrassed because they only speak like 3 words of English.
- ✖ I don't want my friends to see the way they dress.
- ✖ They're always saying that everything's so much better "back home". Boring!
- ✖ Like, they don't even know how to use a cell phone. When I ask them to take a picture of me, they hold the phone upside down!
- ✖ It's so funny the way they enunciate.

There are many parents who are super adapted to the American way of life and don't see this as an issue at all. However, there's a bunch of folks who strive with this every single day. And you know what? It is ABSOLUTELY NORMAL. Cultures collide at home, and this may be difficult for every member of the family.

Quite possibly for you, too. Even though you're of Hispanic descent, going to Mexico, Guatemala, El Salvador, _____ (write the country of your election here), is seems as far and foreign as a safari in Africa.

But please take note that it is complicated for them too. Their little daughter, the one they pictured following the traditions of their homeland, is now a young lady with a barcode or a Mickey Mouse cartoon tattooed and her back, with this thing called iPod permanently glued to her ears.

The truth is that nobody's guilty of anything.

Many, many parents feel insecure being so far away from their country. In order to feel protected, they've locked themselves up in a Hipanobubble (does this word even exist? Probably not, but it certainly should).

What do we mean by this? Well, some parents actually feel threatened in foreign societies, and that's why they only go to Spanish-speaking shops and they shut their ears as soon as they hear something in English. They even look for Mass services in Spanish so they can pray the Padre Nuestro instead of Our Holy Father.

Darío Sánchez, a Family Therapist based in San Diego, told us about the importance of being social. It's crucial that parents avoid self-exclusion and instead make an effort to integrate to the society in which they're living. Also, it is really important that they realize that you need to be part of that society as well, that you're obviously seeking to be recognized and accepted.

And it is SUPER IMPORTANT that you understand your folks. You're situation and theirs is not the same: being born into a new culture (like you) is VERY DIFFERENT from arriving into a new culture with deep-rooted traditions and customs.

Tolerance is vital. Try to put yourself in their shoes (whether it's their own traditional shoes or a cool pair of Nike sneakers).

As you've seen, both parents and kids have to catch on and show respect. Making them feel bad about their origins is REALLY NOT FAIR, because if we took their encephalogram (you know, a super mega x-ray shot from their heads), we'd certainly realize that:

- They feel really sad when you reject them, because they gave up their lives to provide you with a better one.
- It hurts when you make fun of them, because they feel so proud of you.
- It's painful to see that the price of pursuing a better life is to lose a part of their children.
- Even though they've found recognition at work, the only recognition they're after is yours.

The thing is that neither their problems nor yours are easy to handle. But the fact of the matter is that the more you understand them, the more they'll understand you.

It feels like home here

You're the type of Mexican girl who supports the American team in a US—Mexico soccer match. Obviously, this is TOP SECRET: not even in your wildest dreams would you discuss this at home—not to mention telling Grandma!

Or maybe you're the type of girl who knows nothing about your homeland's traditions, but you can explain every single aspect of Thanksgiving. Actually, you know so much, that you could even write down your turkey's family tree.

Don't freak out! This is absolutely normal.

An important amount of Hispanics who have lived in the US since they were little babies go through this. And it has NOTHING to do with carelessness or lacking affection towards your origins.

So chill out! Inhale, exhale, inhale, exhale, relax... and... stop inhaling and keep reading.

There are several reasons that explain this feeling.

- First of all, growing up with traditions from another country is totally different from growing up in a place where those traditions are just stories, you know, the "Once upon a time" type.
- Second, in general terms, Hispanics in the US are usually associated to illegal immigration, crime and social disturbance.

And that's why you obviously don't want to be identified with that. Not a tiny bit. It's not that you don't like being Hispanic; it's just that you don't find it cool to be connected to negative ideas.

Ok, it is true that some Hispanics do behave that way. Because of them, we've all been stereotyped for being Latinos. But the matter of the fact is that the vast majority of us are hard-working, honest, professional and dedicated people.

And nicknames like *wetback, spick, frijolero, dirty Mexican* (even if you're not Mexican at all), as well as comments like: "You're only getting accepted into College because you're a minority, you know?" constantly make you realize the way we're perceived.

Third, we asked a bunch of girls who live in the US (whether they were born there or not), what they like about living in the USA. Here are their answers:

- Rules are respected here.
- I feel safe.
- I like the way of life.
- There are so many things here.
- People don't mess around with your life.
- We are all respected for being in a powerful country.

Let's be honest: who doesn't like that? And besides, if you add the fact that you've lived here like, all your life, and that perhaps you're even a US citizen, no wonder America feels like home.

But you know what's super important? To realize that you're one of the few fortunate girls in the world who has two cultures to enjoy! You can take advantage, and make the most of each.

Just as there are young Hispanics who feel very proud of their heritage, there are also many others who just... don't. That's why we think that taking the best of both worlds is, after all, the best option. Just think how much you'd miss out if you left one culture out:

- The cultural richness that is present in all Latin American countries.
- The impressive natural landscapes that these countries guard—sites visited by millions of people from all over the world.
- Having roots from some of the most advanced civilizations that have ever existed.
- The second most natively spoken language in the world—and the second most studied too.
- The amazing traditions (and beautiful, too) that most countries admire.
- Our human warmth and our joy; forgetting the way we make friends… and even the way we dance and celebrate.

It's like having a treasure and not being able to enjoy it. Especially because it is part of you, of your own story.

You know what? People from all over the world love Latinos. Personally speaking, our best passport in the entire universe is being Mexican.

We honestly hope that you (and no one else but you…) have the opportunity to enjoy both cultures and take advantage of all of the good stuff that each one has.

We're getting a divorce

It was a Sunday, and my parents were fighting as usual. They started out talking quietly without realizing that we noticed every little thing that was going on. But all of these "discussions" more or less followed the same pattern.

After 15 minutes of screaming at each other, they snuck out of their room like nothing happened. And then they were super affectionate to me and my sister. I think it was because they felt guilty.

So then we got in the car, like every Sunday, to eat out. Mom said something that pissed dad off. Finally my dad just threw the door open and got out of the car when we'd barely stopped. I was scared, and my sister started crying, my mom was just standing there with the door open. She started yelling at my dad so much that my sister and I just slid further and further down the back seat. It was like we were not there.

Finally we all just went home again. My mom chased my dad into their room and Natalia and I were sitting on the living room floor—listening to them shouting and throwing things. I felt horrible and my sister would not stop crying.

Suddenly there was a silence that lasted a long time. After a while, my dad came out and went out the backdoor. He never came back and never slept in our house again.

About two weeks later we all got together to listen to the words I knew they were going to say and that we didn't want to hear: "We're getting a divorce."

Isabel, 15.

Why divorce hurts?

Julia Borbolla, a psychologist says: "Imagine you're on a plane and see that the pilot and the co-pilot fight all the time. One moves the lever forward and the other one moves it back. You may have no absolutely idea how to fly a plane, but it's obvious that if they don't sort things out, and agree on something, you're all going down together."

When you're a teenager, your sexuality wakes up and you realize that your parents are also sexual people. If they get divorced, they suddenly become available! This can be really confusing. And you can end up being the guardian: "Where are you going? What time are you coming home?" This is just one of the frustrations and new situations that can really wear you down—right when what you actually need is for things to calm down.

Some young people who have experienced their parents divorce tell us:

Everything hurts. It hurts to remember watching my dad leaving the house with suitcases. It hurts when I feel like I lost my security, that maybe my mom is going to be poorer. It hurts when I think we're going to a small apartment, maybe to another school. Now she has to work and spend less time with us. I hate seeing my mom sad and hear her crying.

I felt like I had my heart ripped in half and that I will never feel safe again. My dad was looking after me. It hurt when I had to go into my parent's room and I didn't see him in the morning, or smell him anymore. I felt like I would die without his help. He hugged me, but without his kisses and support everyday I was lost.

It hurts to no longer see my dad. And I feel like it was my fault because they argued about my grades. Maybe if I had or hadn't done some little thing... then they would have stayed together. And choosing between the two of them was horrible. I felt really powerless when I imagined seeing my mom with another man or my dad with a younger woman. I don't do anything with my dad anymore.

It hurts that they used me as their messenger and spy and as some kind of negotiating point. I felt totally abandoned and betrayed because I thought my parents would always be together. I really just felt totally different from all my friends.

My parents are divorcing, what can I do?

- Try to talk about your feelings with an adult. It's totally normal to feel fear, anger and loneliness.
- You can cry over what's happened. That's also completely normal and it's going to help you to get through the whole process.
- Write to your parents about how you feel. They're as busy as you are, but they may take the time to read and that can give them a little time to reflect on what you really need or want.
- Understand that in a divorce there is no "good" or "bad". Everyone suffers and everyone loses.
- Don't judge your parents as a couple, but try to think of them as a man and a woman.
- Maybe you just reject the idea of seeing your parents rebuild their lives. It can seem unbearable, but with time they will probably do it, so cool down a bit. Try to understand them and respect them. Be nice and treat their new partner (if they have one) as they treat your friends.
- Don't take advantage of the situation to manipulate them or to get money, concessions or special permissions. This eventually turns against you, and you'll fell really bad about it.
- Don't take sides and try to stay out of their problems. Don't be the messenger, the referee or the reporter of what's going on in "the other house."
- Try to build support and unity with your siblings.
- You definitely want to avoid using alcohol or drugs. You might feel reassured (or oblivious) for a moment, but if you're hooked for life, you totally lose.

- Do not seek sex with lovers or do anything in order to feel loved or to mask your loneliness. The only thing that will happen is that you'll feel sorry and increasingly empty.
- Understand that divorces happen for a thousand reasons, but none of those reasons are your fault.
- Despite the fact that this episode is so painful, you can use it to learn something about being more mature in a relationship and the true value, and difficulty of all these things.

Most of the young people we talked to for this book told us that after all the problems, the pain and the anguish, the overall mood in their homes eventually improved. And most of them prefer a thousand times over, how they're living now. Even if it hurts a lot at the time, eventually people get used to the way things are going to be. If the decision is made then all you can do is focus on making yourself a better person, enjoy your parents separately and try to be happy with everything that you have. Take it easy.

My Mom's Boyfriend / My Dad's Girlfriend

If you go through a divorce or the loss of one of your parents, sooner or later they are going to start rebuilding their lives. It might be the best thing that could happen but it could also mean you have new friends, cousins (siblings?), and they have a new boyfriend or girlfriend, and could remarry. It makes sense.

When you're used to having "exclusive access" to your dad or mom, the new partner can bring a lot of problems.

But parents need company for many reasons: loneliness, sadness, wanting to be happy, feeling guilty or fearing economic problems.

You might feel that just when things are settling down after a divorce, this person shows up and you freak out because there is really "no time for me." But by trying to understand, empathize with and think like your parents, you really can achieve a tremendous amount of personal growth in just a short time.

Here's another situation. "Some stranger suddenly wants to be my new parent. She/he wants to impose new rules, educate me and above all, to steal the attention that once came exclusively to me" (of course, you don't like it at all). In this case, it seems perfectly normal to feel jealousy, anger, betrayal and abandonment along with other negative emotions. "My mom asks me to try to love him, or at least to like him, but he's not even related to me."

A relationship with a stepfather or a stepmother can be super difficult to navigate and it can really draw out feelings of guilt and anger. Eventually, things will adjust and although it might seem unbelievable at first, if everyone does their best, the situation can really work out better for everyone.

This doesn't mean that person will be your new mom or your new dad. Just respect their right to privacy and treat him or her as you would have your parents treat your own friends or your boyfriend.

It's also important to know that most new couples are trying, primarily, to make each other happy. They may smile again and hopefully, feel the joy of life once again. After everything your parents have been through, it may be the least they deserve.

If you realize that with time, you may just like your step parent after all, then don't feel bad. The affection from and for a father or a mother is not something that you'll find with anyone else. They know that too.

You just opened up another part of your heart. With all of the changes and unexpected hassle, in the end, doing so is one of the things that costs the least and can reward you the most.

Violence at home

It's a sad reality but many families and many homes still run under a violence scheme. The factors and variables that result in domestic violence are too numerous to count.

Every day in the news you can hear stories that take place on Harmony Street but sound like something from "Nightmare on Elm Street."

A big part of the problem is entertainment, because it is loaded with violence, from comedy to drama to children's programs. And every bit of it is treated as absolutely normal. Even music is involved; the sexual content of songs is censored with beeps but the words regarding violence and death are left as they are.

On any given day, you can hear a lifetime's worth of violence and carnage, right down to sarcastic and cruel verbal comments lobbed casually at other people. Sometimes you walk out defeated and disrespected, and no wonder you just become bitchy. After seeing and hearing this a thousand times, what message do you think you take with you?

The more violence we see the more accustomed to it we become—so much that we hardly notice it.

"Don't talk back to me!" That's what my mother always told me. The problem was that once she was so mad, that she slapped me across the face and left a horrible red mark. I missed a week of school.

It's horrible but every time my mom yells and walks in I'm so afraid I close my eyes and put up my arms to protect myself. She hits me with whatever is at hand. Once it was a heavy spoon and she hit me so hard it left marks on my arm.

> I was really ashamed. I didn't want anyone to notice the bruises.
>
> **Amanda,** 18 years old

In some homes, this type of violence against children is either totally common, or more dangerously, the dark secret of parents. It's called "domestic violence" and it takes a number of forms: psychological, physical, emotional or sexual. Remember that no one—inside or outside your family—has the right to mistreat you.

If you live in a home with some type of violence, finding a trusted adult and telling them is absolutely vital. It's not easy, but unless some serious steps are taken, the situation will not improve.

Domestic violence is a crime punishable by law and it may imply imprisonment; you have the right to live safely and in peace, just like everyone else. Women, in particular, can become accustomed to abusive environments. Please don't let this happen to you.

If you haven't experienced anything as important and devastating as this kind of situations, count yourself among the lucky. It may seem unbelievable to you, but it is very real and it is something you should be aware of.

Parents who abuse their children were almost always mistreated themselves. When they were small there was no one there to help them. It's not an excuse, but as a result, they do not know how to control and channel their anger now that they have children. They simply don't know how! Emotionally unstable, many also have problems with alcohol or drugs. Whenever they feel frustrated or upset, they will lash out instead of saying what their feelings are. It is understandable, but it cannot justify violent or abusive behavior.

Children who are beaten and don't receive full support will suffer depression and low self-esteem. The worst thing is that they are likely to become abusive parents themselves. The cycle can continue from generation to generation and the problems end up messing other areas of their lives.

If you know someone suffering from any type of abuse, or you're in an abusive situation yourself, ask for help.

WARNING!

if you can understand this message, we urge you to read up on the subject below. (And you should keep reading it, even if you don't get this message.)

●●● Chat conversation

"Hw ya doin'? I'm OK. Wanted to tell ya I <3 you so much. Never 4get it, pls take care ok? Kisses XOXO."

The Internet

Our Daily Bread

●●●

These days everybody is sort of stuck on the Internet. Maybe even your parents! They might even try to teach you a trick or two that they learned at work. But let's face it—you're probably way ahead of them already.

The truth is that the Web goes way faster and further than anybody really knows, and that includes your parents, you, and all of your friends. Even the masters of the universe don't really know in how many ways it is changing now.

There's no question that online you can find, create, buy, sell, exchange, watch, listen, play, contact, blog, mail, post, and tweet in the same way that the whole world is doing it. But, that's the problem. It really is—"the whole world." And here, we have to point out that not everyone in the world is "good." In fact, there are a lot of people that use the Internet to try to take advantage of someone else.

The Web is defined as an interconnection—in this case with millions of other computers, literally. It is a web, a knitting of connections. So watch out, because just like with a real spider's web, it might catch you and make it very difficult for you to get out. Use it, enjoy it, have a great time with it, but keep your eyes wide open and be sure to know where you're navigating.

For starters, we want to tell you something that should be in your list of things to watch out for. There are many sites with messages like:

"Are you the kind of girl who can't relate to people, especially with the opposite sex? Do you feel lonely? Don't have any girlfriends, though you'd like to have a few? Are they bullying you and mocking you? Don't worry. Here you are among friends. We understand you and we'll help you to get in touch with new, better friends."

Sounds harmless, right? Well, it's actually a trap conceived especially by a world-wide gang of pedophiles, sex abusers and people who assault children and teenagers. They'll approach you during your moody periods or your day-to-day problems, the circumstances that everyone experiences at some point, and they'll use them to trick you—or anyone like you. Boys, girls, anyone can be a target. If you add to that the fact that many young people already have to put up with self-esteem issues, feeling lonely and all of the normal problems of growing up, well, they can make easy targets for some really bad people.

At the beginning, of course, they won't say they're planning on abusing you. Actually they won't say it in the end, either. They'll just invite you to do apparently innocuous things and then make you feel like you wouldn't dare to tell anyone about whatever is going on. These people can convince and manipulate you very subtly—so you don't want your weak points to be obvious.

You may feel that with them you've found an identity or feel that you belong to something bigger. They may make it seem like you've found a club of friends and—really the worst part—is the brainwashing and slow process of manipulation and smooth talking. At some point you've been totally drawn in and may feel that they've really done you a favor.

You have to keep not one, but both eyes open and focused on this fact. Don't think that this only happens in other countries. We got only the best advice from a psychologist who specializes in teens and she told us that she's actually handling a lot of cases in which girls like you have been deceived and damaged.

Woow, candy25 is online

How do they operate?

First they'll try to persuade you to take some kind of bait. It will likely be disguised as some innocent invitation to meet and have a soda or ice cream in some innocent place. There they will let you know that you can trust them and maybe make you believe that they are your true friends. But from that point on, they'll be using your personal info—stuff that you have provided unaware of what they are after. They'll be recording your tastes, hobbies, places you visit, your friends and everything else. Gradually they'll smuggle something into your life—maybe, a picture that they took of you, or they might threaten to tell your parents some of the things you entrusted them. It's very important that they don't seem like bad guys at all. They're usually attractive, young, good looking, and they may give you presents or things that they know you want. They can be very seductive and they've probably carried out this whole plan at least once before.

●● Be very careful!

All of the above should put you on high-alert. Remember, these people will go to extreme lengths to hide their intentions so there aren't any tell tale signs. They are well aware that what they are doing is illegal so their security is always dependent on secrecy and silence.

A high level of awareness could help you to avoid doing something you regret.

Remember also that if you ever feel isolated, increasingly friendless or belittled around somebody else, you might check back with this book for further advice.

Along with the scenario described above, there are many other traps you may face without knowing. When you least expect it, you're being stalked and besieged by someone who could be part of a criminal organization that kidnaps and even enslaves young people for prostitution or pornography.

Of course the Internet is still amazing and there are zillions of things that you can enjoy without any risk. But you must keep your defenses up, click with awareness to avoid being trapped in a very seriously dangerous net. At the end of this section, we have some more recommendations for a safe use of the Internet.

Social Media (SM)

Whether it's Facebook or Twitter or _____ (jot down the name of the newest and most fashionable network here), any of these networks, besides providing you with a lot of fun and the benefits of seeing your friends all together, also expose you to the outside world. And that can create a whole slew of problems.

We love social media because anybody can feel accepted into any kind of group and you really can have new friends and even re-invent yourself exactly the way you want. Or at least, you can push yourself further toward how you'd like to imagine yourself.

You can gain online popularity while at school no one notices you. If you're different or sort of "out there" so what? A social network encourages similar people to find each other and people who previously wouldn't have accepted you at all may now be friendly. Is the trick all in your nickname? Maybe. You can say whatever you want here while, at school, you may feel completely forbidden from expressing at all. That's all part of the really positive influence that these networks have on us.

There are plenty of reasons why everyone is fascinated with social media. But, just as they can help you find your lost uncle on the other side of the world or help you out with your homework team, they can also contribute to your disconnection from the real world. You become a zombie staring at your smart phone. Social networks can also de-personalize you, prevent you from actually speaking with your friends, or really confront you with some alarming and irresponsible attacks. That doesn't help anyone's self-esteem. For some people, social networks become an addiction that interferes with all of their non-Internet related activities.

The point is that you can have a lot of fun and you can even learn a lot but you have to behave thoughtfully and take care of who you are giving all of your information to.

BOR: Basic Online Recommendations

We talked with a bunch of specialists, including experts in technology, to get tips that will help you protect your data and confidentiality when you're online:

- Never fill out any questionnaires or registration forms that request your address, phone number, school, city, schedules, etc. Even if you only fill out your phone number, you're opening a chance for the recipient to find out where you actually live.

- Always use a neutral nickname.
- Setting up face to face meetings with anyone you've met online should be avoided completely.
- Likewise, don't post where you are going to be.
- Don't send pictures in real time that give away where you live or where you are.
- Keep in mind that your "friends" in a chat or any social network might not be as young as they claim to be. 50-year-old adults with bad intentions will fake being 14-year-old girls. Anonymity opens the chance for anyone to say that they are someone else. But there is NO LEGITIMATE REASON for any adult to fake being a teenager, or to want to socialize with people under 18.
- Hackers will frequently send requests to sign up for social media and other networks. If they ask you to click a link or exchange personal info or passwords: WATCH OUT. Don't click or download anything that is not sent by someone you know and trust.
- Don't ever post messages like: "I'm going off on vacation, from October 5 to 13." You may as well post: "You're welcome to break into my house from October 5 to 13." Remember: you can't know who is following you online or watching your updates or checking out your every move.
- Never reply to emails, chat requests or tweets from someone you don't know at all.
- Be conscious of the pictures you upload and those uploaded by your friends in which you appear. They cannot only undermine your reputation but they may also cause serious problems between you and some of your friends.
- Don't upload pictures where it is easy to identify your neighborhood. Don't forget, mean people frequently get information about their victims through this kind of photos.
- Don't post messages that indicate your daily routine.

CLICK

- Don't give away your passwords to anyone and change them once a month.
- Don't ever leave your accounts logged in. When you least expect it, someone could post or send out anything under your name.
- When you're no longer using an account or a profile, don't just leave it floating there in cyberspace. It's much better to cancel them because there are people who scan the internet for inactive accounts to use them for whatever purpose. However difficult they may be to find, almost all social networks provide a way to cancel and delete your account.
- Don't ever send sexually explicit or even merely suggestive pictures of yourself in underwear or bathing suits, nude or near nude. There are plenty of people willing to steal these photos and place them all over the Internet, including sites that will use them as pornography.
- When a social network asks you to let all your contacts know that you have joined always say NO.
- When you open a profile or account in any social media site, always upgrade the privacy settings to the maximum level.

●●● I chat with:

Friends:

_____
_____
_____
_____
_____
_____
_____
_____
_____
_____
_____

●●● I follow:

In Twitter:

_____
_____
_____
_____
_____
_____
_____
_____
_____
_____
_____

CLIC

CLICK

Chapter 3

What's up with...

my looks

Self-esteem

ASSERTIVENESS

my inner image

your body is talking to you

masks

Self-confidence

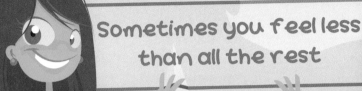

Your inner image

Sometimes you feel less than all the rest

Self-esteem

Don't you hate it when you walk towards a group of girls and they all suddenly shut up when you arrive? It feels like they were talking about you, doesn't it?

How about when you're not invited to a party? You pretend you don't care but you can't help but wonder, why didn't they invite me? What do I have? Why don't they like me? It's easy to feel totally worthless.

Even though the word "self-esteem" sounds like some boring thing that you've heard in school, we're almost positive that you'll want to deal with it more directly after you read the following pages.

Why?

Self-esteem is courage, the level of confidence and of love that you have for yourself. Basically, it's how much you believe in yourself regardless of what's going on around you, the stuff, people, ideas or prejudices you're up against. However, feeling like the greatest thing alive doesn't mean that you have a high self-esteem, it just means that you're either stuck up or you're hiding something—most likely some dark thought about yourself.

Have you ever felt that your boyfriend, parents or friends don't show you enough love? Well, we've got news for you: this happens when you don't accept yourself.

The label you decide to stick on your head will be the one that everybody reads. If you feel secure, you'll look secure; but if you feel ugly, then you're going to look ugly.

If you're confident in yourself, everybody else will believe it. If you like how you are, the rest of the world will like you, too. Maybe not every single person, but enough of them so that the others won't make any difference. Self-esteem is one of those things that the rest of world can smell from for away.

Frankly, low self-esteem just brings problems into your life. It might make you feel like a misfit or a malcontent or it might just make your mind blurred. Extreme problems can come up too, like alcoholism, depression, bulimia, anorexia and in the most hardcore of situations, even suicide.

When your self-esteem is high, the rest of the world just gets better. Your relationships with your friends, teachers and guys improve a lot. At school everything works out better and you become an attractive girl—for real.

The causes of low self-esteem

Self-esteem issues usually begin at home. Everything your parents tell you (whether it's positive or negative) influences the way you perceive yourself. If they told you things like:

Even if you can't recall the precise moments, these phrases get stored in the hard drive of your subconscious, and they're always running in the background noise of the worst and best of situations.

For instance, if you're at work or at school and someone asks: "Who wants to be in charge?", and you feel fit for the job, just as you begin to raise your hand, all of the stuff you've heard for the past years starts coming up as if it were an avalanche: "No, you don't know how to do it", "Don't be stupid", "Ugh, let your sister do it". Then you put your hand down, and with that, you bring yourself down as well.

133

For better or for worse, many parents say these things without being aware of the importance they will have in defining your future. Still, you need to give your parents a break. Part of growing up is learning that all other people have too many things going on in their minds! It's only normal that they make some mistakes when trying to bring you up so don't even think about throwing it back in their faces because you will really only make them feel bad for something they never meant to do.

jump to page 229

All contact with the outside world affects your self-esteem too. From the days when you fed bunnies in Preschool, all the way to the beauty salon or the most prestigious university.

Here are some examples:

● Say you're with a bunch of friends talking about boys. You're anxious to tell the girls your own story. So you decide to wait for the person speaking to finish before opening your own mouth, and just when you speak up: "The other day something so…" someone else interrupts and takes over the conversation. "It's OK. I'll speak whenever she's done," you try to think. Yet it happens again and again. Nobody is paying attention to you, and so your self-esteem bottoms out, right? This has happened to every one of us.

You go on a date with a guy and you have a blast. You're even pretty sure that the guy is totally into you—but just like that he stops texting you. No calls. No note. Nothing. The first thing that comes in your mind is: "What did I do wrong?" Your first reaction is to blame yourself before considering what else could have happened:

This guy does not know what i'm worth	What a fool, he didn't get to know me	i'm too much for him
	He's totally missing out	He went on vacation

Is it natural to just assume the worst? He didn't like you after all? The cleavage wasn't enough? Your shoes didn't match your nails? You know what? You simply aren't confident enough in yourself.

Physical appearance

Body appearance is one of the things that affect our self-esteem the most. When we spot someone with a peculiar or obvious physical characteristic, lots of people will make fun of him or her by saying things like: "It's not like Laura is ugly, she's just a bit manly" or "George is not chunky, he's a blimp."

Anything can affect our self-esteem negatively, like a part of our body that we consider different or unattractive: too chubby, too thin, too tall, too white, too dark, small ears, nose of a toucan, acne...

But did you know that even handsome and beautiful people often feel horrible and different? These feelings are all directly linked to self-esteem issues—not to any actual physical appearance issues. How many successful people are also unattractive? Or put differently, how many happy and successful people are also just very odd looking? The point is, self-esteem makes even weird-looking people seem beautiful.

If your self-esteem concerns spin around your physical characteristics, let us tell you straight up: there's a bunch of things that can be changed: your weight, acne and cellulite, among others. But guess what? There's a whole slew of other things that won't ever be altered, like your height, build, features and the color of your skin. That's it. Period. Nobody will change them. Well, Michael Jackson might be a sort of exception. But do you really wanna go there?

It'll be way better if you came to good terms with your body and your appearance and learned how to live with the whole package now. You were born with it and you'll die with it. So you might as well start feeling proud of your physical peculiarities now so you can enjoy them for a while. They're a huge part of what makes you unique and unrepeatable.

Masks

Lots of people end up wearing masks when their self-esteem is low.

❌ The "boooring" mask: people who are timid, withdrawn, isolated and bored all the time. You can notice their insecurity from miles away.

➕ The "it's OK" mask: depressed people who feel very bad, but who act as if everything's OK in front of other people.

✖ The "bully" mask: this is the aggressive person who bosses everyone else around and conducts him/herself as something of a leader. In plain words, this person tries to show the world how secure he or she is, just to hide the true sense of insecurity within him or herself.

❌ The "Artificial Self-Esteem" mask (ASE): this one feels like they're worth nothing in front of other people. Compensation comes from stuff that everyone else supposedly values: designer clothes, cars, vacations… The point is always to show off so everyone knows how much you spend: "Check out my new Louis Vuitton. It was so expensive!" They feel worthless so their value depends on material stuff—even if it's a fake Armandi or Versanchez.

➕ Pity Boyfriends represent another classic "ASE" behavior. You know they are jerks but end up going out with them anyway just to feel "saved". Insecurity can never be compensated with bits of love and security in an otherwise unfulfilling relationship.

How can I pump up my self-esteem?

Now, here's the most important secret to pump up your self-esteem: once you get to know all of your "special" peculiarities, get out and find your qualities—all of them. We all have them, and they're the most important thing.

You decide what you want people to notice in you: your body appearance or your qualities as a person. For instance, you could be:

Chubby	but a great leader.
Really tall	but super funny.
Super skinny	but a great friend.

Always keep in mind that people see what you want them to see. If you go to a place and think: "Oh my god! Everyone can see my love handles!" or "This makes me look so ugly" or "Everybody in here hates me," well that is what people will actually sense and see. Serious business, huh?

But if you arrive feeling secure about yourself and you think: "I look pretty good!" or "I am absolutely gorgeous" or "I can hang around with everybody", well, that is what you end up projecting.

People don't mind or even notice a person's body appearance whenever he or she is genuinely appreciated. Instead they say things like: "She's such a cool girl" or "She threw a party that rocked!" or "She's adorable! The day I cried she came over to ask if everything was OK."

I have big teeth

But im super cool

Nobody is ever going to say something like: "She's too skinny and too dark, even if she is friendly?" This person makes everybody see her qualities, not her physical appearance. That's why it's so important that you realize that:

Your value is determined by who you are, not by the way you look

Our self-esteem cannot be based either on the stuff we own or on the affection we receive from anyone else.

What you can control, though, is the way you feel about yourself under any circumstance. Nobody can crush your self-esteem unless you allow them. People may try to hurt you by calling names, but they will fail because you are smart enough to reject their ideas.

Don't let anyone make you feel bad. Believe in yourself and be yourself. Love yourself, indulge yourself, be nice to yourself and find support in yourself too. You'll become not only a popular, unique and attractive girl, but also a person who is generally happier.

Spotting people with high and low self-esteem

High

▲ People who stand out from the rest. They might make jokes and be popular, they are confident.
▲ They have good communication with their parents, teachers and friends.
▲ They're in control of their own lives.
▲ They feel capable of doing just about anything.
▲ They speak well about other people.
▲ They live life without concentrating on their problems.

Low

▼ They're anxious—all the time.
▼ They get upset—easily—all the time.
▼ They feel basically unhappy.
▼ They get depressed.
▼ They feel controlled by circumstances and people.
▼ They're really critical about everybody else.

Self-confidence

Movies, TV, magazines and even the internet can make us believe that self-confidence is obtainable through things like diets, breath mints, fashion trends, exercise equipment (like those that promise you'll lose 20 pounds by just exercising three minutes a day), cars and clothes… Fortunately, it's a lot easier than buying a bunch of products. What you can be sure of is that self-confidence is something super valuable that we can all get through different means.

How can I become self-confident?

The word confidence has its Latin root in *confidere*, a word that actually means "to believe", and as the old saying goes, "Seeing is believing." But for our purposes here, it is a lot better to say "Believing is Seeing." For example, picture the hottest guy in school, ok? Most girls like him and want to be his girlfriend, but they think: "He's so hot, but it'll never happen. Why try?" But those who do things the other way around ended up with something real. We are talking about those who thought things like: "I've got so many qualities he'd fall for", that is the type of girl who gives a fight.

The women who have dated Tom Cruise—how many have there been anyway?—first thought that the whole thing was possible. Then they got what they wanted because of their self-confidence. (Note: This book can help you pump up your self-confidence, but we cannot promise that you'll end up dating Tom Cruise.)

Want to boost your self-confidence? Check this out:

- Believe in yourself. Keep a "record of achievements," like a piggy bank of accomplishments that you're proud of. It can be just a small secret pad of paper. Read it and cool down whenever your self-confidence is low, like it's your secret weapon. It's OK to lose track of the stuff that once cheered you up at bad moments, but picture your goals and get rid of the usual inner voice that says: "That's too hard," "You won't be able to do it," "You're so bad at that". Confront it by saying: "Would you please shut up? Stop screwing around with me!"

- Discipline. You won't believe it but the more disciplined you are in the little things you do, the more respect you'll feel for yourself. Your self-confidence will soar everytime you achieve something. For example, skipping dessert and going out for a jog instead. Discipline actually generates personal security because it makes you feel that you're in control.

- Start believing in what you want. If someone asks you "How are you doing?" and you're feeling a bit blue, the best thing to do is to answer back: "Great, how about you?" You already feel way better. Negativity is contagious, so watch out!

Always bear in mind that the bird doesn't sing because it is happy but rather it is happy because it sings—unless it's Woody Woodpecker, in which case, he only sings to make other people as crazy as he is.

What's my personality?

"She's got such a personality!" This expression is likely to cross your mind when you spot a movie star at the airport or when you bump into some extraordinary person in the street, right? We'd all love it if people thought the same thing of us but, really, what is personality? How do you get it? What is it based on?

What you can notice about someone with personality:

She feels comfortable with herself.
She likes herself.
She's proud of who and what she is.
She digs herself.

How she projects what she projects:

The way she walks.
The way she talks.
Her eyes are all lit up.
How she dresses.
Her overall appearance.

When we talk about clothing, it's not as though it's taken her years to get ready, or as if she's planned everything to make a big impression on us. Certainly not that she conforms in every manner to some external standard whether it comes from a designer, or a magazine or a fashion mafia. Personality does not only come from cool clothing or the amount of time you spend doing your hair. It comes from the inside. It's the sort of thing that is so easy to spot, that it takes your breath away. It isn't very easy to explain but it's definitely something we can all attain, you know?

You've got to be AUTHENTIC

How come babies make everybody go crazy. It's not what the baby does, nor all the money the little thing has. We feel attracted to babies for who they are: there isn't any superficiality, hypocrisy, pretense or fakeness involved. They transmit their true feelings through their own language, smiling and crying, and they do it transparently. You don't ever wonder if they're being honest, do you?

That's the key: get rid of the masks and be who you are. Get rid of fears and negative thoughts like: "What if they don't like me," "What if my nose starts bleeding and everyone notices that my blood isn't blue?", "What if they perceive me as..." So what?! Babies are authentic and adorable because they simply are who they are. Just don't wear diapers to school to find out if everybody likes you or not. Please.

Personality is something that everybody has. It's just a question of letting it flow and not pretending to be someone you aren't—someone that you believe is better than the real you! Believe in yourself, get to know yourself and acknowledge the good stuff that you are and that you have.

Don't be scared to show your true self and to make an effort to feel attractive. We're sure that people will be saying: "Now, she's got personality!" even if you're not perfect and bubbling.

Has anyone ever made fun of you? Taken advantage of you? Made you feel less than the rest? Do you get the feeling that people abuse your good intentions? Have you ever been victim of a wedgy or bra-strap snapping?

If so, what did it feel like? Did you do something about it?

Everybody has gone through these things at least once in their lifetime. What makes it different, however, is the way we react to this kind of issues.

Most people try to calm down by thinking stuff like: "There's no point in complaining", "Don't make an issue out of this." "It doesn't matter—they won't pay attention to me anyway", "I can't do anything about it" or "Things are just going to get worse if I answer back". This kind of frustration makes our self-esteem plummet.

You won't solve anything by backstabbing or punching the bully in the face as if you were in some kind of mud-fight. In the end, you still end up frustrated, possibly punished and you may even regret what you've done. The solution is to be assertive.

Don't know how to say no? How can i be assertive?

Being assertive means:

✖ Being able to say "No" whenever you want.

✚ Saying "No" to stuff that you don't like, you really can't do, you really don't want or to things that make you feel uncomfortable. It's so easy.

✖ Speaking up for your rights with certainty and politeness.
✦ Being straightforward without being rude.
✖ Nobody is born being assertive, nor is it something that just happens. Practice it.

With the help of a group of Psychology students in New York, Dr. Moriarty directed a study about assertive reactions. The students were invited to take part in situations that crushed the rights of other persons.

One of Dr. Moriarty's students began to play loud rock n' roll music right next to a group of students that had to concentrate on some difficult homework. Here are the results:

◉ Eighty percent of the students didn't say a word. Only later did they admit they were annoyed by the music.
◉ Fifteen percent of the students asked the guy with the music to turn the volume down, but refused to do it again after an aggressive reaction.
◉ Only five percent insisted until the jerk actually lowered the music.

TEST:
How assertive are you?

5=ALWAYS
4=ALMOST ALWAYS   2=SELDOM
3=SOMETIMES   1=NEARLY NEVER

WHEN I GOT SOMETHING TO SAY:

I simply say it.   ☐

I stop to think about the best way to say it.   ☐

I weigh the consequences before speaking.   ☐

To avoid trouble, I first ask the person what the problem is.   ☐

I can describe the stuff that annoys me without going mad.   ☐

I express my feelings.   ☐

I don't insult or blame people.   ☐

I propose solutions when they're necessary.   ☐

I say things loud and clear.   ☐

I look straight into the eyes of the person I'm talking to.   ☐

TOTAL: ☐

50= VERY ASSERTIVE GIRL
25 OR LESS= MAKE A REAL EFFORT TO SPEAK UP FOR YOURSELF.

What we have to do is to spot the stuff that makes us angry, identify exactly how we feel and be straightforward about it without losing our objective.

I don't know how to say no. How can I be assertive?

- Chillax every time you say hello. Everybody likes being greeted with phrases like: "What's up?", "How's it going?", "How are you doing?", "Hey there!" It's way better than a timid "Hi" or waving hello without saying a word.
- Express your feelings when you're giving opinions. Instead of saying: "That movie sucks", say something like "*I* didn't like the movie" or "*I* liked it very much".
- Accept gifts. If someone gives you a compliment, take it and answer positively: "Thanks! I love this shirt too". If you reply something like "Oh, really? It's so old", you're basically throwing the gift back in your friend's face.
- If you're asked to do something that doesn't seem reasonable or something that smells fishy, answer back with another question: "Why should I do that?"
- Get things clear. If someone's just explained to you how to do a certain task and you didn't understand get things straight. Simply go back and calmly say: "I didn't quite get you. Could you explain it to me again, please?
- Don't stay quiet if you disagree. If you're thinking different than everybody else, just feel confident and give your own point of view: "Well, I see it in a different way", "I think that...", "I believe that there are things that haven't been taken into account, like...".
- Stand up for yourself. Don't ever let anyone make you feel as if you're nothing. Say something like: "You're fifteen minutes late." "Please get your own food" or "Would you mind kissing your own boyfriend?"

The benefits

- You become the lead actress of you own life.
- You don't wait passively for things to happen to you.
- Your self-esteem increases.
- You can calm down. Your thoughts and your actions go together.
- You feel free once you learn how to say "no."

It's definitely worth it being assertive. It's the kind of thing that makes you feel happy with yourself once you put it into practice.

Chapter 4
What's up with...
my sexuality
Kisses
HIV / AIDS
Condoms and pills
Virginity
Sexual harass-ment
Making out
STDs
Rape drugs

What is sexuality all about?

We're connected to sexuality from the very moment we're born until the day we die. It demands great responsibilities, for the choices you make will be of great importance for the rest of your life.

Understanding and maneuvering the world of sexuality in an intelligent and safe way is something that takes time. All of the things you learn at school, the "conversations" you have with your parents and the stuff you read, will definitely come in handy.

Above all though, the most important thing is that you keep yourself well-informed. If you want to make the best choices, you need to consult as many sources as possible—and not just stuff from your friends' stories.

How to calm down your STRESSED parents when talking about sex.

The terrifying moment of: "Let's have a talk."

It basically means that your parents want to talk about sex with you—it may be more frightening for them than for you. Immediately after the dreaded phrase is uttered, they get a bit tense and start walking in circles. They sweat, they don't hear the phone ringing, they can't keep their eyes fixed in one place…

Poor guys! They feel very uncomfortable and nervous, so give them a hand. It'll go pretty smooth if you have open-minded parents, but if not, then it is important to be patient.

Back in the old days sex was extremely taboo. Your parents probably didn't exchange a word about it with their own parents. And for sure they don't talk about sex as naturally as you do. Help them out! Pay attention to them and understand that they're doing it because they love you. Keep in mind that it's really not easy for them, but their experience and advice is definitely worth listening to.

When does it start?

The first sexual sensations generally begin during puberty. There's something new going on; for instance, interest in the opposite sex suddenly appears. The guys you used to regard as goofy little boys now look really hot! (Though let's face it: some didn't actually change at all.) You turn red when the guy you like walks by, you start getting butterflies in your stomach and stuff like that. But watch out! You don't want to become one of those butterflies that men love to collect.

Sexual attraction

When you like a boy, a very personal sensation awakens in you. It's cool—and weird, too. The thing you find most attractive in a guy may give your best friend a headache.

All five senses play an important role (way important, actually) in sexuality. After all, we perceive the whole world through them: sight, smell, touch (men dig this one, obviously), hearing and taste.

The limbic system in our brain is in charge of processing the information that our senses receive. At the same time, it is responsible for sending messages to different parts of our body so they react sexually to them. In other words, it's a really wild flow of information that will keep you busy and happy for the rest of your days.

Sexuality: stages

Desire

Sexuality would be something mechanical if it weren't for desire. This stage is totally psychological. Desiring a guy means wanting to touch him and to be with him. It's about fantasizing or just wishing to get to know him better—and it can be all about, at least, bumping into him!

153

At this point, you've got to be clever enough to decide between managing the desire or letting everybody—or anybody—know about it. And such gossip spreads like wildfire.

Now remember: every single action, no matter how insignificant it may seem, has its consequences.

Physical contact

Your skin is a super sensitive receptor. Even the slightest touch (a brush on your arm, holding hands or a bumped shoulder) can provoke a series of signals that are sent to your brain and that alter the whole chemistry of your body —seriously. Here's a list of things that may happen: sweaty hands, blushing, saying silly things in complete confusion, asking his name twice, asking his age on five different occasions, giving the dumbest of answers. The reason that all of this occurs is simple: as he talks and asks you questions, you're thinking: "How do I look?", or "Am I being that obvious? I hope not!"

If you start liking each other and the initial crush you've had on him begins to evolve in both ways, it would seem that your lips are closer than ever to meeting.

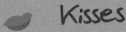 Kisses

Kissing, making out, snogging, (weird, yet used in Britain, Harry Potter fans!)... Regardless of how it's referred to, kisses are awesome and magical. They take us to a dimension that no words can describe. It can be magical, also, because the jerk you've just kissed disappeared afterwards... Lighting fast!

Kissing is about sharing all the senses—that's why it's a personal and delicate thing. It can be the perfect meeting between two people, although the magic side of it doesn't show up with just anybody. Kissing a random guy will simply bring a random, empty feeling. Besides, if the guy wears braces, you will need to mind your poor lips.

The wide variety of kisses depends on rhythm, intensity, desire and the mix of all the feelings involved. Just as you can kiss someone in a cool way (you know, that sort of exchange that comes when you say hello or good-bye), you can also give intense kisses that are charged with love and passion (the sort of smacks that make you go: "Can I have my tongue back, please?")

Your first kiss should be awesome. It's a whole new experience, so enjoy every single instant of it: this moment could stick with you for the rest of your life.

When you're about to get that first kiss, a sense of nervousness and vulnerability might come over you. After all, we're talking about the first intimate contact with a guy in your life, so you sort of feel vulnerable. Worries burst into your head, like: "What's he going to think about me? And what about my body, my mouth, my breath? Should I have chewed gum? Why are my knees shaking?" It's absolutely normal to feel nervous during your first sexual experience.

With braces, forever and ever

smuack

155

KISS

I don't know how to kiss

Don't know how to kiss? No big deal. Even though the first kiss is like bungee jumping, when there's chemistry things simply work out. (But if he's got a bad breath issue, well, it might actually feel more like a freefall.) The more relaxed and calm you are, the better kiss you'll get and give. Now, if you're lazy about it, don't complain later that the whole thing was a waste of time. Don't know what to do? You basically have two options:

- Trust the guy and tell him. He'll take the lead. Don't want to tell him? Just do what he is doing. Keep in mind that no cheat sheets are allowed!
- If you don't want to kiss him, say so. Nobody can make you do something that you don't want.

I'm about to have a mental breakdown

The more comfy you feel with this guy, the faster you'll probably overcome anxiety—that is, just relax and chill out. Keep in mind that men, as we've already mentioned, also feel insecure and have practically the same worries you do.

Nasty kisses

It can also happen that the kiss that you dreamed of all your life turns out to be not what you expected. Maybe the guy was too nervous and screwed things up.

Making out

Term hated by parents worldwide. Also referred to as "hooking up," "messing around" or "getting down." Anyway, the thing is that making out is likely your second sexual experience, so you might as well learn something about it.

Making out is about kissing, hugging, caressing and touching—all at the same time of course. You've both given some limited permission to your counterpart for the hands to wander. While this is taking place your sense of smell catches a substance called pheromone, which is generated by our bodies to keep desire elevated. That's why it is said that the best sexual stimulant in the world is the scent of the man you love. Now if your boyfriend hasn't showered lately, he's likely to attract… only flies.

Since every person has different ideas related to the sexuality of humankind, making out can be natural and logical for some people—others just think it is totally inappropriate. The most important thing is that you're aware of what you really want, and that you feel comfortable and secure about the level you're willing to take it to. Only you.

Now, if your man has super proper manners, do not be surprised to receive a formal invitation like this one:

And then, of course, there's still a chance that he might turn out to be a complete jerk. Instead of being the teddy bear you had in mind at first, he could turn out to be more of a cheap octopus with more tentacles than you can keep track of.

Making out is the path that leads to making love, so be cautious if you don't feel like "doing it" right away. If you cross the line, it could be hard to go back to just kissing. Remember, you're calling the shots.

If you've chosen to make out with your boyfriend, it's only natural that you get nervous the first few times. You know nothing about it, but once you've tried it you'll think: "Where has this been all my life?"

Convinced? Relax and have fun. There's nothing to feel guilty about.

Don't get too excited, though. If you hook up with just any guy who likes you, you're going to end up with a reputation you don't want. Be selective and be careful.

Sexual arousal

It's time that you learn the true meaning of "arousal." When your brain receives some sort of stimulus (like when you spot the guy you dig), it starts emitting specific signals that provoke the increase of both your blood pressure and your heartbeat. This is the point in which your heart begins to feel like it is skipping beats.

Once this dynamic has been set in motion, your genitals receive a higher influx of blood, your senses become more acute and the sensitivity in your skin can go so wild that you'll think you're melting. If a keen sexual interest develops, lubrication occurs and your nipples can harden.

Manual stimulation

First of all, keep in mind that if you let the heat of the moment escalate, you may enter a stage of intensity that may be harder to control. Your body is likely to sense pleasure and demand more in return, but you must ask yourself whether you're ready or not.

Second, when letting a guy touch your sexual organs, there is a risk of contracting an infection that only a doctor can treat (even though your vagina has resources to balance and protect itself). That's why it's really important to have clean hands if you choose to go ahead.

Sexual intercourse

Let's put it in the old standard terms: kisses are like first base, making out is something like second base, heavy petting can be third base and of course, actual sexual intercourse is going all the way to home plate. In real terms, sexual intercourse means penetration, whereas in romantic terms it signifies the conclusion of love: perhaps the most intimate and honest physical union between two people.

Orgasm

MEN 0 WOMEN 1

The orgasm is supposed to be the culminating point in sexual intercourse, anxiously searched by a great number of people. It happens when both, arousal and muscular tension, reach the highest point and once certain muscular contractions (which you cannot control) take place in the genitals, the uterus and the anus.

It's way too hard to describe an orgasm. There are so many types! Everyone experiences it in different ways. For some people, it's a terrific accumulation of tension and rigidity that provokes an awesome explosion of feeling and physical re-action or a pleasant, but powerful sense of relief. So if sex is like scoring a home run, orgasm is something like winning the World Series.

But it's totally possible to play without winning the World Series. There are many women out there who haven't expe-rienced an orgasm in their lives—whether it's because their body wasn't ready or because their sexual partners haven't stimulated them properly. In some cases they don't know how to stimulate themselves. Some women discover orgasms years after becoming sexually active, and only once they feel truly comfortable with their sexuality and their bodies.

Other women have orgasms with absolutely no problem at all. As matter of fact, however, the inventor or researcher who manages to perfect a method to bring every woman to orgasm, could indeed end up being very wealthy.

Unlike men, women are multi-orgasmic. That means that girls can have several orgasms during sex whereas men can only have one orgasm per sexual engagement. Final score: Girls, two? three? five? —Guys, one.

Relaxation

After having an orgasm you can feel a tremendous sense of physical relief and relaxation. You relax and your body returns to its normal state. Both your heartbeat and your breathing return to a normal rhythm. And the bad thing is that many guys fall right asleep just as you're feeling closest to him.

Draw your own paradise here:

THE SECRET LIFE OF MASTURBATION

This topic is pretty much kept underground. Why? Well, it's a pretty private matter. Lots of girls do it, and nearly every guy you meet does it too. At the same time there are girls who don't feel any need whatsoever for it or who simply never feel like it—and there are some guys like that too.

The *Random House Unabridged Dictionary* defines masturbation as "the stimulation or manipulation of one's own genitals." At its best, masturbation is a good way to get to know your body. It gives you the chance to find out what provokes pleasure in yourself—and the way you react to it. That certainly doesn't mean that girls who don't masturbate are freaks or sexually repressed. Actually, many people don't masturbate until they've reached full adulthood or once they're in a mature and stable relationship. As we've already mentioned, there are people who never do it and who have never encountered any problem at all. The important thing is that you feel comfortable whether you do it or not.

Part of our problem is merely that there are thousands of myths and stories about masturbation and its consequences. None of them are true. All of them have been created to control you, and to control the way you behave. Actually, all babies instinctively touch their genitals in order to discover their own bodies and plenty of them begin repeating it once they find the pleasure in it.

Masturbating is not dangerous at all—really. If you think about it, it's absolutely safe sex because there are no risks of getting pregnant or contracting a disease. There's also no pressure or anxiety since it's done all alone. It's a very good way to know yourself and the only risk that exists is catching an infection if you don't wash your hands well before doing it.

Men enter puberty a little later than girls do, more or less between ages 10 and 14. The whole thing starts when the hypothalamus (though it sounds like an animal, it's actually a region in the brain) and the pituitary gland send a signal to set off the production of testosterone.

The main sexual organs of men are the testicles and the penis. You know all the alternative names. At around age 18 the penis stops growing, and most guys are content, if not truly proud, with what they've got.

A big penis during sex might hurt, although a small one can be nearly unnoticeable. But most guys fit somewhere in between and they are perfectly happy and the chances of meeting either extreme are not really noteworthy.

Culture dictates that men are very sexual. And while this can be as damaging for young men as it is for young women, it wouldn't be surprising to find out that a guy's main interest in you is sex. So watch out! Perhaps you're in a relationship that seems the most sincere in the whole wide world: he brings you flowers, he writes deep letters of love, and promises the moon and the stars... but after all, maybe he's only trying to make you fall in love with him in the interest of having sex with you. There are also guys who truly fall in love and respect every single choice you make.

Just as you have concerns regarding the whole sex issue, men also have their own—especially when it comes to the erection of the penis

WHAT'S UP WITH ERECTIONS

Average Erection

ASLEEP

(moment in which the penis gets larger and harder due to the concentration of blood there).

Men get erections when there's some sort of physical stimulation or simply when sexual thoughts cross their minds. Erections can also occur just like that, without any cause at all. In other words, guys can have erections practically anytime of the day. That's why sometimes a guy's boxer shorts are tented up in the morning.

So if you're with a guy (say your brother, a male friend or a cousin of yours) and his little friend gets a bit too anxious, be cool and ignore them both—give him a break!

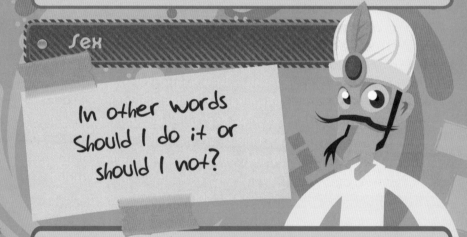

sex

In other words Should I do it or should I not?

At a certain point in life, we have all asked ourselves whether we should have sex or not. This same question buzzed around the heads of your parents, your grandparents and even your boyfriend (even if he pretends to know the *Kama Sutra* from cover to cover). Having sex requires you to be responsible for yourself.

Everyone's got his or her own beliefs, theories and line of education about having sex or not. And really all points of view need to be respected. Just remember that you shouldn't feel pressured into doing something that you don't feel like doing or that makes you feel uncomfortable. Going ahead or not going ahead is a personal choice that you need to arrive at independently and drawing on your own best resources (independent values, advice and knowledge).

Mixing sex with love and responsibility is among the most intense and amazing forms of communication, union and love that can possibly exist between two people. It involves every part of our being: your soul, your heart, your intelligence and of course, your body.

But sex can also be an unsatisfying experience—and often even a traumatic one—if it's made under pressure, or just for selfish or physical pleasure. So, it's super important that you don't rush things—you don't want to end up feeling used, empty, afraid or lonely. Take all the time you need to get to know your boyfriend, and develop love so that both of you are able to take this step responsibly.

If you choose to do it, live it and don't feel guilty. Just as you can feel bad about it, it can also be a great experience if handled consciously and sensibly.

You can protect your body against an unwanted pregnancy or even a sexually transmitted disease (STD), but you must also protect your heart and your self-esteem.

Don't let it happen to you

Many teenagers have said that their sexual life started without them really wanting it to. This may happen because sometimes you are full of doubts and under all sorts of pressures, like when you have a boyfriend who's older than you and he pressures you to do things. When it comes to girls, the top reasons for starting to experience sex are:

✖ "I couldn't say no." It is way important to learn how to say no—especially when you feel pressured. If you still don't know how to refuse certain things, check out our section "Don't know how to say no? (How can I be assertive?)"

✖ Alcohol and drugs. Your senses get screwed up after having a few beers or consuming any type of drugs including marijuana. You may end up being more co-operative than you intended to be. Be careful with any alcohol! Sex can seem fun in that precise moment—but then, the remorse can be unbearable and it may also be only the beginning of the repercussions.

✖ Fear. The idea of hurting a boyfriend or being dumped for the pretty girl next door can be so frightening that you may end up consenting to sex. If that's what he wants, any girl can give it to him (the girl next door or the girl who lives across the street, and the girl at the convenience store). You are different and he should love you because of that—not because of the sex you can offer. It isn't that way? It's good that you realize it so you can blow him off. Remember that girls who respect themselves are way more interesting to men, and that's why men classify women in two categories: the ones you fool around with and the ones you take seriously.

✖ Pressure and Manipulation from a Guy: "If you love me, prove it." This phrase should be banned from movies and TV programs! Even if you feel a bit uncomfortable, the best thing to do is to be straightforward with him. For sure, it is way better than going along with some "proof" you don't believe in.

✖ Pressure and Manipulation from Female Friends: those who've already had sex can also pressure you, although not directly, by making comments like: "It is the best thing ever!" and "Getting laid is out of this world," but far worse, "You're a loser if you don't do it." Maybe what you need is new friends who are more mature. It is also possible that what one of your buddies is actually suggesting, is that she needs a companion who can help her face the problems she's created for herself by having sex at a very early stage of her life. You can be that companion without making all the same mistakes. Because, believe us, no true friend is going to insist that you share her mistakes.

✖ Heartache. It is important that you realize that many girls have sex just because they want to feel loved or accepted. And physical love may seem like a good substitute for "actual love." Ironically, girls in this situation end up feeling even lonelier. Love and acceptance is something you need to achieve by yourself, alone. Any substitute for that is going to be a poor and problematic imitation.

✖ Media. In one way or another, sex is everywhere in the media and it's portrayed as something marvelous with little or no repercussions. The images, situations and dramatic scenarios presented in the media are barely real. The ads are made by professionals models who've just met and technology that alters everything until the end result is anything but close to reality. If you want to be influenced by media, consider an opera, a real opera (not a soap opera).

Some of the risks

⦿ Getting pregnant will turn your life upside down.
⦿ Putting your body in a guy's hands—literally—when there's no honest communication or true love, or when you're just under blind confidence, will turn out to be a really bad experience. If these elements describe your relationship already, then this is not the place to experiment with sex.
⦿ STDs like HIV/AIDS are serious business. A study conducted by The Medical Institute for Sexual Health re-

vealed that you're four times more likely to acquire an STD than to get pregnant.

- Getting tagged as a "hoochie mama" or as a slut is no picnic. We've made a big point already about judging yourself on your own terms. But why make things even more difficult in your life?
- Guys are worse than any tabloid or gossip magazine. They may even be worse than a gaggle of your girlfriends —and their gossip hurts.
- Awful feelings of guilt can take months to process. So you want to be sure that what you do can be done without guilt, and that means doing it conscientiously and with certainty and security.

What if you wait?

- You'll feel more comfortable with yourself.
- You're far more likely to be free of regrets.
- You definitely won't be worried about pregnancy, STDs and unwanted responsibilities.
- It's been argued that the longer a couple waits to have sex, the more special the "first time" is. They also enjoy a greater sense of control over their relationship.
- Remember: you have tons of time ahead to enjoy sex with whomever you want and whenever you want. Wait-

ing now guarantees that when the time is right, the sex will be better.

- When we are young we usually feel very mature—but we are not. Playing a game that involves your heart, your life and a lot more requires that you operate with all the advantages you can.
- If your sex life starts under better conditions, then your relationships, life, self-confidence and control will be based on better terms too.

Set the rules

If, all of a sudden, that cute boy you're going out with turns into a swift little monster—going way faster than you wanted—you need to be in a position where you can stop him for whatever reason. If any action makes you uncomfortable in the slightest, it's up to you to stop it. He must cease upon request. Immediately.

Guys may think that, "A man can get as far as a woman lets him." It's true too. If a guy insists on going further, be straight and repeat it loud and clear so that he gets the message. Any guy who is worth it is going to understand that sex is absolutely consensual and he'll accept your choices. But respect also needs to be a two-way thing. You may find that he's the one saying no and you're the one who feels like devouring him! You need to respect him too.

Why is it called "making love"?

Strictly speaking, two people make love when they love and respect each other, when they wait for the most suitable moment and when they do what is perfectly natural and healthy in a consenting, mutually supportive relationship.

Having sex, though, is something very different; a merely physical act for which pleasure is the main goal. Love and respect are not necessarily present.

Abstinence

Some people consider it a forbidden word, but abstinence is actually a good option for lots of teenagers. The concerns surrounding unwanted pregnancies and STDs have become so hardcore that lots of young people consider abstinence.

In interviewing 30 young guys, we found that 7 of them had chosen to remain abstinent (yes! Those horny warriors). For all the pressure out there—and it's just as forceful for guys—both male and female teenagers would rather just chill out when it comes to sex.

Attention!

The point is that having sex or not having sex is up to you. You can even choose to never, ever have sex.

Already made up your mind and decided to have sex? Go ahead, just take care of yourself and be it responsibly. If you've met someone who's decided to be abstinent, you have to give it to him: instead of tagging him as a lame, you should acknowledge and respect their tenacity because no doubt they're as jumpy as you are. Their hormones also go wacko when they're near to somebody they like, the difference is they've decided to endure it and have fun in other ways. They want it? They're dying for it! And whether you believe it or not, guys do respect and fall for girls who have chosen to remain abstinent.

The first time

Be responsible if you choose to do it

A gazillion things happen the first time you have sex. As we've already mentioned, the most important thing is that you feel comfortable and confident with your choice and with yourself.

If you choose to do it, talk things over with your boyfriend beforehand. Since there isn't a 100% effective method that can prevent pregnancies, ask him the following questions: What does it mean to you? How are we going to protect ourselves? What will we do if I do get pregnant? His answer will give you a good idea of how seriously this guy's taking you.

There are many guys out there who will promise you the moon and the stars. Unfortunately it's an entirely different story when they find out that the girl they've been sleeping with is pregnant. They also feel scared, play dumb, and some will even disappear from the face of the Earth. Talking straight from the very beginning will make him think, and hopefully make him more aware and responsible.

Love-Making Expectations

Most girls have waited ages for this moment. You've heard so much about it that you're pretty positive about the magic that will take place when it happens. Stars will come streaming down from the sky, the bed you're in will elevate, you'll feel on top of the world and you'll be jumping for joy. And yes, you'll be jumping alright... when your cell phone rings and it's your dad calling!

The first time is usually a pretty awkward experience. Awesome, fantastic, magical? Maybe, but not likely. The responses to polls on the matter do not favor the magical idea much. It's only logical; there are tons of thoughts, doubts and feelings—at times contradictory—that float between you and him. And often you don't even know how things should be working. But you know what? Future encounters won't have a thing to do with the first one.

When penetration occurs for the first time, you're likely to experience some mild pain as well as light bleeding. This happens because some hymens are not elastic enough and will tear apart when penetrated for the first time.

If you're too stressed or nervous, things can get a bit more painful as your vagina dries and tightens up. This is also typical on the first time, but as you relax and become more sexually active, your vagina will expand and lubricate better up to the point in which no pain is felt at all. Lubricants or lubricated condoms will ease the pain.

The lubricant issue might sound weird, but it's pretty basic. You don't want his nervousness or yours making things tougher.

Guess what?...
I'm pregnant

This is Mariana's story

Shit! How am I going to tell my parents? They're going to kill me! I'm such an idiot. And Joel? What is he going to say? I thought it would never happen to me. It just happened. I guess the condom broke. And it was me who criticized Susana when she told me that she'd gotten pregnant after doing it once. "You can't be serious!" I thought. And then I'm the one who gets pregnant—I'm so stupid. What am I going to do? I'm not even done with high school, and I probably won't be going to College either. Now what? What if Joel doesn't give a crap?

Joel totally freaked out when I told him. He got nervous; he didn't want to have it. He asked: "How are we going to afford it? Where are we going to live? We're only 19…"

As Mariana spoke to us over the phone—still in the voice of a teenager—about the things that crossed her mind when finding out she was pregnant, we could hear the three month-old baby in the background.

Mom was shocked when I told her. She broke into tears. My dad is scary, so I wrote him a letter instead. They didn't want me to have the baby either, but after discussing the whole issue with them, I decided to have it. It's been pretty hard for them to accept the whole thing.

I had to leave school too. I felt terrible and had to home school my way out. But I'm happy with my choice despite losing so many things. I don't have time to hang out with my friends or time to party on the weekends. I live with my parents and Joel comes around to see the baby. Even though he's very affectionate towards our baby, he gets bored and sad. For me it's tough because I've got to help both my baby and Joel to get ahead…

Now it's time to ask Mariana what kind of advice she'd give to girls her age.

Protect yourself or don't do it. If you are already pregnant, let me tell you that what's coming ahead is not a walk in the park. Your life changes entirely. Even though giving birth might scare you, I think the sense of regret is the worst part.

Pregnant? Symptoms

- Lack of menstrual periods.
- Change in the size and sensitivity of your boobs.
- Morning nausea.
- Darkening of the area around the nipples (areola).
- Fatigue.
- The color of your vulva changes.
- Increase of vaginal discharge.
- Frequent urination.
- Food cravings.
- Metallic taste in the mouth.
- Light dizziness.

Some girls get pregnant due to carelessness. Others might do it to try trap a guy thinking that he'll then love her. Do we need to say this is NOT recommended by any means? Maybe it was one of those wild nights when you just didn't care—and remember that alcohol can play an important role here—or maybe you simply thought it would never happen to you.

But what if you do get pregnant? Then what are you going to do?

There is no easy way to handle an unwanted pregnancy. Once it's been confirmed, you have a serious matter to confront and very few options to choose from.

Before doing anything, talk about it with the baby's father as well as with an adult who loves you. Keep in mind that any choice will be difficult and painful, and you won't be able to go back once it is made.

There are three options if you decide to have the baby: get married, raise the kid as a single mother or give it in adoption.

Getting married

A child should be one of the most incredible experiences to come into the life of a couple. But bringing a baby into the world is an enormous responsibility. Nature's wisdom gives us 9 months to prepare ourselves as best as we can to face this extreme change. Are you going to live together? Where? How are you going to afford your living expenses? Will you get a job? Who will take care of the baby?

Being a single mother

Not ready for marriage? Maybe the father is not ready either. In any case, marriage requires a lot of courage, and having a baby alone does too. Single mothers rely on a lot of people including family and friends but this option is increasingly common and accepted. It's still difficult for almost everyone—especially for the mother who needs to seriously reorganize her life and her priorities in order to care of a child.

Giving the Baby Up for Adoption

Giving up a child for adoption demands a lot of courage. Under certain circumstances it is perhaps the best choice, but it is also the least often chosen. There are loads of infertile couples out there that are eager to adopt and so the results can be quite satisfactory. In the US, any reasonably sized city will offer a center that is always looking for homes for babies born to mothers unwilling or unable to care for them. They should also be able to provide advice, guidance and support to the mother.

Abortion

Since 1973, abortion has been a legal option for American women. Although it's been almost four decades since the US Supreme Court of Justice determined its status, abortion remains a very sensitive and serious issue subject to constant ethical and political debate. State laws heavily regulate the way abortions are performed in the US.

22 percent of pregnancies end in abortion, and 50 percent of those are for women under the age of 25. Women aged 20–24 get 33 percent of all abortions, and teenagers receive another 17 percent.

Abortions can have negative consequences in some women. Physically speaking, there's a risk of infertility, perforation of the uterus or peritonitis, the inflammation of the abdominal cavity. Worst case scenarios might call for the extraction of the uterus but also in psychological terms, abortions can cause depression and a sense of guilt that, in the words of some women who have undergone the procedure, can last years or even a lifetime.

That's why abortion is one of the toughest and most painful choices you can face. If you're thinking about having an abortion, check out your local legislation and find out what type of restrictions apply.

There are people and arguments to be made in defense of the legality and availability of abortion but the best option is definitely not to have to make this painful choice at all.

Be smart. Think things through and don't let the heat of the moment sway your decisions. You're worth a lot, so protect yourself thoroughly or opt for abstinence so you don't risk it.

Sexual preferences: heterosexuals, homosexuals, bisexuals and transsexuals?

Chances are you've met men and women that feel attracted to people of their same sex. You probably know that they are called **homosexuals**, **gays** or **lesbians** in the specific case of women. Their attraction to people of the same sex is both physical and emotional.

Heterosexuals are those who feel attracted to the opposite sex.

Persons who feel attracted to both women and men like—it really doesn't make a difference to them—are called **bisexuals**. And there's more: **transsexuals** are those who feel *identified* with a gender that differs from their assigned sex. They feel like they were born having the wrong sex because who they are internally does not match the body they posses. They look at it and they're like: "Whoa! That's not mine." Many transsexuals behaved like a person of the opposite sex when they were little. This happens in one out of 30,000 women as well as in one in 12,000 men. So, yes, probabilities are higher in men than in women.

A man who enjoys dressing like a woman is known as a **transvestite**, but here's some news that's going to actually surprise you: he isn't necessarily a homosexual.

Are you born that way or do you become that way?

It's like the "hen or the egg" question. Some experts claim that homosexuality is part of nature. Various investigations have focused in the determination of its possible causes.

Some say that there is a physical difference in the hypo-thalamus—that's a specific area in your brain that controls sexuality, among other things. Other investigations claim that it is has a genetic or hormonal origin, or even that it is linked to pregnancy and birth.

Researchers have also said that it is related to a certain type of education or a specific environment.

What is for sure is that it is not something you choose and it is obviously NOT a disease—and we hope this idea doesn't even cross your mind.

Popularity

- Her wardrobe is so impressive... I'm positive her dad owns Saks Fifth Avenue.
- She is so hot... that sometimes I even think I dig her!
- She is at every single party... she must get paid to go.
- Loads of guys are drooling all over her... I'm sure she's made a pact with the devil.
- So many people know her... she even appears in a GPS map!

And the truth is that... Ugh... I... I totally wanna be her!

This popularity issue can turn into a nightmare—you know, like the ones in which you dream about peeing and... well, you actually wet your bed.

Popularity is like a close relative of acceptance, sort of a first-cousin.

And who doesn't dig being accepted? It's absolutely natural. The problem, however, lays in the fact that, in order to be popular, one's got to carry The Hollywood Kit at all times:

money, beauty, designer brands, friends, stuck up pets (even more conceited than the proprietor) and even Botox (yes, some pets can be quite demanding!).

Nowadays, this matter is totally out of control.

There's no problem in wanting to look hot, wearing nifty outfits and feeling cool about your looks. It's normal. Chaos comes, however, when you stop being yourself in order to become this hyper-ultra-mega-super Queen Bee. Though thinking about it... having a few workers around doesn't seem such a bad idea, after all.

In many occasions we want to feel accepted because we sense rejection, or even insecurity. As if "I'm worth a lot just because I'm popular". And this is where the problem begins, because the more we seek popularity, the higher the risk of rejection. So, if your self-esteem had already hit rock bottom, after this it will surely be buried down so far that you'll start considering a mud mask.

The most important thing is to be yourself; doing what you love to and being exactly who you are. The least popular thing in the world is a Wannabe—well, there is something even less popular than that: two Wannabes.

Being a Wannabe is like being a huge red light: everybody notices it, and everyone rejects it. As matter of fact, the Wannabe is not only NOT COOL, but a liar as well.

Most popular girls are not as happy as they seem to be—even though it seems to be the opposite—because they're always trying to please everybody else and stop remaining true to themselves.

"What? Go to McDonald's and eat McNuggets? With no makeup on, wearing a pair of sweatpants and a dull ponytail? You've got to be kidding me. What are the members of our High School community going to say about this behavior!"

Popular girls are always hanging out with a bunch of people. But did you know that sometimes they feel very lonely because their "friends" are not at all sincere? In many occasions, these "friends" are around to take advantage of their popularity.

Not all popular chicks are the same. There are authentic popular girls who like dressing popular and enjoy acting popular; who have loads of money and are complete "party animals". Perhaps they're a natural-born leaders, or maybe extraordinarly charming. The important thing to keep in mind is that being popular is not a choice: if one's not naturally popular, trying to fit in will only bring pressure and pain... every time you're blown-off for being a Wannabe.

Oh, by the way, please note that popularity only exists in school. It comes to an end the very day you graduate! Finito! GAME OVER!

In the real (grown-up) world, popularity is no longer the main objective, and success becomes the goal to attain.

There are well-respected computer geniuses... those who used to be catalogued as geeks. There are heaps of famous singers... who used to be treated like freaks. There are so many doctors who save lives... and who used to be part of the nerd bunch. There are great fashion designers... who back in High School would only care about their looks. So many world-changing ecologists... that everybody used to laugh at. Tons of extraordinary moms... who used to think they had no purpose in life and ended up choosing the toughest job of all.

Well, these people are who they are today because back then, when they were younger, they decided to be who they truly are and decided to do what they really enjoy. They chose not to be something they weren't.

Long story short... you pretty much have two choices:

- You can try to please and impress everyone around you, forgetting about yourself and showing the world the fake version of you.
- Or you can do what really moves you, putting an end to all the lying.
  And you can also have true friends whom you share interests with... and enjoy school to the max. It's only up to you. You choose.

> Keep in mind that the greatest popularity of all consists in having one true friend who loves you and respects you unconditionally.

Am I gay?

I'm freaking out a bit. I'm not sure if I like women or not. I have this friend and I love being with her. I like her eyes, her face—even her hands. But I honestly don't know if that's because she dresses really nice... or because I'm gay. I'm a bit concerned that, when another girl gets too close and chats with her, I get way more jealous than normal and try to make the chic go away. I feel like I'm doing everything I can to convince myself I'm not gay, but deep inside I believe I'm fooling myself.

Most of the times I say "I like that guy" I'm lying. I say it just because everyone is saying how hot he is. But the thing is, there is a boy I do like. I'm so confused.

I feel embarrassed when I think about what my parents and brothers are going to say or what is everyone else going to think. Once, when I was tipsy at a party, the idea of kissing one of my girlfriends crossed my mind, but I'm not sure if I thought of it because I wanted to be cool—like in the videos—or because I really wanted to kiss her. I'm scared. That's normal, right?

Georgina
16 years old

Some experts believe that, in periods of transition such as adolescence, some youngsters may have a homosexual experience. In occasions it can be brief and irrelevant, a passing thing. Other times, it can become a lifestyle years ahead.

Talking about adolescence—it is quite common that during your sexual awakening you have stimulating sexual experiences with another person from the same sex. You may even have fantasies with other chics! That has nothing to do with you being gay or not. Don't feel guilty. Think about it, it's logical: your period, your boobs, hair everywhere, your hormones! These are working for the first time and are making you experience so many sensations. So if by chance you feel a weird flutter as you see one of your girlfriends walk by, you are not necessarily gay.

It's also super normal that you have the sort of doubts like: "Am I gay because I like to hang out with my girlfriend all the time?", "Because I check her out quite a lot?", "Cause I get really jealous that my best friend hangs out more time with another friend of hers?", "Because I just love it when she gives me a hug?"

In many occasions, a girl experiences these things because she needs to feel secure, understood and supported. Or maybe because you really admire your friend and you just want to learn from her. Once again, it has nothing to do with you being a lesbian.

There is a chance that you don't feel any type of attraction towards anyone or anything. Perhaps you still don't know who you like. No worries, though! Confusion is very normal during adolescence.

So far so good? (Now that sounded like a teacher giving an explanation, right?). Cool, let's continue. Another group of specialists think that there are girls and boys who have felt different since they were little children. However, as society didn't seem to understand or accept them, they choose to remain silent for a long time—or forever.

There's a lot of disinformation regarding this matter. There are no formulas that determine how long a person with these doubts should take to define his or her sexual preference. The important thing you should bear in mind is the following: if you think this is your case, seek proper information with trustworthy people or in reliable internet sites and books. And remember: the choice is yours only.

The day you are completely sure, you will be able to confront your fears. You—and nobody except you—will know when it's time to take steps. Basic thing to keep in mind: when you either believe or know you're gay, you may experience anxiety, pain and depression. You may even have suicidal thoughts because you don't seem to understand yourself or because of your deep fear of rejection. You may even think about homophobia (hate towards homosexuals): a lot of people make cruel jokes about gays—and then realize, in angst, that "That's me." It's not easy, but you must remain calm and recognize that, if you're sure you're gay, it is not something you chose; you will not be less or more happy than the rest of us; there are many, many girls in the same situation you are in; and the time to confront the situation will arrive.

In the meantime, if you have any doubts, the best thing you can do is seek information and orientation with a specialist in Sexology or Psychology. We suggest you read a lot about this matter—you need to be properly informed and realize that you are not the only one.

Check this out:

A report from *Surgeon's General, All to Action to Promote Sexual Health and Responsible Sexual Behavior* from 2001 states: "No child can consider him or herself homosexual. Most people consolidate their homosexual identity during adolescence and adulthood."

Coming out

"To come out" is the most widely known expression to refer to the moment a person is totally convinced about being gay and chooses not to hide it anymore—or "in the closet." The original phrase is "To come out of the closet", actually. If this is your case, you must be prepared to confront situations and problems that in most cases are not easy, such as gaining acceptance from:

Yourself. This is basic, the first step to take. Accept the way you are, acknowledge you're not doing anything bad, and recognize the fact that being gay is characteristic of you: every person's got loads of characteristics, and this one just happens to be yours. If you still get depressed with the matter, don't talk about it yet. You must be strong enough to confront prejudiced people as well as their reactions. Get the best information you can regarding the topic in well documented books or seek professional help from a therapist.

Society. When it comes to sexual diversity, people react in different ways based on what they believe to be right or wrong. You have both sides: persons who do not approve—and those who don't consider it to be problem at all. It is really important to know beforehand that people who do not approve gay feelings or gay behavior may criticize you, call you names, bully you or even discriminate you. This is called homophobia.

Your girlfriends. Breaking the news may surprise some of your girlfriends. However, you have to always bear in mind that just as some may accept the way you are… well, some others may chose to reject you. It's normal. And it is also normal that your girlfriends freak out just a bit: they knew nothing about it and you will have to explain to them that you are not going to seduce them, you won't attack them or convince them to become gay (that has nothing to do with you sexuality). Tell them that it isn't a personal choice, or a disease that a doctor can cure. These are some of friends' typical fears.

Your Family. This may be the hardest of all. Reactions of unease, anger and disappointment can get bad, mainly because the news slams right into the expectations your parents had for you. Maybe they had pictured you married to prince charming with three kids, and all of a sudden, well, things are not like that anymore. In most cases it comes as a big surprise to them—they didn't see it coming. Actually, it's like a loss for them. They feel as if they've failed and ask themselves questions like: "What did we do wrong?" Sometimes they even mistakenly feel guilty. Give them a break! Just like your friends, your siblings and pretty much everyone else, they don't have the proper information. They don't know what's really going on. So find a good moment to come out to them (not when you're coming home drunk from a frat party you sneaked in or when you're angry because of other things). You may immediately receive love and support, or rejection and nasty words. You need to be patient, you need to let them know that you love them and that you need them more than never before. You've had some time to figure things out, but the news hits them like a bucket of cold water. In some cases, they're just scared—like you may have been—and they simply do not know how to act. In the event your parents reject you, please keep in mind that most parents, with time, come to understand—or at least show tolerance. You really need to be strong and convinced of your sexuality in order to surpass all the obstacles and find personal peace. This cannot put your life to a halt: a person's true value is way more than a sexual preference. There are no "normals" and "abnormals". We are all equal and we must respect everybody's sexuality.

Obviously, you can achieve true happiness. And remember that there are various laws that protect sexual minorities against discrimination.

Expert advice

There are lots of institutions, organizations and support groups who can help you through this difficult and crucial process.

Look for one in your hometown and reach out to them. You can keep a log here:

special thanks

Thanks to Darío Sánchez, who provided us with further details to elaborate this chapter.

Darío Sánchez
M.A. in Family Therapy
San Diego Ca.

Tel. 001 6192068744
mail4dario@yahoo.com

Girls who helped us with this topic

Thanks to all of the girls who helped us in writing this chapter with their experiences, thoughts and concerns!

Maria Angelica Villegas Gastelum, 17 years old
Claudia Yanina Morales Morales, 18 years old
Jocelyn Puente, 18 years old
Danna Mirlet Melendez, 18 years old
Dalia Archundia Gutierrez, 16 years old
Ana Lilia Hernández Madrazo, 18 years old
Valeria D. Labra Cortez, 16 years old
Karla Ximena García, 15 years old
Miriam Sarahi Lara, 18 years old
Lucero Itzel López Patiño, 18 years old
Manuella Mejía
Tania Ruiz Galindo

Unwanted Sex

"The music was wild and there we were, Rodney and me, talking, kissing, smoking and dancing a little bit. He was 19 and I had just turned 16. It was about one in the morning when I started to feel dizzy, so I went to the bathroom. I definitely drank more than I should have. Rodney followed me all the way and came in to the bathroom right after I did. He locked the door and I stayed quiet. Then I did absolutely nothing while he was kissing me.

I was leaning on the wall when I felt his hand unbuttoning my jeans. Though I was really drunk, I actually got scared because I'd never had sex before. A bunch of thoughts started going through my mind: "What are you going to do now? You've let him get to this point, you can't tell him to stop now. You're not going to lose your virginity on a bathroom floor, are you? You are so drunk."

All of a sudden Rodney pulled me over in an aggressive way so he could get on top of me and I really began to struggle. I really just wanted to scream and leave that place but I didn't. At that point I was actually really beyond scared. But he kept me down—seriously—with all of his strength. Somehow I managed to push him back with one of my legs and I got out of there.

After thanking Martha (now much older) for sharing her experience with us, we asked her a couple of questions:

How did this experience affect you?

I blocked the whole thing for a couple of years. Emotionally speaking, I was wrecked and the fact that I kept it to myself had a negative impact as well. I was scared and I felt guilty too. I realized I hadn't taken good care of myself and I really hated men for a long time. I learned that I was being pretty arrogant when thinking that I could hit on any guy I wanted to and flirt around like it was a game with no consequences.

Why do you think it happened?

Alcohol played a major role, definitely. I was really drunk. I learned that you're more vulnerable to sexual abuse when you're drunk or high.

Is it sexual abuse?

Sexual abuse appears in a lot of different forms, even with no physical contact; for example sexual harassment, uncomfortable comments, exhibitionism, being forced to watch certain type of images, strange or unfamiliar physical contact, anyone touching your privates without explicit consent, any type of blackmail involving issues of your privacy and consent, anyone attempting to take advantage of a given situation, whether it's a teacher asking for a special favor, or someone demanding "payment" for a favor.

Don't let it happen

Any form of sexual abuse is an issue of power, self-control and personal security/insecurity. It's not about sex, much less about "I love you so much." Being the victim of sexual abuse is humiliating and results in feelings of both guilt and vulnerability. These can have a terrible impact that takes years to recover from. Here are some facts to keep in mind from now on:

- About 80 percent of rapes—defined as "unwanted penetration"—occur between people who actually know each other. It can be a friend, a boyfriend or a relative. We're talking about people you trust!
- Alcohol plays a definitive role in 2/3 of all cases of rape and sexual abuse. Just like drugs, it can make your reason falter and even provoke the loss of consciousness—sometimes to the point in which you don't resist the violation.
- Watch it! In many cases women are willing to participate in a degree of sexual activity. But when it comes to stopping or when a limit is reached, some men may not accept the limit; they simply will not care and may even try to force the activity further. That's why it's important to state loud and clear: "No, I don't want to." Make your limitations very clear and repeat them as many times as needed. This statement could be crucial in an extreme case where law enforcement is involved. But it can also eventually sink in and protect you.

The abuser's relationship to the victim:

- **27%** uncle
- **19%** cousin
- **16%** a stranger
- **14%** friend of the family
- **11%** unknown relationship
- **9%** older brother
- **4%** couple
- **3%** dad/stepdad
- **2%** grandfather
- **1%** priest

Did you tell someone about the abuse?

never:	84%
yes:	16%

How to spot someone who wants to do something to you?

It's important that you realize that incidents of sexual abuse and rape are not uncommon. Think about the guy you're dating, the type of people you hang out with and the people that you're sure you are comfortable with—and why. Observe the way you're treated. If the kid you're going out with is always insisting on taking you to lonely places, or exhibits sudden changes of personality or behaves aggressively, then be extra cautious!

Can it happen to any girl? Yes, it can. Can it always be prevented? No, but you can reduce the chances of it happening to you —especially when you're young. It's a question of being cautious:

HOME

- Don't let anyone (whether it's your uncle, your big brother, your cousin, your stepfather, your neighbor or anyone else) touch your private parts without your consent. Studies reveal that 38 percent of cases of sexual abuse take place at the victim's home. Another 38 percent of cases occur at the house of a friend or relative.
- Sexual abuse may provoke guilt and shame, but it's really important NOT to remain quiet. EVER!
- The abuser might try to intimidate its victim by saying it was not a question of abuse, but rather seduction. DON'T LET IT HAPPEN.
- Do not touch any adult's genitals under any circumstance.
- If something strange does happen, talk to an adult you trust immediately and tell him or her exactly what's happened. Speak up. The longer you keep the secret the harder it may be to let it out. Please, speak immediately.

ON THE STREET

- Rapes or sexual assaults can and do happen in public places right in the middle of the day; therefore, calling attention to a potential situation is never a bad thing.
- Avoid extremely crowded places, like buses or subways, if you need to use them be aware of who is pressed up against you and what they are doing. Don't be afraid to shout.
- If you notice that you're being followed, again, you can shout. Run or walk quickly into a shop or any busy place with people.
- Obvious dodgy areas or places you're not familiar with, require extra caution. Every city has streets that have "sexual abuse" written all over—try using different routes. The same rules apply if you're in the country, or a big park or tourist area. Don't go alone into unknown areas.
- If you've got no other option and you have to walk through this kind of areas or streets, be sure you can move quickly if you need to. No flip-flops. Walk firmly, feel confident and look ahead.
- If possible, carry a cell phone in your hand. You can pre-dial 911 so you're able to quickly hit the "call" button if you need to.
- If you're on foot, on a sidewalk or boardwalk, be cautious of unknown turns and stay closer to the street rather than the wall.
- Avoid getting into elevators alone with someone you don't know and trust.
- Be very wary of any vehicle pulling over to ask directions. You can answer back—but keep your distance! If you're the one driving, keep your windows up and lock the doors at all times. Don't stop if you think you're being followed. If a car bumps into you make sure you're in a well-populated area before stopping to investigate. If you have a cell phone, call 911 before getting out of the car. And don't give rides to strangers.
- Street smarts need to be in effect at all times.

- Anyone staring at you in a way that makes you uncomfortable should be avoided. Don't think twice about moving or letting your host know you're uncomfortable.
- Drugs and alcohol diminish your capacity to defend yourself. Drink sensibly. Also, you really want to avoid any drugs or drinks that come along, especially unannounced, from people you don't know.
- Trust your instinct. If the guy you're hanging out with begins to act strangely, or if any weird situation comes up—just leave. Don't hesitate to make a scene if you need to.
- Sexual abusers will use powerful sedatives—sometimes with the help of a bartender or waiter—to take advantage of girls at clubs and bars. Victims feel paralyzed or extremely drowsy. Once the vision has gone hazy, the victim enters a state of near unconsciousness that seriously affects her memory. Most of the time the victim won't even remember a thing. Don't accept any drinks from strangers.
- Expensive drinks or dinner never entitle someone to take advantage of you, much less to mistreat you.
- Avoid sharing rides with people you've met at parties or bars. Even if he seems like the nicest guy on earth, after a night of drinking and partying it's better to leave with people you know and trust.
- It's never too late for a Self Defense course like karate or judo. Even if you don't re-discover your life and re-do your whole image, a short course can really boost your self confidence and let you walk with your head held high where ever you go.
- Stand up for yourself! Even if a guy insists that you go further than you want, don't listen to any excuses. "Stop acting like a child", "You're so lame", "Look at me! Do you think you can leave me like this?" Don't give in and don't feel intimidated! He's just trying to scare you so that you shut up and let him do what he wants.

PAY CLOSE ATTENTION

Date Rape drugs

CHECK THiS OUT

These are drugs that most commonly facilitate the sexual assaults of people, meaning, anyone who plainly does not want to have sex. The effect that these drugs cause, makes victims more or less helpless, unable to refuse and, afterwards, confused about what actually happened. In some cases they may not even know what went wrong or be able to remember anything.

KETAMINE

Known as "Special K," "Vitamin K," "Kit Kat" or "Keta." A general anesthetic—yes, the kind that completely knocks out the patient—it is rarely used for human surgeries but is frequently used in veterinary practice. Ketamine is easily diluted in drinks because it is tasteless and colorless. Victims suffer unconsciousness and amnesia almost immediately. However, it will also distort visual and auditory perception and could produce a deep sleep.

Victims speaking to authorities after a rape often offer unreliable testimonies, and this doesn't help anybody. In many cases the drug has been combined with cocaine or crystal meth (MDMA) and inhaled. That combination is sometimes called "CK" or "Calvin Klein." But there are lots of ways that it can be presented or slipped to you without your even noticing it. So be careful!

GHB

Also known as "Liquid Ecstasy", GHB is a depressant that affects the central nervous system, and will induce sleep or amnesia. It also dangerously alters functions of the will; it dissolves in beverages or food, and causes deterioration in judgment and alterations in perception.

Recommendations

- Keep an eye on your drink all the time.
- Don't accept drinks that have not been opened in your presence or prepared in front of you.
- And then make sure they're from sealed containers.
- Don't accept drinks from strangers or people whom you've just met.
- At parties or clubs, stay in a group with your friends, talk about the risks beforehand, and look after each others' drinks.
- If you come to a party with a group, then leave with the same group.
- If you think you've been a victim of a sexual assault, you need to tell your family and the authorities immediately and get medical attention.

Do not feel intimidated

If you are ever in a situation in which a fellow insists in having some sort of sexual interaction against your will, SPEAK UP! A reaction on his side is likely: he might protest and try to make you feel scared, guilty or threatened: "What's wrong with you? Don't be a girl", "This is ridiculous", "You got me like this, you can't just go", "Everybody will find out you're a slut". Who knows, unbelievable things are said to intimidate. DON'T BUY IT. DON'T BE SCARED. He just wants your fear and your silence so he can get away with this.

We must insist: talk about any violation with your parents or with an adult you trust, and with the police if necessary. Don't feel shy about it. On the contrary, you'll feel relieved once you let it out. There is nothing worse than dealing with a humiliating situation on your own, and the fact is it doesn't have to be humiliating. Nobody's got the right to force a woman to have sex against her will—not even in a marriage.

The security of sexual abusers depends entirely on the silence of their victims. Everything is over once you talk about it, so regardless of who he is, you shouldn't feel guilty about anything! It doesn't matter if you drank too much, if you let him kiss you or if you went willingly into a dark and dodgy place. An abuser's actions are still solely his responsibility, not yours.

If you or someone you care about has been a victim of sexual abuse or rape, here are some institutions where you'll find help:

Helpcenters

▶ After Silence

▶ Male Survivor

▶ Pandys

▶ Women's Health

STDs
Sexually Transmitted Diseases

Bear in mind that men you've just met, no matter how nice and decent they seem, are still strangers to you. You don't know every aspect of their personal life. That guy who looks like a prince tonight may have been at a strip club just the night before.

Just swearing to being healthy and free of any "weird thing" is not proof enough. It can get you into trouble and can even threaten your life. If he's got genital herpes it could mean a lifetime of unpleasant maintenance, or if he's got HPV, do you really think he's going to tell you about it?

Nobody talks about STDs—sometimes not even to best friends because it's an uncomfortable issue frequently mixed up with a lot of shame. STDs are also quite common, but you won't hear about them at parties, at school or when you go out with your friends. And in fact, you know what? Lots of people will even try to hide it from their own doctor.

We're providing this information because we don't want you to find yourself saying: "Oh, I didn't know" or "If only someone had told me about it", We know that this is the type of things that don't cross your mind as the night heats up at a party or wherever, when people are concentrating on having fun.

It's not easy to meet a person who's recovering from anorexia or drug addiction, much less to find someone willing to talk about it. It's totally admirable and worthy of respect, but it's even harder—if not impossible—to find someone willing to talk about having an STD.

Can you picture why it's so difficult? "Hi my name's Mark and I have genital warts." Or "I really like you, you know? Oh, by the way, I have herpes—they're really contagious. What do you say? Come on, let's go."

In most cases, having an STD is a painful situation that is confronted all alone in your bathroom. Check out these facts:

* In the 1950's only five STDs were cataloged. Today there are over 50. Seriously.
* Twentyfive of those are very common among teenagers and 30% of them have no cure.
* Eigthy percent of STDs have no symptoms. How can you cure something you don't even know you have?
* You're then spreading the disease without knowing it, eventually becoming infertile with pelvic inflammation, that could even result in cancer. It's serious business no matter how many jokes are made about it.
* One of the most common illnesses today is Human Papillomavirus (HPV). More women die due to this virus than from HIV/AIDS. And as we've already mentioned, you're 4 times more likely to get an STD than you are to get pregnant.

Do I need to get tested for an STD?

Think about this: Have you had sex with somebody who has had sex with anybody else? If your answer is yes, then you do need to be tested for STD. It's a question of going to the doctor and getting some blood tests. As matter of fact, it's suggested that you get tested every 6 months if you are sexually active even in a monogamous relationship (that is, even if you have just one sexual partner).

The most important thing is that you stop thinking "It's never going to happen to me. No symptoms, no disease. No penetration, no risk." STDs are not only spread through semen and vaginal fluids. Sometimes genital contact is enough to pass on an infection or a disease and, in some other cases, saliva or blood can transmit the illness.

That's why condoms don't provide complete protection. The risk of getting an STD is real even if you've had intimate contact with just one guy.

The truth about STDs

THIS IS SOOOO FALSE

- The risk of getting an STD is present only with penetrative sex.
- Washing your genitals after sex prevents the spread of STDs.
- When infection takes place you know it because your whole body starts itching.
- The only serious threat is HIV/AIDS. The rest of STDs disappear with treatments you get pretty easy from your doctor or the pharmacy.
- Once the itch stops, you no longer need to treat yourself.

- STDs are very contagious.
- The best way to stay away from them is to avoid having sex altogether.
- Symptoms do not all appear immediately. Some will not appear at all.
- The only way of controlling or curing STDs is by following a doctor's prescribed treatment.
- Some illnesses stay in your body even though they seem to disappear, and they also can resurface later.
- If not treated properly, many STDs can cause death.

Please get informed and think about it thoroughly. Just imagine that anyone can engage in sex—even animals. Having sex or not doesn't make us more of a woman or a man; in contrast, determination, integrity and self-respect do make you a better person! Besides, nothing can beat the experience of making love with the person you love, free of troubles, fears and doubts.

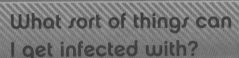

What sort of things can I get infected with?

Here's a list of the most common STDs, how they're spread, their symptoms and the normal course of treatments. Your doctor or gynecologist can give you much more information.

Gonorrhea

✱ What is it?

Bacterial infection.

✱ How do you catch it?

Vaginal or anal contact as well as oral sex.

✱ Symptoms

Men experience more trouble than women (females might not have any symptoms at all). Men undergo intense pain on urinating or whenever the penis secretes fluid. Women may experience increased vaginal discharge, pain or difficulty urinating and may have swollen labia or bleeding after intercourse.

✱ Prevention

Avoid sexual intercourse until the affected person is completely cured. Condoms and spermicides lower the risk of getting infected, although not completely.

✱ Treatment

Antibiotics.

✱ Long-term implications

If gonorrhea is not treated properly, there is a risk of infertility and pelvic inflammation.

Crabs

✱ What are they?

Parasitic insects that establish themselves in the pubic hair of human beings and feed on blood. May be able to live in people's heads and armpits as well.

✱ How do you catch it?

By coming in close physical contact with an infected person, including sharing underwear, sheets or pajamas. Pets may carry these insects too, but the species which infect humans are of three types and will not leap from pets to people or vice versa.

✳ Symptoms

Lots of itching. Tiny red spots may appear in your under-wear due to the insects' bites. And the insects themselves are often, but not always, visible.

✳ Prevention

Avoid intimate contact with people who have pubic lice.

✳ Treatment

Similar to treatment for head lice or for bed bugs—all of which are closely related. An over-the-counter medicated shampoo will take care of all but the most severe infections. Clothing and bed clothes must be washed thoroughly, and treatment might need to be repeated.

✳ Long-term implications

None.

Herpes

✳ What is it?

There are two types of herpes. Oral herpes may appear as cold sores around the mouth. Although extremely common, oral herpes is not cataloged as an STD. On the other hand, genital herpes is an STD characterized by the odor, itch and sores that appear on and around the genitalia. Oral herpes may occasionally show up later in the genitals of an infected person.

Once the virus that causes genital herpes makes its way into a person's system, it installs itself in the nerve base of the vertebral column and stays there permanently. Symptoms can emerge either at the time the virus is contracted or afterwards. As the virus never leaves the body, outbreaks of sores can come back sporadically; it is known that stress and fatigue trigger the reappearance.

✳ How do you catch it?

Through oral, genital or anal contact with a person with active, open sores. The virus can pass through simple skin contact, although semen and vaginal fluids can transport it as well.

✳ Symptoms

During the first genital outbreak sores can break, bleed, fester and itch, and thereafter the healing process will take between seven and 14 days.

Occasionally, fever symptoms can accompany an outbreak (headache, body aches, fever and fatigue) as well as urination pain. Following outbursts are usually milder, at times looking like infections or simple allergic reactions but will repeat regularly if not treated.

✳ Prevention

Always protect yourself with a condom and use spermicide. Female condoms are even better because they cover a wider area of the genitals. The risk of catching the virus is still latent at times when the sores aren't visible.

✳ Treatment

Certain type of ointments (anesthetic gels, for instance) may reduce the itch and sense of discomfort and accelerate the healing process, but advances in antiviral drugs have led to reduction in the number of outbreak days from an average of 20 per year to 10 per year in infected persons. Good sleep and proper nutrition also help.

✳ Long-term implications

Herpes is a virus that never leaves a person's system. That's why extra care and special habits are required in case of acquiring it:
✳ Wash your hands thoroughly during outbreak periods.

* Avoid touching your eyes and face after coming in contact with blisters. Herpes can travel to your eyes and could cause blindness under certain circumstances (ocular herpes).
* If pregnant, it is suggested to give birth with a c-section. An outbreak would put the baby's health at risk so keeping the doctors informed about genital herpes is crucial.

Human Papilloma Virus

*What is it?

HPV is a common sexually transmitted virus associated with the virus that provokes the emergence of warts throughout the human body.

*How do you catch it?

Through the skin, or from oral, anal or vaginal contact with a carrier.

*Symptoms

It is usually painless, and, occasionally, itchy warts may appear throughout the genitals. Their appearance depends on the specific area where they develop. Warts in the external genitals are harder and tend to have a whitish or brownish color while those that develop in the vagina or the cervix are softer and more pink.

*Prevention

Certain things like condoms and diaphragms can reduce the risk, although it is important to notice that the virus can still travel through skin contact despite protection. Many persons with genital warts do not know they are infected and many others carry the virus but simply ignore it.

*treatment

Once the HPV has been detected, the warts can be frozen, cauterized, cut off or treated with a laser. The body's immune system is able to get rid of the virus eventually or at least to reduce it to un-detectable levels. It is not clear to researchers whether the virus can then still be spread.

✱ Long-term implications

Untreated warts can keep growing until some sort of irritation provokes their breaking and bleeding. In very few cases, some of this virus' side effects are associated to pre-cancerous cells in the cervix as well as with cervical cancer itself. Pap smears detect this type of cancer—treatable and curable in early stages. Every woman must get it done once a year, although those who've been diagnosed with HPV must get a pap smear every 6 months.

NOTE:

most recently an HPV vaccine has been developed. this vaccine may prevent infection with certain species of human papillomavirus.

Consult your doctor for further information!

Chlamydia

✱ What is it?

Bacterial infection in the genitals.

✱ How do you catch it?

Through skin, anal or vaginal contact with a carrier. Oral sex passes the virus on too.

✱ Symptoms

A sense of burning appears in the genitals particularly when urinating. The smell and consistency of vaginal discharge changes; cramps may appear.

✳ Prevention

Make sure that neither you nor your boyfriend has Chlamydia. Wear a condom and use spermicides when practicing anal, vaginal or oral sex.

✳ Treatment

Prescription antibiotics if diagnosed at an early stage.

✳ Long-term implications

If not diagnosed and treated promptly, the infection can damage a person's urinary tract and sexual organs. Diseases related to pelvic inflammation may appear in women, who could then lose their capacity to have children.

Hepatitis B

✳ What is it?

Virus that affects the liver.

✳ How do catch it?

Hepatitis B is transmitted through body fluids including saliva. Kissing an infected person can pass on the virus, as can oral, anal or vaginal sex. Sharing personal hygiene products such as razor blades, toothbrushes and nail clippers can also spread the disease, as can infected needles used for piercing or tattooing and those used by drug addicts.

✳ Symptoms

Skin rash, fatigue, nausea, vomiting, body pain, abdominal pain, loss of appetite and a yellowish look of the skin. Some people do not present any symptoms at all.

✳ Prevention

There is a vaccine that prevents acquiring Hepatitis B. However, since this virus is highly contagious, it is still recommended that you avoid intimate contact with an infected person. Both male and female condoms (used with sper-micide) reduce the risk of catching the virus, although one must keep in mind that the virus can still be spread through kissing.

✳ treatment

The vaccine is effective even after being exposed to the virus. Shots of Immunoglobulin E can also help by strength-ening the body's immune system and fighting the virus.

✳ Long—term implications

This disease can be effectively controlled as long as there's enough rest, a proper diet, complete abstinence from al-cohol and a good medical treatment. Keep in mind that Hepatitis B is a chronic illness. The risk of liver damage and death is latent if it not handled professionally.

Syphilis

✳ What is it?

Bacteria that enters a person's bloodstream after sexual contact. It provokes ulcers, sores and skin rashes.

✳ How do you catch it?

Through oral, anal and vaginal sex. Kisses may spread the bacteria if sores are present in the mouth.

✳ Symptoms

Syphilis manifests itself in different stages. First, an ulcer appears in the spot in which the bacteria landed. At this point, the most contagious, the sore will fester though it will dry later.

If not treated properly, the bacteria can keep spreading throughout a person's system and begin to provoke skin rashes, fever and headaches. Healing does not occur when the sore is dried up for the illness is still present—as is the risk of acquiring it.

✳ Prevention

The use of male and female condoms (with spermicide) will reduce the risk, although sex with a person infected with Syphilis is strongly discouraged.

✳ Treatment

Antibiotics.

✳ Long-term implications

Untreated Syphilis may injure vital organs, provoke brain damage and, if untreated, it will eventually cause death.

Bacterial Vaginosis

✳ What is it?

Bacterial vaginosis is the most common type of vaginal infection (vaginitis).

✳ How do you catch it?

The cause of this infection is not really well known. However, it is related to an unbalance in the amount of bacteria in the vagina. Most of these bacteria are usually, benign, but there are some that are harmful to the body. BV shows up when there is an increase in the amount of harmful bacteria.

Some of the situations that increase the risk of catching BV, are:

✳ To have a new sex partner or to have many of them.
✳ Vaginal douching.

The relationship between sexual activity and BV is not that obvious, however, it is a fact that this illness is not contracted by the use of public bathrooms; wearing somebody else's pajamas, swimming or by touching specific objects. Furthermore, women who have never had sex can also develop BV.

✳ Symptoms

Women with BV may have abnormal vaginal discharge, meaning bad smell and, more specifically, fishy odor—especially after having sexual intercourse. The discharge may also be white and clumpy; grayish or yellowish. BV may also cause burning sensation when urinating and/or vaginal itching.

Beware of the fact that many women take some of these symptoms for granted, so you must be super careful to acknowledge them properly since BV may, if untreated, lead to more serious stuff like Pelvic Inflammatory Disease (PID)!

✳ Prevention

Among the steps that may help prevent BV, you may keep a good daily hygiene routine, especially when you are having your period; to have only one sexual partner, avoid vaginal douching and not to wear spray deodorants to conceal your natural vaginal odor.

✳ Treatment

Antibiotics, medicated creams or gels to be applied internally with a device designed specifically for this purpose. It is very important that you let your doctor know if you are taking some other type of medication.

✳ Long-term implications

In most cases, BV does not have long-term implications, however, if it is not treated and duly contained, it may increase the risk of catching other STDs.

it was enough to be worried about catching a cold!

Acquired Immune Deficiency Syndrome (AIDS)

It's almost impossible to meet someone who hasn't heard about AIDS, but what it is exactly? AIDS is an illness caused by a virus that spreads through blood, vaginal fluids and semen. The Human Immunodeficiency Virus (HIV), responsible for AIDS, attacks the immune system and makes an infected person much more prone to illnesses due to the lack of defenses and protection.

No cure for AIDS has been found. However, there are many treatments on the market that can more or less control the disease. The virus commences to silently destroy a specific type of cells called lymphocytes CD4. It's because of this subtle action that years can pass by before a bearer knows that he or she is HIV positive. It's important to notice that being HIV positive is not the same as having AIDS, although an HIV positive person could develop the disease with time.

HIV can be transmitted if unsafe sex (oral, anal, vaginal) is practiced with an HIV positive person. Also, the virus can make its way into someone's system by using unsterilized surgical materials, razor blades, tattooing needles and previously used syringes. An HIV positive mother may pass on the virus to her baby during pregnancy or while breastfeeding the child.

Symptoms

No symptoms are noticeable during the initial phases. After a while, an infected person's lymphatic ganglia swell up and a massive loss of weight takes place. Heavy sweating occurs during the night, infections appear frequently and fever can occur from time to time—as well as diarrhea and headaches. A sense of tiredness and fatigue frequently takes over the person. HIV can be avoided by using either male or female condoms with spermicide (in charge of killing the sperm).

Don't count on luck. Protect yourself

We don't need to say that HIV/AIDS is a life or death matter. We haven't given the issue so much space and importance out of mere curiosity. Lots—and lots—of people are dying or have died in the last several decades because of this disease.

When you're young you might think that the choices you make don't matter much. But choices about your health and safety can have the biggest repercussions and ramifications later on.

As we've already said, science has not yet found a cure or a vaccine for AIDS. So it doesn't matter how many beers you've had, or how much you like the guy or if it'll be your only chance to be with him. Don't do it if you haven't got a condom. Living the most incredible moment in the universe is not worth risking your life.

NOTE:

If you think that you may have caught the virus, or you've had an unprotected sexual experience with someone whose status you don't know, wait three months after the encounter and get tested for HIV. Discuss the results with your doctor. If you test positive, your life will change, but it won't end.

Oral sex

It's when the mouth comes into contact with the genitals. It's really important to be cautious as many diseases (like AIDS and Herpes) can be passed on this way. Viruses are not visible, so you'll never know if your partner bears the virus. If you choose to do it, remember that the use of condom does greatly reduce the risk, though again, not by 100 percent.

Anal sex

Someone's penis or finger penetrating the anus is more commonly practiced than you might think. Many people find it exciting as many nerve endings are located there in the rectum but it can also be painful and risky since there is a chance that the tissue in the rectum can tear and bleed. There is absolutely no decrease in the transmission or acquisition of STDs—though because there is no risk of pregnancy there is sometimes confusion about the relative "safety" of anal sex. Anal sex is NOT safe sex and you must use a condom to reduce the risk of STDs.

Things get worse if the penis is introduced into the vagina afterwards. Don't do it! Wash the fingers and penis and replace the condom.

Sexual Protection

Wow! That guy sure has Super Powers!

Contraceptive methods

If your guy and you are going to be fooling around, it is crucial that you get information regarding the subject. If you're sexually active, keep in mind that no matter what method you use, there will always be a risk of getting pregnant or catching an STD.

Once again, only abstinence is 100 percent effective!

Protection can be increased if two contraceptive methods are employed at the same time, like using a condom and taking the pill. Of course, this will only be more effective if we're talking about birth control pills!

Check this out: according to the Fact Sheet of Planned Parenthood, Federation of America:

- Three in 10 American teens experience pregnancy.
- For teens who did not use contraception during the first sexual encounter, 43 percent of girls have been involved in a pregnancy.

Trying any contraceptive method is better than doing nothing at all. There are different sorts, each one with both advantages and disadvantages.

CONTRACEPTIVE PROTECTION METHODS:
CHART OF EFFECTIVENESS

Type of contraceptive	Effectiveness vs. STDs	Effectiveness vs. pregnancy
Condom	High. Besides abstinence, the male condom is the best protection against STDs.	88% Effectiveness increases if used with spermicide.
Diaphragm + spermicide	Low. Spermicides can protect you against HPV and Gonorrhea.	82%
Fertility awareness	None.	Very low.
Suppositories, foam, jellies	Low. Can protect you against Chlamydia and Gonorrhea.	79%
Contraceptive pills	None.	99%
Coitus interruptus	None.	38%
Female condom	None.	90%
Intrauterine device	None.	98%–99%
Tubal ligation	None.	99%
Sponge	None.	64%–94%
The Morning After Pill	None.	80–95% Though it depends on how much time has passed after the sexual encounter.
Contraceptive implant	None.	99%
Vaginal ring	None.	99%

Things that simply won't work

Birth-control myths and misconceptions go back as long as women do. These are some of the most flagrantly untrue.

✚ Consuming lots of lemon. This is good for a cold, nothing else.
✚ Coca-cola is an effective spermicide.
✖ Taking just one contraceptive pill on the day you plan to have sex.
✖ Jumping up and down after sex will make the semen come out.
✖ Pulling out before ejaculation.

Common contraceptive methods

The Pill

Visit your doctor and ask him or her to prescribe the type of pill that best suits you. Birth control pills contain small doses of hormones that stop ovulation but there are different brands with different hormone concentrations—that's why the intake frequency changes—so you need to speak to your doctor.

Some pills must be taken the day your period begins. Some other pills have to be taken 7 days after your period ends. And if not taken at the same hour everyday, the pill loses its strength and effectiveness. This all seems a bit complex, but don't worry! Your doctor will know what type of pill is the best for you and he or she will be happy to explain their use. It's not complicated.

Besides being a pretty safe birth-control method, the pill regulates menstrual cycles and reduces pain during your period. There are some side effects though, especially during the first three months of intake:

- Weight gain
- Growth of body hair
- Breast pain
- Headache
- Depression
- Nausea

Despite these side effects, the pill is one of the most popular birth-control methods. Many women prefer the pill to any other method. It's also important to mention that neither smokers nor girls with breast problems can take birth-control pills. So, again, you need to speak to your doctor.

intrauterine Device

The intrauterine device (IUD) is a T-shaped device made of plastic or copper. A doctor will install the IUD in a woman's uterus upon request and then check every six months to be sure it's in the right position. Its mission is quite simple: make the uterus an inhabitable place for a fertilized egg. Its effectiveness rate is around 98 percent and it may work properly for three or five years without the need of changing it. However your period can get a bit rougher on you, the IUD is known to provoke more cramps and more bleeding especially when you first start using it.

Diaphragm

A diaphragm is a two to four inch cup made of rubber that women introduce into the neck of the uterus before having sex. The mission of this small, removable object is to prevent semen from getting anywhere beyond the cervix. Talk to your doctor before getting one. He or she will tell you what type of diaphragm suits you best.

Once it's been put inside, a woman needs to cover it with a spermicidal gel. When sex is over, it needs to be left inside the uterus for at least seven hours while the spermicide does its job.

It's important to check each time that the diaphragm is in good condition before insertion. Women can insert it up to four hours before sexual intercourse, and if inserted properly there should be no pain. Wash it right after taking it out and store it in its case.

Condom

Known as "prophylactics" back in the old days, condoms are sort of latex sleeves that tightly cover an erect penis. The mission is to trap pre-ejaculate fluid and semen once ejaculation takes place, stopping it from reaching the uterus.

There are tons of types: lubricated, ribbed, printed, in all sorts of colors and flavors. By the way, don't be surprised to find a musical condom out there!

Condoms can be bought at any drugstore. And as you already know, condoms protect you from catching certain STDs—HIV/AIDS included. Regarding birth control, condoms are 88 percent effective, although that protection will increase if combined with other vaginal contraceptives.

Do's and Don'ts of Latex Condoms

- There's not that much difference when it comes to sensation—especially for women. But no matter what they tell you, men still feel 95 percent the same as if they didn't use a condom.
- Condoms cannot be reused! A brand-new condom must be put on every time you have sex.
- You can't start to put one on—realize it's backwards—and then turn it over. If the outside—the wrong side—of the condom is smeared with pre-ejaculate fluid then it's useless. You need to start again with a fresh one.
- Musical condoms, those with funny pictures on them, the kind that are big enough to wear to a party or on your head, don't work. They've been made for jokes and satire.
- Your "Romance" might be interrupted to get the thing on. But you know what? It's definitely, totally worth it.
- Don't open up the individual package with your teeth! There's a chance that you'll perforate the condom without knowing it. Tear it carefully from the corner.
- A very small number of guys are truly allergic to latex and spermicides.

How are condoms used?

- The condom is applied on the erect penis before having sex. You should twist the tip of the condom with your fingertips, half a turn, before you slide the rolled part down the shaft of the penis so that no air gets stuck inside. That way it won't break because of air pressure. Don't let the penis touch the vagina without a condom—all the fluids on the tip of the penis contain sperm.

- The tip of the condom should protrude about half an inch to provide a reservoir for the semen. Once ejaculation takes place, it's important to get rid of the condom safely before the erection disappears. First, press the base of the condom firmly. Then, as you take the penis out of the vagina, hold the rest of condom tightly against the penis until it's outside the vagina completely. You've got to be really careful, because you really don't want a condom full of sperm to get stuck or to spill.

- Once it's out, simply dispose of it in a garbage bin.

- Don't use Vaseline! The condom's latex is badly damaged by contact with petroleum jelly and becomes fragile and compromised. Avoid putting on two condoms as friction may actually tear both of them.

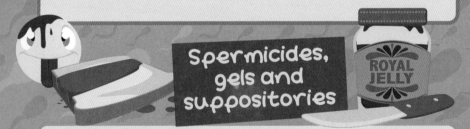

Spermicides, gels and suppositories

Spermicides are chemical substances applied inside the vagina. Their mission is to kill or immobilize sperm without harming any sexual organ.

Spermicides need to be applied 15 minutes before a sexual encounter and they can usually be applied with your fingers or with a special applicator. Just follow the instructions. The effect of spermicides lasts about an hour, and their effectiveness rate is 79 percent. Without a doubt, things get much safer if combined with another birth-control method like a condom or a diaphragm.

Coitus interruptus

Coitus Interuptus is simply "pulling out," an attempt to ejaculate outside the vagina, interrupting intercourse by taking the penis out of the vagina prior to ejaculation. The effectiveness rate is really not very good because there is sperm in all of the male fluids that are released during sex, prior to ejaculation. And it really offers no protection against STDs either.

The Female Condom

This tube-shaped latex membrane is introduced into a woman's vagina in order to prevent semen from passing beyond the neck of the uterus. Just as with male condoms, it comes lubricated to ease insertion.

Women who have used it say it feels a bit strange, especially at first. However, besides being 90 percent effective, it does a great job in protecting you from STDs as it covers a wider area of the vagina than the male condom.

NOTE:

it's not recommended that you use both male and female condoms at the same time because they will stick to each other.

Contraceptive implant (implanon)

AKA the contraceptive chip. The implant is like a little wire that's got the same size as a match. Doctors put it in the inside of an arm and even though it can't be seen, it can definitely be felt.

It's highly effective when it comes to birth control and has a lifetime of three to five years. After being inserted (simple procedure, no doubt), the little wire slowly liberates a synthetic hormone called Progestagen Etonogestrel—used in most modern contraceptive pills.

The implant is easy, quick to insert and remove. One can stop using it anytime and, once it's taken away, ovulation comes back in just about five days. Watch it: the use of this implant must be discussed beforehand with a professional.

Vaginal ring (Nuvaring)

This is a small, thin plastic ring about the same size as a condom. It offers protection for a month, and you can even introduce it yourself quite simply. The ring can remain steady for up to three weeks, and during this period, it liberates certain components every 24 hours as to constrain your system from ovulating. These hormones get access to your body via the vaginal tissue.

One may remove the ring three weeks after (some women suffer from minor bleeding afterwards). A week after the ring was removed (exactly one week), one must insert a new one. This method is 99 percent effective, and again, you must discuss its use with a doctor.

The Rhythm Method

The Rhythm Method is about having sex during the infertile days of the woman's cycle—that is, when there's no ovulation. In order to find out when you're fertile, simply follow the next steps:

- Check out your body temperature. Normal human body temperature is 98.6° F, but when you ovulate it increases about 1° F to 99.6 degrees. A woman's fertile days are three days before ovulation and three days after. The best time to check your body temperature is in the morning, before getting out of bed.

- Take a look at your vaginal discharge. During the fertile days a woman's vaginal discharge becomes transparent and thicker, something like an egg white.
- Then it's all about math. In a 28-day cycle, the riskiest days to get pregnant are the 13th and the 14th. Keep in mind that women are fertile from the 10th to the 17th day. The effectiveness of this method, however, is pretty low because a) you have to have a really strict control and b) you have to be super regular for it to work. Nevertheless, used in combination with another method, it can increase your overall protection.

Emergency contraceptives

BREAK IN CASE OF EXTREME EMERGENCY

If something unexpected happens despite taking care of yourself (the condom broke, for instance), in many places you can visit your doctor or a hospital and ask for the "morning-after pill."

This pill provides hormones that alter the uterus' endometrial lining in such a way that the ovum cannot be properly embedded thus interrupting a potential pregnancy. As a consequence, menstruation will follow. The pill needs to be taken within 72 hours after having sex. And only your doctor can approve this relatively extreme method.

As you've seen, Sexuality is a big universe of human experience. It's up to you—and nobody else—to make it a wonderful experience. But if you don't make a conscious effort to approach it with calm and deliberation, it can turn bad quickly. It's up to you!

Chapter 5
What's up with...
my mind
TO EAT OR NOT TO EAT
EMOTIONS
DRUGS
DEPRESSION
SUICIDE
BOOZE

If you think that your body experiences a massive amount of changes, just wait till you hear about the ones that take place in your mind. For sure you're already aware of some of them, like those abrupt mood changes or maybe the feeling that you're losing yourself—all triggered by the fact that you no longer know who you are, who you were or where you're heading.

Insecurities, doubts and confusion make you discover many versions of yourself that you didn't know existed. But keep in mind that having several versions of yourself doesn't give you the right to have several boyfriends.

Emotional issues

Existential doubts have been part of humankind since prehistoric times. So don't get all wound up or start feel guilty. You know something? The vast majority of adults still haven't found the answers to some of their questions. Have you ever felt that you act in a certain way when you're alone, but when you're with someone else you act totally different?

Has it ever happened to you that one day you're feeling timid and on the next you simply don't care what people think? Sometimes you're the sweetest girl on earth, but other times you couldn't care less about anything. What about clothing? One week you dress like a good schoolgirl and a few days later you're the rocker from hell, right? Chillax! Just remember that it's all gonna be over soon. Go with the flow.

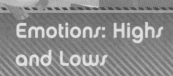

Emotions: Highs and Lows

Humans have all sorts of emotions. On one hand, you've got the ones that are awesome, fun and enjoyable, like love, satisfaction, achievement and many more. On the other hand, you have the ones that hurt and that can be really hard to deal with. Every person feels and handles these emotions in different ways.

Emotions are feelings, not actions. It's true, sometimes you can't control what you feel, but you are able to control what you do about it. If you ever feel that you don't have enough strength to deal with a negative emotion and you're harming yourself or others, please ask for help.

Emotions you DON'T like

I feel lonely

Has it happened to you that you feel as lonely as a cloud even though you're surrounded by a bunch of people? You might even be at your own birthday party and feel like not even the dog will wag his tail at you. Have you cried for hours in your bedroom or felt that nobody loves you? Well, it's important that you know that this can also be normal. Everyone you know, male or female, has been through this at least once.

I feel anxious and distressed

Have you ever felt like your belly is a big pit into which all your confidence is plummeting? Both anguish and anxiety are states of unease and fear that arise when confronting a situation with a high degree of uncertainty—that is, when we don't know what's going to happen. Just as you can fear something specific, you can also be frightened by the unknown.

If you feel anxiety or distress, try this: hang out with your friends and have a good talk, find an interesting class or a challenging workshop, work out your muscles or exert yourself physically, meet your boyfriend and enjoy some good kisses (actually, this is one of the best pastimes you can find).

However, if either anxiety or distress is seriously affecting your day-to-day activities, you could also consider seeking professional help. There's nothing to be frightened of—many, many people go through the same thing. It is very normal, and in most cases therapy or medicine will let you manage the problem in a better way.

I'm depressed

Depression sucks and it happens to loads of people. You may feel depressed because you broke up with your boyfriend, things at home aren't going well, you're grades aren't as good as they should be. Sometimes you're depressed and you don't even know why, but it does happen.

The best way to fix things is by confronting depression and figuring out what's got you hitting rock bottom. Sometimes, opening your feelings up and talking things through with someone you love, can cheer you up and make you feel better. However, some depressions can be so extreme that you just can't get out of the hole on your own—here's when the help of a professional is needed.

CAUTION

OMG! I'M SO DEPRESSED

IF DEPRESSION'S BEEN HANGING AROUND FOR OVER TWO WEEKS AND...

- ▶ You've cried nearly everyday,
- ▶ You feel tired, guilty or desperate,
- ▶ You don't get excited anymore about the things you used to enjoy,
- ▶ You're irritable and upset (and it's not because you have the M-syndrome),
- ▶ You're beginning to exhibit self-destructive behaviors,
- ▶ You've even thought about putting you life to an end...

...chances are that you're suffering from a major depression. In this case, the best thing to do is to find either a psychologist or a psychiatrist. Sometimes therapy is enough, but some other times it can be combined with prescription medicine. There's a special treatment for each problem.

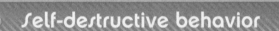

Self-destructive behavior

Whenever anyone puts him or herself into a dangerous situation, either physically or emotionally, it's time for the rest of us to get involved. This type of behavior can be triggered by many things, like going through a painful situation in your life, or by running away from grief or sensing a future risk that you don't know how to face or that simply scares you.

Self-destructive behavior can be expressed in various ways. Just as you may stop putting effort in the things you like, you may also begin to deliberately harm yourself. This is a very serious issue.

Suicide

A huge number of teenagers think about suicide but the problem remains largely taboo and unspoken. Some teenagers, regrettably, take their thoughts into action.

Suicide is one of the toughest things in the world to understand. Besides hurting themselves, people who commit suicide make things very painful for everyone else, especially those dealing with the aftermath: guilt, anger, sadness, impotence and further depression.

When we go through difficult moments, our minds sometimes play games with us. It's then that we think that life couldn't possibly get any worse, that our problems have no solutions and that it's just not worth going on... but the truth is that those beliefs are always wrong, and there are solutions to everything, even for the toughest problems. And there are people out there who can tell you how they've dealt with issues you would not believe existed, like:

➤ Not having a boyfriend. Being of no interest to anybody.
➤ The death of an important member of the family or, in some cases, of the entire family.
➤ Divorce.
➤ Drug addiction.
➤ Breaking up with that loved one and going through unbearable pain.
➤ Problems with one's parents.
➤ Being heavily indebted. Being threatened.
➤ Feeling as if one's the smallest person on Earth, and having huge self-esteem issues.
➤ Even that big problem you're going through right now.

Remember: everything must come to an end. Anxiety and tough moments pass, and things ALWAYS change—along with our feelings. Even the most negative and intense ones.

Even though some problems have no remedy, the best path one can take is acceptance. Try to learn from it. You'll discover mental growth when confronting these issues. You'll become more mature. You'll realize that no matter what tough experiences you've been through and how much you've suffered, you can always enjoy life again.

The real problem is not the complexity of any given issue, but the reluctance of a person to escape from it or to solve it. But a step as radical as death is definitely not the solution.

If suicidal thoughts have crossed your mind when facing a problem, it's really important that you talk about it with someone you trust. Try sitting down and chatting about it with a friend, a doctor, a therapist or a teacher that you like. There are also help lines that can provide you with professional counseling.

Now, if you ever hear a friend talking about suicide, please take it seriously. Quit playing, have a conversation, talk things through and seek professional help immediately.

If he or she rejects your help, go quickly to an adult and explain the whole situation. You may also call a helpline to find out what you can do.

Suicide myths

m= myth
F= fact

Before taking action, 80 percent of people who have committed suicide mention it to somebody. If anybody has mentioned the idea, help him. Help her.

m. Youth suicide stats has decreased.
F. Suicide is the third leading cause of death among persons aged 15-24.

m. Only people with specific characteristics commit suicide.
F. Any person, no matter whom, can commit suicide. Men and women, rich and poor, young and adult… People from the city or from the country… Christians, Muslims, Jews…

m. When somebody talks about suicide, change the subject so the idea goes away.

F. On the contrary. Take the person very seriously. Listen, pay attention. Give the person the chance to say how he or she feels and express your concerns. Look for help lighting fast.

m. Most people who want to commit suicide in fact just want to die.

F. Most people who want to commit suicide are confused. They're not sure if they want to die or not. Almost always, suicide is somebody's way of asking for help.

IS SOMEONE YOU KNOW THINKING ABOUT SUICIDE? RED ALERTS:

- Talking constantly about suicide is a big red flag.
- Giving away or neglecting personal possessions.
- Planning to put an end to their lives.
- Keeping pills, a gun or any other type of weapon.
- A history of self-destructive behavior or hurting themselves.
- A radical change from hardcore depression to a carefree disposition from one day to the next.
- Reluctance to see friends or to study; loss of interest in personal appearance.
- Self-exclusion from the rest of the world or a sudden appearance of new friends.

Drugs

What are drugs?

Marijuana, ecstasy, crystal meth, blunts, LSD, crack, acid, coke… it doesn't matter, they're all the same.

Drugs are either synthetic or natural substances that have effects on your body and your mind. Some of these can be permanent and provoke changes in both your feelings and behavior.

Drugs are part of our reality, and that's why we'd like to provide you with the best information possible.

Why do people get high for the first time?

Curiosity or "just to try it." This gets into peoples' minds all the time and, unfortunately, inside their noses, mouths and into their veins too. The idea of "just trying it" is way more dangerous than most people think because it's extremely easy to become an addict. Did you know that 7 out of every 10 persons who "just try" a drug, continue to consume it afterwards? What started out as curiosity can end up being a nasty problem for the rest of your life.

Sometimes we don't know that we have emotions laying somewhere: unfelt and un-experienced in the unconscious part of our minds. They're just waiting for the right moment to come out.

For example, you think you feel great and tell yourself you feel great without realizing that some part of you is actually sad. Maybe it's your parents getting divorced or a guy you've broken up with—or maybe it is something much less significant. It could even be something small that would make you laugh if you really confronted it. The point is you don't know why it makes you sad—but deep inside it's quite common to feel that you're not being totally honest with yourself. And that little bit of dishonesty extends into all other parts of you. These situations are perfect scenarios for drugs to play a role in one's life. So it doesn't matter if you're having the time of your life, if you're fired up, or if you're going out on a date with the guy you're dying for. If you're ever in the "to try, or not to try" dilemma, don't think that "nothing's going to happen," because something always happens!

GIRLS CONSUME DRUGS...

- To experiment and find out what it feels like.
- To avoid being kicked out of their group of friends.
- To avoid being the target of mockery.
- To escape reality and avoid problems.
- To prove that nothing's going to happen. "I've got a group of friends that's been on coke for two years and nothing's wrong with them. They're so cool." Even though everybody reacts differently, drugs lead you to the same point—sooner or later. Some people face problems within months after beginning to consume drugs, some problems take longer to develop. The consequences can be devastating in either scenario.

If you had some kind of X-ray vision, you'd be able to see the damage that drugs cause in your friends' bodies as well as the daily rise in their drug addiction. People who get high can do so for five or even 10 years but, eventually, they end up in rehab, jail or in a cemetery.

Do drugs cool down your problems?

People who offer you drugs will say things like:

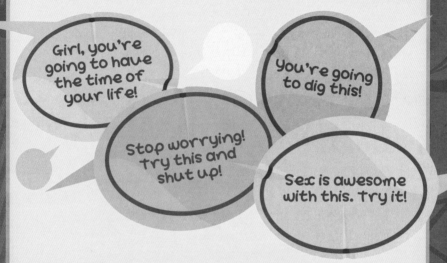

Girl, you're going to have the time of your life!

You're going to dig this!

Stop worrying! Try this and shut up!

Sex is awesome with this. Try it!

Is it true? In most cases, yes.

- You may have the time of you life, forget your problems and relax... The question is: for how long?
- It's always the perfect hook. Just when you think that nothing's going to happen, things start happening. At the beginning, quite often everything turns out to be just as they'd told you. But as you get accustomed to a drug, the problems that had disappeared come back a hundred times harder, and faster.
- Tranquility becomes anxiety, distress, fear and loneliness.
- At the beginning some drugs demand a small intake to feel high, but as the addiction grows, the quantity you need increases as well. Eventually you are consuming

more drugs merely to maintain the feeling of being on drugs, rather than actual tranquility, and life without drugs becomes hellish.

- Keep in mind what tolerance is all about. When your body gets used to any given substance, it will ask for a greater quantity to get the same effect. When you least expect it, you're consuming too much. If this weren't enough, some people actually boast about how much drugs they "can take"; they have no idea that their body gets hooked on a lifelong addiction.

- Eventually, in trying to get rid of your problems you'll be creating a far bigger mess. That's why when people are complete drug addicts and facing the physical and emotional problems drugs bring, they say: "I had no idea what I was gething into."

- At first, you'll hear you're friends say: "Come on, do some coke/pot/acid. You won't believe the feeling." What you will end up feeling is how deep you've gotten in such little time.

Good news, bad news

The bad news is that there are a lot of people out there who already have addiction issues. The good news is that there are ways of controlling them. Addiction is an incurable, progressive and mortal illness, but it can be controlled eventually. Usually that happens only when the victim's life is in total disarray already. Being an addict is the same as being sick.

Just like with eating disorders, conquering addiction requires guts and perseverance. The real problem is the addict's reluctance to confront the fact and take steps to fight the addiction. It is very difficult and, just like with anorexia, the struggle may include multiple relapses and years of work.

The first step consists in accepting that you have a problem. If you've made it to this step, just face it and start working on it as soon as you can. Get your act together and remember that when it comes to drugs, the farther you go, the harder it's going to be to get back. If you just can't give up on drugs on your own, you'll need a support group or serious rehab.

Legal drugs

ALCOHOL

Note: Federal drinking age is 21. Since alcohol is part of reality, we feel obliged to discuss this issue in this book.

Adolescents are very curious about experimenting with that happy-go-lucky feeling one gets with a couple of beers. Maybe you've already done so in secret, or perhaps your parents let you have a glass of wine or beer on some special occasions. Maybe you're the type of gal who uses alcohol to perk yourself up at parties.

The thing is that drinking alcohol is a two edged sword. On one hand, you can enjoy it and have no problems if you do it responsibly or... you can go wacko, drink too much and get yourself into heaps of trouble. In the worst of scenarios, you can become an addict or just be involved in one of the serious accidents that kill far more people than does the addiction.

You'd be better off if you took a look at this. You don't want a beer to become your new BFF, do you?

Girls and alcohol

"Oh my god! Did I get shitfaced last night or what? Ha, ha. Did you see that girl puking in the bathroom? She was so wasted. Can someone get me a beer? I am so hung over!"

We couldn't help over-hearing these phrases on vacation on the Mayan Riviera. A group of five or six girls were putting on suntan lotion and laughing it up about the night before as they sat down next to us. Turning around to take a look at them, we were shocked to realize they were barely 15 or 16 years old. They looked pretty, well cared for and, certainly, they seemed to be well-educated girls. If we hadn't seen them we would've never believed they'd made those comments.

Years ago, getting wasted from so many drinks was something you'd only see in guys. Today it's as common to see girls drinking as much as guys. That's why we chose to include this section in this book. If you have the right information, we hope you'll make the right choice.

GABY

New Sensations

The whole "growing up thing" includes confronting the inevitable presence of cigarettes, alcohol, drugs and other substances that alter our moods and our minds.

Far and away, alcohol is the most available, the most consumed and the most accepted.

As a teenager, you have a chance to experience life with a higher degree of freedom when you're not at home or when you're far away from your parents. You want to try things out—and try yourself out, too. Lots of us drink beer, drag on a cigarette, we ignore the rules and we want to have some fun.

Experimenting with new and wonderful sensations catches our attention and you know what? It also happened to every one of us who are now adults, and we understand every bit of it!

Some of the effects of alcohol

WE WILL, WE WILL, ROCK YOU.

- Booze makes many people feel good. It also works as a stimulant and gives them a bit of self-confidence.
- It takes about five to 10 minutes for booze to go from your intestines to your bloodstream. The effects of alcohol can last several hours, though it all depends on the quantity of alcohol, how fast you drink it and the size of your body. Besides, quite frequently you can feel dizzy and clumsy as alcohol makes its way out of your system.
- The next morning you'll often wake up with a headache, a hangover, feeling wrecked or however you want to name it. This generally gets worse as you get older.

THINGS THAT INCREASE THE EFFECTS OF ALCOHOL

- Empty stomach.
- You're on your period.
- Being too tired or too stressed.
- Drinking too fast.
- Heightened emotions, happiness or sadness.
- Playing one-shots.

HOW MUCH ALCOHOL DOES IT HAVE?

- One beer 5%
- Wine 12%
- Tequila, whisky, vodka, rum and gin 40%
- Soft Drinks 0%

RISKS

- When you drink till you drop, you put yourself in danger. Everyone will make fun of you, even those who got you drunk. It happens when anyone drinks loads of booze really quickly and it happens to everyone who grows up outside of a severely restrictive community. Why do you think people run from those communities and go straight to a bar?

- If one of your friends passes out from being drunk, and he or she can't wake up or breathe properly you need to lay him or her down on their side—in case they vomit so that they don't choke. If their breathing is irregular you need to seek medical attention.

- Excessive drinking can play games with your memory too. Alcohol impairs your attention, your motor coordination, as well as your sense of balance. Driving under the influence of alcohol—any alcohol—is totally off limits.
- Excessive drinking can provoke a loss of appetite, vitamin deficiency, stomach and skin problems and sexual impotence. Long term drinking will damage your liver, your pancreas, your heart, and even your nervous system.
- Who will ever want a serious relationship with a girl who's constantly drunk?

RISKS THAT ARE PARTICULAR TO WOMEN

- Women get drunker way faster than men. After drinking the same amount of alcohol (it doesn't matter if you dance way more than dudes), alcohol levels in a girl's system will increase 25 or 30 percent higher than in a guy. Never try to compete or to keep up with men drinking. Girls are smaller but, more importantly, they produce less of the enzymes that process alcohol in the body.
- Women are more vulnerable to the negative effects of alcohol, both short and long-term. After drinking as much as a guy, a woman's ability to detect a risky situation decreases a lot: "Can I drive?" "Shall I sleep with him?" "Should I tell him to wear a rubber?"
- The risk of sexual violence increases in proportion to the amount of alcohol consumed.
- Alcohol, more than one glass daily with a meal, also causes serious and irreversible damage in unborn babies.

Risks for teenagers

- Important: the brain is not fully developed until you turn 23. This can make young people much more vulnerable to the effects of alcohol than an adult with a fully-developed brain.

Genetic risks

- A person with an alcoholic parent or close relative is more prone to have problems with alcohol. If you have a close relative who's an alcoholic, it's really important that you start making smart choices when it comes to alcohol.
- Daring to be yourself commands the respect of the people around you, including your closest friends. Try to make your choices independently of your friends' influence and pressure.
- Drinking doesn't make you look more mature or sexier. On the contrary, stop drinking whenever it suits you and you'll demonstrate you're an intelligent woman. When everyone is trashed, imagine being the classy one at the party. Composed, calm and having fun. You won't regret that.
- If you have serious issues with alcohol or you want to help out a friend with his drinking habits, take a look at the sections "Good news, bad news" and "My friend's an addict, what should I do?"

It's about 10 o'clock at night and there we were, me and five friends, each with a pill in our hands, ready to swallow them and jump in the pool. So I washed it down with vodka and 30 minutes later it was totally kicking in.

After a while, I come to the conclusion that the thing that was making me feel weird was alcohol. I was the one who bought the pills, so I was in charge. I washed another one down without anyone noticing—it kind of sucked that they were all high and I wasn't.

Wow! Then it kicked in for real. All of a sudden, a feeling of completely like 'wow' came over me. Everything was slow, in harmony. And we all felt so good... I love the universe and all our problems vanished just like that. I just wished we could stay like that forever.

An hour and a half later I was like "I need another pill" —the effect was gone. This time I was going to take two; that should double the effect. Everybody says that pills leave your head fried, but I'm on holiday with my friends... what could happen?

By 4 o'clock in the morning I'd already taken 6 pills and smoked two joints. I had a terrible headache and the idea of getting out of the pool scared me to death. I was totally paranoid; shadows crossed my eyes, my friends wanted to go to bed and the only thing I thought about was more pills.

The comedown is horrifying. I felt totally depressed and kept having panic attacks.

LAURA

Laura is 27 years old and is now in rehab. She began using all sorts of drugs when she was 16. With an overwhelming honesty that we really appreciate, she tells us her story in order to prevent other teenagers from getting the wrong idea about drugs.

ECSTASY

WHAT IS IT?

Also known as "E", "X" or "XTC", ecstasy is a pill made from a substance called 3,4-methylenedioxy-N-methylamphetamine (MDMA). Since this book is not interested in jawbreakers, we can just call it E. E can be found in pills, capsules or in powder.

Ecstasy pills used to be sold in raves, discos and big parties, but they're consumed almost everywhere nowadays —however, they still have that "big party" reputation. Most pills have an image on them and are named after all sorts of things, like clothing brands, movies and cars. Dealers often mix them with other substances, making them even more dangerous.

EFFECTS

It takes anywhere from 30 minutes to two hours before a dose takes effect. The "trip" lasts between two and six hours—a time in which shyness disappears and everything seems trouble-free. Ecstasy can provoke an openness to feelings, and seems to heighten awareness and increase a person's capacity to perceive beauty. It can also cause shakiness, jitters, involuntary eye movement, loss of appetite, nausea and vomiting.

RISKS

The experience of the "trip" is followed by a comedown, or crash. Since facing reality again can seem a little rough, some users prefer repeating the trip as quickly as possible. The symptoms of a crash can last for several hours to several days. Consuming high doses repeatedly or regularly can cause anxiety attacks and vertigo.

EXTRAS

It is very common that drug dealers give away pills for free to get you hooked on them. But sometimes, not even they know what's in them. In some pills it has been possible to find rat poison, so, if after reading all of this you still give them a try, don't be surprised if you have a very low end.

MARIJUANA

WHAT IS IT?

Marijuana is a plant also known as Cannabis (*indica* or *sativa*). Its flowers and leaves can be either smoked or eaten in cakes and brownies. One of its closest relatives is hashish, which is smoked as well.

EFFECTS

People consume marijuana to feel relaxed. The high includes changes in perception and a sense that problems are eased. The sense of the passing of time can also be affected. In high dosages, marijuana may affect the vision and provoke hallucinations.

RISKS

Marijuana reduces a person's capacity to concentrate and short-term memory. It can also trigger heart problems and mental disorders in susceptible people. Consumption during pregnancy can cause low birth weight.

EXTRAS

The danger of marijuana use comes from driving or operating machinery when the senses are seriously impaired. Some people will form a psychological dependence on the drug, and heavy use can cause paranoia and social withdrawal. It is also illegal for recreational use as are all the drugs in this section and therefore, possession of even small quantities can get you into serious legal problems.

COCAINE

WHAT IS IT?

Cocaine is a white powder that is extracted from the coca plant. It is usually inhaled (snorted), though it may be injected or smoked as well. In general, the one that is smoked is a highly potent form of cocaine.

EFFECTS

The "trip" is really short: between 20 and 40 minutes but when smoked, the effect is even shorter—around 15 minutes, although it gets to be more intense. Cocaine induces users to a strong sense of well-being—even self-confidence, loss of appetite, aggression, sexual arousal and euphoria.

RISKS

Cocaine is highly addictive—people who consume it go through a really tough time trying to stay clean. Street grade cocaine from a random dealer is almost certainly impure and likely more toxic. The "good stuff" is more addictive. Injecting cocaine can cause death by overdose or heart failure. Snorting cocaine damages the entire upper respiratory tract and nose, and smoking it will definitely affect your respiration.

Cocaine will also accelerate a person's heart cycle and cause anxiety, dizziness, paranoia and nausea. It may also provoke violent behavior.

EXTRAS

Inhaling cocaine during pregnancy increases the risk of miscarriage as well as premature birth. The effects of the drug can also pass on to a baby through breast milk, provoking irritability and loss of appetite.

CRYSTAL METH, AMPHETAMINES AND SPEED

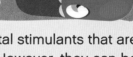

WHAT ARE THEY?

Amphetamines are physical and mental stimulants that are used for certain medical treatments. However, they can be bought illegally as tablets or capsules and can be injected into the bloodstream.

Both amphetamines and methamphetamines—along with some chemically similar stimulants—are known colloquially as speed.

EFFECTS

Amphetamines are among the most dangerous drugs you'll encounter. You feel fine for a few moments; hunger and tiredness vanish as your pupils get big, your throat dries up and you lose motor coordination. Other negative reactions include paranoia, headache, increased heart rate, diarrhea, vertigo, dizziness, shakiness and sexual impotence. Convulsions can occur if consumed in high doses.

RISKS

If consumed frequently, amphetamines, especially crystal meth, will provoke severe malnutrition and irreversible brain damage that affects a person's capacity to speak and think. Little by little, users start requiring higher doses to get the desired effects.

EXTRAS

Mothers who consume amphetamines give birth to babies with heart problems or with a cleft palate. Overdose can result in coma or even death.

METHAMPHETAMINES

WHAT ARE THEY?

Crystal Meth, like amphetamines, while used particularly in common cold remedies, is often consumed illegally. Also known as meth, ice or glass, methamphetamines are often found in a bitter-flavored white powder, tablets or capsules. Although they're usually inhaled, they can also be eaten, smoked or injected.

EFFECTS

The "trip" of crystal meth is similar to that of amphetamines. A state of hyper-alertness and euphoria is more common than a relaxing effect and an increase in blood pressure and body temperature will frequently cause increased heart rate.

RISKS

"Amphetamine Psychosis"—a state of mixed paranoia, auditory and visual hallucinations, extreme irritability, lack of sleep as well as an erratic and aggressive behavior will result from regular use. A psychological dependence on the drug will lead to anxiety attacks in the drugs absence, and users' cravings for sugar and sweets, especially soft drinks, lead to catastrophic dental problems that are notorious, disgusting and widespread among "Meth Heads."

EXTRAS

Meth badly affects people with heart problems—especially hypertension. If consumed during pregnancy, babies can be born with heart problems.

OTHER DRUGS

Another kind of substances you have to keep an eye on is opiates, that come from the opium poppy plant. In contrast to the drugs listed in the previous pages, opiates have an analgesic effect and will depress the nervous system. The most common drugs of this family are heroin and morphine.

There will always be someone who'll offer you drugs and that there will always be "suitable" moments. Be careful.

My friend's an addict, what should I do?

Making a friend accept his or her addiction is one of the most important steps—and one of the most difficult ones. Quite frequently they're simply not ready to face the problem and, sadly, they may have to hit rock bottom before they realize they have a problem at all.

The best thing you can do is let the person know that you are aware of his or her addiction. Chances are you won't hear from them ever again.

Help them by not helping them at all

In case your friend does not acknowledge the problem, the best thing you and the family can do is let him or her face the consequences of his or her actions. Trying to "help out" can actually be harmful, like lending her money, covering him, helping her out if she faces legal problems, letting him spend the night at your place under the influence, or stuff like that.

Your friend will possibly acknowledge the problem once he or she hits rock bottom. This will be the best time to ask for help in a specialized organization, a support group or in a rehab clinic.

In many occasions, friends, as well as family, become "addicted to the addict." This means that their love or pity ends up contributing to their drug addiction and preventing them from facing the problem. If this happens, it's really important that they attend a support group to learn how to deal with issues like these.

Also, many people choose not to confront a buddy's addiction because they're scared of losing his or her friendship. On the contrary, helping a friend out in this type of situations is priceless; whenever full recovery is achieved, he or she will come to realize that you acted like a true friend, like someone who really cared for him or her—unlike the rest of the "friends" that were around. This will definitely tighten your friendship and may keep you close forever.

Remember: It's not the easiest thing in the world, but getting your own act together and helping out a friend who's facing this sort of problems is something that only true friends do.

WHERE THE MOST HIDEOUS MONSTERS REST IN PEACE.

Write down the name of your ex boyfriends. Include the dates in which you went out together.

R.I.P.

Kissed toads

GABY VARGAS
YORDI ROSADO
Quiúbole con...
BILINGÜE
TU CUERPO
EL LIGUE
TU IMAGEN
LAS DROGAS
INTERNET
EL SEXO
Y TODO LO DEMÁS...
AGUILAR

AGUILAR

D. R. © Gabriela Vargas y Yordi Rosado, 2013.
De esta edición:
D. R. © Santillana Ediciones Generales, S.A. de C.V., 2013.
Av. Río Mixcoac 274, Col. Acacias
México, D.F., 03240

Esta obra se terminó de imprimir en septiembre de 2013
en los talleres de Impresora Tauro S.A. de C.V.
Plutarco Elías Calles No. 396 Col. Los Reyes
Delg. Iztacalco C.P. 08620. Tel: 55 90 02 55

Primera edición: septiembre de 2013
ISBN: 978-607-11-2719-8

D.R. © Diseño de portada, diseño de interiores e ilustraciones:
Christian Michel, Infección Visual, www.infeccionvisual.com

Se utilizó la familia tipográfica "Chalet" para el cuerpo de texto y títulos, así como
la fuente "House Cut" creadas por House Industries, www.houseind.com

Quiubole con

EL ÍNDICE

Capítulo 3

Quiúbole con... mi imagen

Capítulo 4

¿Quiúbole con... mi sexualidad

zZz

Capítulo 5
Quiúbole con... wi' wente

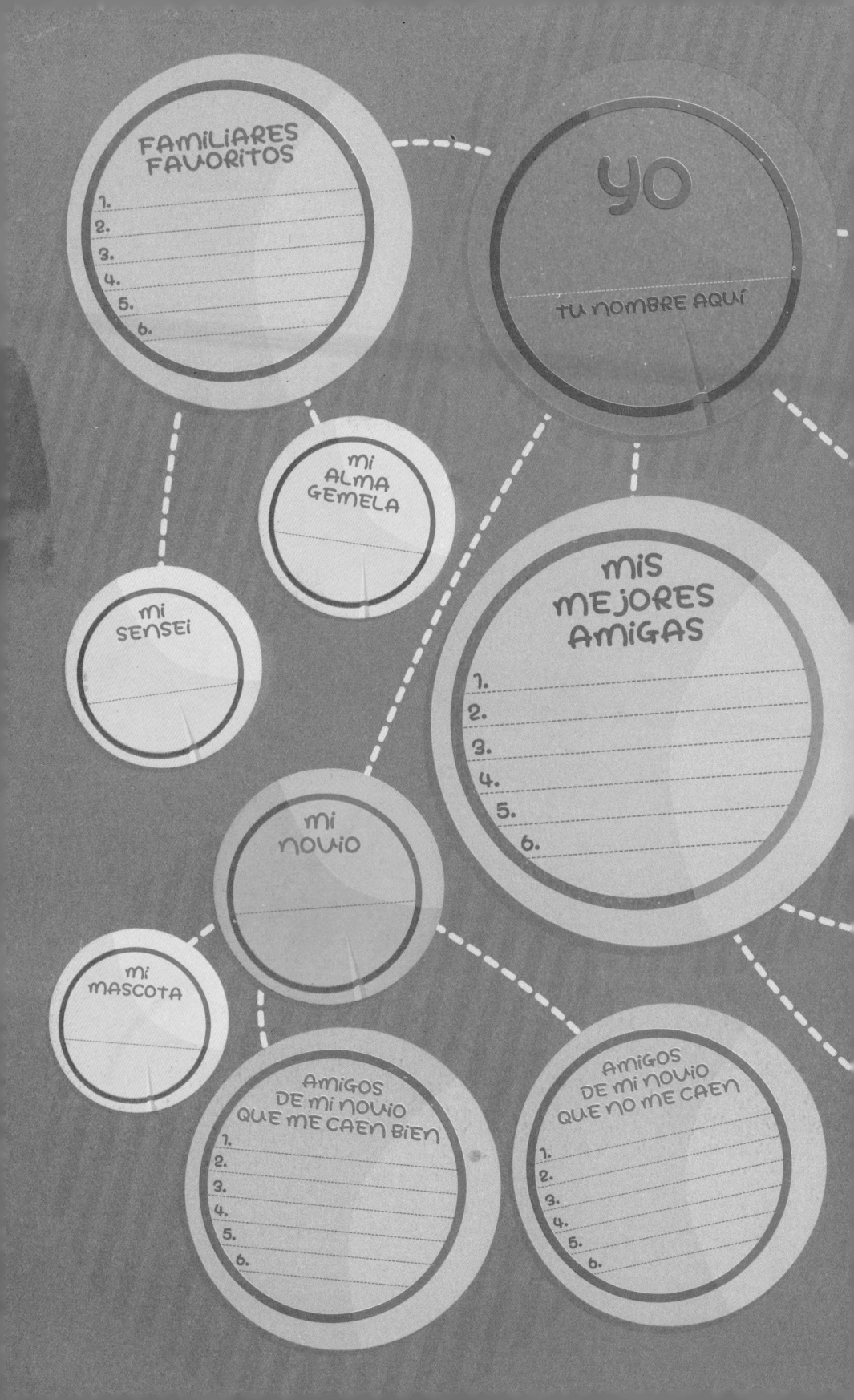

"CÍRCULO DE AMISTAD"

NIÑOS QUE ME GUSTAN

1.
2.
3.
4.
5.
6.

Como dicen que cada cabeza es un mundo (y si estás leyendo esto... es un hecho que tienes una cabeza)... Te dejamos este organigrama o lo que es lo mismo "dibujito para organizar", con el único objetivo de que apuntes quiénes son tus mejores amigas, tus galanes, tu confidente y bueno hasta tu mascota. Así que... ¡ARRÁNCATE!

MI CONFIDENTE

LOS POSIBLES

1.
2.
3.
4.
5.

MI AMIGO INVISIBLE

MI AMIGA no. 1

MIS NO TAN AMIGAS

51.
52.
53.
54.
55.

LOS IMPOSIBLES

1.
2.
3.
4.
5.

Advertencia: Te pedimos, te imploramos y te suplicamos que llenes los espacios con lápiz, porque en cualquier momento... puedes cambiar de OPINIÓN ¡...Mua...ja...ja...ja! (perdón, intentamos que sonara como una risa macabra, pero escrito no está tan fácil).

El prólogo

Como posiblemente
no te gusta leer
los prólogos...

No te
preocupes,
¡nos lo saltamos!

¡¡Hola!! El objetivo del *Quiúbole con...* es que encuentres de una forma divertida, alivianada y al mismo tiempo profunda, toda la información de lo que te inquieta y te sucede, de lo que te va a pasar y de las cosas que de plano a veces sientes que por más que le echas ganas, no te pasan.

Sabemos que en ocasiones te puedes sentir súper sacada de onda porque crees que las cosas sólo te ocurren a ti: relájate; verás que lo que platicamos en este libro le pasa a muchas niñas como tú, y verás también que la diferencia es cómo lo toma y lo resuelve cada quién.

Puedes leer *Quiúbole con...* por secciones de acuerdo a lo que te late; o lo puedes leer de principio a fin.

El libro está dividido en cinco grandes temas que son: tu cuerpo, tus relaciones, tu imagen interior, tu sexualidad y tu mente.

Queremos decirte que cuando hicimos este libro, los dos aprendimos y nos divertimos mucho. Quizá la mezcla de Gaby y Yordi te parece medio loca y te preguntas: "¿Por qué dos personas tan distintas se juntaron para escribir este libro?" Bueno, porque creemos que justamente por la diferencia de edades, de sexo y a veces de manera de pensar, el libro se hace más interesante y se complementa.

La idea se nos ocurrió mientras corríamos en las caminadoras del gimnasio. Como nos dimos cuenta de que, por más que nos esforzáramos, jamás seríamos estrellas

en los 100 metros planos, y ni siquiera de la mini olimpíada de Xochitepec, corrimos, pero a entrevistar niñas que nos platicaron y nos ayudaron a entender lo que te preocupa y lo que tienes ganas de saber.

También entrevistamos a muchos especialistas en diferentes temas, que nos asesoraron para asegurarnos de que la información que vas a encontrar aquí, es totalmente confiable.

Como es lógico, a veces los dos discutimos sobre nuestros diferentes punto de vista, sobre si meter "x" chiste o no, sobre qué temas te interesarían más, y qué palabras utilizar para que le entendieras mejor, pero la finalidad del libro siempre estuvo súper clara: informarte de la manera más objetiva y neutral posible, para que tengas herramientas y tomes tus propias decisiones sobre todos los rollos que vas a enfrentar en este momento de tu vida.

En fin, ojalá lo disfrutes tanto como a nosotros nos gustó y nos divirtió hacerlo. Estamos seguros de que si este libro te sirve para algo, nuestro trabajo habrá valido la pena.

GABY Y YORDI

Entre los nueve y los 13 años parece que diario es tu cumpleaños. Todos los días te levantas y tienes algo nuevo ¡pero en tu cuerpo! Y también, como en tu cumpleaños, te encuentras con cosas padrísimas y con otras que dices: "¿Qué es esto? No, gracias, no lo quiero". La bronca es que una vez que lo tienes no hay cambios ni devoluciones, no puedes regresar a la tiendita y decir, ¿sabe qué?, siempre no.

En tu cuerpo empieza una revolución tan cañona que de plano no te la crees. Cuando notas las primeras señales dices cosas como: "Qué raro, me están creciendo las bubis...", y hay de dos: o le das gracias a Dios porque escuchó tus plegarias y le dices a tus blusas con escote: "Ahora sí, van a chambear", o te niegas rotundamente a aceptarlo y te tapas lo mejor que puedes. Pero es muy chistoso porque primero te da pena, luego como orgullo, y si te crecen mucho, como si fueras modelo de revista con mucha, pero mucha "pechonalidad", pues como que otra vez te vuelve a dar penita. Entonces te pasa que sientes como si fueras en la carretera y de repente te encuentras un letrerito que dice:

ACAPULCO
20 KM

BIENVENIDA
A LA ADOLESCENCIA
POBLACIÓN: TODAS TUS AMIGAS

CUERNAVACA
YA TE PASASTE

JOJUTLA
PRÓXIMA SALIDA

La adolescencia es también conocida en las altas esferas de los adultos como:

¡La edad de la punzada!

¡La edad del "me vale", y si a mis papás no les late que me valga, "pues me vale"!

¡La aborrecencia!

¡La época de los pubertos!

Es una época muy padre, divertida, súper chida, pero a veces, medio complicada.

Además de los rollos en tu cuerpo, vas a notar que tu manera de relacionarte con los demás también empieza a cambiar; tú misma te sientes y piensas diferente. ¿Ya sabes?

En conclusión, los juegos que antes jugabas de niña ahora pueden ser súper densos, porque si empiezas a jugar con tu novio al doctor (con inyección y toda la cosa) ¡aguas! Puedes terminar jugando al papá y a la mamá, ¡pero de a de veras! Y de ahí en adelante, a jugar todos los días a la comidita... Bueno, pero eso es otra cosa.

El caso es que entras a una de las épocas más padres de tu vida. En este capítulo vamos a platicar de todas estas cosas nuevas que tu cuerpo experimenta; pero antes de continuar, te proponemos que hagas este test, para saber qué tan adolescente eres.

Test de la aborrecencia

IMA
INSTITUTO MEXICANO DE LA ABORRECENCIA
POR UNA SOCIEDAD CON UNA ADOLESCENCIA FELÍZ

ÁREA PARA RESULTADOS

AUTO TEST No.1
ENTRADA A LA ABORRECENCIA

Nuestro test ha sido desarrollado por los más selectos especialistas en el ramo. Lea cuidadosamente cada punto antes de contestar, evite copiar o usar cualquier método que implique hacer trampa en la evaluación.

¡Mucha suerte!

(SÍ) (NO) Te sientes incomprendida y con más presiones.

(SÍ) (NO) Te vuelves enojona, tipo "Grinch" en intercambio navideño.

(SÍ) (NO) Si antes tu paciencia era de 10, ahora es como de 3.5 (y aquí el .5 no sube).

(SÍ) (NO) Ahora para ti, lo mejor de la vida es salir con tus amigas.

(SÍ) (NO) Te preocupa mucho verte bien.

(SÍ) (NO) Cuestionas todo lo que viene de tus papás: permisos, forma de vestirse, forma de hablar y demás.

(SÍ) (NO) Estás hipersensible.

(SÍ) (NO) Tu grupo de amigas es tu tesoro más valioso.

(SÍ) (NO) Hace más de dos años que no tocas tus barbies (casi casi ni para limpiarlas).

(SÍ) (NO) Un segundo estás feliz y al siguiente ¡estás llorando!

(SÍ) (NO) Les contestas mal a tus papás por todo (no importa si no te preguntaron nada).

(SÍ) (NO) No te entiendes ni tú misma.

HB 2

• QUIÚBOLE CON EL TEST • MEX •

SÍ NO Tienes mil broncas con tus papás. Ya no quieres que se metan en tu vida y cuando te regañan sólo les das el avión.

SÍ NO El niño que antes sólo se te hacía mono, ahora te parece guapérrimo, es más, te mueres de ganas de comértelo a besos ¡hasta sus brackets te parecen sexys!

SÍ NO Ahora ves tus bubis más que tus cuadernos.

SÍ NO Ya no te diviertes con las mismas cosas de antes.

SÍ NO Tu autoestima está súper inestable.

SÍ NO Antes estabas de acuerdo con todo lo que tus papás te decían; ahora sus recomendaciones ya no te laten tanto.

SÍ NO Así como el planeta tiene sus elementos (agua, fuego, tierra y aire) tú tienes los tuyos (fiestas, ropa, amigas y música).

Si tu forma de ser coincide con 1 a 3 afirmaciones eres adolescente.
De 4 a 10 la adolescencia se te sale por las orejas.
De 11 a 19 podría aparecer tu foto en la enciclopedia de la adolescencia.

Las bubis

Los pechos se conocen de muchas maneras: bubis, senos, bubs, chichis, en fin, como quieras decirles. El caso es que las bubis se han convertido en un icono de la sexualidad en la mujer (algunos hombres también las tienen: son luchadores de lucha libre y generalmente usan copa 38 B).

A ciertas niñas les da pena que les crezcan y caminan estilo Notre Dame, o sea medio jorobadas; tratan de usar sudaderas gigantescas con la cara de Winnie Pooh para

que los nuevos bultos se confundan con los cachetes del osito (así el pobre Pooh se ve como con 8 kilos más de como es realmente). A otras, les urge que sus pequeños montecitos se conviertan en los Alpes Suizos.

Las bubis empiezan a aparecer gracias al estrógeno; seguramente dirás: "Estro... ¿qué?" No te preocupes. El estrógeno es una hormona que estimula el crecimiento de tus glándulas mamarias, y para protegerlas crea unos colchoncitos de grasa a su alrededor. También en tus bubis se construye una red de conductos para que, en un futuro, cuando seas mamá, la leche pueda salir por los pezones.

¿Qué tipo de bubis tienes?

Ya que les dices "Bienvenidas a mi vida", empiezas a voltear a ver todas las bubis que se te cruzan enfrente (este ejercicio también lo hacen los hombres, ¡pero durante toda la vida!): observas las grandes; las divorciadas, que son las que no se hablan porque cada una ve para un lado distinto; las amigas, porque están siempre pegaditas; las de brújula, porque una se dirige al norte y la otra al sur; las medianas; las soñadoras, porque ven siempre hacia el cielo como pidiendo un deseo; las deprimidas porque ven hacia el suelo; las copas, A, B, C, D y Copa Davis, en fin... descubres que hay de todo tipo.

¡Más chicas! ¡Más grandes! Aunque sea parejas, ¿no?

En el tamaño y forma de las bubis no hay reglas y es súper importante que sepas que todas son normales. Quizá sientas que las tienes más grandes, ya sabes, tipo naranjas o más chicas que tus amigas, tipo limones. No te obsesiones. La verdad es que no hay niña que esté totalmente contenta con ellas. Siempre quisiéramos que fueran más chicas o grandes, redondas o parejas. También es muy común que sean asimétricas; es decir, una más grande que la otra, o una ve para el frente y la otra para un lado. No es que estén bizcas, es normal. Con el tiempo se emparejan, así que tranquila, no te agobies.

Vas a notar también que su tamaño cambia de acuerdo con tu ciclo menstrual (más adelante platicaremos de esto). Cerca y durante tu periodo tienden a ser un poquito más llenitas y sensibles; o sea, como que se inflan, ¡pero no cantes victoria porque luego regresan a su tamaño normal!

Cada mujer es diferente, hay bubis que se desarrollan casi completamente en tres meses, y otras que tardan hasta 10 años para desarrollarse por completo. Ahora que si ves a tu tía de 55 años y no tiene nada de nada pero aún conserva la esperanza, habla con ella y dile: "Tía, siéntate, tenemos que hablar…"

Gigantescas calabazas

Diminutos chícharos

Enormes sandías

Perfectas manzanas

Exprimibles naranjas

Redondos melones

Güerita… ¿Cómo las tiene?

También vienen en todos los tamaños y colores. Son especialmente sensibles a los cambios de temperatura. Puedes notar que si hace frío se ponen más chiquitos y duros; igual sucede cuando te excitas sexualmente. Si se te marcan en la camiseta y lo único que pasa es que tienes frío, puedes ponerte un brassiere más grueso, unos parches especiales del color de tu piel que venden para eso, voltearte hacia otro lado o ya de plano ponerte una chamarra de esquimal. Ahí sí olvídate de que se te vean los pezones: con trabajo se te verá la cara.

Si no encuentras los parches ponte unas curitas... son como la versión pirata de los parches, pero funcionan.

En este aspecto, los hombres se portan casi todos como niños. Si él nota que te diste cuenta de sus miradas y te sentiste incómoda se va a sentir terrible y apenado, así que no dudes en hacérselo notar.

IZQUIERDA

DERECHA

Algunos pezones son invertidos, o sea, como que les da miedito, porque se ven como metidos hacia adentro. Es normal y saldrán con el desarrollo más o menos a los 18 años. Otras veces puedes notar un pezón más grande y duro que el otro; también es normal. Si notas algún cambio raro en ellos ve con el ginecólogo para que te revise. Si te salen vellitos alrededor puedes dejarlos tal cual, depilarlos con pinzas, cortarlos con unas tijeritas o hacerte depilación láser, sobre todo si no quieres parecerte a la prima del hombre lobo.

Para proteger tus bubis, mantenerlas en su lugar por mucho tiempo (o sea, que no se cuelguen como calcetines con canicas) y evitar que reboten con el movimiento como gelatina de tiendita, es muy cómodo y necesario usar algo que las sostenga. Y es aquí donde viene nuestra famosa...

Oración a San Corpiño de los tirantes

San Corpiño de los tirantes, dulce compañía, no me desampares ni con mi mamá ni con mi tía. Protégeme de los vendedores mirones y de los brassieres con varilla. Apártame de desear el pecho ajeno, y de usar corpiño con relleno. Cúbreme con tu manto milagroso, y que comprar mi brassiere no me dé oso.

Crónica de un brassiere anunciado

La primera vez que tu mamá te va a comprar un brassiere, corpiño o camisetita enseña-ombligo, obvio, te mueres de la pena. Primero porque a ellas les encanta introducirte al famoso mundo de la mujer. ¡Pero que no se claven!, no enfrente de todas sus amigas. La típica frase en la reunión es: "A Paulina ya le compré sus brassiercitos... ¡Aaayyy, están muy monos porque están chiquititos!" ¿Qué necesidad tienen tu tía Licha y tu tía Nena de saber que tus bubis se te están desarrollando? ¡Ah, no! Tu mamá es feliz divulgándolo.

Cuando llegas con ella a comprarlo típico que le pregunta en voz alta veinte veces a la que atiende: "¿Cuál le podrá quedar a mi hija?" ¡Por si alguien no se había enterado de que estás comprando tu primer brassiere! Para colmo, no falta que esté por ahí un niño que se te hace guapo... y te quieres morir. Por si fuera poco, tu mamá te acompaña al vestidor para ayudarte a abrocharlo. ¡No, por favor! Ya después tú verás si te consigues un segurito o si te lo amarras de plano con estambre del ocho, pero ese rollo nada más te da pena y te incomoda.

Ruégale a "San Corpiño de los Tirantes" que a tu mamá no se le ocurra acomodarte los tirantes del brassiere frente a sus amigas, porque eso sí es nefasto.

Por otro lado, también está la niña que se muere de ganas de usar brassiere porque todas sus amigas ya lo usan, y el día que se lo compran lo presume a todo mundo. Casi casi le toma una foto y se lo manda por correo electrónico a todas sus amigas, con el título de "la primera hamaca de mis bubis"

Cualquiera que sea tu caso, ubica que tu mamá sólo te quiere ayudar y no se da cuenta de que estos detalles dan pena o te hacen sentir mal. Dilo. Seguro te va a entender muy bien.

Me quiero cambiar de ropa, de escuela... ¡y de bubis!

Existen un buen de remedios para cambiar un poco tus bubis, como los brassieres con relleno, ponerte las hombreras de las blusas ochenteras de tu mamá, las famosas bolitas de kleenex, calcetines y hasta maquillarte en medio de las bubis tipo artista de televisión.

Lo más importante es que ninguna mujer necesita cambiar de pechos para ser mejor o peor. Unas bubis más grandes no pueden definir tu seguridad como persona ni tu forma de sentirte frente a la vida. Tú eres mucho, pero mucho más que un par de bubis.

Cuando alguien tiene bubis muy grandes pueden darse algunas broncas como: dolores de espalda, problemas crónicos del cuello, hombros lastimados por el peso que recae en los tirantes del brassiere y hasta tu novio las puede agarrar de almohadas. En fin, puede ser muy molesto. En estos casos se puede recurrir a una reducción de senos, que no deja de ser una cirugía pero te puede ayudar a sentirte mucho mejor.

Hoy en día es muy normal escuchar acerca de implantes y cirujanos; sin embargo, la decisión de operarte es algo súper serio y personal. Por más avances científicos que existan, ciertas mujeres tienen complicaciones muy

delicadas después de implantarse unas prótesis, y a otras les quedan muy bien, sin problema alguno.

Lo que sí es muy importante es que sepas que no te debes operar si no has cumplido 18 años y que, a pesar de que a algunas mujeres les dan seguridad personal, ningún par de prótesis te hace mejor o peor persona. Sin embargo, si ya lo platicaste en tu casa, si puedes y quieres sólo toma todas las medidas de seguridad posibles.

Los famosos genitales

Las hormonas me atacan

por unas caderas más redonditas

Urge cambio de cuerpo

mucho tráfico

Si de repente sientes que en tu cuerpo hay una revolución no te preocupes, es normal, simplemente se trata de un gigantesco ejército de hormonas que están haciendo marchas y plantones adentro de tí. Primero tus caderas empiezan a redondearse y la cintura se nota más. En tus genitales externos vas a notar el crecimiento de un vellito de color más oscuro que en el resto del cuerpo. Tus genitales internos también están cambiando mucho. Ahora que, si te quedaste dormida en las pláticas de la escuela y tus órganos sexuales te parecen más extraños que un 10 en matemáticas, échale un ojo a lo siguiente.

Es importante que te familiarices bien con lo que sucede allá abajo. Parte de tus genitales se localizan dentro de tu cuerpo y los que están por fuera no se ven mucho que digamos.

Los de afuerita

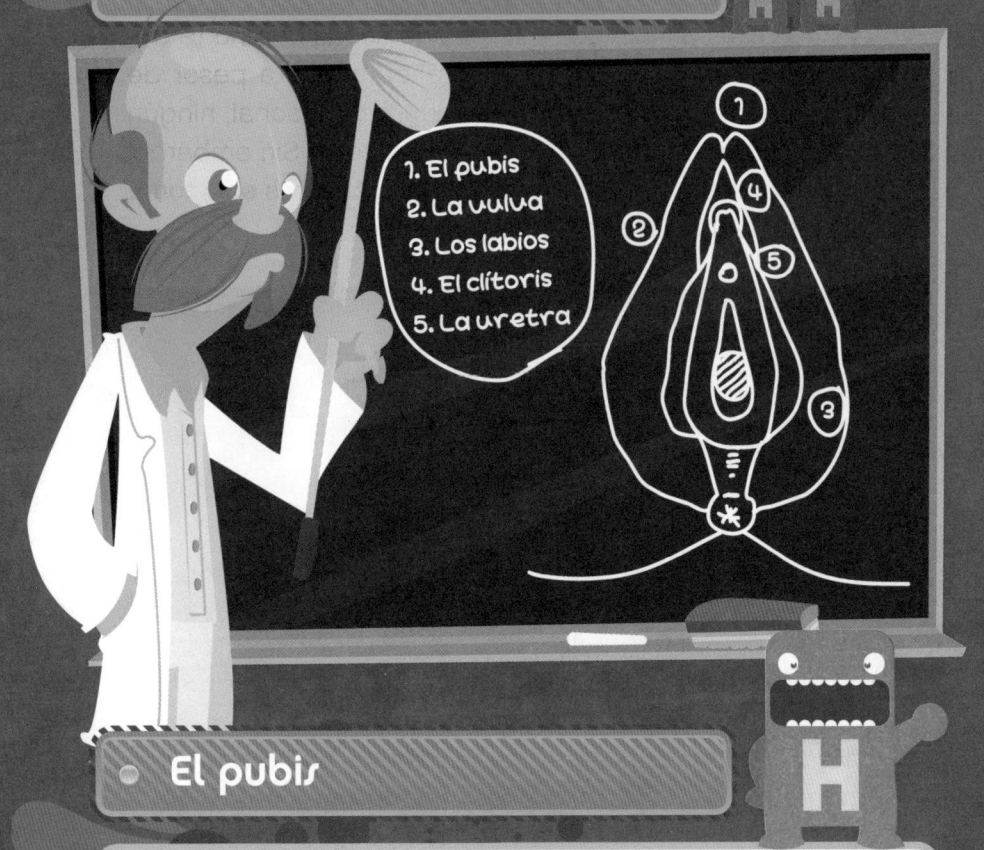

1. El pubis
2. La vulva
3. Los labios
4. El clítoris
5. La uretra

El pubis

Digamos que es el comienzo de la zona genital; es la parte que se eleva un poco sobre el hueso púbico y donde aparece el vello durante la pubertad.

La vulva

Incluye los labios exteriores y el clítoris. Es bueno que conozcas esta parte de tu cuerpo, pero como eso está cañón (a menos de que seas contorsionista de circo), la puedes conocer en persona si tomas un espejo y lo colocas entre tus piernas.

Los labios

Igual podrás ver que hay unos labios más grandes y externos que son los que protegen a los demás genitales, por eso se cubren de vello. Más adentro, están otros labios más chiquitos que sirven como puerta hacia la vagina; éstos no tienen vello, son mega sensibles y, por supuesto, por más puerta que parezcan... no tienen timbre.

El clítoris

En la parte superior vas a ver algo como un pequeño botón, formado por miles de terminaciones nerviosas súper sensibles que se estimulan cuando lo tocan. Durante la excitación sexual y el orgasmo, que es la culminación de la excitación, su tejido se hincha. Su única función es la de generar placer sexual, o sea que este órgano ¡pura diversión y nada de chamba! Una vez que pasa la excitación y el orgasmo el clítoris se relaja y regresa a su tamaño natural y a descansar.

La uretra

Es un tubito por donde viaja la orina (léase también "pipí, piz, del uno", etc.) desde la vejiga hacia el exterior; se localiza entre el clítoris y la vagina. No es un órgano sexual.

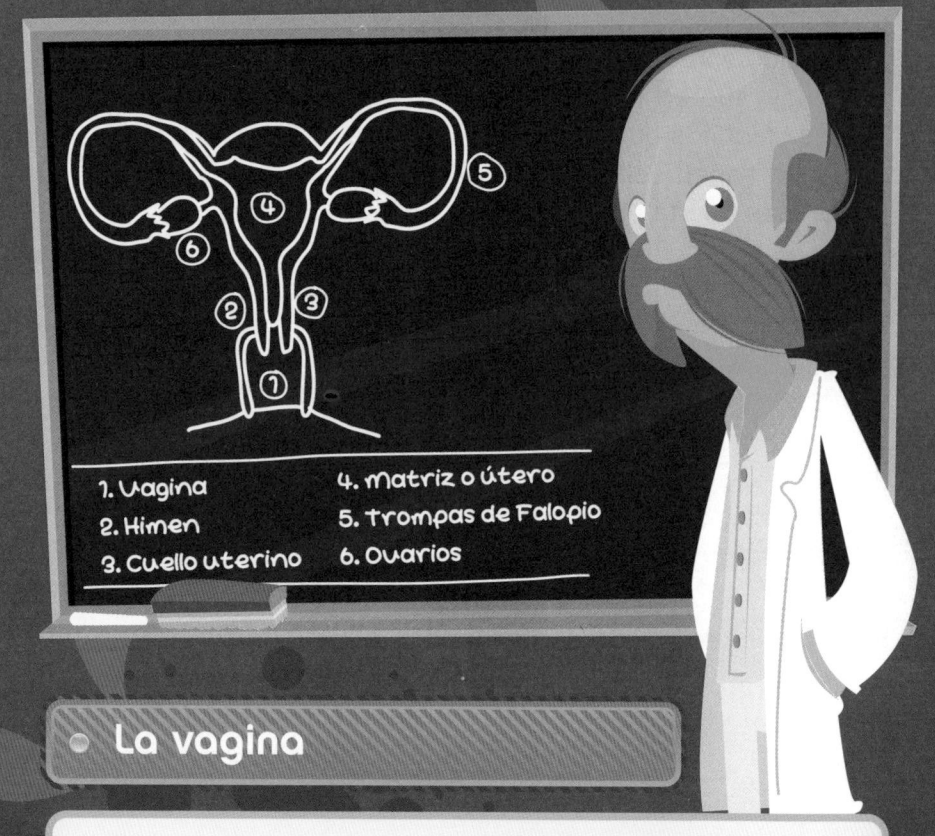

1. Vagina
2. Himen
3. Cuello uterino
4. Matriz o útero
5. Trompas de Falopio
6. Ovarios

◉ La vagina

Es el canal que comienza en el útero o matriz y termina en la vulva, tiene paredes súper elásticas y llenas de pliegues. Le da salida a la menstruación, recibe al pene y sirve como conducto para que el bebé nazca. Sus paredes casi nunca están secas y el grado de humedad varía de acuerdo con tu periodo de menstruación. Puedes ver que entre más cerca estás de que te baje, más seca está la vagina, y cuando se acerca la ovulación (aproximadamente de 10 a 15 días después de que te baje) es cuando más húmeda está.

Cuando se produce la excitación porque viste algo que te gustó en una revista o en la tele, el cerebro se pone las pilas y da órdenes a ciertas glándulas para que hagan un

liquidito que lubrique la vagina y se prepare para la penetración. La maravilla es que ésta tiene su propio sistema de
defensas para las infecciones; a esta defensa se le conoce
como flora vaginal y tiene gérmenes que mantienen ácidas
sus paredes.

Cada vez que te baja las células del útero y de la vagina
se destruyen o se cambian. Ésta es la mejor limpieza fisio-
lógica, así que por la limpieza de adentro no te preocupes;
por fuera sí date tus buenas bañaditas.

El himen

Es famosísimo por el rollo de la virginidad. En realidad es
una membrana híper delgada permeable (o sea, perfora-
da), que se encuentra a la entrada de la vagina y la cubre
en parte. A veces esta telita de tejido se puede desgarrar
o romper por hacer ejercicios bruscos y deja salir unas
gotitas de sangre en algunas mujeres, así como durante
las relaciones sexuales. Así que el rollo de que una mujer
virgen debe de tener el himen intacto, no es cierto. Además para un hombre es imposible sentir si la mujer tiene
himen o no.

El cuello uterino

Es como la puerta de entrada al canal que conduce a la
matriz. Cuando una mujer embarazada está a punto de dar
a luz, el cuello uterino se hace grande hasta que prácticamente desaparece para permitir el paso del bebé al nacer
(iouch!).

Matriz o útero

Normalmente es del tamaño de una pera volteada hacia abajo, excepto cuando te embarazas. Sus paredes son gruesas, musculosas y súper elásticas para guardar a uno o más bebés. Por dentro están como forradas de una mucosa llamada endometrio que fija e inicia la alimentación del bebé. Cuando no hay bebé en la matriz el recubrimiento se desprende con las capas vaginales cada mes, y esto es lo que provoca la famosa y nada sencillita menstruación.

Las trompas de falopio

Son un par de tubitos flexibles que salen de la parte superior del útero y se acercan muchísimo a cada uno de los ovarios. Cada mes se encargan de transportar el óvulo liberado hacia la matriz después de la ovulación. Si en el camino se unen el óvulo y el espermatozoide, las trompas se encargan de trasladar al huevo recién formado hasta la matriz para que se fije en el endometrio.

Los ovarios

Son del mismo tamaño y forma de las almendras. Si no sabes de qué tamaño son las almendras no te preocupes, son más o menos del tamaño de… de… un ovario. Bueno ya, en serio, éstos se encargan de guardar en unas pequeñas bolsas, llamadas folículos, todos los óvulos (alrededor de unos 300 mil) que a lo largo de los años liberarás cada mes, desde la pubertad hasta la menopausia.

La glándula pituitaria (se oye rarito, pero así se llama) produce hormonas que viajan por la sangre y le echan un grito a los folículos para que liberen un óvulo maduro.

Lo grueso es que en cada uno de los miles de óvulos se encuentra toda tu información genética o ADN: color de ojos, pelo, forma de tu cuerpo, etcétera. A este proceso se le llama ovulación, y es por eso que algunas mujeres, a la mitad de su ciclo, sienten una especie de cólico pequeño o dolor en la parte baja del abdomen. En estos días puedes estar fértil. Pero en especial estás de mírame y no me toques...

No manches con la mancha misteriosa

A veces, en tus "chones" te puedes encontrar con una especie de mucosa amarilla o blanca y no sabes bien por qué aparece. Bueno, pues es normal y se llama flujo.

Este flujo es un sistema de limpieza natural de tu vagina. Por lo general notas que aparece uno o dos días antes de tu periodo. Hay dos variaciones de flujo: normal y anormal.

NORMAL

ANORMAL

Es húmedo, transparente o medio blanco y no provoca comezón. Una vez que está en tus calzones y le da el aire se puede volver amarillento.

La cantidad de flujo puede variar de acuerdo con la fluctuación de hormonas. La excitación sexual también provoca que éste aumente.

Si el flujo se hace espeso, huele feo y tienes comezón en los genitales debes ir al ginecólogo porque es probable que tengas una infección y es súper importante atacarla de volada.

Espacio para tel. del Ginecólogo

Andrés... el que viene cada mes

O "Ya me bajó"

"Quiero felicitar a Margarita que abre sus pétalos para convertirse en una bella flor"

¡Ah, y si ven al mesero me lo mandan de volada!

¿Anda borracho?

Qué importa, de todas maneras habla bien bonito.

Hay muchas formas de decirle: la menstruación, el ciclo, la regla, Andrés Rojas, el periodo, etcétera. Tus tías generalmente te dicen: "Bienvenida al club".

Cuando te baja es uno de los cambios internos más importantes y más significativos en tu cuerpo. De entrada, es la señal que indica que pasas a otra etapa de tu vida en la que ya puedes embarazarte (nada más ¡aguas! no te adelantes). Es el cambio que algunas personas llaman cursimente "de niña a mujer"; es lo típico que dice un padrino borracho en unos xv años, pero es cierto.

Como decíamos anteriormente, cada mes, a causa de la producción de hormonas de una glándula llamada hipófisis, un óvulo tuyo crece, madura y se lanza a las trompas de Falopio (Falopio no es ningún elefante). Allí puede ser fecundado por un espermatozoide durante las siguientes 12 a 24 horas.

El rollo es que, al mismo tiempo que ocurre esto, en el útero, como ya vimos, se hace un revestimiento (el endometrio) para recibir al óvulo que ya fecundado se llama huevo. Es un tipo de cuna para que el huevo caiga "en blandito". Si el óvulo no fue fecundado este revestimiento, cuna o como le quieras llamar, se empieza a desprender y produce un sangrado que se llama... ita-tán!: ¡menstruación!, o sea, ¡ya te bajó! Sí, la temida y escalofriante regla (de hecho, debería existir una regla que prohibiera las reglas).

NUEVE

datos interesantes que toda mujer a la que le baja debe saber, o lo que es lo mismo: nueve puntos que a cualquier hombre le valen.

Los nueve básicos

1. La menstruación se regula en dos o tres años.

2. La duración de tu periodo puede ser diferente al de tus amigas; es normal. Éste puede ser de entre dos y ocho días (de cuatro a seis promedio); lo importante es que sea regular.

3. El ciclo normalmente dura entre 21 y 35 días (28 promedio), más o menos un mes.

4. Los ciclos pueden cambiar de acuerdo con el clima, la alimentación, el estrés (como cuando estás en época de exámenes), la edad, los viajes, el subir o bajar de peso, el que estés enamorada o bien embarazada (esto último no sólo hace que la cambies, sino que hasta pierdas la menstruación). En fin, mil cosas afectan.

5. Te va a bajar por unos 40 años, con excepción de los periodos de embarazo y lactancia. Es decir, unas 400 o 500 veces en tu vida: son un buen, ¿no? Así que tómalo con "filosofía", calma y aprende a "disfrutarlo" (bueno, sabemos que tampoco vas a llegar a una fiesta a interrumpir la música y a decir por el micrófono: "Perdón, perdón… un momentito por favor… ¡quiero decirles que estoy súper feliz porque… porque ¡me está bajando!… y quiero que todo mundo lo celebre. Hoy es mi noche. ¡Arránquese mariachi!") También puede ser que no te moleste mucho, además, se vale hacer berrinche, es completamente normal.

6. Tu primer sangrado puede ser café y no rojo, es normal.

7. A veces puedes notar que ya empieza o termina tu menstruación al dejar pequeñas manchas de color café en tu calzón. Si te empiezas a pelear con todo el mundo en tu casa, también puede ser un buen indicativo de que está llegando Andrés.

8. La mejor forma de saber a qué edad te puede bajar es preguntándole a tu mamá, hermanas o a tu abuelita cuándo les bajó a ellas, ya que mucho de esto es hereditario.

9. Si ya tienes 17 años y no te ha bajado, mejor ve con tu ginecólogo a ver qué pex.

¡Ouch! Me está bajando

AAyyy mi pancita

El rollo es que cuando te baja por primera vez te puedes sentir incómoda, porque finalmente lo que ves es una mancha de sangre. También porque aunque calculas las fechas en que te va a bajar es como examen sorpresa: nunca sabes exactamente cuándo va a llegar.

De entrada, queremos decirte que con la regla demuestras (la primera de muchas veces en la vida) que eres más valiente que los hombres, ¡imagínate a uno de tus amigos el primer día en que le baja!, entraría muy macho al salón, con paso firme y la mirada amenazadora, como escaneando la situación, y de repente: "Ay, ay... mi panza, ay güey, me duele... ay, mi panza, mi panzita... ...aaghhh. No se rían, les juro que nunca han sentido algo así. Aaaaay... ¡mami!, imamita!"

En muchas familias, la primera vez que le baja a la niña parece fiesta nacional. Si la tuya es una de esas, prepárate para que 15 minutos después de haberle dado la noticia a tu mamá ya lo sepa toda la casa y algunas de sus 35 amigas íntimas. Lo peor es que tu papá se acerque a felicitarte, con el típico: "¡Felicidades mi hijita, ya eres toda una señorita!", o que te regale flores: ¡No, por favor!, te va a caer de la fregada, vas a querer decir: "Papi... si en serio me quieres, te pido de la manera más atenta que... ¡Te calleeeeeeeesss, ...ah, por favor!"

La neta es que cuando tu papá te lo dice lo único que quiere es que sientas su apoyo y lo más probable es que él mismo no sepa ni cómo decírtelo, así que no te claves.

También es pésimo que el primer día que te baja sientes que todo mundo en la calle te ve y piensa: "Mira, a esa niña hoy le bajó". ¡Tranquila! Tómalo con calma. Nadie lo piensa, nadie lo nota.

Dime qué tipo de menstruación tienes y te diré quién eres

La regla tipo suegra:

Es la que amas cuando se va y odias cuando regresa.

La regla hermano:

Todo el día te está molestando.

La regla pizza:

Es la que te urge que llegue.

La regla Dormimundo:

Te tumba en la cama todo el día.

La regla cometa Halley:

Nunca sabes cuándo va a llegar.

La regla espinilla:

Es la que molesta desde antes de llegar.

La regla de fin de semana:

Ni se siente.

La regla chon de hilo dental:

Todo el día te recuerda que está ahí.

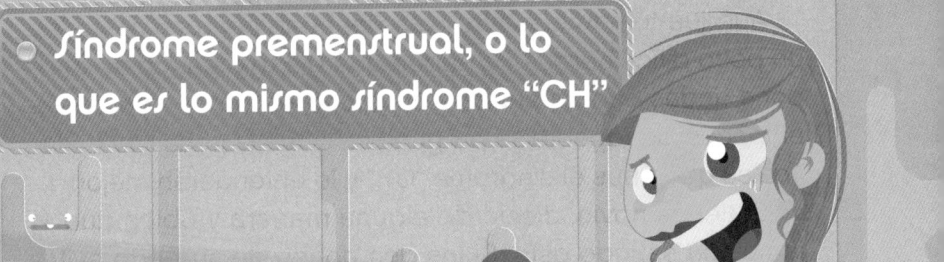

Síndrome premenstrual, o lo que es lo mismo síndrome "CH"

Cuando tu ciclo menstrual llega a la tercera semana el cuerpo se prepara hormonalmente para desprender el endometrio y desecharlo a través de la menstruación. Esto provoca que tengas una serie de cambios en tu cuerpo que pueden variar, desde dolor de cabeza, depresión y mal humor, hasta irritación, ganas de chillar por todo, granitos en la cara, cólicos, dolor de bubis, cansancio, pancita chelera, retención de agua, etcétera.

El coco de los síntomas premenstruales es el síndrome "CH" (léase "ché") por chípil, chillona y chocante. Este síndrome te hace caer en irritabilidad, depresión y mal humor. De hecho, en esos días a veces ni tú misma te aguantas; pero tranquila, porque si tú misma te odias o te chocas al rato tú misma, ¡te perdonas! Ahora, no te preocupes, puedes llorar porque tu perro no te movió la cola, porque no prende el foco del refrigerador o porque te acordaste de tu lonchera del kinder de Hello Kitty. ¡Tal cual! Tú no te preocupes.

Hay quien afirma que es precisamente en "esos días" cuando, por estar más sensible, desarrollas mejor tu creatividad, por lo que si sientes el síndrome "CH" aprovecha para escribir, pintar, oír música, meditar o ya de perdis hacerle una cartita a tu galán.

Aunque tus amigas y tu novio puedan comprenderte, es un poco difícil porque no saben qué día te toca (como tampoco andas con un anuncio en la cabeza de "ya me bajó"), entonces, de repente se preguntan: "¿Qué le pasa hoy?" Platícales que traes el síndrome "CH" y lo entenderán mejor.

Si tienes novio, díselo de alguna manera y ubica que él jamás ha sentido esto. Si los dos ponen de su parte evitarán muchos enojos y resentimientos.

El cólico

El cólico es un dolor en la parte baja del abdomen y algunas veces da la vuelta hasta la parte baja de la espalda. ¡Generalmente es perrísimo! Esto se debe a que los músculos del útero se contraen para eliminar el flujo menstrual. Duele, pero cada vez es más fácil de controlar. También puedes sentir cólico en el momento de la ovulación, entre 10 y 15 días después de que te bajó.

A algunas mujeres súper rayadas cada mes les pasa desapercibida esa etapa y no tienen ningún síntoma; para otras, el síntoma puede ser desde un dolor light antes y durante los dos primeros días en que les baja hasta ser insoportable y mandarlas knock-out a la cama.

Hola... mi nombre es CÓLICO

Y me apellido todo el día

39

¿Cómo aliviar el cólico?

Existen algunas pastillas buenísimas para aliviarlo. Algunas que te pueden servir son Sincol, Analgen o Advil, pero si está muy grueso el dolor puedes usar Buscapina. Siempre debes preguntarle a tu mamá o a tu doctor antes de tomar cualquier medicamento porque puedes ser alérgica. (Consulta a tu médico antes de tomar cualquier medicamento.)

Puedes descansar con una bolsa de agua caliente sobre el abdomen, o frotar las manos para calentarlas y ponerlas en el vientre. También hay parches que se pegan, los pones en el chonino y se conservan calientes por doce horas, inclusive ya hay un calzón llamado Termo Panti que tiene una compresa de gel que se calienta automáticamente cuando la activas, para que te aliviane cada vez que estés en tus días.

Checa

Estas cosas evitan los cólicos:

- No levantes cosas pesadas ni te quedes parada mucho tiempo.

- Bájale a las grasas, los condimentos y las carnes rojas.

- Haz ejercicio para mejorar tu circulación.

- Bájale a la sal, al azúcar, a la cafeína y al alcohol.

- Come más verduras y carbohidratos.

- No te claves en la cama, trata de seguir tu vida normal.

- Tómate dos gotas de "aguantitis"; o sea, "aguántate". Éste es el método más barato pero menos recomendado.

Con amarillo te puse lo más importante

Come frutas y verduras

En estos días también es normal sentir las bubis mucho más sensibles e hinchadas. Para evitar mayor dolor en este caso aléjate de cualquier amigo torpe que tengas, porque es la Ley de Murphy y en esos días se tropiezan con tus bubis cada dos segundos y creen que el dolor se quita con un chistosito "¡ay, perdón!"

Otro síntoma premenstrual puede ser un dolor de cabeza que te quieres morir, además del cansancio y a veces dolor de espalda. Con todos estos síntomas te puedes sentir fatal, pero no te preocupes; conforme más veces te baje aprenderás lo que puedes hacer para controlar el dolor y sentirte mejor.

Cuando te baja por primera vez debes ir al ginecólogo para que te revise. Anota en un calendario las fechas de cada menstruación, los días que dura y cuándo tuviste cólicos para que lleves un control. Estos datos son muy importantes para el ginecólogo (ojo con perder el calendario, porque es típico) ya que hay mujeres cuyo ciclo menstrual es de 24, 28 o 30 días, y otras son completamente irregulares.

Protección: toallas contra tampones

DUELO DE TITANES

ALITA SAGRADA VS PUFFY-PUFF

La mayoría de las niñas usan toallas protectoras; a otras les laten los tampones, mientras que algunas usan una combinación de los dos. En realidad, es cuestión de gustos y de lo que a ti te acomode.

¿Cuántos necesito?

Al principio vas a querer usar todo un paquete de toallas en un día. Con el tiempo vas a encontrar la medida aproximada de cuántas necesitas según tu flujo. Como dijimos, hay que cambiarlas cada tres o cuatro horas para que te sientas limpia, no huelas mal o manches la ropa. Aquí sí aplica la frase: "No manches".

Los tampones me dan terror

Los tampones son unos tubitos de algodón comprimido que se insertan dentro de la vagina para darte protección interna; además tienen un cordón para que los puedas sacar sin bronca. Por lo tanto, no les tengas miedo. Al imaginarte cómo se ponen te puede parecer una película de terror, pero la verdad no es tan tétrico como parece.

Capítulo 2
Quiúbole con...
mis RELACIONES
LAS TÉCNICAS CUPIDO
EL ROLLO DE LOS HOMBRES
EL TRUENE
EL FREE
mi novio FORMAL
mis GALANES
mis AMIGAS
EL LIGUE
mi CEREBRO y su CEREBRO

Los hombres

Lo que un hombre observa primero en una mujer...

O lo que es lo mismo, "ya te vi".

Cuando un hombre te acaba de conocer y quiere bajarte el cielo, la luna y las estrellas, dice frases como:

ÉL: Lo primero que vi fueron tus ojos.

TÚ: (piensas) ¿A 50 metros de distancia?

Decimos "piensas", porque a pesar de que sabes perfectamente que no es cierto, prefieres quedarte con la duda pues se siente más bonito.

Estás en Cancún, con bronceado de seis días y con un súper bikini, y el niño llega y te dice: "Hola, qué bonita nariz tienes." Ay, no manches, es tan malo el comentario que da lo mismo que te diga: "Qué bonito omóplato tienes."

ÉL: ¡Hola, qué guapa estás!

TÚ: Gracias.

ÉL: Oye, ¿cómo se llama tu amiga?

(O sea, adiós, perro del mal, aquí si aléjate y cuéntaselo a quien más confianza le tengas.)

El asunto es que para que un hombre se acerque a decir frases como éstas (no te asustes, son de las menos afortunadas), necesita haberte echado una miradita antes en la escuela o en algún centro comercial.

En la Universidad de Georgetown, Washington, se hizo un estudio sobre esto, basado en la pregunta: "¿Qué es lo que vemos de los demás en un abrir y cerrar de ojos?" y éstos fueron los resultados:

45

¿LE VISTE LAS POMPIS?

TIENE BOCA DE BESO

ESA FALDITA ¡GUAU!

UYYYY VISITE SU PANZITA

¡WOOOW! QUE OJAZOS

26%

¿CÓMO VISTE?

YO LE VI LAS BUBIS

31%

CARA

43%

CUERPO

LO QUE UN HOMBRE VE PRIMERO EN UNA MUJER

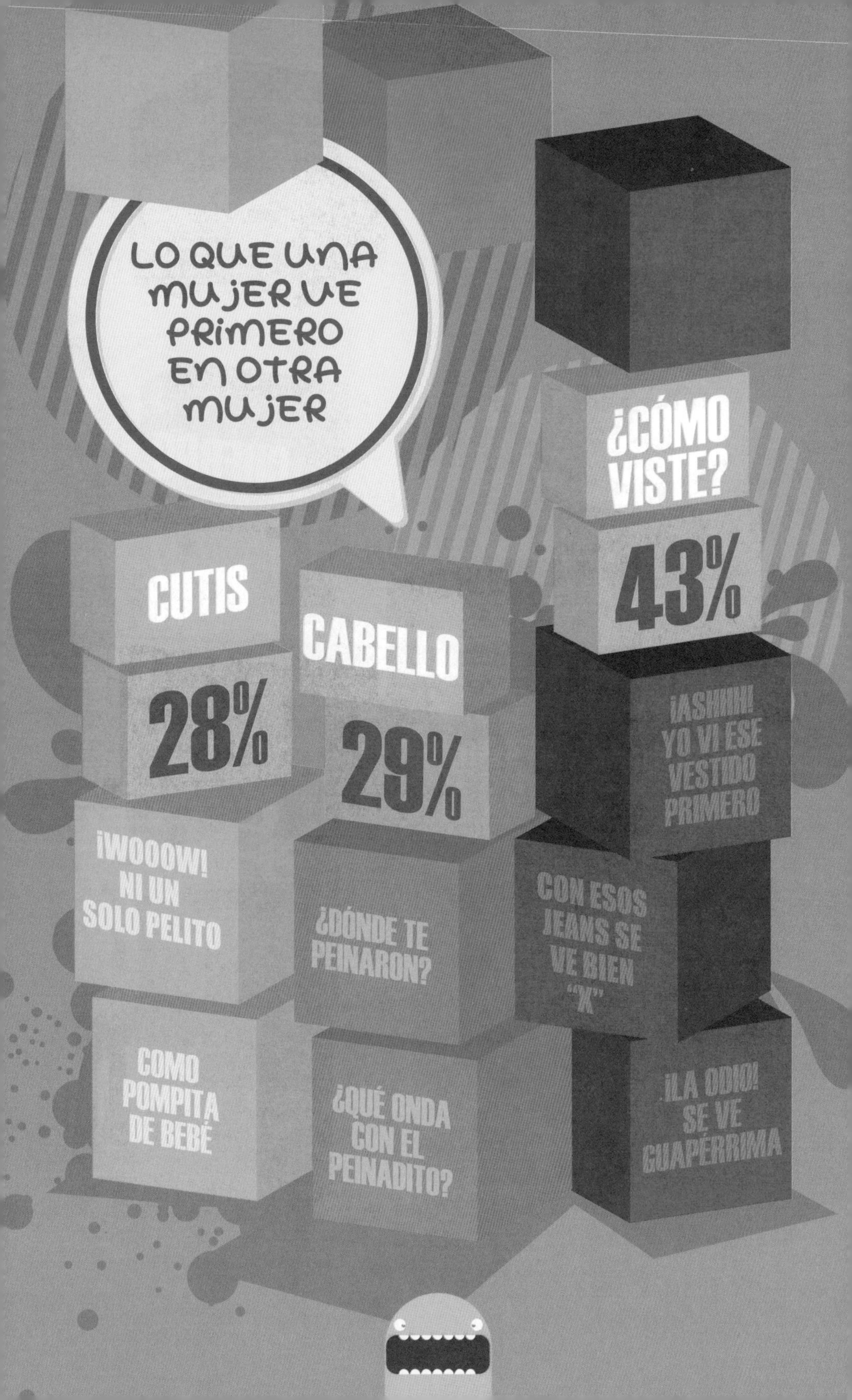

¡LA ODIO! SE VE GUAPÉRRIMA

¿QUÉ ONDA CON EL PEINADITO?

COMO POMPITA DE BEBÉ

CON ESOS JEANS SE VE BIEN "X".

¿DÓNDE TE PEINARON?

¡WOOOW! NI UN SOLO PELITO

¡ASHHH! YO VI ESE VESTIDO PRIMERO

29% CABELLO

28% CUTIS

43% ¿CÓMO VISTE?

LO QUE UNA MUJER VE PRIMERO EN OTRA MUJER

NO ME LATE
QUE SE VEA
COMO
CRUZÁZNAISER

YA QUE
SE CAMBIE
ESOS
JEANS

ME ENCANTA
EL AZUL
PROFUNDO

TIENE
CARITA DE
NIÑO

GORDITO
SIMPÁTICO

LA CORBATA
LO HACÍA
VERSE
¡WOW!

ESOS OJITOS
HIPNOTIZAN

CUANDO LO
VI ME
DESLUMBRÓ

ME
ENCANTA
MUGROSITO

24%

25%

21%

CUERPO

30%

SOLO
OJOS

CARA
SONRISA

¿CÓMO
VISTE?

LO QUE UNA
MUJER VE
PRIMERO
EN UN
HOMBRE

¿Qué es el ligue?

El ligue es un cambio de señales juguetón e interminable que una pareja comparte; o lo que es lo mismo, es cuando a dos personas se les salen las hormonas casi casi por las orejas.

El ligue es súper divertido; de hecho, deberían convertirlo en deporte nacional; ¡ah! sí, los latinos ganaríamos muchas medallas!

El asunto es que a veces lanzas una señal y te la rechazan. Después vuelves a mandar otra con más fuerza, esperando que esta vez San Antonio y el Santo Niño de Atocha te hagan el milagrito. Pero si ese milagrito hace un rato que no se te cumple, no te mal viajes y checa las cinco etapas del ligue. Pon un buen de atención en este capítulo porque con inteligencia, si te aplicas, te puedes volver una experta y ligarás hasta con los puros ojos, sin que los hombres se den cuenta.

Como puedes ver, los hombres se fijan primero en el cuerpo y las mujeres en lo que traes puesto.

La forma en que te vistes habla todo el tiempo de quién eres, habla de tu forma de ser, de tu ánimo, de tus gustos, y a veces hasta de si le echan cloro o no a tu ropa cuando la lavan.

Si en alguno de estos puntos no te sientes a gusto, no te preocupes, porque precisamente en este libro te vamos a ayudar a que los mejores. Recuerda: "Nunca tenemos una segunda oportunidad para causar una buena primera impresión".

Fases del ligue

Estas fases son súper importantes ya que con ellas puedes darte cuenta de cómo avanza tu proceso de ligue. Incluso, puedes ver cómo algunas de tus amigas que parecen mosquitas muertas se convierten rápidamente en arañas ligadoras.

Ahora que, si mandas y recibes millones de señales, y cuando el chavo se pone frente a ti y te dice con voz profunda: "Hola, ¿cómo te llamas?", tú te apanicas y te sales casi casi por la puerta de emergencia, no te preocupes, no es miedo… es ¡pavor! Pero entre más sepas del ligue más rápido lo dominarás.

Fase 1. Captar la atención

Primero, los hombres y las mujeres marcan su territorio, como perritos frente a un árbol; ya sea en una fiesta o en un antro, pueden marcar su territorio mediante una mesa, una silla o una esquinita de la pared para recargarse (por alguna razón que la ciencia aún no ha podido explicar, a los hombres les encanta hacer ésto). Una vez con el territorio marcado, fíjate muy bien cómo, si están en el ligue, empiezan a hacer este tipo de cosas...

Se estiran, se paran derechos con los hombros para atrás, meten la panza, se ríen a todo volumen, exageran los movimientos del cuerpo.

LOS HOMBRES

Enfatizan más el movimiento de la cadera, se empiezan a hacer churritos en el pelo con sus dedos, se ponen rojas, levantan la ceja y sonríen.

LAS MUJERES

Fase 2. Reconocimiento

El contacto visual es básico pues define el futuro del ligue: La persona observada puede responder de tres maneras:

- Sonreír o hacer evidente que cruzan miradas (casi todas las mujeres usan la técnica "cachorrito", o sea, sonríen sin abrir la boca y mueven la cabeza hacia un hombro, tiernamente). En este caso, si el galán está muy cerca,

dirá para sí el típico "¡mi vidaaa!" y después tratará de platicar contigo. Si está lejos, girará su cuerpo hacia donde tú estás para acortar corporalmente la distancia y el juego de miradas podrá seguir un rato, hasta el momento de platicar (si él giró el cuerpo, significa que ¡el ligue va bien!). Existen algunos miedosos que después de verte toda la noche se van como si no hubiera pasado nada. En estos casos, no te preocupes, lo que pasa es que ese chavo es muy inseguro o tímido, así que él se lo pierde y tú te lo ahorras.

- Desviar la mirada: En este punto, si te intimida la mirada del tipo, automáticamente harás lo que se llama "gesto de desplazo", lo que significa que estás en el juego pero quieres desviar su mirada a otra cosa; entonces, puedes peinarte, jugar con tu bolsa, mandar un mensajito en tu celular (aunque ya no tenga pila), sacar tu cartera para dizque buscar algo, ajustarte la blusa, tocarte la oreja o lo que sea, en este caso lo que tu cuerpo dice es: "Sí me gustas, pero como no puedo aguantarte la mirada, hago algo para que no me dejes de ver." Ahora que, si no te gusta el monito, le das la espalda y bye, bye. Esto se conoce como el "gesto de ya me fui..."

- Planea tu estrategia. Cuando tienes claro que a la que está viendo es a ti (y no a la modelo de junto), entonces debes pensar qué vas a hacer para que él se acerque; o sea, busca la forma de tener un encuentro casual. (Para más detalles, consulta el plan B en la página xx).

Fase 3. Hablar

Generalmente, la plática empieza con frases poco significativas o halagos: "Se pone bien aquí, ¿no?", "¿No conoces a...?" (esa frase es la más típica y tonta de los hombres, sin embargo funciona), "¡Qué bonitos ojos tienes!" (a veces están tan embobados que te lo dicen aunque traigas

puestos lentes obscuros), "¿Con quién vienes?", "¿Tienes un cigarro?", en fin.

El hecho es que te dicen algo que necesita una respuesta para abrir el canal de comunicación. Esta plática se diferencia porque hacen la voz más suave, en tono más alto y como cantadita. Es muy importante el tono con el que se dicen las cosas. Un ejemplo básico es la típica amiga que habla con una chava por celular y al ver que tiene una llamada en espera de su galán, le dice a su amiga: "No güey... cómo crees güey, a ese lugar va pura wila de cuarta," e inmediatamente le contesta al galán, y cambia el tono de voz : "Hola bebeeeeee, ¿cuánto me quieres cachorritoooo?"

Aunque te parezca increíble, tu voz revela tu intención, tus emociones, tus antecedentes, tu educación, y si te tomas unas cubas extra, hasta tu estado etílico.

Gaaaallo advertencia

La voz puede atraer o repeler de inmediato al sujeto ligable. ¡Cuida que no se te salga un gallo!

Fase 4. Tocar

Después de esto, llega un momento súper interesante: el contacto físico. Comienza con lo que se llama "claves de intención". Como que no quiere la cosa nos inclinamos hacia la persona con la que estamos ligando. Pon atención y fíjate cómo acercamos el pie o el brazo al pie o al brazo de la otra persona.

Por insignificante que este contacto sea, lo sientes hasta... el intestino delgado. Es como si la piel de los dos tuviera sensores láser, y en ese momento grabas cada contacto en el disco duro de tu cerebro. Lo que es muy típico, es

que cuando te sientes con un poco más de confianza, hasta le dices: "¡Ay, qué chistoso!", y le pegas en el brazo, y ya un poquito más aventurera le tocas varias veces la rodilla como recargándote. Por otro lado, a los hombres les cuesta mucho trabajo tocar (aunque su cuerpo se los suplicaimplora), lo típico que hacen es tomarte de los hombros y como que te dirigen hacia donde vas. No importa si la puerta del lugar esté en frente de ustedes, su cuerpo, con tal de tener contacto físico con el tuyo, te dirige como perro lazarillo (bueno unos no tienen nada de lazarillos y sí mucho de perros). En fin, aunque estos contactos son casi imperceptibles a la vista por su rapidez, son súper importantes porque el otro, aunque se haga el que no se da cuenta, ¡claro que lo nota!

Como te decíamos, si la otra persona corresponde con una sonrisa, se inclina hacia delante, te empieza a tocar (de forma casual) más de lo normal, o te toma de los hombros, ¡estás lista para la quinta etapa del ligue! Pero si él, para corresponder, se avienta sobre ti ¡aguas! porque está muy prendido o te estás ligando un experto en lucha libre.

Si, por el contrario, de plano no hay respuesta de su lado, no te preocupes, a veces algunos chavos son muy poco aventados, o está en otro canal y no quiere ligar.

Fase 5. Sincronía del cuerpo

O lo que es lo mismo "me gusta copiar ¿y qué?"

Esta fase es chistosísima porque conforme los dos se sienten con más confianza, empiezan a hacer los mismos movimientos. Primero, se alinean de manera que los hombros de los dos quedan frente a frente. Si no, checa y verás.

Este movimiento puede darse antes o durante la plática. Después, si él toma un vaso, tú lo haces al mismo tiempo, si uno cruza la pierna, el otro hace lo mismo, si uno se mueve a un lado, el otro se mueve de la misma forma. Haz de cuenta que están bailando una coreografía, ¡y todavía no ponen ni la música!

Aunque el verdadero amor es mucho más complejo y profundo, este rollo del ligue es el paso inicial, y si no se maneja de manera inteligente, puedes perder a tu próximo novio en sólo... cinco etapas.

Enfermedad "Nomepelan aguda"

También conocida como síndrome de no ligo nada.

> SÍNTOMAS <

UNO

Crees que cada vez que sales con alguien la riegas en algo.

DOS

Consideras que el novio de tu amiga está mal proporcionado (o sea, te lo deberían de propocionar a tí).

TRES

Has llegado a pensar que eres una súper heroína, nada más que te tocó ser "la mujer invisible".

CUATRO

Lejos de sentirte bonita, te sientes fea.

CINCO

¡Tienes mucho éxito! Pero con los chavos más feos que conoces.

SEIS

Entre más te maquillas y peinas, sientes que pareces más a un payasito dominguero.

Si no tienes suerte en tus primeros intentos de ligar...

No te preocupes, sólo tienes "nomepelan aguda" y nosotros te vamos a recetar la medicina adecuada.

El rollo de sentir que no te pelan es muy común, y aunque crees que estás sola en ese mar de lágrimas, no te preocupes; hay muchísimas niñas que tienen el mismo problema pero no te das cuenta, porque tampoco se la pasan gritando: "!Tengo 'nomepelan aguda'! ¡Me recetaron 2 cucharadas de besos de Ben Affleck, un apapacho y medio de Tom Cruise y 5 gotitas cada 12 horas de Brad Pitt! ¡Una ambulancia por favor!"

Cuando tienes un buen rato sin que ningún chavo se interesa por ti, quisieras que en las tiendas donde rentan smokings también rentaran novios, y te encantaría llevarte uno solamente para sentirte mejor y demostrarte que no estás tan mal, o ya de perdis para que tus amigas te vean.

Ojo, cuando pasas por esto puedes sentirte como una tonta si llegas a hablar con un chavo, o empiezas a cooperar más en el rollo sexual con tal de que te haga caso. Incluso, algunas veces hasta analizas palabra por palabra la última conversación (que sólo duró un minuto y medio) para ver en qué la regaste o qué dijiste mal.

En fin, todo esto te lleva a sentirte triste y confundida, te preguntas qué es lo que los chavos no encuentran en ti, y cuando piensas así sientes un hoyo horrible en el estómago; de hecho, cuando ves al chavo platicando con otra, puedes llegar a sentir odio. En fin, es una mezcla de coraje, tristeza, desesperación y vacío. ¿Ya sabes?

Ninguna persona vale únicamente por su apariencia física. Es verdad que existen chavas que parece que físicamente les tocó todo y no tienen este problema. Eso es real, pero recuerda que aunque ellas no tienen ese problema, tienen otros.

Lo importante es que estar gordita, no ser tan guapa, tener muchos granitos o tener una nariz muy grande, no es la razón por la que los hombres no se acercan.

Lo que realmente hace que un chavo no se acerque es la falta de seguridad de una persona, la falta de amor por uno mismo; en otras palabras, la poca confianza que tengas en ti.

Los hombres se dan cuenta de eso inconscientemente y no se acercan. Seguro has escuchado el típico caso de alguien que no tenía novio o novia y nadie se le acercaba, pero cuando empezó a andar con alguien le llovieron pretendientes. Bueno, esto es completamente real y sucede precisamente porque cuando alguien tiene novio/a se siente más seguro pues ya no tiene que buscar a nadie, y los demás notan esa seguridad y se acercan a ligar.

Lo que debes hacer cuando te sientas así, es simplemente buscar esa seguridad en ti. La gente vale por lo que es como persona, no por cómo se ve. Por eso, muchas veces encuentras a niñas cero guapas que andan con unos súper galanes: esto es porque ellas saben quiénes son, las virtudes que tienen y lo que valen.

Hicimos una encuesta donde preguntamos a muchos hombres que es lo que más los conquistaba de una chava, y las respuestas fueron:

UNO	DOS	TRES
Que sea segura.	Que no quiera ser como todas las demás.	Que no sea fácil, pero tampoco imposible.

Así que es momento de que te relajes, te valores y no te preocupes: esa persona que esperas va a llegar. Y aquí te vamos a dar el mejor consejo para encontrar galán: el secreto es que tengas amigos sin ningún interés romántico, que salgas con ellos, te hagas su amiga y, especialmente, que te diviertas mucho en tu vida. Una vez que dejes de preocuparte todo el tiempo por tener novio y empieces a disfrutar la vida, te darás cuenta de cuántos hombres darían todo por estar con una mujer de tu nivel.

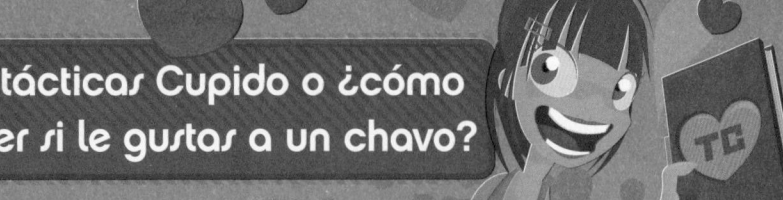

Las tácticas Cupido o ¿cómo saber si le gustas a un chavo?

Algunas señales son muy obvias, a veces te topas con el niño al que casi casi se le escurre la baba cuando te ve en la escuela; la verdad es muy fácil identificarlo porque maneja la "Hansel y Gretel líquida" o sea que deja un caminito de baba por donde pasas. Se convierte en tu amigo secreto y te deja chocolates de la tiendita o flores. Pero hablemos de los que no son tan obvios (de hecho casi todos). Los hombres son muy predecibles en este aspecto y es fácil detectar cuando quieren aplicar sus "*tc*" (Tácticas Cupido).

Después de platicar con muchos chavos, te damos información sobre sus "*tc*" más comunes.

"tc en la escuela"

molón – Fregón

En la escuela, es típico que cuando le gustas a alguien automáticamente te empieza a molestar. Te jala el pelo con pequeños tirones por atrás y luego se hace el tonto como para que no te des cuenta de que fue él, pero por supuesto, le interesa que lo sepas porque ese jaloncito significa: "Aquí estoy, ¡mírame!"

También te mete el pie como muy maldoso, te empuja, te arremeda (esto es, si el niño no está en la universidad, porque si hace esto y está en la maestría, entonces sí ni cómo ayudarlo). En fin, hará todo lo posible por molestarte y que tú creas que realmente lo hace por patán: en realidad se muere por ti sólo que no tiene el valor de decírtelo.

Guarura

Cuando el tipo no va en tu salón, te sigue durante todo el recreo, así como que no quiere la cosa, pero el monito casualmente siempre está donde tú estás: en la tiendita, afuera de los baños, en la sección del patio donde te gusta estar; en fin, te sigue como guarura (algunos vienen armados con una rosa adentro de su chamarra de deportes). Todo eso lo hace porque le encanta verte y a veces, aunque no lo creas, cuenta los minutos para salir al recreo y encontrarte. Ahora que si cuando pasa cerca sus amigos lo empujan hacia a ti, pues está más que obvio.

Cooperador

Otro truco es que te llama por teléfono como para checar cosas de la tarea. Los trabajos de equipo son su mejor oportunidad; después de que la maestra dice la frase mágica, "hagan sus equipos", el monito voltea para todos lados rogándole a Dios que nadie te escoja. Se hace tonto y actúa desinteresado, como si no le quedara de otra y te pregunta: "Pues, ¿tú y yo, no?"

"TC en las fiestas"

A veces el niño se quiere acercar a ti en una fiesta, si tú y él son un poco más grandes, pues él se acerca para hacerte plática y punto; pero si están más chavos es muy cómico, porque él planea todo nervioso durante un buen rato en qué momento se va a acercar a ti.

Indeciso

Cuando te quedas sola cinco segundos, dice: "Ahorita, ahorita...", y al momento en que se decide y camina hacia ti, llega otra amiga y ya valió todo. Otra vez a esperar. El caso es que así se la pasa toda la fiesta y al final, jamás se te acercó. ¡Ah!, pero ahí no acaba el asunto. El chavo pide tu teléfono con alguien y te llama un mes después... ¡Sí! Un mes después, y aunque por teléfono se hace el muy cool, en realidad está sudando del otro lado mientras dice: "Hola, ¿te acuerdas de mí? Estaba vestido de amarillo pollo". ¡Imagínate!, si con trabajos te acuerdas de cómo ibas vestida tú.

Distraído

A veces se acerca a todo un grupo de niñas y hace preguntas abiertas: "¿Cómo se llaman?, ¿cuántos años tienen?, ¿no les late ir a 'x' lugar?" En realidad lo único que le interesa es saber tus datos; de esto te puedes dar cuenta muy fácilmente porque al ratito sólo a ti te llama por tu nombre. Es el único dato que espera su cerebro.

Autodirigible

También existe el autodirigible, es el que empieza a bailar en un extremo del reventón como muy en su rollo y termina "casualmente" bailando a tu lado y luego empieza a bailar contigo, así como: "¡Ay!, qué chistoso, el aire me empujo hasta aquí."

Así que si identificas una "*tc*" y el niño te gusta, analízalo y dale una ayudadita, porque luego los hombres son tan miedosos que son capaces de estar así todo el ciclo escolar y después, cuando los encuentres seis años después con tu novio "peor es nada", ellos te van a decir: "No me lo vas a creer, pero tú siempre me gustaste."

Secretos para que los hombres se claven

¿Por qué algunas mujeres tienen cinco tipos muriendo por ellas, mientras que otras creen que no hay niños disponibles sobre la tierra? O, ¿por qué a algunas las tratan como reinas y a otras los chavos se la pasan bateándolas? ¿Por qué, con el tiempo, un hombre pierde interés por una mujer?

Hay niñas que, sin ser la última chela del estadio, tienen una manera de comportarse con los hombres que las vuelve irresistibles. A veces te dan ganas de preguntarles: "¿Cuál les aplicas? ¿Qué les haces?" Pues aquí te vamos a dar algunos secretos.

Empecemos porque, aunque los hombres no siempre lo reconozcan, a ellos les encanta el reto, la conquista y lo difícil de alcanzar. Es por eso que les gustan los deportes, lo extremo y todo este tipo de cosas donde se proyectan.

Cuando una niña es bien rogona, le habla a cada rato al niño con pretextos que nadie le cree, siempre le inventa salidas o dice que "sí" a cualquier insinuación de tipo sexual, ¡eso es pésimo!; además de que te delatas, estás destruyendo el instinto natural de conquista que el sexo masculino tiene, y les das súuuper flojera.

Al contrario, si juegas el papel de la "inalcanzable", la difícil de obtener, de volada despiertas en ellos el deseo de logro y conquista. Al mismo tiempo logras que el niño te valore y se sienta muy suertudo contigo. Esto puede sonarte anticuado y parece no ir de acuerdo con la moda. Créenos, los consejos que te vamos a dar suenan como de la abuelita de tu abuelita, ¡pero funcionan! Si no nos crees, manéjalos para que te convenzas.

1.- Siéntete "Laaa niña"

Ubícate como la mujer que a todos los hombres les latería tener a su lado. Lejos de ser un asunto relacionado con el físico, como te habíamos dicho, es una actitud, un estado de ánimo, siéntete orgullosa de ti misma, siéntete súper iguauu! O sea, piensa, actúa y camina como si fueras top model.

2.- Ponlo a chambear

Salir con alguien es como bailar las tranquilitas, deja que él tome la iniciativa. No seas la primera en empezar a platicar o invitarle un chupe. Tampoco te quedes viendo al tipo como si estuvieras planeando la luna de miel y los nombres de sus hijos. Evita hablar hasta por los codos, contarle cosas muy íntimas o entrar en conversaciones densas y filosóficas en las primeras citas (es de flojera). Hay que ser inteligentes, interesantes y misteriosas. No le digas cosas como: "Con nadie me la paso tan chido como contigo," o "de tanto que les he platicado a mis amigas y a mis papás de ti, ise mueren por conocerte!" Vete leve.

3.- Juega a "la difícil"

Si te habla el jueves para invitarte a salir un viernes, contéstale buena onda, pero segura y dile: "Qué mala onda pero tengo plan." Aunque te quedes súper loser en pijama viendo en la tele un programa que es la repetición de la repetición. Él tiene que captar la idea de que tú eres una mujer con tantos planes y actividades que eres como salón de fiestas para graduación, o sea, que te debe apartar con anticipación. Si la invitación es el viernes en la tarde es obvio que ya alguien más le dijo que no. Y ser plato de segunda mesa... ipara nada!

4.- Di bye, antes que él

Aunque te encante platicar horas y comentar con pelos y señales todo lo que te pasó, no te quedes más de 10 minutos en el teléfono. Si es necesario cómprate un cronómetro, ¡pero ubícalo! Le puedes decir: "Oye, te tengo que dejar...", o bien, "Oye, perdón, tengo mil cosas que hacer," eso lo deja con ganas de platicar más y seguro se preguntará: "¿Estará saliendo con alguien? ¿Por qué me habrá colgado tan rápido? ¿La habré aburrido?"

5.- Sé la más linda

Sé buena onda y ríete de sus chistes, pero sin exagerar (no te veas muy emocionada). No te sientas con la obligación de llenar los silencios en la conversación. En general, deja que él haga toda la chamba como abrir la puerta del coche, retirarte la silla, etcétera. Es básico decir "por favor" y "gracias" a todos estos detalles, así como nunca, pero nunca, criticar el lugar, la comida o el servicio aunque estén nefastos. Trata de ver lo positivo en todo.

6.- Contrólale las salidas

Los hombres se enamoran más rápido que las mujeres. Igual, se desenamoran más rápido también. Por eso es importante que dosifiques las veces que se vean aunque el instinto y las ganas de verlo te estén matando. En el beso de la despedida, cuando el niño pregunte: "¿Qué vas hacer mañana?" muérdete la lengua y contesta: "Voy a andar como loca." Si no resistes la tentación y a todo le dices que "sí", notarás como poco a poco su interés se aleja.

7.- Es muy importante

Es muy importante que te des tu lugar y de repente no lo peles, porque la neta eso les encanta a los hombres y se

pican gruesísimo. Si por otro lado no te das tu lugar y estás como loquita atrás de ellos todo el tiempo, los vas a aburrir y se van a sentir tan seguros que no te van a tomar en serio, lo único que vas a conseguir es que se aprovechen de ti sacándote un free, se lo platiquen a todos sus cuates y luego no regresen.

¿Qué hacer cuando no ligas ni un resfriado?

Si ya aplicaste todo lo anterior y el susodicho no te pela, o de plano tienes muy poquito tiempo para ligártelo y él ni se inmuta, o simplemente sientes que no te ve y presentas el síndrome de "cuerpitis ausentis", no te preocupes, esto le pasa a 11 de cada 10 mujeres encuestadas.

> No puedes hacer mucho porque el cuate puede considerarte una wila.

> Y no puedes hacer poco porque tus amigas te lo pueden bajar.

Plan "B"

- Ríete mucho, debes verte como la niña más buena onda sobre la Tierra (nada más no te pases, no te vaya a salir contraproducente).
- Si estás en el bar o en un antro, puedes empezar a bailar y a cantar la rola que tocan en ese momento mientras volteas a ver al niño que te gusta y discretamente, con

ritmo, como que lo señalas con el dedo así de: "¡Tú!, sí, tú". Nada más no lo hagas si la canción es un narcocorrido.

- Puedes usar la típica de que te acercas a la barra donde esta él, y como que no quiere la cosa, con tono de "ay, que casualidad", ¿ya sabes?, le pides la hora o un encendedor.
- Levanta un poco la voz (sólo un poco, no te vayas a convertir en vendedora de La Merced).
- Arréglate lo necesario para que te veas bien y llámale la atención (no exageres con los mega escotes, las minifaldas y el maquillaje panquecito, que es cuando son kilos de maquillaje, que le puedes meter un dedo y se queda el hoyito) porque pueden hacer que en vez de verte como una niña atractiva te vean como wila cero atractiva).
- Dale unas dos vueltas al antro para que te vean y tú a ellos. Ahí vas a notar quién te ve y a quién le gustaste. Generalmente, el o los niños tratarán de tropezarse o chocar contigo y decirte "perdón..." La próxima vez que sus miradas se encuentren, sonríe y ahí ya empezó el ligue. No des más de dos o tres vueltas en el antro porque va a parecer que estás de promoción (si en tu vuelta de reconocimiento nadie te voltea a ver, no te preocupes; el ligue llega cuando menos te lo imaginas).
- Busca sentarte junto a él como de casualidad, pero no llegues al grado de balconearte feo.
- Utiliza el arma secreta de todas las mujeres: la mirada. Voltea para verlo, no lo veas, vuelve otra vez a verlo, no lo peles, y si no entiende esa señal es que es un bruto.
- Si ya se dio lo de las miraditas, puedes ir al baño del lugar sola o con una amiga. Si le interesas, seguramente él se va a parar y tratará de encontrarte en el camino para platicar.

AGENCIA DE INVESTIGACIÓN
QUIÉBOLE CON LOS CLAVADOS

● Advertencia: no vayas con más de una amiga. Los hombres generalmente son muy inseguros y muchas veces les preocupa si llevas a más amigas porque piensan que los puedes batear y quedarán en ridículo frente a más personas.

● Si te empieza a ligar el más feo de su bolita, tú déjate, piensa que ese chavo puede ser el pasaporte hacia el que te gusta. Recuerda que el fin justifica los medios... aunque ese medio esté muy piñata.

● A los hombres les late saber que le gustan a alguien, pero que no sea muy obvio. Por ejemplo, el chavo nunca se ha fijado en "x" niña, pero en el momento en que alguien le dice que a esa chava le gusta, empieza a pensar en la posibilidad, y empiezan las frases como: "No está nada mal", "hasta eso, me cae bastante bien", "ella también me gusta un poco" o "siempre me ha gustado, pero perdí las esperanzas hace como un año".

Ahora recuerda que también existe la posibilidad de que cuando le digan: "Le gustas a tal", él diga: "Ah, órale... ¡A mí no!"

¿Qué no hacer ni por equivocación?

● Nunca te pongas jarrísima para llamar su atención. Es lo peor que puedes hacer. Lo único que vas a lograr es perder el estilo y verte cero atractiva.

● No te acerques y le preguntes: "¿Qué haces?", porque te puede contestar: "Aquí, agarrando un vaso, ¿y tú?"

● No importa cómo te vistas; puedes ser fresa, rockera, fashion, emo, pandrosa, dark, punketa, recatada, o de

plano muy sexy, el asunto es que los hombres no soportan a las chavas sucias o a las que les huele mal la boca, que estén mal peinadas, traigan la ropa manchada o que tengan las uñas mordidas y demás.

- Di las menos groserías posibles porque a los hombres no les gustan las mujeres que hablan con muchas groserías. Un "güey" o una que otra grosería no tiene bronca, pero no más.
- Nunca, nunca y nunca jamás le pidas el teléfono a un niño ni su chat personal (WhatsApp, etc.). Si por dentro estás que te mueres porque te lo pida y casi se despiden, tranquila, cuenta hasta 10 y respira porque si se lo pides se va a sentir súper seguro y si no te lo pide, no pasa nada, ya habrá otra oportunidad para que se aviente, pero si tú se lo pides ten por seguro que ahí sí no va a pasar de un free o algo así.
- Pueden hablar de sus cuentas de Facebook y de Twitter, pero no lo estés estoqueando deja de contestarle 2 o 3 días para que se pique.
- En la etapa del ligue, donde se hablan por teléfono diario, por favor no le llames cada cinco minutos para preguntarle: "¿Qué haces?", pues le vas a dar chance de que te conteste: "Nada, aquí pensando en lo insoportable que podría ser un noviazgo contigo."
- Y si de plano el chavo que te late no te ve ni reacciona, ¡aléjate corriendo y tira tu zapato rogándole a Dios que el chavo se sepa la historia de la Cenicienta!

Las relaciones son así, de estira y afloja, así que en estos casos échale muchas ganas, pero por favor no te la pases estirando poco y aflojando mucho porque eso se llama de otra manera.

Tipos de hombres

Aunque es difícil encasillar o etiquetar a los hombres, algunos de plano hacen todo lo posible para que los ubiques en cierto tipo.

Así que nos juntamos con un grupo (muy amplio) de chavas para conocer qué piensan sobre los tipos de hombres, sus características, dónde los puedes encontrar, qué poderes y armas tienen para conquistarte, qué contras tienen y su sex appeal, o sea, qué tan peligrosos son a la hora de los besos (nivel de 1 a 5). Y aquí está lo que nos dijeron:

TIPO DE HOMBRE:

INTENSO CURSI

CARACTERÍSTICAS:

Clavado, muy amoroso y más tierno que el último elote que le sobra a la marchanta. Se olvida de su vida para "ayudarte" a vivir la tuya. Es tan detallista que podría poner una papelería completa, con el material que le sobra en su casa.

LO ENCUENTRAS EN:

En la zona de tarjetas y moños de tiendas tipo Sanborns.

DISFRAZ:

Se viste como tú quieras, no tiene estilo propio.

FRASE:

"¿A dónde quieres ir?" "…no, tú dime."

PODERES:

Conoce más de 70 formas de cómo doblar cartitas.

PROS:

Siempre tomarás la última decisión en todo y llorará contigo en las películas.

SOSPECHOSOS CON DICHAS CARACTERÍSTICAS:

CONTRAS:

No te deja ni respirar y puede ser muy peligroso cuando descubre que existen gomitas de dulce con forma de corazón.

ARMAS:

La cara de cachorrito que pone cada vez que le dices NO a algo.

NOTAS DE LA AGENTE:

ENEMIGO:

Los chavos que te tratan mal, pero que aún así tú los pelas.

NIVEL DE CALENTURA:

1 2 **3** 4 5

Le bajamos pero les bajamos .5 porque son de los que preguntan "¿Te puedo dar un beso?", y al final quedan en 2.5.

AMIGOS QUE ENTREN EN ESTA CATEGORÍA:

71

TIPO DE HOMBRE:

CHISTOSITO

CARACTERÍSTICAS:

Simpático, seguro, sangre ligera, cuando te lo van a presentar y preguntas ¿es guapo?, te contestan: es súper chistoso. Son el alma de la fiesta, a tal grado de que si cobrara por ir, muchos le pagarían.

LO ENCUENTRAS EN:

En medio de la bolita, contando un chiste.

DISFRAZ:

Boxers con todo tipo de payasadas y playeras con personajes o chistes. Si está medio gordito, se pone la playera, aunque parezca chorizo a punto de explotar.

FRASE:

¡Ah, verdad!

PODERES:

Todo mundo lo quiere (esto no incluye a maestros, directores y emos).

PROS:

No le teme al ridículo (lamentablemente tú sí).

CONTRAS:

Es difícil hablar en serio con él.

ARMAS:

Te hace reir y te empieza a gustar.

ENEMIGO:

Lugares donde no puede hablar (misa, velorios, buceo).

NIVEL DE CALENTURA:

1 2 3 **4** 5

SOSPECHOSOS CON DICHAS CARACTERÍSTICAS:

NOTAS DE LA AGENTE:

AMIGOS QUE ENTREN EN ESTA CATEGORÍA:

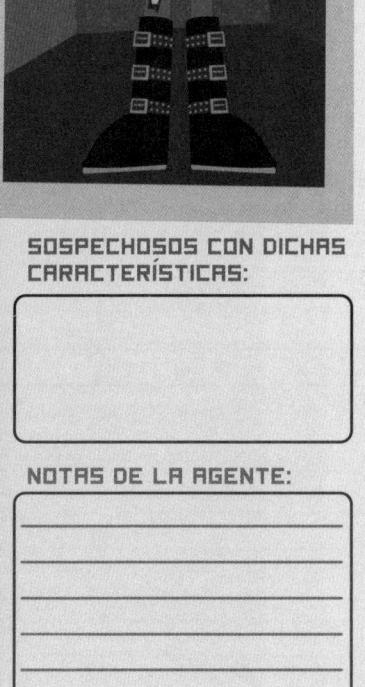

TIPO DE HOMBRE:

ALTERNATIVO PANDROSO

CARACTERÍSTICAS:

Se lleva la vida leve, es culto, inteligente y puede hablar profundo hasta de un vaso con agua, ama las bandas de garage o rock, pero odia a la banda Timbiriche. No soporta a la gente superficial y presume a sus amigos hippies (entre más sucios estén, más los presume). Nunca ha bailado Caballo dorado o La macarena.

LO ENCUENTRAS EN:

Librerías, festivales de música "propositiva", exposiciones, muestras de cine, bares con música en vivo, hoyos funkies, partidos de los Pumas y detrás de cualquier disc jockey o nube de humo que huela medio rara.

DISFRAZ:

Jeans rotos y muy, pero muy por debajo de la cintura, playeritas deslavadas con letras o figuritas con "onda", Converse, Vans o cualquier tipo de tenis, colgije con hojita de marihuana en plateado, pulseritas con más de 2 años de permanencia (muchas veces ya olvidaron de qué eran o por qué se las pusieron).

SOSPECHOSOS CON DICHAS CARACTERÍSTICAS:

NOTAS DE LA AGENTE:

AMIGOS QUE ENTREN EN ESTA CATEGORÍA:

FRASE:

¿Qué t-r-a-n-z-a ? Te invito a una t-o-c-a-d-a (hablan súper lento).

PODERES:

Siempre está relajado y cae bien.

PROS:

Nunca se pelea por tonterías y es cero inseguro.

CONTRAS:

No es romántico, ni detallista y le da flojera socializar.

ARMAS:

Su backpack (traen hasta cables para conectar aparatos).

ENEMIGO:

Los fresas que se combinan hasta el reloj.

NIVEL DE CALENTURA:

1 **2** 3 4 5

TIPO DE HOMBRE:

WILO - ZORRO

CARACTERÍSTICAS:

Le da alas a todas, tiene muy buen verbo, su control de calidad es bajo, o sea, le tira a lo que se mueve. Todas mueren por él, pero saben que andar con él es un suicidio estúpido (o aceptar a 15 socias). Busca diversión, no quiere nada en serio.

LO ENCUENTRAS EN:

El antro de moda o, como acostumbra decir este espécimen, "donde haya más".

DISFRAZ:

Como nunca le falla la cara de seductor, se puede colgar cualquier trapo y se le ve bien.

FRASE:

"Eres la más guapa del antro… te lo juro." Y "¿Me prestas 200 para la cuenta?"

PODERES:

Tú sabes que te está choreando, pero lo dice tan bonito que le crees (o por lo menos le quieres creer).

PROS:

Sirve para darle celos a tu novio y, de que te la pasas bien, te la pasas súper bien.

CONTRAS:

Si te pide tu teléfono, ve sacando tu rosario.

ARMAS:

Tiene maestría en ligue y cursos de faje en el extranjero.

ENEMIGO:

Un Wilo master (cualquier wilo que le haya bajado una chava a otro wilo).

NIVEL DE CALENTURA:

1 2 3 **4** **5**

Con más de tres cervezas el .5 sube a 5.

SOSPECHOSOS CON DICHAS CARACTERÍSTICAS:

NOTAS DE LA AGENTE:

AMIGOS QUE ENTREN EN ESTA CATEGORÍA:

TIPO DE HOMBRE:

TETAZO

CARACTERÍSTICAS:

La piensa 10 mil veces antes de acercarse y cuando llega no sabe qué decir. Su plática es de flojera. Es buenísimo en la escuela. Sólo se enoja cuando todos le quieren copiar o cuando le salió una nota mal en sus clases de violín.

LO ENCUENTRAS EN:

El laboratorio, analizando un mechero de Bunsen.

DISFRAZ:

Pantalón arriba del ombligo, siempre se faja y cuando llega a usar jeans, son nuevos y están planchados.

FRASE:

"¿Qué onda mi NIÑA, cómo TAS?" (literal).

PODERES:

Es fiel… (sí leíste bien ¡es fiel!).

PROS:

Podrás identificar a la perfección plantas fanerógamas y criptógamas.

CONTRAS:

Cuando te esté platicando, no vas a saber cómo cortarlo.

ARMAS:

Sus conocimientos impresionarán hasta a tus papás.

ENEMIGO:

Las horas libres en la escuela.

NIVEL DE CALENTURA:

1 2 3 4 **5**

Han esperado tanto, que cuando tocan a una mujer por primera vez, pueden causarle quemaduras de segundo grado.

SOSPECHOSOS CON DICHAS CARACTERÍSTICAS:

NOTAS DE LA AGENTE:

AMIGOS QUE ENTREN EN ESTA CATEGORÍA:

TIPO DE HOMBRE:

BUENA ONDA

CARACTERÍSTICAS:

Es agradable, te cuida, cero perro, y siempre te da tu lugar.

LO ENCUENTRAS EN:

Como ex novio de chavas luciditas que según ellas les "dio flojera".

DISFRAZ:

No notas mucho cómo se viste, pero siempre se ve bien.

FRASE:

"No te preocupes, yo te ayudo."

PODERES:

Sabe escuchar (aunque parezca imposible, algunos hombres lo logran).

PROS:

Te vas a sentir respetada, querida, y tus amigas lo van a adorar.

CONTRAS:

Algunas chavas se sienten tan seguras, que se les sube.

ARMAS:

Les da súper buena vibra a tus papás.

ENEMIGO:

Las chavas que sólo ven el físico.

NIVEL DE CALENTURA:

1 2 3 4 5 Ninguno

Viene en diferentes presentaciones.

SOSPECHOSOS CON DICHAS CARACTERÍSTICAS:

NOTAS DE LA AGENTE:

AMIGOS QUE ENTREN EN ESTA CATEGORÍA:

TIPO DE HOMBRE:

PATÁN

CARACTERÍSTICAS:

Nunca cumple lo que promete. Maneja muy buen verbo y si no le crees, por lo menos te marea. Su raza es Galán spaniel cruza Mamilón de las praderas, y por más que parezca NO tiene pedigree.

LO ENCUENTRAS EN:

Viendo tu escote y el de cualquier mujer a 150 metros a la redonda.

DISFRAZ:

Camisa garigoleada, abierta hasta el ombligo, o playera en cuello "v", tres tallas más chica.

FRASE:

"¿Ya pediste tu taxi?"

PODERES:

Te baja el sol, la luna y las estrellas (y si te descuidadas, hasta la blusa).

PROS:

Te volverás muuuuuy popular (pero por ser una de las cinco novias).

CONTRAS:

Vas al baño y cuando regresas, ¡ya está con otra!

ARMAS:

Baila bien y siempre te dice lo que quieres escuchar.

ENEMIGO:

Las chavas que no toman.

NIVEL DE CALENTURA:

 1 2 3 4 **5**

SOSPECHOSOS CON DICHAS CARACTERÍSTICAS:

NOTAS DE LA AGENTE:

AMIGOS QUE ENTREN EN ESTA CATEGORÍA:

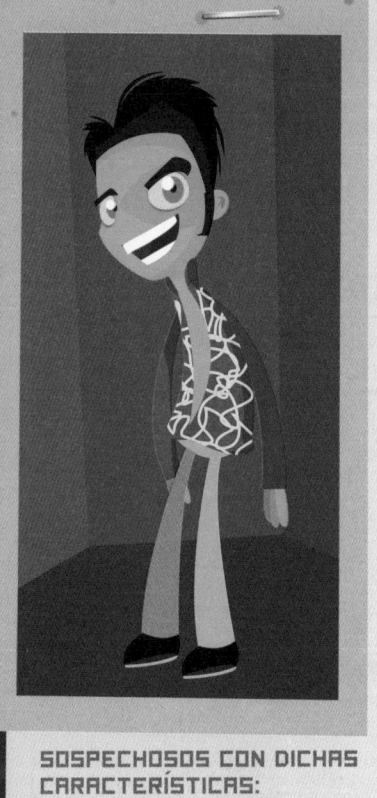

TIPO DE HOMBRE:

AMIGOVIO

CARACTERÍSTICAS:

Es, pero no es. Odia la palabra novia y la frase "te quieren conocer mis papás". Cero compromisos, pero 1000% química.

LO ENCUENTRAS EN:

Tu agenda con 5 tachones, pero siempre vuelves a poner su teléfono (tal vez tú nunca lo borraste).

DISFRAZ:

Le vale; como sabe que se gustan cañón, es lo último que le preocupa.

FRASE:

"Para qué echamos a perder nuestra amistad."

PODERES:

Es mago… hoy lo ves, la próxima semana no lo ves.

PROS:

Te la pasas bien con él y como no tienen obligaciones casi no se pelean (ésta es la teoría, porque en la práctica es como los experimentos de química… nunca salen como te dicen).

CONTRAS:

Te puedes súper enamorar y, obvio, él no va a querer nada.

ARMAS:

Sabe lo que te gusta y lo que odias de los hombres.

ENEMIGO:

El chavo que quiere en serio contigo.

NIVEL DE CALENTURA:

1 2 3 4 **5**

SOSPECHOSOS CON DICHAS CARACTERÍSTICAS:

NOTAS DE LA AGENTE:

AMIGOS QUE ENTREN EN ESTA CATEGORÍA:

TIPO DE HOMBRE:

MEJOR AMIGO

CARACTERÍSTICAS:

Hay de dos, o está secretamente enamorado de ti, o está secretamente enamorado de ti.

LO ENCUENTRAS EN:

La comida en casa de tu abuelita, la kermesse de tu escuela, el veterinario cuando tu hamster está enfermo, etcétera.

DISFRAZ:

Hace como que le vale, pero se pone lo que le chuleas a los demás.

FRASE:

"Tú te mereces algo mejor."

PODERES:

Siempre te consuela.

PROS:

Realmente lo quieres.

CONTRAS:

Realmente te quiere (pero dar unos besotes).

ARMAS:

Usa la información de lo que te choca de tu ex, para hacer todo lo contrario.

ENEMIGO:

Cualquier hombre que te guste (aunque dizque le hecha porras).

NIVEL DE CALENTURA:

1 2 3 4 5 6

SOSPECHOSOS CON DICHAS CARACTERÍSTICAS:

NOTAS DE LA AGENTE:

AMIGOS QUE ENTREN EN ESTA CATEGORÍA:

TIPO DE HOMBRE:

INALCANZABLE

CARACTERÍSTICAS:

Galán, sonrisa colgate, no hay una sola chava que no lo conozca, de hecho hasta alguna parte de su cuerpo es famosa (pompas, brazos, etcétera). Si te lo encuentras, hay un 110% de posibilidades de que no te voltee a ver.

LO ENCUENTRAS EN:

Las fotos grandes de las revistas de sociales.

DISFRAZ:

Si le pones uno de príncipe, está igualito al de la Cenicienta (si no es tan galán se parece al de Pocahontas).

FRASE:

" ", (sólo habla con sus amigos).

PODERES:

Todas quieren con él (nota: pero él no quiere casi con ninguna).

PROS:

Si anduviste con él, tendrás algo que contarle a tus nietos.

CONTRAS:

No importa cuántas veces te lo presenten, siempre te dice "mucho gusto". Y si andas con él, olvídate de tu nombre, serás la novia del súper galán…

ARMAS:

Sabe que todas quieren con él.

ENEMIGO:

El maestro acomplejado que siempre lo quiere tronar por galán.

NIVEL DE CALENTURA:

1 **2** 3 4 5

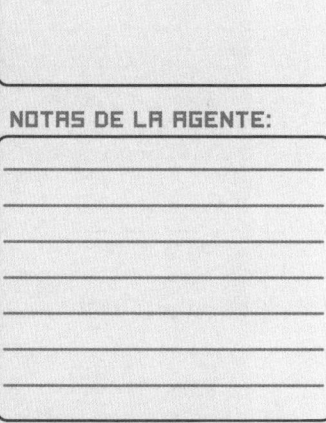

SOSPECHOSOS CON DICHAS CARACTERÍSTICAS:

NOTAS DE LA AGENTE:

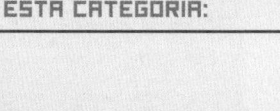

AMIGOS QUE ENTREN EN ESTA CATEGORÍA:

Si te preguntas si un tipo de hombre puede cambiar, la respuesta es Sí... se puede poner peor. No, ya en serio, algunos toda la vida son así y para otros es sólo una etapa.

También cada tipo puede tener sus combinaciones. O sea, puedes encontrarte un intenso-wilo o un alterno-patán. Si te encuentras una de estas mutaciones, no te asustes, sólo cuídalo, aliméntalo y sácalo a pasear.

> A ver Roberto hazme 4 veces como pollito.

> Pío, pío, pi pi.

Palabras y frases que nunca le debes decir a un hombre

Imagínate a un cuate que mida más de 1.75 metros, súper rudo, con cara de pocos amigos y que sea como un monstruo de 110 kilos; en fin, el típico al que todo mundo le tiene miedo, pero al que de repente su novia le pide que le haga como pollito chicken, y este gigantón acepta y con todo y sus 110 kilos!, esto no quiere decir que sea medio teto, sino que más bien los hombres, al igual que las mujeres, tienen fibras muy sensibles y bajo ciertas circunstancias salen a la luz pública.

Por lo tanto, debes pensar que, así como un hombre se preocupa por tratar de no herirte con ninguno de sus comentarios (o por lo menos eso intenta), tú debes procurar lo mismo con él, recuerda: un hombre sentido vale por dos... pero dos mujeres.

Y aunque así como entre hombres y mujeres existe gente muy segura de sí misma que no tiene ningún problema con estas cosas, no está por demás darte algunos tips.

Cuando tu galán todavía tiene algunas inseguridades le molesta hasta que le digas que otro cuate está guapo. (Evita decirlo, pero ni de loca dejes de voltear a verlos.)

No lo hagas sentir menos con cosas materiales que otro niño tenga y él no te pueda dar.

No le presumas el trabajo de otro cuate o lo compares en el nivel laboral o de la escuela, a menos de que el objetivo sea su superación y realmente tengas bases.

No critiques a su familia (una cosa es dar un consejo y otra criticar). Además, si él le llega a contar a su familia, no te la vas a acabar, porque a él se le olvida... pero a la familia nunca.

Cuando se peleen nunca se digan groserías, nunca se agredan. Una vez que cruzas esa línea es muy difícil regresar.

No le digas que las cosas que le gustan son tonterías.

No lo presiones para ir al nuevo antro de moda o algo así (si no ha accedido, lo más seguro es que no tenga dinero o no lo dejen entrar y le da pena decirte).

No le cuentes los súper detalles que tenían contigo tus ex novios.

No le platiques de cómo tu familia adoraba y trataba al ex, porque va a empezar a alucinar a tu familia desde ese momento. Mejor dale tiempo a que se los gane.

No queremos decir que con este tipo de comentarios se acabará la relación, pero por lo menos sí te vas a ahorrar dos o tres broncas innecesarias y lo harás sentir mucho mejor.

CHECA ESTO

¿Cómo saber cuando tu novio te engaña?

No importa cómo le digan: poner el cuerno, dobletear, tener una socia, doble frente, o como sea, se siente CAÑONCÍSIMO. Si creías que cuando tus papás te ponían alcohol en una herida ibas a gritar, espérate a este grito.

La neta es que a algunos hombres (si es que se pueden llamar así), les encanta el 2 x 1, y cuando menos te lo imaginas, ya pasaron de coqueteo 1 y cerrada de ojos 2, a ser licenciados en infidelogía con todo y maestría.

El especimen Infidelius estupiduz, ataca con la tranquilidad de que su pareja se encuentra distraída con el resto de la manada; es por eso que aquí te damos algunos argumentos que él usa para buscar onda en otro lado; así que si cachas al especimen cortejando a otras niñas, conviértelo más que de inmediato en Infidelius estupiduz ABANDONADUZ, Pero a la de iya!

♥ Su celular tiene clave, pues según él, tiene números muy importantes o dice que se le marca solito a cada rato (siempre que quieres hacer una llamada de su celular, él marca la clave).

💔 Facebook, Facebook, Facebook, ah, y Twitter, dime quién lo tagea y te diré dónde ha estado.

💔 Se pone nervioso cuando abre sus redes sociales frente a ti y jamás, jamás, te deja navegar sola por ellas.

💔 Tiene una mejor amiga, a la que jamás puede ver contigo.

💔 Cada vez que están juntos por mucho tiempo, busca la forma de separarse de ti con cualquier pretexto, para marcar algún teléfono.

💔 En su celular tiene casi siempre mensajes de texto borrados.

💔 Normalmente insiste en buscar besos o algún tipo de faje y de un día a otro, como que ya no le importa.

💔 Supuestamente está en un lugar en el que puede contestar su celular y por más que lo intentas, obvio no contesta.

💔 De repente te cambia el apodito cariñoso; por ejemplo, siempre te ha dicho "cosita" y de la nada te comienza a decir "bebus" (lo más seguro es que así se dice con la otra "bebus").

💔 Cuando se le olvida su celular en TU casa, regresa más que inmediatamente a buscarlo.

💔 Van al cine y se le sale que ya vio la película (aquí de volada vas a verlo tartamudear y ponerse nerviosito para explicarte con quién la vio o te pondrá el pretexto de que lo leyó en un artículo muy, muy amplio sobre la película). ¡Aaaja!

💔 De la nada se niega rotundamente a ir a una fiesta o a "x" antro (tal vez ese día, también vaya a ir tu socia).

💔 A veces frente a ti contesta el teléfono y se pone súper nervioso y cortante, se aprieta muchísimo el teléfono contra la oreja para que no escuches que es otra mujer (generalmente tiene registrado el teléfono con nombre de hombre; esto lo aprendió en alguna película de James Bond).

💔 En la navidad te da regalos muy chafas o de plano no te dá (... ya se gastó el presupuesto).

♥ Generalmente se te pierde una tarde o un día completo y casualmente en esos momentos "olvidó" su celular en casa o se le acabó la pila.

♥ Al llegar a tu casa, está hablando por teléfono y siempre cuelga antes de estar contigo.

♥ Regresa de un viaje o un fin de semana que no lo viste y se empieza a portar muchísimo más lindo de lo normal. (La famosa situación francesa… La colé entre le paté).

♥ Estás en su casa y al contestar tu suegra el teléfono, dice "no está", cuando en realidad está toda la familia (aquí la suegra está metida hasta las manitas).

♥ Cuando escucha el tema de infidelidad en la tele, radio o alguna conversación, le saca la vuelta, le cambia al canal o se le ocurre ir al baño.

♥ A ti te late que algo pasó y tratas de verlo a los ojos, pero él escapa la mirada. Esa ya es señal ROJA de alerta.

Bueno, aunque estas son algunas de las señales que puedes tener cuando alguien aplica la infidelidad, tampoco queremos que te conviertas en espía profesional. Si tu novio encaja en uno o dos de estos puntos, relájate, lo más seguro es que no pase nada y que sea otra cosa (esa bolita que te está saliendo en la frente es granito, no cuerno).

Pero si tu galancito cae constantemente en más de 5 puntos, es muy posible que te esté engañando.

Ahora, si es tu caso, seguro te preguntarás si debes tronarlo. Nosotros, ¡ni lo dudaríamos! Sin embargo, eso sólo depende de ti. Lo que te podemos asegurar es que si lo hace una vez, es muy probable que lo vuelva a hacer. No te engañes.

Aunque a veces nos cuesta mucho trabajo reconocerlo, y no lo queremos hacer, es mejor afrontar la situación. ¡Qué caso tiene estar con alguien que NO quiere estar contigo!

Si ese es el rollo, es mejor no aferrarse y tomar esta relación para aprender, para darte la oportunidad de conocer después a un hombre fiel que te de el lugar que te mereces. (Sólo como dato: los hombres fieles, sí existen.)

Por otro lado, también es un hecho que cualquiera puede equivocarse y mega regarla. Si ese es el caso, y en verdad estás muy enamorada y lo perdonas de corazón, te sugerimos que le armes un súper pancho, lo cortes, luego dejas que te ruegue un buen rato, que le cueste trabajo y, si decides perdonarlo porque en verdad lo notas arrepentido, le des otra oportunidad y tal vez pueda servir la experiencia para que te valore y te aprecie más. Date siempre tu lugar, si no lo haces tú, ¿quién lo hará?

Ahora que si lo vuelves a cachar en lo más mínimo, no pierdas tu tiempo. No vale la pena.

Por más dolor que sientas, date la oportunidad de amar a alguien que verdaderamente te ame.

Noviazgo

¡PAPIS!
Les presento
a mi novio Lennon,
nos casamos en un mes

Tener novio es padrísimo y, por supuesto, es más que un ligue: es una relación amorosa, digamos que es oficial. En el noviazgo se pueden dar todo tipo de emociones: amor, emoción, diversión, entrega e ilusión. Pero también tiene su lado difícil; quizá exista confusión, enojos, truenes, celos y muchas cosas más, pero todo es parte del mismo paquete.

Así que no te preocupes si un día te sientes entre mil estrellas, y al otro sientes como que te estrellaron mil veces: ¡felicidades! Tienes un noviazgo en toda la extensión de la palabra.

TIPOS DE NOVIAZGO

Noviazgo recreo:
porque no dura nada.

Noviazgo siamés:
se la pasan tan embarrados que parecen uno, en lugar de dos.

Noviazgo paparazzi:
porque se andan escondiendo de todos.

Noviazgo de bajo aprovechamiento:
porque se la pasan tronando.

Noviazgo Greenpeace:
preserva la especie, o lo que es lo mismo, es cuando te haces novia del hermano de tu mejor amiga.

Noviazgo titanic:
se aman hasta la muerte.

Noviazgo karate:
son novios pero se la pasan de la patada.

Noviazgo panadería:
uno es un pan y el otro puros cuernos.

Adentrándonos más en este rollo de la manita sudada, ¿te ha pasado que de repente sientes que tu novio y tú piensan muy diferente?, ¿estás súper clavada y te preocupa que no sienta lo mismo por ti?, ¿un día lo amas y otro lo odias? Bueno, pues es completamente normal.

En esta edad, los sentimientos cambian todo el tiempo sin avisarte. Además, si hay mucha diferencia en edad, cultura, educación, valores o costumbres el asunto se complica un poco.

Lo mejor es que también esas diferencias hacen que tú y él se complementen. Y cuando el amor es grande, dice "quítate, que ahí te voy".

Tips para el rollo de los novios

> Las relaciones tienen altas y bajas, disfruta las dos.
> Respeten su espacio; cuando todo el día andan de pegotes es agobiante.
> No seas absorbente ni controladora: ¡lo alucinan! Tampoco permitas que él lo sea contigo.
> Olvídate de preguntarle todo el tiempo: "¿Me quieres?" o, "nunca me dices si te gusto, si estoy guapa..." ¡de flojera! A veces los hombres son tímidos, o simplemente no se les ocurre decirte estas cosas.
> Platica con él sobre lo que les late y lo que no.
> Las peleas constantes apagan el amor. Si te peleas de vez en cuando es normal, pero nunca con agresión verbal y mucho menos física.
> Los celos son aceptables cuando son normales; cuando son enfermizos hablan de una persona súper insegura.
> Nunca dejes que él te obligue a hacer algo que no quieras.
> Si hay engaños es mejor terminar.
> Cuando truenas sientes que te vas a morir. Tranquila, no te mueres, sientes horrible pero siempre pasa y te vuelves a enamorar, escucha bien: ¡siempre!

Las relaciones maduran cuando encuentras a la persona correcta. Olvídate de sólo pasarla bien, vas a querer estar con esa persona no sólo un rato, sino toda la vida.

Mis amigas

Tener una buena amiga

¡Qué importante es tener una buena amiga! Ella puede comprender mejor que nadie lo que te pasa, lo que sientes, lo que te preocupa, simplemente porque, por lo general, está viviendo lo mismo que tú. Con ella puedes llorar con confianza, contarle tus depresiones, saber con un intercambio de miradas lo que tú y ella piensan y reírte a carcajadas hasta que el estómago te duela.

No hay dos iguales

Estás de acuerdo en que algunas amigas son esporádicas; ya sabes, las conoces en vacaciones y nunca más las vuelves a ver. Otras son amigas que ves sólo en una clase, en un deporte o en cualquier otra actividad, también están las reciclables; las típicas que la amabas, luego te peleaste a muerte y otra vez son medio amigas. Sin embargo, tienes LAS AMIGAS, el grupito con el que te sientes más identificada y donde están las que más quieres.

Aunque es posible que la amistad entre un hombre y una mujer se dé, por lo general hay cosas que sólo le confías a una amiga, ¿ya sabes?

Las amigas y el teatro

Las amigas son como los lugares del teatro: hay amigas *vip* (casi siempre son dos o tres) que comparten tus mismos valores y forma de pensar, y con las que te abres sin temor a ser criticada. A ellas las sientas en la primera fila. Hay amigas, las de tu grupito, por ejemplo, que sientas en la zona de preferencia; cuídalas mucho. A otras las mandas a gayola y di que les tocó lugar. A unas pocas las sientas en los palcos, a otras tantas las acomodas en medio porque son como del montón, y de plano hay algunas que te caen nefasto y nada más les dices: "Perdón, pero ya se me agotaron las funciones y tú no alcanzas ni en la reventa."

Como en todas las relaciones, la comunicación abierta y honesta será la clave para que tu amistad dure mucho tiempo y sobrepase los conflictos que inevitablemente tendrán. Si andas insoportable y les tiras mala onda a todas, ojo, porque a ti también te pueden cerrar el teatro.

Me cuesta trabajo hacer amigos

"Llevo en la secundaria como dos meses y desde que entré no tengo amigas. Cuando llegué no conocía a nadie y la neta me la paso sola porque me cuesta mucho trabajo hacer amigos. En el recreo sólo me siento en el patio a hacer la tarea mientras veo cómo los demás juegan y se divierten. ¿Me entiendes? Es deprimente, ¿no? Yo creo que como soy tímida y callada los demás piensan que soy rara o mala onda. ¡No sé!", nos cuenta Liz.

Es cierto, no a todo el mundo se le facilita hacer amigos, es cuestión de temperamento. Con eso naces y no vas a cambiar; lo que sí puedes hacer es ser más accesible. Por ejemplo:

Si ERES iNTROVERTiDA

Los introvertidos, como Liz, a veces se sienten bichos raros. Por lo general comparten poca información acerca de ellos mismos, y si lo hacen, hablan de su forma de pensar más que de sus sentimientos. Son personas a las que les gusta pensar, profundizar en las cosas y son excelentes observadores y amigos. Saben escuchar muy bien y son muy pacientes. Generalmente se sienten como dedo en el recreo y como no tienen con quién platicar, se ponen a leer o a hacer la tarea, o ya de plano leen su tarea tres veces, nada más para hacer tiempo. Si éste es tu caso, relájate, no estás sola, a muchas personas les pasa. Una forma en la que puedes empezar a hacer amigos es, aunque te cueste un poco de trabajo, acercarte a alguien que te lata y hacerle preguntas.

Preguntarle, por ejemplo, sobre algún tema que vieron en clase, sobre quién le corta el pelo, sobre algun programa de televisión de moda o algún deporte, y poco a poco platicarán sobre temas distintos. Otro día la invitas a comer, juntan el lunch y así empezará la amistad.

Es bueno que ubiques que a veces la gente puede confundir el ser tímida con ser sangrona, por lo que te sugerimos sonreír mucho y tratar de abrirte para que esto no te suceda. También te recomendamos que si pasan el lunch juntas no te abalances el primer día sobre sus cacahuates gourmet, o sea japoneses con Miguelito de agua y chile.

Si ERES EXTROVERTiDA

Los extrovertidos son aquellos que apenas acabas de conocer y ya te contaron su vida entera. A ellos les gusta estar llenos de actividades, conocer mucha gente, ir a muchos lugares y experimentar mil cosas a la vez.

Hablan hasta por los codos (y vaya que hay codos muy expresivos) y son muy malos para escuchar. Hablan sin

pensar, por eso es común que metan la pata o se metan en problemas. Si ésta es tu forma de ser, hacer amigos se te facilita mucho; sólo procura interesarte en ellos, cuidarlos más, iah!, y de vez en cuando cierra la boca para que sepas cómo se llaman, si tienen hermanos, si andan con alguien... en fin, cosas básicas.

Conflictos y complicaciones

Entre dos o más amigas siempre habrá situaciones externas o internas que pongan a prueba su amistad. Hay veces que la amas y dices: "¡Qué haría sin ella!", y otras en que la odias y dices: "¡Ashhh! ¡Qué voy a hacer con ella!" Es inevitable. Para aliviar cualquier circunstancia es necesario platicar mucho, tener paciencia y confianza.

Sentimientos que se dan en una amistad

> Admiración: "Mi amiga Laura es guapísima, tiene a mil galanes muertos por ella. Además, es la más aplicada del salón y es la mejor amiga de todas".
> Posesión: "¿Cómo que quedaste de ir al cine con Paola? ¿No vamos a estudiar juntas?" Casi casi le dices "idiota".
> Indignación: "Siempre me copias en lo que me pongo." "El sábado ni se te ocurra ponerte la blusa lila porque yo me la voy a poner, ¿ok?"
> Envidia: "Mi papá no me deja ir al concierto del sábado y Ale ya tiene boletos y además va a ir icon Pepe! ¡Grrrrr! Ojalá que al vocalista le dé una enfermedad rara y se cancele."

- Competencia: "Cristy es una de mis mejores amigas, pero ni modo, le tengo que ganar en las calificaciones, y si no, por lo menos que yo me vea más guapa el día que las entreguen, ji, ji, ji."
- Celos: "Desde que tienes novio, ya ni me pelas," o "mi mejor amiga es buena en todo y le gusta a todos los niños. ¡Claro!, ¿a quién no? Es alta, flaca, tiene el pelo divino y es perfecta. ¡Ay!, la odio, pero si yo fuera hombre ¡creo que andaría con ella!"
- Solidaridad: "No te preocupes, yo me voy a tu casa en la tarde para explicarte mate. Está muy fácil, vas a ver. ¡Claro que puedes!"
- Decepción: "Mi mejor amiga le insinuó a José Pablo 'sin querer', que muero por él, lo que es cierto, pero me dio mucho coraje. Ya me pidió perdón mil veces, pero la verdad no siento que sea sincera."
- Afinidad: "Con mis amigas me la paso ¡súper!, nos encanta ir los viernes a comer y después al cine."
- Amor incondicional: "Regina tiene mil broncas en su casa y además es gordísima y no es muy bonita, aun así la quiero mucho y trato de ayudarla."
- Traición: "Claro, mi amiga se fue con Eugenia porque ella sí fuma y yo no. ¡Estoy furiosa!", o "el secreto que le confié a Lupe se lo contó a todo el mundo." Aunque es peor: "Laura me bajó a mi novio, y también ya se lo pasó a todo el mundo."

¡Es neto! En una amistad, todas estas cosas se pueden dar y más. ¡Es muy normal! Lo importante es reconocer si lo que sientes son tonterías pasajeras o a lo mejor en realidad no es tu amiga. Si algo no va bien no te lo calles, platica con ella y aclaralo, porque una buena amistad influye de muchas maneras en tu vida: hay que cuidarla. Es algo que dura para siempre, especialmente las que haces durante esta etapa, y es lo mejor que te puede pasar. Pero no olvides que la amistad es como una calle de doble sentido: dar y recibir, es la regla del juego.

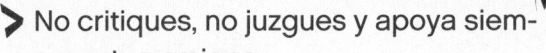

Sé una súper amiga

> No critiques, no juzgues y apoya siempre a tus amigas.
> Atrévete a hablar con sinceridad las cosas que otras se callan.
> Cuando una amiga te cuente algo que le preocupa escúchala con atención.
> Si alguien molesta a tu amiga defiéndela.
> Si no te piden un consejo no lo des.
> Guarda bien ese secreto que te contaron.
> Permite que los demás sean como son, no los trates de cambiar.
> "La única manera de tener un amigo, es siéndolo", R. W. Emerson.

CHECA ESTO

Me traen de bajada / bullying

Odio ir a la escuela, hay dos niñas que no dejan de molestarme. Cada vez que estoy cerca de ellas dicen cosas horribles de mí, delante de mí, y se ríen. Me empujan, me esconden mis cosas, y me avientan bolas de papel con baba a la cara.

Un día me escribieron en mi mochila "eres una teta" y cuando llegué y lo vi, me di cuenta de que me estaban grabando. Se murieron de la risa y después lo subieron a internet. Cuando lo vi sentí lo peor que he sentido en mi vida; pensé en tomarme unas pastillas de mi mamá, para morirme y no volver a la escuela.

Primero eran sólo dos niñas, ahora, es casi todo el salón. Dicen que cuando no voy no se divierten. Las odio, pero por más que intento no puedo decirles nada. ¡No sé qué hacer!

Susana, 14 años

Nunca falta. Todos, en algún momento de la vida, supimos lo que se siente que los demás se burlen de ti: del apodo, de los zapes, de la tristeza que te da y demás. A esto en inglés se le conoce como *bullying* y lamentablemente ha crecido cada vez más. De entrada, queremos que sepas que esto pasa en todas las escuelas y en el caso de los zapes, en todas las cabezas. Sin embargo la manera en la que nos enfrentemos a esta bronca marca la diferencia entre ser feliz en la escuela o pasártela súper mal.

Los papás, a veces, no le dan importancia a este rollo. Piensan que este tipo de acoso es típico cuando pasas de la niñez a la juventud. Sin embargo, esto ha aumentado y el que te traigan de bajada es un tema que les pega a miles de chavos y chavas; y de acuerdo a las investigaciones, los daños psicológicos pueden ser gruesos y reflejarse incluso cuando seas más grande.

Les preguntamos a algunos expertos y a varios jóvenes. Nos pareció interesante compartir contigo sus respuestas:

¿Qué hace que a una chava la traigan de bajada?

"Su forma de actuar, la manera como se viste, si está fea, si es muy gorda, si siempre trae el pelo sucio, si habla chistoso, como de otro lugar, que huela feo, que sea tonta, "teta" o medio wila, su peinado, el color de su piel, que tenga malas calificaciones, que sea tímida, introvertida, freaky, rara, que no conozca niños, que se vea vulnerable —todo esto hace que la puedas molestar—, que sea atacable..."

¿Qué tanto pasa esto y a qué se debe?

"Es muy frecuente, en especial en la etapa de preescolar y en la adolescencia. Puede ser por una sobreprotección de

los papás. Si al niño siempre le han solucionado todo, no sabe cómo construir sus defensas. El niño se acostumbra a ser el tonto, el flojo y desarrolla tolerancia a los insultos, una baja autoestima y ninguna herramienta de defensa. A eso le sumamos a niños o adolescentes, que quieren tener poder sobre otros. Cuando logran que se enojen, que lloren o que se pongan tristes, sienten que ellos tienen el control."

Si ya te traen de bajada, ¿qué puedes hacer para que te dejen en paz?

Aquí te damos algunas sugerencias que investigamos entre jóvenes, expertos en problemas juveniles y en algunos libros:

- Simula que no te importa, aunque por dentro te mueras. Ríete, tú misma has burla de lo aparentemente "chistoso" que tienes. Eso es lo mejor para desanimarlos a seguir.
- No les des poder, si te pones triste o te ven llorar, logran su objetivo y la cosa se pone peor. Si cuando los ves en un lugar, les sacas la vuelta y te vas por otro lado, consiguen lo que quieren. Mejor júntate con una amiga y pasa exactamente por ahí. Que vean que no tienes miedo (aunque obvio, sí lo tengas).
- Otra forma es que si las cosas ya se pasan de la raya, reconoce que te molesta y te enoja que te traigan de bajada. Contéstale a la que te moleste, para que te respete. Todos tenemos defectos, así que encuéntrale uno y dícelo. Esto funciona cañón, porque se da cuenta de que ella también tiene defectos que todo mundo puede ver y burlarse de ellos si se hacen públicos. Y aunque al principio haga como que no le importa, va a sentir que se muere. Sus amigas van a quedarse calladas, pero en el fondo van a pensar "sí es cierto, tiene las cejas de azotador ...ji,ji,ji". La mayoría de los que molestan, lo hacen porque son muy inseguros y tratan de cubrir esto al molestar a los demás. Así que si le dices su defecto,

y se lo repites varias veces, va a sentirse vulnerable y te dejará de molestar. Ahora, nada más no lo sigas haciendo, no te vayas a convertir en uno de ellos.

- Háblalo con tus papás o con un maestro, pero para pedirles un consejo, no para acusarlos. Es muy difícil salir de una de estas situaciones sola.
- Habla a solas con cada una de las que te molestan, enfréntalas. Aunque te suene raro o suicida, esto pueda ayudar muchísimo. Primero porque se necesita mucho valor y eso lo notan ellas; y segundo porque por lo general a ellas en algún momento también las trajeron "de bajada". Así que es muy probable que te dejen de molestar.
- El lenguaje corporal es importante: evita caminar encorvada, mirando hacia el suelo, como si no existieras, porque esto empeora las cosas. Camina segura, pisa fuerte.
- Si te molestan por algo de tu apariencia física, tipo el peinado, o de tu forma de vestir, puedes cambiarlo. Seguro el primer día se van a burlar, pero después se van a acostumbrar y te van a dejar de molestar. Nunca metas reversa.
- Escribe una lista de tus cualidades, acepta tus "diferencias" con orgullo. No te achiques y no faltes a la escuela. Reclama tus derechos y, sobre todo, construye la imagen de lo que quieres ser y trabaja para obtenerla.

Cuando estaba en cuarto de primaria, había una chava muy guapa que se llamaba Sofía. Un día me empezó a molestar en frente de todos, diciéndome que mi papá estaba muy moreno. Los demás se empezaron a burlar y a esa edad me pegó horrible. Lo siguió haciendo por algunas semanas, hasta que decidí hacer algo.

Un día en la tarde se me ocurrió empezar a decirle "salami" (no te rías, ubica que estaba en cuarto). Le dije a un amigo que me ayudara a decirle igual. Al día siguiente, llegué a la escuela y le dije "hola, salami". Obvio, al principio

no entendió. Después cada vez que estábamos cerca de ella, decíamos "¿huele a salami, no?", y empezamos a jugar todo el día con la palabrita. A los demás del salón se les hizo chistoso y siguieron con la broma.

Bueno el asunto es que ese día, Sofía terminó llorando y suplicándome que no le volviera a decir "salami". Lo hice, y ella dejó de molestarme.

Jamás me imaginé que una cosa tan tonta me ayudara a resolver un problema que en ese momento me agobiaba tanto.

Como ves, esto funciona. Lo único importante es utilizarlo sólo para defenderte. **Jamás para convertirte en uno de ellos.**

yordi

Otra cosa súper importante es recordar que el mundo es como un espejo. Como te ves, la gente te ve. La etiqueta que te pongas, va a ser la que los demás lean de ti. Y sobre todo, ponte buza, porque: "La gente te tratará como tú permitas que te trate" Así que… ¡Mucha suerte!

NOTA:

Si tú eres de las que por caerle bien a los demás, por sentirte superior, por diversión, por llamar la atención o sentirte aceptada, zapeas y traes de bajada a alguien, piensa en el daño que le puedes hacer a esa persona, y que a veces ese daño es de por vida. Ponte en sus zapatos y pregúntate si te gustaría que te lo hicieran a ti. Acuérdate de que todo lo que haces en la vida, como búmeran, tarde o temprano regresa a ti…

Ahora que si ves que tu amiga molesta a alguien y a ti no te late, aléjate cuando lo haga. La gente que molesta quiere público, para demostrar su poder, si no lo tiene, su rollo no funciona. Trata de convencer a la que molesta de que le baje, en buen plan.

HUELE A SALAMI

TODO EL MUNDO LO HACE

La necesidad de pertenecer es un asunto súper grueso que toca las fibras de la esencia humana. Sin embargo, en la etapa de la adolescencia en la que estás, pertenecer o no a un grupito de amigas es un factor de supervivencia y hasta una razón de vida. La presión de grupo afecta muchos aspectos de tu vida.

La mayoría de las niñas entre 12 y 19 años hacen lo que hacen porque "todo el mundo lo hace", no importa si se trata de mentir, irse de pinta, tomar unos drinks, vestir a la moda, fumar, meterse a una clase de algo o no, tener relaciones o no. Son cuestiones que se reducen a una frase tipiquísima: "Todo el mundo lo hace".

Se siente tan nefasto la angustia de no pertenecer, que eres capaz de vender a uno de tus hermanos con tal de que te pelen, así que mejor platiquemos de este rollo.

"En la escuela, mis amigas me tienen en el congelador porque soy buena gente con una niña a la que todo mundo en el salón le tira mala onda. La pobre me da lástima. A mí no me gustaría que fueran así conmigo, pero mis amigas no lo entienden y no sé qué hacer," nos cuenta Andrea.

Que no te pelen por una razón tan simple como ésta o por algo más importante, es muy difícil de superar para cualquiera, porque te pone en una situación súper vulnerable, asunto que el grupito de tus amigas conoce bien o intuye; por eso ponen a prueba a sus miembros, ya sea con méritos o con ritos de iniciación para tener el privilegio de "pertenecer".

Esta presión puede ser tan cañona que logra que una niña haga cosas que jamás haría por su propia voluntad. Si alguna vez te ha pasado esto, creemos que para tomar tus decisiones es importante que sepas qué es lo que nos mueve a los humanos a responder a lo que se conoce como:

Presión de grupo

Seguramente te vas a encontrar con gente que piensa que debes ser o actuar de cierta manera y va a tratar de influir para cambiarte. Esto te confunde muchísimo, especialmente si viene de alguien que te importa, que crees que es tu amiga o de algún galancito que te guste; además, quizá todavía no estás muy segura de quién eres tú.

A veces los consejos y las sugerencias te ayudan y te dan buenas ideas para ver qué onda. Pero si te llevan hacia una dirección que te hace sentir incómoda, hasta en lo más mínimo, porque va en contra de tus valores y principios, te obliga a hacer cosas que no quieres y que ponen en peligro tu vida, tu libertad, o te causa problemas con tu familia, la escuela o con otras personas, hazle caso a tu intuición y ¡no lo hagas!

"Es que si no haces lo que todas hacen, tus amigas te hacen sentir como bicho raro: se burlan de ti, te critican, te hacen menos, o simplemente te hacen a un lado," continúa Andrea.

¿Por qué tendemos a ceder a la presión de grupo?

Porque estas actitudes de rechazo tienen que ver con nuestros miedos más grandes: el miedo al abandono, al ridículo (cuánto miedo nos da hacer un súper osote, ¿no?), al fracaso o al rechazo que todos llevamos dentro. ¿Quién no tiene estos temores? ¿Se siente horrible? ¡Claro! Por lo que, dado el caso, no es fácil encontrar el valor suficiente para oponernos. Al mismo tiempo, pertenecer a un grupo nos hace sentir súper chido porque te sientes poderosa y aceptada (la frase se oye como de super héroe, pero es neto).

¿Cómo hacerle frente?

- Aprende a decir "no": dilo convencida, fuerte y claro. Te vas a dar cuenta de que al principio tus amigas igual te rechazan, pero luego, te lo aseguramos, en el fondo te admirarán por tu firmeza y te van a respetar más que antes.

- No te creas el "todo mundo lo hace": no es cierto, no todo el mundo se pierde en la jarra, no todo el mundo fuma mota, no todo el mundo lloró con las mismas películas, no todo el mundo tiene relaciones sexuales ni dice mentiras. Este es un rollo que por el simple hecho de escucharlo, hace que mucha gente se lo crea y haga "x" cosa.

- Tampoco te creas el "una vez y ya": este es otro de esos rollos que en el momento se escuchan fáciles y te convencen: "Una vez y ya, no te va a pasar nada. ¡Ay! ¿Qué tanto es tantito?" De hacerlo, pueden arruinar tu vida o te pueden dar la confianza para seguir en algo de lo que después ya no podrás salir: pisarle al acelerador, entrarle a las drogas, robar o tener relaciones con alguien que no conoces y sin cuidarte, nada más porque te dijeron y porque están de moda los deportes extremos.

- No te engañes con el "a mí no me pasa": y, ¿por qué no? Pregunta a las personas que en un segundo tuvieron un accidente y están en una silla de ruedas o les pasó algo drástico en sus vidas. A cualquiera, incluso a ti, te puede pasar todo.

- Escucha a tu cuerpo: el cuerpo es súper sabio, por medio de sensaciones te avisa de volada cuando algo no le late o no estás actuando bien. Es un mecanismo natural de conservación. De hecho, hay estudios que dicen que tu intuición es más certera en muchas ocasiones que tu propia razón. Así que ya sabes: ¡Hazle caso a tu cuerpo!

- Establece alianzas: busca a alguien que se sienta de la misma forma en que te sientes tú. Es más fácil resistir la presión cuando te sabes apoyada.

Por último, recuerda que tú eres tú, que tu vida la construyes sólo tú, y que tus verdaderas amigas son aquellas que te aceptan tal y como eres y a quienes no necesitas demostrarles nada. Así que di no a la presión de grupo y... y... y ¡no al consumo de huevos de tortuga! (bueno, no tiene nada que ver, pero se nos ocurrió).

INSTRUCCIONES

En todas las escuelas hay bolitas, así que sigue las siguientes indicaciones para completar el anuario:

- Sal al recreo / descanso de tu escuela.
- Voltea a las esquinas del patio.
- Identifica a las bolitas (si la bolita que identificaste está en medio del patio, es normal, son la bolita "véanme").
- Apunta el nombre de la bolita en el dibujito correspondiente.
- Ve a la tiendita y cómprate algo (esto no sirve de nada para llenar el anuario, pero está rico; no?).
- Selecciona a las integrantes de la bolita y escribe el nombre de cada una en las placas fotosensibles (o sea en la fotito).

Aunque la gente por naturaleza hace grupos donde se identifican, es súper importante que ubiques que ningún grupo, bolita o persona es o vale más que otro.

Cada quien tenemos gustos y afinidades distintas y eso es lo que nos hace sentir bien con nosotros mismos. El respeto a los demás es súper importante.

Acuérdate que cada persona somos un individuo y eso es lo que nos hace especiales. Si todos fuéramos iguales... qué flojera.

Mi Familia

Ahí naciste

Puedes escoger a tus amigas, a tu novio, a tu escuela, pero lo que no puedes escoger es a tu familia. En ella naciste. De ahí eres. En el mejor de los casos, la familia es una fuente de amor, apoyo y consuelo. En el peor, es fuente de dolor, frustración y gran pena. A veces, es una combinación de las dos cosas.

Es chistoso, pero muchas veces cuando eres chiquita ves a tus papás casi perfectos; crees que cómo son ellos contigo respecto a tu educación, a los valores que vives en tu familia, a cómo se tratan entre sí, o te tratan a ti y a tus hermanos, así son los papás en todas las casas.

Cuando creces y te haces un poco más independiente, empiezas a ver a tus papás y a tu familia desde otro ángulo, así como de: "Ah, caray, como que me los cambiaron." ¿Ya sabes? Te das cuenta de que son personas como cualquiera, con defectos y cualidades. Al mismo tiempo, descubres cómo funcionan otras familias, lo que te ayuda a ubicar mejor a la tuya; comprendes cómo tu familia ha influido en ti, en lo que te gusta, en lo que estás de acuer-

do y en lo que de plano no, así como lo que te gustaría cambiar (una vez más, acuérdate de que por mucho que quieras, no puedes cambiar a ninguno de tus hermanos, ni regalarlos en una rifa).

El sube y baja en las relaciones

En todas las familias hay cosas que te gustaría cambiar, cosas que a lo mejor te molestan o son dolorosas y no te queda más que aprender a vivir con ellas.

Asimismo, en todas las familias los hermanos se pelean, se odian y se adoran. En este proceso de cambios que vives, la relación con tus hermanos y con tus papás puede tener varias etapas y altibajos. Es normal: todo mundo los tiene.

También sucede que a tus papás de repente los adoras, los admiras y, de pronto, ¡los quieres matar frente a tus amigas! En ocasiones te dan orgullo y en otras quieres desconocerlos. Típico que estás con tus papás en el centro comercial y ellos, como es domingo, se fueron en pants a desayunar, todos fachosos, y a la salida te encuentras al galán que te fascina: "¿Son tus papás?" "No, para nada... ni los conozco. Deben de trabajar aquí. Pobrecitos, se ven cansados." O cuando tu mamá les enseña las fotos al niño que te gusta de cuando eras bebé y estás encueradita, quisieras desaparecer el álbum y, si se pudiera, a tu mamá también; o de plano cuando tu papá canta una canción súper retro y tú y tus cuatro amigas van con él en el coche y tú muriéndote de pena ajena.

Diferentes tipos de papás

Antes de seguir con el tema de los papás, debemos tomar en cuenta que en las familias hay de todo: las de ambos papás, las de un papá o una mamá; las que viven con los abuelos, con una tía o quizá con la nueva persona con la que tu mamá o tu papá se casaron. Así que al decir "papás" nos referimos a esa persona esencial en tu vida, con la que compartes lo bueno y lo malo, las altas y las bajas de todos los días.

¿Qué les pasa?

Como dijimos en el capítulo anterior, cuando la adolescencia te llega, por lo menos tu cuerpo te avisa, te manda señales: un pelito por aquí, una bolita por allá, cólicos por… TODOS LADOS, en fin. El asunto es que cuando tú cambias, también a tus jefes les afecta. La bronca es que a ellos nadie les avisa. Sólo piensa: cuando menos se lo esperan, su hijita, que era un niña que jugaba con las muñequitas que le regalaban, ahora sólo quiere jugar con los muñecotes (de carne y hueso) que ella escoge.

Entonces las soluciones que antes tenían para resolver las broncas, ya no les funcionan ni tantito.

Llevar la contraria: deporte nacional

¿Sabes por qué de repente les quieres llevar para todo la contraria? Lo que pasa es que, cuando somos niños, nuestros papás son nuestro modelo a seguir: queremos ser como ellos. Y realmente nos parecemos mucho, prime-

ro, por la herencia genética (carácter, habilidades; bueno, hasta las orejas de Dumbo que odias de la familia, cuando menos te imaginas… tómala, ahí las tienes); y segundo, por la educación que recibes de tus papás.

La cuestión es que una de las principales características de la adolescencia es que necesitas buscar individualidad. Tu instinto te pide que seas tú misma y ¡zaz! te das cuenta que llevas años tratando de ser como tus papás. Entonces inconscientemente decides llevarles la contraria en muchas cosas porque necesitas dejar de parecerte a ellos, para empezar a ser tú.

Ahí empieza el problema y, a veces, aunque te juren y perjuren que el cielo es azul, tú dices: "Pues yo lo veo rosa y punto." Entonces te ponen una súper castigada y se te va acabar lo rosa de tu vida (va a empezar a ser medio marrón).

En realidad, ni tus papás ni tú tienen la culpa. Se trata simplemente de una etapa que ninguno escoge: las dos partes la tienen que vivir y resolver. De hecho, ellos la pagan sin deberla.

No hay papás perfectos

Es una realidad que en todo el mundo no existe el papá y la mamá perfectos, ¿estás de acuerdo? A veces hay divorcios, problemas, discusiones, papás ausentes, hermanos postizos y demás.

Sin embargo, en la mayoría de los casos los papás te quieren y se interesan por ti como nadie más en el mundo, aunque a veces no parezca.

La relación con los papás puede ser conflictiva a cualquier edad; en la adolescencia

el asunto se pone más denso por los cambios que vives, especialmente en cómo ven tú y tus papás el asunto de la independencia. Ellos pueden sentir que pierden el control de tu vida, mientras que tú te matas para obtenerlo. La realidad es que te aman tanto, que les da pavor que te pase algo, por eso se ponen tan chockys contigo.

A ver pa, apúntale...
Voy a casa de la Jeny,
de ahí nos vamos al cine...
...y regreso en un mes.

El origen de la mayoría de las broncas

La base de todo conflicto es la falta de información. Te damos aquí un buen tip: Entre más les demuestres a tus papás que pueden confiar en ti, más se harán a la idea de que eres capaz de ser responsable y cuidarte a ti misma. ¡Te conviene!

Si mantienes a tus papás informados sobre lo que haces, a dónde vas y con quién te llevas, ayudarás a alivianar sus miedos. Cosas tan sencillas como decir la verdad y llamarles por teléfono para decirles dónde estás (hasta donde se pueda), harán que ellos se tranquilicen y que la relación sea de mutua confianza; incluso, decirles cosas que sabes que no están bien como: "Me fui de pinta." Muchas veces, lejos de regañarte, agradecen que les tengas confianza y entienden, por lo general, que de vez en cuando es normal.

Por otro lado, si no los informas funciona todo al revés: sus miedos crecen y entonces te presionan para saber más de ti, te dan menos permisos, tú te enojas; vienen los castigos, te encierras en tu cuarto y se dejan de hablar. Por supuesto, la relación se deteriora, se desgasta y todos pierden, sobre todo tú.

Me dan pena mis papás... ¡ni siquiera hablan inglés!

Se oye horrible, pero es la neta, a muchos chavos (no a todos) les pasa esto. Platicamos con muchas niñas que están ya muy adaptadas a la *cooltura* de Estados Unidos y nos platicaban cosas como estas:

- ✖ Me da mucha pena que sólo sepa 3 palabras en inglés.
- ✚ No me gusta que mis amigas vean como se viste.
- ✚ Me da flojera que siempre dicen que en su país toooodo es mejor.
- ✖ No sabe usar ni un celular, se lo doy para tomar una foto y ¡¡lo agarra al revés!!
- ✖ Me da risa como pronuncia algunas palabras.

Aunque hay muchos papás que están súper adaptados a Estados Unidos y no tienen ni medio problema con esto, hay otros a quienes sí les cuesta mucho trabajo; y ¿sabes qué? "es normal", porque en tu casa hay un choque de culturas, y puede ser difícil para todos.

Posiblemente para ti, por más hispana que seas, ir a México, Guatemala, El Salvador, _____ (pon aquí TU país) es tan difícil y extraño como ir de excursión a África.

Y para ellos también es complicado, porque la hija que ubicaban de chiquita con las tradiciones de su país, ahora la ven con un código de barras, un Mickey Mouse tatuado en la espalda y un iPod soldado en los oídos.

La verdad es que nadie tiene la culpa.

Muchos de los papás han llegado y se han sentido muy inseguros fuera de su país y para sentirse protegidos se han encerrado en una *hispanoburbuja* (¿existe esta palabra? Seguro no, pero debería existir).

Nos referimos a que algunos, al sentirse amenazados, sólo van a la tiendita de la esquina o al súper latino donde hablan español, cierran inmediatamente sus oídos cuando escuchan inglés y hasta buscan la misa que dan en español para rezar el "Padre nuestro " y no el "Our Father".

El Lic. Darío Sánchez de San Diego, con Maestría en Terapia Familiar, nos platica que es súper importante que los adultos no se aíslen y que inviertan tiempo en integrarse a la sociedad en la que viven.

También tienen que saber que necesitas formar parte de una sociedad en la que vives todos los días, y que obviamente en todo momento necesitas aceptación.

Por otro lado, también es muuuy importante que entiendas la situación de tus jefes y ubiques que no es lo mismo nacer en una nueva cultura —como en tu caso— que llegar a ella cuando ya tienes todas tus costumbres y raíces arraigadas.

Es por eso importante que tengamos tolerancia y nos pongamos en sus zapatos (sean unos tradicionales de su país o unos Nike ultramodernos).

Como ves, ambos deben agarrar la onda y respetar, pero lo que no se vale es hacerlos sentir mal, porque si le sacáramos un encefalograma a algunos papás (o sea unos mega Rayos X de la cabeza) nos daríamos cuenta...

- Que se sienten muy tristes con un rechazo de sus hijos, porque ellos han dejado su vida para darte una mejor a ti.
- Les lastima que te burles de ellos, cuando tu para ellos eres su más grande orgullo.
- Les duele que el precio del dinero y de vivir mejor, sea perder una parte de sus hijos.
- Y que seguramente han tenido mucho reconocimiento en la chamba, pero que el reconocimiento que más les interesa es el tuyo.

En fin, el asunto es que ni los problemas de ellos, ni los tuyos son sencillos, pero lo que sí es un hecho es que entre más los entiendas tú, más te entenderán ellos.

Me siento más de aquí que de allá

¿Eres de las mexicanas que juega México *vs.* Estados Unidos en *soccer* y le vas a Estados Unidos? (Aunque obvio ni de loca lo dices en tu casa… ¡y mucho menos a tu abuelita!)

O de las que no se sabe casi nada de las tradiciones de su país, pero puedes explicar el Thanksgiving tan bien, que conoces hasta el árbol genealógico del pavo que te estás comiendo.

No te preocupes, es completamente normal.

A muchos de los latinos que han vivido en Estados Unidos desde chiquitos les pasa esto, y no tiene nada que ver con no querer o tenerle cariño a tu cultura de origen.

Así que tranquila… inhala… exhala… inhala… exhala… relájate… y… y… y mejor deja de inhalar y sigue leyendo.

Hay varios puntos que hacen que te pase esto:

- Primero , que no es lo mismo vivir y crecer con las tradiciones de un país, a que casi nunca las hayas vivido y solo te las cuenten así como cuento de… había una vez.
- Segundo, que la reputación en general de los latinos en Estados Unidos, se relaciona con ser ilegales, cometer delitos y alterar el orden.

Eso obviamente hace que no tengas ni tantitas ganas de que te identifiquen con esto. No es que no te guste que te relacionen con ser latino, simplemente no te late que te etiqueten con cosas negativas.

Es cierto que algunos latinos se comportan de esa manera y han hecho que nos etiqueten en general, pero la realidad es que la mayoría somos personas trabajadoras, honradas, profesionales y muy entregadas.

Sin embargo un comentario como llamarte *wet back*, frijolero, *dirty mexican* (aunque ni siquiera seas mexicano) o hasta los más light como: "Te van a aceptar en la universidad porque eres *minority*", hacen que tengas muy presente cómo nos ven algunos.

Y como tercer punto (la tercera es la vencida), le preguntamos a varias niñas latinas que viven o nacieron en EUA qué les gustaba de vivir ahí y contestaron lo siguiente:

- Aquí se cumplen la reglas
- Me siento segura
- Me gusta la forma de vivir
- Hay de todo
- La gente no se mete con tu vida
- Todos nos respetan por estar en un país poderoso

Y siendo realista, ¿a quién no le gusta eso?, y si además le sumas que llevas toda tu vida viviendo ahí y tienes la nacionalidad norteamericana, pues claro que este país es una gran parte de ti.

Algo mega importante es que te des cuenta de que eres de las pocas afortunadas en el mundo que itiene dos culturas para aprovechar y disfrutar! ¡Puedes tomar lo mejor de cada una!

Y aunque hay muchos jóvenes latinos que se sienten orgullosísimos de sus raíces y no dejan de gritar cada vez que pueden de dónde son, hay otros que de plano no.

Por eso creemos que la opción es disfrutar lo mejor de los dos mundos. Piensa que sería una pena que dejaras a un lado:

- Una cultura tan grandiosa como las que tenemos en todos los países latinoamericanos.
- Países con riquezas naturales tan grandes que muchísimas personas viajan miles de kilómetros para poder estar ahí.
- Ser parte de las raíces de una de las civilizaciones más avanzada que ha existido en la historia.
- Un idioma que es el tercero más hablado del mundo y que miles de extranjeros están tratando de aprender.
- Unas tradiciones tan bonitas e interesantes que la mayoría de los países admiran y estudian.
- La calidez, la alegría, nuestra forma de hacer amigos, la calidad humana que tenemos… bueno hasta el ritmo para bailar y vivir la fiesta.

La verdad es como tener un tesoro y no utilizarlo, y especialmente porque es parte de ti, de tu historia.

Hoy podemos decirte que la gente de todas las nacionalidades adora a los latinos y que para nosotros, como autores de este libro, nuestro mejor pasaporte en el mundo ha sido ser mexicanos.

Esperamos que tú (y tú y tú y tú y tú y tú…) que tienes dos culturas, las ames, las goces y aproveches todo lo bueno que tiene cada una.

Nos vamos a divorciar

Es domingo y mis papás, para variar, se están peleando. Empiezan a hablar dizque bajito para que no nos demos cuenta; pero nos hemos vuelto unas expertas en cacharlos. ¡Las discusiones son tan seguidas!

Después de como 15 minutos salen de su cuarto, como si no pasara nada, aunque los dos andan de cara y no se dirigen la palabra. Pero cuando nos hablan a nosotras son súper cariñosos, yo creo que es porque se sienten culpables.

Nos subimos al coche, pues vamos a comer a un restaurante. No sé qué le dice mi mamá a mi papá que él se súper encabrona, avienta la puerta y se sale del coche. Yo me asusto horrible, y mi hermana que es más chavita se pone a llorar; mi mamá le empieza a gritar a mi papá, tanto, que ni nos pelan; has de cuenta que no estamos.

Total que todos nos bajamos del coche y nos metemos a la casa. Mi mamá persigue a mi papá hasta el cuarto y ahí se quedan peleando un buen.

Natalia y yo nos quedamos sentadas en la sala y sólo escuchamos gritos y cómo se avientan cosas. Siento horrible y mi hermana no para de llorar.

De repente se hizo un silencio que dura mucho. Mi papá, después de un rato, sale de su cuarto y se va. Nunca regresó a dormir a la casa.

Como dos semanas después nos juntaron para decirnos la frase que sabía que nos iban a decir y que no quería escuchar: "Nos vamos a divorciar".

Isabel, 15 años

¿Qué duele y por qué duele el divorcio?

La psicóloga Julia Borbolla nos dice: "Imagínate que tú vas en un avión y ves cómo el piloto y el copiloto se pelean todo

el tiempo. Uno mueve la palanca para adelante y el otro para atrás. No tienes idea de cómo manejar el avión, pero sabes que si no se ponen de acuerdo, tú te caes con ellos."

Cuando de adolescente despiertas a tu sexualidad, te das cuenta de que tus papás son sexuados también (o sea que tienen relaciones), y que además si se divorcian, ¡quedan disponibles! Esto te confunde mucho, y te conviertes en el vigilante: "¿A dónde vas? ¿A qué hora llegas?" Y como chava, te frustras porque tu mamá no se va a dejar. Eso te desgasta mucho.

Algunos jóvenes que han vivido el divorcio de sus papás nos dicen:

"Duele todo. Duele acordarme de ver a mi papá salir de la casa con maletas. Duele sentir que voy a perder mi seguridad; que quizá mi mamá no va a tener dinero para pagar lo que siempre hemos tenido. Que a lo mejor nos vamos a un departamento más chico, a otra escuela; que ella ahora tiene que trabajar y está menos con nosotros. Duele ver que mi mamá está triste y la oigo llorar."

"Sentí como si me hubieran arrancado la mitad de mi corazón, como que nunca me iba a volver a sentir segura. Mi papá me cuidaba. Duele horrible pasar por el cuarto y no verlo en las mañanas, no oler su loción. Sentí que me iba a morir sin que me cargara, me abrazara, sin sus besos y que me diera todos los días la bendición."

"Duele ya no ver a mi papá. Sentir que por mi culpa, por mis calificaciones, ellos discutían. Duele pensar que si yo hubiera hecho o no hubiera hecho algo… a lo mejor seguirían juntos. Duele tener que elegir entre los dos y que la familia se termine. Duele la impotencia; el imaginarme o ver a mi mamá con otro señor o a mi papá con otra mujer más joven. El sentir que no voy a tener el apoyo de mi papá, que ya no voy a jugar con él."

"Duele que me usen de mensajera, de espía o como si fuera yo algo negociable. Duele sentir que me abandonaron. Sentirme traicionada porque pensé que mis papas siempre estarían juntos. Duele que se critiquen uno al otro; sentirme diferente a mis amigas."

Como hijo, ¿puedes hacer algo?

- Trata de platicar tus sentimientos con algún adulto. No te los guardes. Es normal sentir miedo, coraje y soledad.
- Llora lo que tienes que llorar, es completamente normal y te va a ayudar a sacar el dolor y superarlo.
- Escríbeles a tus papás lo que sientes. Están tan ocupados en lo suyo, que quizá no te volteen ni a ver.
- Entiende que en el divorcio no hay "buenos" ni "malos". Todos sufren y pierden.
- No juzgues a tus papás como pareja, sino como han sido contigo como mamá y papá.
- Quizás rechaces la idea de ver que tus papás rehacen su vida, y te sientas mal. Aliviánate (aunque sabemos que cuesta un poquito de trabajo) y trata de entenderlos y respetarlos. Sé amable y trata a su nueva pareja como ellos tratan a tus amigos.
- Evita aprovecharte de la situación para manipular, conseguir permisos, dinero o concesiones. Esto a la larga te trae cruda moral que no te la acabas.
- No tomes partido ni te involucres en los problemas. Niégate a ser la mensajera, el árbitro, la tapadera o la reportera de lo que pasa en "la otra casa".
- Busca apoyo y unión con tus hermanos.
- No trates de sacar tu tristeza usando alcohol o drogas. De momento sentirás que te tranquilizan un poco, pero te engancharán para toda la vida. Seguro pierdes.

- No busques sexo con algún galán para sentirte querida. Lo único que va a pasar es que te sentirás arrepentida y cada vez más vacía.
- Ubica que un divorcio puede darse por mil razones, pero nunca, entiéndelo, nunca por tu culpa.
- A pesar de todo y aunque no lo creas, este episodio tan doloroso te puede llevar a ser una joven más madura, más consciente para entender la realidad y el verdadero valor de las cosas.

Finalmente, la mayoría de las chavas y chavos nos dijeron que después de todos los problemas, los gritos y las angustias, el ambiente en su casa mejoró. Que prefieren mil veces vivir como viven ahora. Después de todo, aunque duele mucho, te adaptas y te acostumbras. Así que relájate, la decisión está tomada y lo único que puedes hacer es enfocarte en hacer de ti una mejor persona, en gozar a tus papás por separado y vivir feliz con todo lo que SÍ tienes.

El novio de mi mamá, la novia de mi papá

Si vives un divorcio o el fallecimiento de alguno de tus papás, lo más normal es que tarde o temprano, tu mamá o tu papá quieran rehacer su vida. Incluso es lo mejor que puede pasar. Esto quiere decir que tendrá nuevos amigos, novio o novia, y es posible que se vuelva a casar. Es lógico.

Cuando el nuevo "novio" aparece, para ti como hija, es muy cañón ya que de alguna manera estás acostumbrada a tener papá o mamá en "exclusiva".

La soledad, la tristeza, las ganas de ser feliz, la culpa o la escasez económica, lleva a los papás a buscar una pareja (aunque a veces parece más dispareja que nada).

La bronca es que cuando las cosas parecen que van mejor, de pronto aparece este extraño/a... así de "un dos tres por mí", y obvio, te sacas muchísimo de onda.

Pero aquí viene otra situación: que ese extraño/a quiera ser tu mamá o tu papá; quiera imponer sus reglas, quiera educarte y, sobre todo, se robe la atención que antes tu papá o tu mamá te tenían sólo a ti. Y eso, por supuesto, como que no te gusta nada... Por lo mismo, puedes sentir celos, coraje, enojo y demás emociones negativas. "Mi mamá me pide que trate de quererlo, pero cómo va a ser, si ni es mi pariente."

Las relaciones con un padrastro o una madrastra pueden ser súper difíciles y tal vez hagan surgir sentimientos de culpa y coraje. Obviamente es muy difícil, pero con el tiempo, las cosas se van ajustando, y aunque te parezca increíble, si todos ponen de su parte, la situación puede mejorar muchísimo para todos.

No es necesario que quieras a la nueva pareja de tu mamá o de tu papá. Solo respétala y trátala como te gustaría que tus papás trataran a tus amigos o a tu novio.

Es importante que sepas que la mayoría de las nuevas parejas tienen como objetivo principal hacer feliz al otro; que vuelvan a sonreir y a sentir el gozo por la vida. Cosa que, después de lo que vivieron tus papás, es lo mínimo que se merecen.

Así que si te das cuenta de que con el tiempo el padrastro o la madrastra te cae bien, incluso sientes que lo/la quieres, no te sientas mal. El cariño de un papá o una mamá es insistituible.

Sólo le abriste a tu corazón otro departamento (aunque al principio le haya salido la renta carísima) y eso es bueno. Esto no le roba nada al gran espacio que le tienes a tu papá o a tu mamá.

Violencia en mi casa

Es una tristeza y una realidad saber que todavía haya algún tipo de violencia dentro de las casas de muchas familias, y esto depende de muchos factores.

De entrada, todos los días escuchamos en las noticias historias que suceden en la calle "Solidaridad", que más bien, se debería llamar "Pesadilla en la calle del infierno II".

La tele, para entretenernos, pasa varios tipos de programas con violencia. Por ejemplo, hay programas cómicos en donde los actores se agreden, se tiran mala onda, se insultan y nos reímos de eso. En las caricaturas, los personajes se cortan la cabeza o se sacan los ojos y la sangre sale como de la manguera de un bombero. Y lo vemos de lo más normal.

En los conciertos, también vemos la violencia en el escenario o la escuchamos en las letras, que a veces tienen más "piiiips", que palabras normales.

Un día, por curiosidad, cuenta todos los actos de violencia que ves y oyes en los medios. Incluye cuando una persona es sarcástica con otra o le habla golpeado, cuando se dicen groserías, cuando se falten al respeto, se hagan caras o simplemente se pasen de gandallas. Después de ver y oir eso mil veces, ¿qué mensaje crees que se nos graba en la cabeza?

Entre más violencia vemos, poco a poco ¡nos acostumbramos! Y ni cuenta nos damos.

"¡No me contestes!..." era lo que siempre me decía mi mamá. El problema no era ése, sino que se enojaba tan fuerte que una vez me cacheteó y me dejó marcadísima la cara. No me mandó a la escuela como por una semana.

Es horrible que cada vez que tu mamá te grita y se acerca, te de tanto miedo que cierres los ojos y levantes el brazo para protegerte. Siempre me pegaba con lo que tuviera a la mano. Una vez, tenía una cuchara de las que se

usan para aplastar los frijoles, y me pegó tan duro que me dejó marcados los hoyitos en el brazo.

Me daba mucha pena que me vieran los golpes.

Amanda, 18 años

En algunas casas, este tipo de violencia a los hijos se da súper seguido, o se da entre los mismos papás. Esto se llama "violencia intrafamiliar" y las hay de varios tipos: psicológia, física, emocional o sexual. Recuerda que nadie tiene derecho a maltratarte de ninguna forma.

Si en tu casa vives algún tipo de violencia, busca a un adulto de confianza y platícale. No es fácil, sin embargo hay que hacerlo para darle solución. Confía en que te va a creer.

La violencia intrafamiliar se considera un delito, que puede ser castigado con la cárcel. Tú tienes el derecho de vivir en un ambiente tranquilo. Todos lo tenemos.

Además, si de chica te acostumbras a vivir con algún tipo de violencia, de grande te parecerá de lo más normal que tu novio o tu marido te maltrate. ¡Jamás lo permitas! Ni en lo más mínimo.

Si afortunadamente no has vivido algo tan grueso como la violencia, te puede parecer increíble que unos papas torturen así a sus hijos.

Hay que comprender que por lo general estos papas a su vez fueron maltratados y no tuvieron a nadie que los ayudara; por eso no saben ni controlar ni canalizar su enojo. ¡No saben cómo! Casi siempre se trata de personas emo-

cionalmente inestables. Muchas de ellas, por lo mismo, tienen broncas de alcohol o drogas. Cuando se sienten mal
o frustrados, golpean en lugar de decir lo que sienten en
forma tranquila. Podemos comprender, mas no justificar lo
que hacen.

Los niños que son golpeados y no reciben apoyo, con el
paso del tiempo corren el riesgo de sufrir depresiones y baja
autoestima. Y lo peor es que también se pueden convertir en
papás golpeadores.

Si sufres de este tipo de abuso, o conoces a alguien que
lo viva, pide ayuda. Aquí te damos algunos centros a los
que puedes acudir. ¡Ni la pienses!

Procuración de la defensa del
menor y la familia
Xochicalco 947, México, D. F.
01 (55) 3003 2200 ext. 228

Apoyo Psicológico por Teléfono
SAPTEL 01 (55) 5259 8121

Centros de Asistencia Infantil
Comunitarios (CAIC)
Congreso 20, México, D. F.
01 (55) 3003 2200 ext. 5301

Apoyo Legal por Teléfono
VICTIMATEL 01 (55) 5575 5461

Apoyo a niños/as Víctimas de
Abuso Sexual
NIÑO TEL 01 (55) 5658 1111

Asociación para el Desarrollo
Integral de Personas Violadas
(ADIVAC)
01 (55) 5543 4700

OTROS TELÉFONOS

¡ALERTA!

Si entiendes este mensaje, urge que leas este tema (pero si no lo entiendes... también)

●●● Conversación

Cm sts? io sty pkm...
Qría dcrt q tkmmmmm, q nunk
C t olvid!
Así q Cdtm ok?

Bss xoxo

Internet

El pan de cada día...

Todo mundo está clavadísimo en internet. Seguro, de vez en cuando hasta tus papás te quieren dizque enseñar un truquito que aprendieron en su oficina. Aquí sí aplica por primera vez aquello de: "Hay papá, cuando tú vas, yo ya vengo."

La verdad es que no es cierto, el rollo de la red va más rápido de lo que sepan tus papás, tú, tus hijos y hasta tu pez beta (en caso de que tu pececito tenga mail).

Efectivamente, en internet puedes encontrar, crear, comprar, vender, intercambiar, ver, escuchar, jugar, contactar, blogear, taggear, skypear, mailear, postear, twittear (¡todo lo que termine en ...ar!) y conectar con todo el mundo. ¡Ahí está el problema!, "con todo el mundo". El rollo es que no "todo el mundo" es bueno, y hay mucha gente que utiliza este medio para aprovecharse de los demás.

Se llama red porque está conectada a millones de centrales, literalmente es una red, un tejido con múltiples co-

nexiones, pero ahora hay que tener cuidado porque, como lo hace una red, también te puede atrapar. Así que utilízala, disfrútala, y pásala increíble, pero abre muy bien los ojos para que sepas dónde navegas.

De entrada te queremos decir algo con lo que te tienes que poner a las súper vivas. Hay unos sitios que cuando los vistitas te dicen cosas como éstas:

¿Eres una niña que te cuesta trabajo relacionarte con los demás, en especial con los del otro sexo? ¿Te sientes sola en este mundo? ¿No tienes amigas? ¿Te gustaría tenerlas? ¿Te traen de bajada y se burlan de ti? No te preocupes, haz llegado al lugar ideal. Aquí te comprendemos y te ayudaremos a relacionarte.

Se escucha inofensivo, ¿no? Pues es una trampa gruesísima hecha por un grupo mundial de pedófilos —abusadores sexuales de niños y jóvenes—, que aprovechan nuestros bajones emocionales o problemas cotidianos, circunstancias que todos en algún momento hemos vivido, para atrapar a chavos y chavas y abusar de ellos.

Si a eso le sumas que muchas niñas, efectivamente, traen la autoestima por los suelos, y se sienten solas, pues se convierten en blanco perfectos de estos patanes.

Lógicamente, al principio no te dicen que van a abusar de ti, de hecho, ni al final; ni que te van a invitar a hacer cosas que aparentan ser inocentes y que en el fondo hacen que sientas que tu corazón se encoge y no te atreverías a contárselo a nadie. Estos sitios regularmente están diseñados por personas preparadas —y muy enfermos—, que de una manera convincente y sabiendo tus puntos débiles, te dicen, por ejemplo, que con ellos vas a tener una identidad, vas a sentir que perteneces a algo, vas a tener un club de amigos, ¡y aquí viene lo grueso! Te lavan el cerebro poco a poco, con dibujitos y palabras cool, hasta que crees que relacionarte con ellos es lo mejor.

Pero no creas que esto sólo pasa en otros países. ¡Estos tipos están en todos lados! Platicando con una reconocida

psicóloga de adolescentes en México, nos comentó que tiene muchísimos casos de jóvenes en esta situación. ¡Imagínate, muchas son chavas como tú!

Woow, ya se volvió a conectar dulcecita25

¿Cómo operan?

Primero tratan de convencerte para que caigas en alguna de sus trampas disfrazada de una invitación a conocerte en algún lugar, haciéndote creer que son tus amigos.

A partir de ahí, usan tus datos personales —que diste al principio, sin la menor sospecha—, te siguen para conocer tus gustos, los lugares que visitas con frecuencia, tus amigas y demás. Poco a poco se meten en tu vida y te empiezan a insistir y a comprometer con alguna foto que te tomaron sin darte cuenta, o te amenazan con decirle a tus papás algo que no te gustaría... en fin. Es importante que sepas que para nada se ven como el malo de las caricaturas. Suelen ser gente físicamente agradables, jóvenes, te llenan de regalos y son muuuuy seductores (saben muy bien su cuento).

●● OJO, mucho ojo, osea aguas, muchas aguas ●

Este tipo de "sitios" y de personas usan símbolos para su identificación. De verdad, ¡Ten mucho cuidado!

⚠ Los triángulos hablan del gusto por los niños.
💗 Los corazones por las niñas.
❀ Y las mariposas indican que les gustan niños y niñas.

Estos símbolos entrelazan un Triángulo grande con uno chico adentro, el grande representa al adulto y el chico al joven, y así sucesivamente.

Ten muchísimo cuidado con estos símbolos en los sitios de Internet, los collares, las pulseras, los llaveros, tatuajes, etcétera.

Es muy importante que lo sepas, para que pongas mucha atención y no te pase nada que puedas lamentar. Acuérdate de que si te sientes sin amigas o menos que los demás, todo está en ti. Checa en este libro el apartado de Autoestima, y cuídate de estos tipejos.

El rollo es que así como existen estas trampas, hay muchas otras, y diferentes situaciones donde cuando menos te imaginas estás siendo seguida o asediada por alguien, en los planes de secuestro de otros, en una red de prostitución o pornografía infantil y tú, ni en cuenta.

Efectivamente, la red es increíble y hay millones de cosas que puedes disfrutar de una manera padrísima, divertida y sana, lo único que tienes que hacer es mantener tus ojos muy abiertos y tus clicks muy cerrados para no caer en las redes de la red. (Chécate, al final de este capítulo, nuestras recomendaciones para cuando estás en línea.)

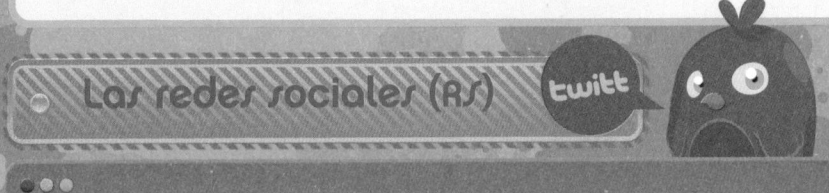

Las redes sociales (RS)

Que si Facebook, Twitter, , o (pon aquí los nombres de las que estén de moda); en fin, cualquiera de las redes sociales, además de darte un servicio, te pueden ofrecer muchos beneficios, el problema es que si no te aplicas, como ya dijimos, también te pueden dar muchas broncas.

De entrada, las redes sociales nos encantan porque te sientes aceptada en un grupo social (tus mejores amigas se llaman cybergirl54, Lily__bsb, conejitapink@2011) y ni siquiera las conoces, pero bueno.

Por otro lado, te pueden dar popularidad cuando en la escuela ni siquiera te voltean a ver; si eres diferente, te da igualdad, te hace pertenecer a un grupo que no te pelaba (el nick aquí es básico), puedes decir lo que quieras mientras en la escuela no dices ni pío; en fin, hay un buen de cosas que nos seducen de las redes sociales.

Pero así como te pueden ayudar a encontrar a tu tío perdido del otro lado del mundo, o a hacer la tarea en equipo sin salir de tu casa, también te pueden desconectar del mundo real (te conviertes en zombie de celular, con eso de que ya puedes traer todo esto en los teléfonos), hacerte sentir mal porque ya no hablas físicamente con nadie: despersonalizarte (o sea que ya ni hablas con tus amigas, sólo les escribes), leer algo feo que alguien escribió de ti (y a veces hasta te lo crees), o este rollo puede hasta causar adicción (en este último caso, nada más no te vayas a querer inyectar el mouse por las venas).

En fin, el rollo es que puedes disfrutar muchísimo las RS, y el internet en general, siempre y cuando tengas cuidado y te protejas con todas las recomendaciones básicas de la red.

RBR (Recomendaciones básicas de la red

Platicamos con varios especialistas, como Javier Matuk, experto en tecnología, sobre puntos importantísimos para que estés lo mejor protegida cuando estés en línea.

- Nunca llenes cuestionarios o ningún tipo de formas de inscripción en donde des tus datos personales como dirección, teléfono, escuela, ciudad, horarios. Con sólo

dar tu teléfono en línea es muy fácil encontrar tu dirección y llegar a tu casa.

- Siempre usa un nick (apodo) neutro en la red.
- Encontrarte con alguien que conociste en la red es un súper volado, mejor evítalo.
- En las redes sociales, nunca, nunca, pero nunca, digas dónde estás, dónde estarás o qué harás. Ni mandes fotos en tiempo real donde sea evidente saber dónde estás. Tipo enviar foto con un monumento muy conocido detrás de ti. Si mandas una foto, que sea un *close up* (toma cerrada).
- Recuerda que algunos de los "amigos" del chat y de las RS, tal vez no sean jóvenes, sino más bien adultos con muy malas intenciones. En el anonimato, cualquiera puede poner una foto de una chavita tierna de 14 años y ser un adulto inmundo y pederasta de 50.
- Muchos hackers mandan *requests* o invitaciones de supuestas redes sociales, solicitando que te metas a cierto *link* para cambiar tus datos y tu clave, ¡aguas!, alguien que ni conoces se está volando tu *password*.
- ¡Cuidado con los mensajes como "me voy de vacaciones con mis papás del 5 al 16 de octubre"!, eso significa, "pueden venir a robar mi casa del 5 al 16 de octubre". (Acuérdate que nunca sabes quién te sigue en tu red o está al pendiente de lo que haces, escribes o envías.)
- Nunca contestes correos, messenger, tweets, o como se llamen, de gente que no conoces.
- No aceptes contacto con desconocidos (mucha gente los acepta para no desairarlos, o supuestamente para no quedar mal), que no te importe: ¡no hagas contacto con gente que no conoces!
- Ten mucho cuidado con las fotos que subes o que suben tus amigos de ti, te pueden causar, hasta tronar con tu novio, o acabar con tu reputación.
- No mandes fotos en donde se pueda averiguar dónde vives o tu nivel socioeconómico. No lo olvides, mucho secuestradores buscan a sus víctimas en la red.

- Tampoco muestres cual es tu rutina diaria, pues puede ser información muy peligrosa en contra tuya.
- Nunca le des a nadie tu *password* (clave), recuerda que la que es tu amiga hoy, puede no serlo mañana.
- No dejes abiertas tus cuentas en la escuela o con tus amigas, cuando menos te imaginas se meten y te publican algo que no quieres y que tú no dijiste.
- Cuando ya no uses tus cuentas, no las dejes volando en el ciberespacio, dalas de baja. Hay quien las busca y hace mal uso de ellas. (Aunque las RS tienen medio escondida esta función porque no quieren que te salgas; ahí está, búscala.)
- Nunca mandes fotos tuyas en ropa interior o semi desnuda como para jugar con tus amigas, hay sitios que interceptan estas fotos y las suben a redes de pornografía de adolescentes.
- Cuando las redes sociales te preguntan si quieres que le avisen a todos los amigos de tus amigos que ya estás dentro, diles que NO.
- Cuando entres a una RS, pon tu perfil y tu cuenta en el la privacidad más alta.

●●● Chateo con:

Mis amigos del chat:

_____
_____
_____
_____
_____
_____
_____
_____
_____
_____
_____
_____

●●● Sigo a:

A estos sigo en el Twitter:

_____
_____
_____
_____
_____
_____
_____
_____
_____
_____
_____
_____

Capítulo 3
Quiúbole con...
mi imagen
AUTOESTIMA
ASERTIVIDAD
mi imagen interior
LO QUE DICE TU CUERPO
LAS MÁSCARAS
LA CONFIANZA EN TI

Tu imagen interior

A veces te sientes menos que los demás

Autoestima

¿Cómo te sientes cuando ves una bolita de amigas platicando y en el momento en que te acercas se callan? Inmediatamente piensas que estaban hablando de ti, ¿no?

¿Qué tal cuando no te invitan a una fiesta? Haces como que no te importa, pero casi siempre te preguntas: "¿Por qué no me invitaron?, ¿qué tengo?, ¿por qué no les caigo bien?" Te sientes poca cosa.

Cuando escuchas la palabra autoestima suena como a plática de flojerita en la escuela. La verdad es que cuando leas lo que es vas a querer saber mucho más de ella.

Para estar bien enterada

Autoestima es el valor, la confianza, el cariño que te das a ti misma. Prácticamente es cuánto crees en ti, sin importar lo que suceda a tu alrededor. Por otro lado, andar por el mundo sintiéndote la gran cosa no es sinónimo de alta autoestima (es sinónimo de ser medio mamila). ¿Te ha pasado

que muchas veces sientes que tu novio, papás, amigos o jefes no te aceptan o no te quieren lo suficiente? Pues te tenemos una noticia: eso pasa cuando no te aceptas.

La etiqueta que te pones será la que los demás lean en ti: si te sientes segura, te ves segura; si te sientes fea, te ves fea.

Si crees en ti, los demás creerán en ti. Si te caes bien, le caerás bien a los demás. Te podríamos decir que la autoestima casi casi se puede oler.

Tener baja autoestima genera un buen de broncas, desde sentirte fuera de lugar o inconforme contigo misma hasta problemas más fuertes como alcoholismo, depresión, bulimia, anorexia y algo mucho más grueso como el suicidio.

Cuando tu autoestima está alta todo tu mundo mejora: las relaciones con tus amigas, con tus maestros y, por supuesto, con tus galanes. En la escuela te va mejor y te conviertes en una niña más atractiva.

¿Te contamos un secreto? Muchísimas personas, más de las que te imaginas, tienen baja autoestima. En la adolescencia pasa mucho porque entras prácticamente a un mundo nuevo y puedes sentir que no tienes las herramientas suficientes para enfrentarlo. Pero no te preocupes: aquí te daremos unos tips para elevar la autoestima.

¿Dónde se genera la baja autoestima?

El rollo empieza desde niña, en tu casa: lo que tus papás o algún adulto te diga, ya sea positivo o negativo, influye mucho en la imagen que tienes de ti hoy en día.
Si te dijeron frases como:

¡Ay! Que mejor lo haga tu hermana/o.

¡Aprende de tu prima!

No, tú no lo sabes hacer.

Tú no puedes.

Hay, ¡qué burra! ¡Qué lenta eres!

SI TE DIJERAN FRASES COMO ESTAS...

No seas tonta.

¡Qué buena eres para hacer esto!

Te felicito, eres muy linda y responsable.

Tú sí puedes.

Qué lista, qué inteligente.

O POR EL CONTRARIO FRASES COMO ESTAS...

Naciste con estrella.

Son frases que, aunque a lo mejor ya no te acuerdes de ellas, se graban y se acumulan en el disco duro de tu inconsciente y están ahí, listas para salir cuando menos o más las necesitas. Por ejemplo, un día estás en la escuela o inclusive en un trabajo y preguntan: "¿Quien quiere ser la encargada de este proyecto?", y tú empiezas a levantar la mano, pero a la mitad del trayecto, recuerdas cosas que te han dicho o que tú te has dicho: "No, tú no lo sabes hacer", "no seas tonta", "¡Ay! que mejor lo haga tu hermana", y bajas la mano, bajas la confianza que tenías en ti por algo que no es verdad, pero que traes hace mucho tiempo en el inconsciente.

Por supuesto, muchos papás, para bien o para mal, dicen este tipo de frases sin saber la importancia que tendrán en el futuro. Además, hay que comprenderlos porque ¡tienen tantas cosas que cuidar en tu educación y formación!, que es lógico que a veces se equivoquen. Lo único que ellos quieren es lo mejor para ti. Así que ni de broma vayas a reclamarles porque nada más los vas a hacer sentir mal por algo que hicieron sin mala intención.

BRÍNCATE A LA PAG. 229

Al tener contacto con la sociedad: desde el kínder, donde le dabas de comer a los conejitos, hasta el salón de belleza o en la maestría con más prestigio, hay riesgo de enfrentar situaciones que afecten tu autoestima.

ALGUNOS EJEMPLOS:

● ¿Te ha pasado que cuando oyes a un grupo de personas platicar de un cierto tema y tú quieres participar, esperas a que la última persona deje de hablar para contar tu súper anécdota? Y cuando empiezas: "Pues fíjate que

el otro día...", nadie te escucha y alguien más toma la palabra, de volada piensas: "No pasa nada, ahora que acabe de hablar esta chava lo digo." Vuelves a intentar y la historia se repite. Entonces, subes el volumen de voz, te paras más derecha y hay quien hasta levanta la mano para pedir la palabra como en la escuela, así de: "¿Puedo ir al baño?", pero nunca te hacen caso. La realidad es que tu autoestima en esos momentos se va al sótano, ¿no? A todos nos ha pasado.

Un niño te invita a salir, se la pasan padrísimo (de hecho sientes que el tipín babea por ti), y al otro día de repente el niño no te vuelve a llamar. Lo primero que piensas es: "¿Qué hice mal?" ¿Te fijas? Tu primera reacción es culparte en lugar de pensar en otras opciones como:

Este chavo no se da cuenta de lo que valgo.	Qué tonto, no pudo conocerme.	Soy mucha mujer para él.
	Él se lo pierde.	Se fue de viaje.

¿Sabes qué? Tú no confías en ti; crees que no te habló porque le caíste mal, tu escote no estaba muy participativo o porque no te combinaba la bolsa con los zapatos. No pienses eso.

Las características físicas

Este punto es de los que más duro nos pega en la autoestima. Cuando vemos a alguien que tiene alguna característica física que llama la atención a la mayoría nos gusta bromear y decir cosas como: "No es que Laura sea fea, simplemente es varonil," "No, Jorge no está gordito, más bien es un tinaco."

Cualquier cosa puede afectar negativamente nuestra autoestima; por ejemplo, alguna característica física que, según nosotros, es diferente o especial (gordos, muy flacos, altos, muy blancos, muy morenos, con orejas chicas, con narices de alcanza queso o con problemas de acné).

¿Sabías que hasta la gente que todos podríamos identificar como muy guapa, se puede sentir horrible y diferente? Ese sentimiento nada tiene que ver con su físico, sino más bien con su autoestima.

Si tu baja autoestima es por tus características físicas, hay algunas que puedes cambiar, como el sobrepeso, el acné, la celulitis y demás (en casos como la obesidad, algunas veces por más ganas que le echas, tu cuerpo tiene una genética que no te permite bajar como quisieras). Y es cierto, hay otras que no puedes cambiar: si eres alta, baja, morena o blanca. Punto. ¡Así eres! Nadie cambia (bueno con excepción de Michael Jackson, pero ve nada más como quedó). Mejor hazte amiga de tus características y aprende a vivir con ellas. Son parte de ti, con ellas naciste, con ellas te vas a morir; siéntete orgullosa de ellas porque es lo que te hace ser única e irrepetible. No quieras tener la cara de "x" actriz famosa o el cuerpo de tal otra. Son tan pocas las modelos y galanes tipo Hollywood "auténticas", que inclusive te sabes su nombre (y si eres medio chismosita, hasta si se están divorciando o cómo se llama su perrito). ¡Imagínate!, a veces no te sabes el nombre ni de los de tu salón. La verdad es que la mayoría de las personas somos normales. Oséase... los raros son ellos.

Las máscaras

Cuando tenemos baja autoestima la podemos esconder tras diferentes máscaras:

✖ La "de flojera": son las personas que todo el tiempo están como tímidas, retraídas y aisladas. A leguas se nota su inseguridad y baja autoestima.

✚ La "no pasa nada": son aquellas personas que se sienten muy mal y deprimidas, pero cuando están con los demás actúan como si no pasara nada.

✚ La "pasada": es la persona agresiva que da ordenes a todos y se maneja todo el tiempo como líder. En pocas y sencillas palabras, trata de demostrar que es la persona más segura del mundo para esconder su inseguridad.

✖ La "doble A" (no "Alcohólicos Anónimos" sino "Autoestima Artificial"): la persona siente que, ante los demás, no vale nada. Entonces busca algo que tenga un valor ante todos, por ejemplo: ropa de marca, coches, viajes y demás. El caso es presumir y encargarse de que los otros se den cuenta de lo que valen las cosas que trae puestas: "¿Ya viste mi nueva bolsa Louis Vuitton?, costó carísima." Aunque en realidad sea piratísima y sea Luis Buitrón, ropa Armandi y lentes Versánchez, como en el fondo sientes que no vales nada prefieres darte el valor de lo que valga la bolsa.

✚ Otra típica del "doble A" es cuando conoces a un niño que sabes que es un golfo y un patán. Te dice que si quieres ser su novia y le dices que ¡sí!, pero en realidad en ese "sí", le dices ¡sálvame!, porque tu autoestima es tan baja que no te importa recibir sólo migajas de amor y seguridad: ¡aguas!

137

¿Cómo levantar mi autoestima?

Aquí viene el secreto más importante para elevar tu autoestima: una vez que conoces tus características especiales, ubica tus cualidades. Todos las tenemos y eso es lo más importante.

Tú vas a decidir qué quieres que la gente vea en ti: tus características físicas o tus cualidades como persona. Por ejemplo, puedes ser:

GORDITA ➤ Pero una chava líder.

ALTÍSIMA ➤ Pero muy simpática.

FLAQUÍSIMA ➤ Pero excelente amiga.

Recuerda siempre: la gente ve lo que tú quieres que vean. Si llegas a un lugar y piensas: "!Ay!, se me nota la llanta", "con esto me veo feísima", o "seguro le caigo mal a todos", eso es precisamente lo que la gente va a notar y a sentir de ti. Está grueso, ¿no? Si por el contrario, llegas muy segura de ti misma y te dices: "Qué guapa estoy", "se me ve un cuerpazo", "me llevo bien con todos", eso es lo que vas a proyectar.

Cuando una persona en la escuela o en algún grupo es muy querida a nadie le preocupa su físico. Todo mundo hace comentarios como: "Es una niña súper buena gente", "ella organizó la última convivencia de exalumnos, es muy movida", o "un día que estaba llorando se acercó y me preguntó si podía ayudarme en algo, la adoro".

toy bien dientón.

Pero soy bien cool.

Nadie le va a decir: "Ay, como que está muy flaca y muy morena, ¿no?" Esta persona se ha preocupado porque la gente vea sus cualidades, no sus características físicas. Por eso es muy importante que te des cuenta de que:

Tú vales por lo que eres, no por cómo te ves

Nuestra autoestima no debe depender de nuestro físico, de lo que tengamos o de cuánto nos quieran; todo eso está fuera de nosotros y escapa a nuestro control.

Lo único que puedes controlar es cómo te sientes contigo misma en la circunstancia que sea. Nadie puede bajarte la autoestima si no le das permiso. Te pueden decir cualquier estupidez para hacerte daño y no lo van a lograr, a menos que te lo creas. No le des a nadie ese placer, cree en ti y sé tú porque una persona que vale no tiene que hacer nada extra para que los demás se den cuenta de su valor.

Quiérete, trátate bien, háblate bonito, apóyate en ti misma y vas a ver qué popular y atractiva te vuelves.

Reconoce a quien tiene autoestima alta y baja

ALTA

▲ Son los que destacan en un grupito, hacen chistes, son populares.
▲ Tienen una buena comunicación con sus papás.
▲ Tienen la sensación de controlar su propia vida.
▲ Se sienten capaces, eficientes.
▲ Hablan bien de los demás.
▲ Viven sin muchas broncas.

BAJA

- ▼ Son ansiosos.
- ▼ Se enojan mucho.
- ▼ Se sienten infelices.
- ▼ Se deprimen.
- ▼ Se sienten controlados por todos y por todo.
- ▼ Critican a todo el mundo.

La confianza en ti

A veces, la publicidad en la televisión y en las revistas nos hace creer que la confianza personal se obtiene de un buen de elementos: la dieta, las pastillas para el aliento, la última moda, un aparato para hacer ejercicio (de esos que bajas 10 kilos con sólo tres minutos de ejercicio diario), un auto, etcétera. Desgraciadamente no es tan fácil. De lo que sí puedes estar segura es de que se trata de algo súper valioso, que todos podemos tener y que hay muchos caminos para lograrlo.

¿Cómo tener confianza en ti?

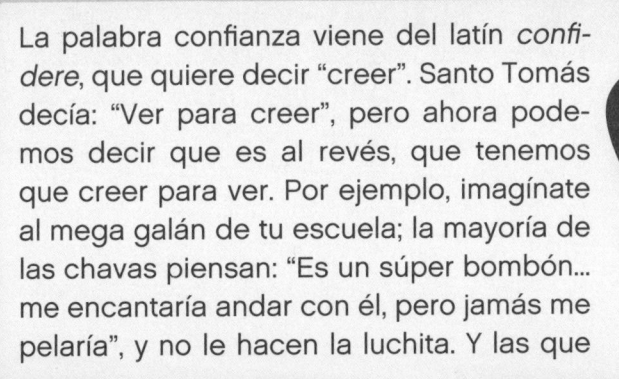

La palabra confianza viene del latín *confidere*, que quiere decir "creer". Santo Tomás decía: "Ver para creer", pero ahora podemos decir que es al revés, que tenemos que creer para ver. Por ejemplo, imagínate al mega galán de tu escuela; la mayoría de las chavas piensan: "Es un súper bombón... me encantaría andar con él, pero jamás me pelaría", y no le hacen la luchita. Y las que

tienen confianza en sí mismas, piensan cosas como: "Tengo muchas cosas que podrían fascinarle"; es decir, creen en ellas, le hacen la lucha y, por supuesto, son las que terminan con el galán que quieren.

He aquí algunas sugerencias para fortalecer la confianza en ti misma:

- Cree en ti. Ten tu "reserva de logros", o lo que es lo mismo "tu guardadito" de momentos en los que te sentiste muy bien y de los cuales te sientes orgullosa. Aliviánate con esa reserva cuando sientas baja la confianza en ti misma. Utilízala como tu súper arma secreta. Es típico que cuando te sientes así, se te va el avión de aquello que te animó otras veces. Imagina lo que quieres lograr y elimina el rollo natural de oír esa vocecita interior que te dice: "Está muy difícil", "no vas a poder", "eres malísima para eso." Cuando escuches la vocecita saca otra que le diga a la primera: "*Please*, ya deja de fregarme y cállate, ¿sí?", y piensa en el último logro que hayas tenido. Eso aunque parezca algo muy "x", cambia completamente la energía de tu cuerpo, y las cosas empiezan a salir bien.
- Disciplina. No lo vas a creer, pero entre más te disciplinas en las cosas pequeñas que te cuestan trabajo, más te respetas. Cuando pospones lo que te encanta, por ejemplo que en lugar de comerte el postre sales a correr, la seguridad en ti misma crece un buen. La disciplina te hace sentir que tienes el control.
- Empieza a creer lo que quieres. Cuando te preguntan: "¿Cómo estás?", y no andas muy bien, lo mejor es contestar: "Excelente, ¿y tú?" El sólo hecho de decirlo te hará sentir súper bien. Jamás, jamás, contestes como esas personas que pertenecen al "Club de la Lágrima Perpetua" que se la pasan de queja en queja. A ellas aplícales la ley de la glorieta: dales la vuelta pues el rollo negativo se pega.

Recuerda que "el pájaro no canta porque sea feliz, sino que es feliz porque canta..."; a menos que sea el pájaro loco y ni cante ni esté feliz, o sea, que sólo se la pase comiendo, y "el que come y canta, loco se levanta", pero como éste ya estaba loco... bueno nos entendiste, ¿no?

¿Tengo personalidad?

"¡Qué personalidad tiene!", seguramente has pensado esto al ver a un artista de cine o televisión, o al ver a alguien simplemente caminando por la calle. A todos nos gustaría que la gente pensara eso al vernos, pero, ¿qué es la personalidad?, ¿cómo la consigues?, ¿en qué se basa? Ahora ten cuidado porque si un niño te dice que tienes mucha "pechonalidad" quizá está hablando de tus bubis, no de tu seguridad; bueno, pero regresemos a lo que nos interesa...

LO QUE SE NOTA

Se siente cómoda ella misma.
Se gusta.
Se cae bien.
Se siente orgullosa de lo que es.

LO QUE SE PROYECTA

Cómo baila.
Cómo habla.
El brillo de los ojos.
Su porte.
Cómo se viste.

Cuando hablamos de cómo se viste, nunca se ve como si se hubiera tardado años para arreglarse o como si quisiera impresionarnos a propósito. La personalidad no viene simplemente de vestir padre o arreglarse mucho, sino que viene del interior; es ese rollo que te impresiona y que es muy fácil de reconocer y no tan fácil de explicar pero que todos podemos alcanzar, ¿ya sabes?

Tienes que ser auténtica

¿Por qué es tan fácil que un bebé vuelva loco a los demás? Seguramente no es por lo que hace, sabe o tiene de dinero, simplemente nos atrae por lo que es, porque en él no encontramos ninguna superficialidad, hipocresía o falsedad. Transmite sus verdaderos sentimientos por medio de su propio lenguaje (llorar o sonreír) que es transparente.

Ahí esta la clave: que seas tú misma, sin máscaras, sin miedos ni pensamientos negativos como: "Y si no les caigo bien", "y si me sale sangre de la nariz y ven que no tengo sangre azul", "y si piensan de mí que..."; ¡que te valga! Los bebés son como son y por eso son adorables. Ahora, por favor no vayas a llegar a una reunión con chupón y pañal, para ver si le caes bien a todos.

Personalidad todos tenemos, sólo déjala salir y no actúes como alguien que no eres. Cree en ti, conócete y reconoce que tienes tus monadas.

Así que no tengas miedo de mostrar tu verdadero yo y sacar el mejor partido para sentirte muy atractiva. Estamos seguros de que vas a lograr que cuando la gente te vea diga: "¡Qué personalidad tiene!" Y si también dicen lo de la ¡pechonalidad! pues ya tienes dos cosas de qué sentirte orgullosa.

¿Alguna vez se han burlado de ti? ¿Te han visto la cara? ¿Te has sentido menos? ¿Has sentido que abusan de lo buena onda que eres? O sea, ¿te resortean el brassiere o te han hecho calzón chino? Si algo de esto te ha pasado, ¿cómo te sientes? ¿Y qué has hecho al respecto?

Todo el mundo ha experimentado esto una o muchas veces. La diferencia radica en cómo respondemos a este tipo de rollos.

La mayoría de las personas intenta alivianarse con pensamientos tipo: "¿de qué sirve que me queje?", "¿para qué hacerla de tos?", "de todas maneras, no me van a hacer caso", "no puedo hacer nada", o "si protesto, me va a ir peor", y demás. Cada vez que nos quedamos con esa frustración, nuestra autoestima se hunde.

La solución, por supuesto, no está en tirar mala onda o querer romperle la cara a quien te molesta, tipo "lucha en lodo". A la larga, también terminamos frustrados y con muy mal sabor de boca. La solución es ser asertiva.

Ser asertiva significa:

no sé decir "no", o lo que es lo mismo, ¿cómo ser asertiva?

Ser asertiva es:

✖ Decir tranquilamente que algo no te late.
✚ Atreverte a decir "no" a lo que no te gusta, no quieres, no puedes, te incomoda y demás. Sólo dos letritas juntas: n+o= ¡no! ¿Ves qué fácil?

✖ Exigir un derecho con seguridad y decencia.

✦ Hablar claro, sin rodeos y sin ser grosera.

✖ Por supuesto, ser asertiva es algo que se aprende. No nacemos sabiéndolo y no lo hacemos así nada más, de repente.

El doctor Moriarty hizo un estudio con la ayuda de sus alumnos de psicología en Nueva York. Los invitó a participar en situaciones en las que hacían pomada los derechos de los demás, para ver su reacción y qué onda con su asertividad.

Uno de los alumnos comenzó a tocar rock pesado a un volumen muy alto junto a otros que tenían que concentrarse en una tarea muy cañona.

Ochenta por ciento de los alumnos no se quejó. Luego admitieron lo mal que la estaban pasando.

Quince por ciento pidió al músico que le bajara pero no lo volvieron a hacer después de que les contestó agresivo.

¡Imagínate! Sólo cinco por ciento insistió y logró que el otro monito le bajara.

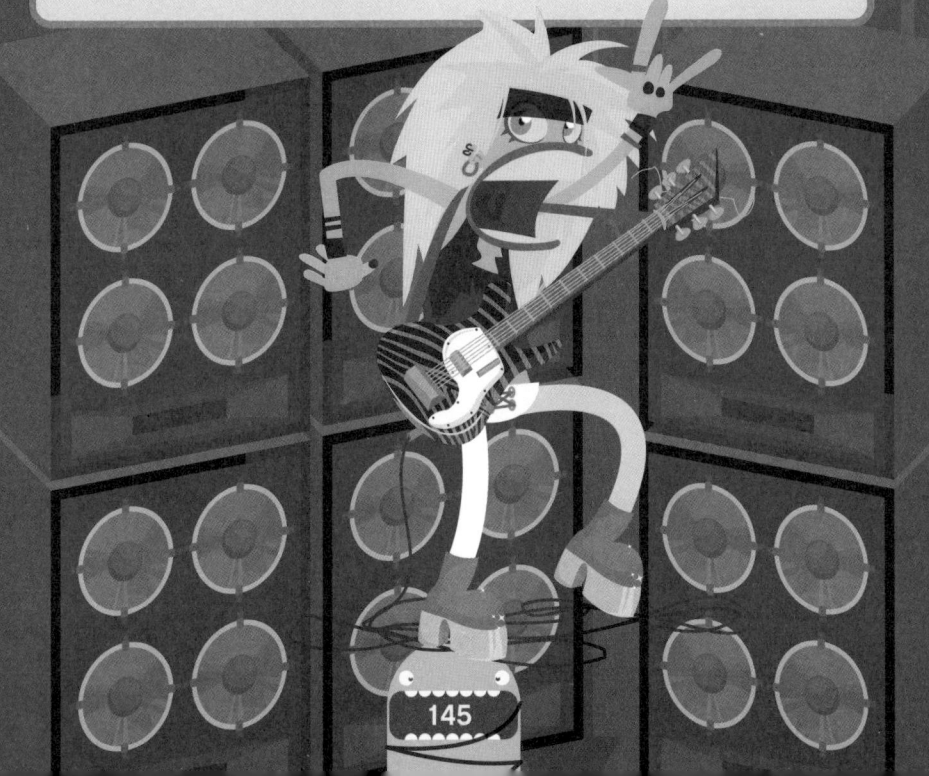

TEST:
Y Tú, ¿qué tan asertiva eres?

INSTRUCCIONES PARA EL LLENADO DEL TEST

5 = SIEMPRE
4 = CASI SIEMPRE   2 = CASI NUNCA
3 = A VECES   1 = NUNCA

CUANDO ME QUEJO POR ALGO:

Lo digo tal cual □

Me detengo a pensar en cómo decirlo de la mejor manera posible sin pasarme □

Considero las consecuencias antes de hablar □

Le pregunto antes a la persona el porqué del problema para evitar broncas □

Sin enojo describo lo que me molesta □

Expreso lo que siento □

No insulto ni le echo la culpa a nadie □

Propongo una solución si es necesario □

Lo digo claro y fuerte □

Miro a la persona directo a los ojos □

TOTAL: □

50 = MUY ASERTIVA
25 o menos = SERÍA BUENO QUE TE APLICARAS MÁS

Lo que tenemos que hacer es identificar qué nos molesta, qué sentimos y decirlo sin rodeos y sin perder el objetivo.

¿Cómo puedes ser asertiva?

- Aliviánate a la hora de la saludada. A todo el mundo le cae muy bien que lo saluden tipo: "¡Quiúbole! ¿Qué onda? ¿Cómo estás? ¡Qué gusto verte!", en lugar de oír un tímido: "Hola", o que saluden con la cabeza sin decir una palabra.

- Al opinar expresa lo que sientes. Por ejemplo, en lugar de decir: "esa película está horrible", di: "A mí no me gustó esa película", "a mí me encanta", "a mí me cae muy bien fulana", y demás.

- Lo tuyo es tuyo. Si alguien te dice un cumplido acéptalo y contesta: "Gracias, a mí también me gusta esta blusa," en lugar de: "¿Te gusta?, pero si está viejísima." Esta última respuesta es como si alguien te diera un regalo y se lo aventaras en la cara.

- Pregunta: "¿Por qué?" cuando te pidan hacer algo que no te parece razonable o no te late, di: "¿Por qué quieres que haga eso?"

- Pide que te aclaren. Si alguien te explica o da instrucciones y tú no entiendes nada, no te vayas confundida y sin saber qué hacer. Al contrario, tranquilamente di: "No entendí bien, ¿me puedes explicar otra vez?"

- Siempre expresa lo que no te late. Si opinas o piensas diferente, di con confianza: "fíjate que yo lo veo de otra manera", "yo opino que...", "creo que hay muchas cosas en las que no hemos pensado, como..."

- Defiende tus derechos. Nunca dejes que alguien te haga sentir menos. Di: "perdón, pero estoy formada y sigo en la fila", "llegaste media hora tarde a la cita", "por favor, trae tu propio lunch", "disculpa, ¿podrías besar a tu propio novio?"

Beneficios de ser asertiva

- Te vuelves protagonista de la vida y no esperas pasivamente a que las cosas pasen.
- Tu autoestima se eleva.
- Te sientes tranquila. Hay congruencia entre lo que piensas y lo que haces.
- Te sientes libre al aprender a decir "no".

Así que vale la pena ser asertivo. Es algo que, una vez que lo pones en práctica, te hace sentir muy bien contigo misma.

Quiúbole con...
Capítulo 4
mi SEXUALIDAD
LOS BESOS
EL ACOSO SEXUAL
EL SIDA
EL FAJE
LOS CONDONES, PASTILLAS, JALEAS...
LAS ENFERMEDADES DE TRANSMISIÓN SEXUAL
LA VIRGINIDAD
LAS DROGAS DE LA VIOLACIÓN

El rollo de la sexualidad

La sexualidad es algo con lo que estamos conectados desde que nacemos hasta el día en que morimos y encierra una gran responsabilidad. Las decisiones que tomes serán súper importantes en tu vida; si se te hacía difícil escoger qué blusa ponerte con qué falda, espérate a ver qué onda con esto. Para vivir bien tu sexualidad es básico tener la mayor información posible.

Entenderla y manejarla de manera inteligente y segura es un rollo que toma tiempo. Y, ¡obvio!, lo que te expliquen en la escuela, lo que tus papás platiquen contigo y lo que leas, te ayudará mucho. Lo importante es que te informes bien y no quedarte sólo con las chocoaventuras que tus amigas te cuentan o ves en los medios para tomar la mejor decisión.

¿Cómo tranquilizar a tus papás cuando te hablan de sexo y se ponen nerviosos?

Cuando escuches la siguiente frase, significa que llegó el momento:
"Laura, Ale, Ana, o Pau, (pon tu nombre aquí), si está muy largo, ponlo acá (   )
quiero que platiquemos."

Esta frase no falla cuando tus papás quieren hablar de sexualidad contigo. Se ponen serios, empiezan a caminar

como locos en el cuarto, miran hacia otro lado, sudan, no contestan el teléfono, en fin. Pobrecitos, se sienten súper incómodos y nerviosos, así que ayúdalos. Si tus papás son abiertos en el tema entonces no tienes bronca, pero si no, es importante que sepas qué pasa.

De entrada es súper natural. Seguro que a ellos sus papás jamás les tocaron el punto porque era ¡tabú! Y mucho menos lo hablan con la naturalidad con la que tú lo haces. Así que ayúdalos, ponles atención y entiende que lo hacen porque te quieren, que les cuesta trabajo pero que tienen experiencia y vale la pena escucharlos.

RAYOS X

¿Cuándo empieza?

Las primeras sensaciones de tipo sexual empiezan por lo general en la pubertad. Obvio, algo nuevo, muy nuevo está pasando. Por ejemplo, el interés por el otro sexo despierta de pronto y los hombres, que antes veías como niños babosos, ¡ahora te parecen unos cueros! (bueno, algunos se quedaron igual). El asunto es que comienzas a ponerte roja cuando ves al niño que te late, a sentir mariposas en el estómago y esas cosas. ¡Aguas! Al rato la mariposa eres tú y a los chavos les gusta coleccionarlas.

La atracción sexual

Cuando un niño te gusta se despierta una sensación muy particular. De hecho, es algo tan padre pero también extraño. Lo que te puede parecer atractivo de un niño a tu amiga le puede chocar.

En la sexualidad, los cinco sentidos juegan un papel súper importante porque percibimos el mundo a través de ellos: la vista, el olfato, el tacto (éste es de los favoritos de los hombres), el oído y el gusto.

Tu sistema límbico en el cerebro interpreta la información que éstos le mandan, y a su vez envía mensajes a las distintas partes del cuerpo para que respondan sexualmente: es una pasadera de información que te va a tener súper ocupada y contentita, como dicen por ahí, por el resto de tus días.

Las etapas de la sexualidad

El deseo

Sin el deseo, la sexualidad se convierte en algo mecánico y nada agradable. Esta primera etapa es totalmente psicológica. Desear al otro es tener ganas de tocarlo, de estar con él, de tener fantasías, de conocerlo mejor, o sea, lo que hoy se conoce como "chocar sus carritos", "darse sus topes", "siempre sí", o como tú le quieras decir.

Pero aquí debes ser muy inteligente para decidir si controlas tu deseo o de plano haces que se enteren hasta tus vecinos (bueno, eso no es muy difícil porque los vecinos se enteran de todo).

Eso sí: recuerda que todas, hasta la más mínima de tus elecciones tienen consecuencias.

El contacto físico

La piel es un receptor mega sensible. Al mínimo contacto con el niño que te late (ya sea que te toque el brazo, te tome de la mano o sientas su cachete al saludarlo), tu cerebro recibe de inmediato señales que cambian la química de tu cuerpo.

Puede pasar que te suden las manos, te pongas roja, el cerebro se te nuble y digas tonterías, así como preguntarle dos veces su nombre, cinco veces su edad o empezar a contestar babosadas. Esto pasa porque mientras te pregunta algo tú estás pensando en cómo te ves, en la forma de disimular que te gusta; en fin, es muy chistoso.

Si los dos se empiezan a gustar y este rollo avanza como debe, puede ser que estén a punto de conocer más de cerca sus boquitas. Recuerda, entre más retardes este paso, estará más loco por ti el niño.

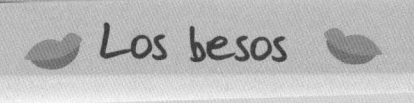

Los besos

También conocido como kiko, kikorete, ósculo (se oye horrible, pero es verdad), en fin, como lo conozcas, un beso es padrísimo y mágico; nos hace entrar a una dimensión que ninguna palabra puede describir. Advertencia: a veces es mágico, porque el cuate después del beso desaparece, así que ¡ojo!

Besar es compartir en todos los sentidos, representa el inicio de una entrega, por lo que es súper personal y delicado. Es la suma perfecta entre dos personas, por eso si te lo das con un cuate "x", se va a sentir exactamente así... "x". Y si además el cuate usa brackets y no sabe besar, prepárate para que tus labios queden como trapeador.

Los besos varían según el ritmo, la intensidad, el sentimiento y el deseo. Cuando le das un beso a alguien, puede ir desde un saludo de buena onda, como: "Hola y adiós", a un beso de cariño, de despedida o uno muy intenso, amoroso y apasionado (esos de: "¿Me regresas mis labios por favor?").

El primer beso, como nueva experiencia, generalmente es padrísimo y siempre lo vas a recordar. Es súper importante que disfrutes cada instante.

También puede ser que estés nerviosa por ser la primera vez y te sientas vulnerable por tener un contacto íntimo con el niño. Aquí pueden preocuparte mil cosas, tipo "¿qué va a pensar de mí, de mi poca o mucha experiencia, de mi cuerpo, del tamaño de mi boca, de mi olor? Hubiera masticado chicle, ¿por qué me tiemblan las rodillas?", y demás. No te preocupes, es natural que te sientas nerviosa en esta primera experiencia de tipo sexual.

Con brackets... juntos para siempre

smuack

155

KISS

No sé besar

¿No sabes besar? No te preocupes: aunque un primer beso es como saltar del *bungee* (si al galán le huele la boca, es como brincar sin cuerda), cuando hay química las cosas se dan solitas. Entre más relajada y tranquila estés, mejor (ahora sí que, flojita y cooperando, nada más aguas, no te vayas a pasar de cooperativa).

Si no sabes qué hacer tienes de dos:

- Decirlo con confianza. El niño te sabrá llevar y si no, copia lo que él hace (recuerda que aquí no puedes sacar acordeón).
- Si no quieres que te bese, también dilo. Nadie te puede forzar a hacer algo que no quieres.

Siento que me muero de nervios

Entre más a gusto te sientas con tu galán, es más probable que te sobrepongas rápido a la ansiedad, o sea, que te alivianes. Piensa que los hombres, como comentábamos, también se sienten inseguros y tienen en la cabeza las mismas preocupaciones que tú.

Besos malísimos

También hay veces en las que el beso que tanto soñaste resulta que ni al caso. Tal vez el niño estaba tan nervioso que la regó.

El faje

Palabra que tus papás con seguridad detestan. También conocido como "fax", "llegue", "agarrón" o ya de plano, lo más cursi de lo cursi, "nos dimos unas caricias" (¡no, por favor!, eso sí suena nefasto). Bueno, el rollo es que el faje, después del beso, es la segunda experiencia de tipo sexual que puede ocurrir.

Un faje es intercambiar besos, abrazos y caricias, es tocar y permitir que te toquen. Como cada persona tiene distintas ideas y valores relacionados con la sexualidad, el faje para algunos puede ser natural y lógico dentro de una relación amorosa, y para otros no tanto. Lo importante es que estés consciente de lo que TÚ quieres y de que te sientas cómoda, segura, de hasta dónde quieres llegar. Sólo tú decides.

Cuando sucede, el olfato capta una sustancia que despide el cuerpo llamada feromona y que ayuda a mantener muy arriba el deseo amoroso. Por eso dicen que el olor del cuerpo de la persona que amas es el mejor estimulante sexual. Ahora que si tu galán no se ha bañado en los últimos tres días, más que atraerte a ti, va a atraer ¡pero a las moscas!

Ahora, tu novio puede ser tan educado que casi casi te manda una invitación que dice:

Tengo el gusto de invitarte este jueves a las 17:00 horas al evento denominado:

"Faje entre Cynthia y Julio"

Que se llevará a cabo en la sala de mi casa.

Posteriormente, agradecemos su presencia en el banquete.

R.S.V.P.

Ropa Interior Sexy Rigurosa

Por otro lado, puede ser un patán y más que parecer "osito de peluche" parezca "pulpo de cuarta" porque sus tentáculos van más rápido que tu vista.

El faje es como la carreterita que conduce a hacer el amor, así que toma tus precauciones si ésta no es tu decisión. Ojo, porque hay una línea muy delgada y, si la cruzas, es difícil regresar sólo a los besitos. Corres el riesgo de que ya encarreraditos los dos, la carreterita va de bajada.

Si decides tener un faje con tu novio, las primeras veces te puedes poner como nerviosita porque no lo conoces. Es natural. Pero una vez que te presentan al faje, le dirás: "¿Cómo no te conocí antes?"

Ahora, no te claves mucho. Si le entras a todo con cada monito que quiera contigo puedes terminar con fama de wila o de pizza, porque se entrega máximo en 30 minutos.

La excitación

Ahora vas a conocer el verdadero significado de la palabra "excitante". ¿Qué pasa en tu cuerpo? Cuando tu cerebro recibe un estímulo (como cuando ves a un galán que te fascina), manda señales para que la presión sanguínea y el ritmo cardiaco aumenten. Aquí es cuando sientes que literalmente ise te sale el corazón! Esto manda un mayor flujo sanguíneo a los genitales, alerta los sentidos y aumenta la sensibilidad en toda la piel, o séase ique te estás derritiendo!

Si el interés sexual es súper en serio, empieza la lubricación vaginal y los pezones se pueden poner duros.

Faje dactilar

Primero, es básico saber que si permites que el faje suba de tono, como ya se dijo, pueden entrar a un punto de encarreramiento mucho más difícil de controlar y detener. Tu cuerpo, con seguridad va a sentir placer y te va a pedir más, pero debes de preguntarte si estás lista y preparada. Y segundo, como el faje dactilar consiste en que el hombre toca los órganos sexuales de la mujer con los dedos, y aunque la vagina tiene una flora bacterial que la equilibra y protege, puedes conseguirte una infección que sólo un médico puede ver y tratar adecuadamente; por lo que es muy importante que, dado el caso, los dedos estén limpios.

El coito

Para entender bien la onda podríamos decir que los besos son llegar a primera base, el faje ir a la segunda y el coito de plano batear un *home run*. En términos muy claros el coito es

la penetración. En términos románticos es la culminación del amor, la unión física más íntima de dos personas, siempre que exista una entrega voluntaria total.

El orgasmo

HOMBRES **0** MUJERES **1**

Tan buscado por muchos, es el punto culminante en una relación sexual. Sucede cuando la excitación y la tensión muscular llegan a su punto máximo, gracias a las contracciones musculares (que tú no controlas) de los genitales, el útero y el ano.

Es mega difícil describir cómo es un orgasmo porque los hay de muchos tipos y cada quien lo experimenta de forma diferente. Hay quienes lo describen como una gran acumulación de tensión y rigidez que termina en una súper explosión o en una sensación placentera de alivio. O sea que, si el coito es un *home run* el orgasmo sería como ganar la Serie Mundial de beisbol.

También es posible no ganar la Serie Mundial. Muchas mujeres no han tenido un orgasmo en su vida, ya sea porque su cuerpo todavía no está listo o porque su pareja no ha sabido estimularlas. Algunas lo descubren años después de haberse iniciado con su pareja en este rollo de la sexualidad; porque con la madurez se sienten más tranquilas y seguras de lo que hacen; otras lo obtienen sin problemas. De hecho, si alguien vendiera mapas para llegar al orgasmo se volvería millonario.

La mujer es multiorgásmica; es decir, puede tener varios orgasmos en una sola relación. El hombre sólo puede tener uno por relación sexual. Marcador final: mujeres 1, hombres 0.

La relajación

Después del orgasmo se siente como si caminaras en el paraíso: te relajas y el cuerpo regresa a su estado normal. El ritmo cardiaco y la respiración se regularizan. Aun sin orgasmo, el cuerpo regresa poco a poco a su estado normal. Lo malo es que muchos hombres se duermen a media caminata por el paraíso.

Espacio para que dibujes tu paraíso ideal:

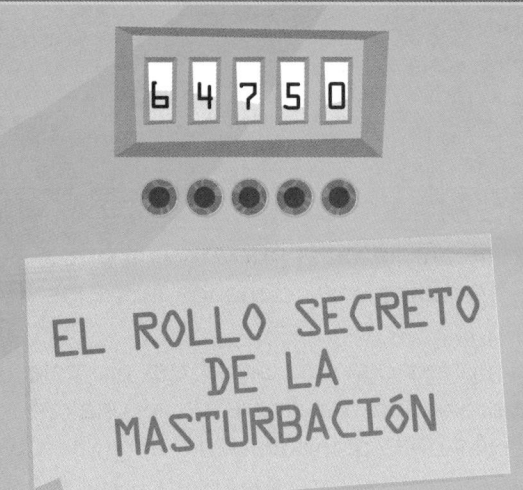

EL ROLLO SECRETO DE LA MASTURBACIÓN

De ley este tema no se toca; ¿por qué? Porque es algo muy íntimo. Sin embargo, en la exploración y conocimiento de su cuerpo, es un hecho que algunas niñas y la mayoría de los niños se masturban. A otras no les hace falta o, simplemente, este tema les tiene sin cuidado.

Según el diccionario, masturbación "es la acción de proporcionarse placer sexual estimulando los órganos sexuales con la mano u otro medio". Es una manera de conocer tu cuerpo y encontrar qué te causa placer y cómo respondes. Esto no significa que si eres de las niñas que no se masturba tienes algo raro; para nada. Algunas personas no se masturban sino hasta que son adultas o cuando tienen una relación madura y estable. Otras, como dijimos, nunca se masturban y no pasa nada. Lo importante es que te sientas a gusto y tranquila con lo que haces.

Existen mil mitos e historias acerca de lo que te puede pasar si te masturbas. Ninguno es cierto. Todos los bebés tocan sus genitales instintivamente para conocer su cuerpo y después lo repiten porque descubren placer en ello.

En realidad no hay ningún tipo de peligro en masturbarte. De hecho, es una manera de tener sexo seguro; no te puedes embarazar ni contagiar. El único riesgo es que pesques una infección si no te lavas bien las manos antes de tocarte.

Los hombres y el sexo

Los hombres empiezan la pubertad un poco después que las niñas, más o menos entre los 10 y los 14 años.

Todo empieza con una señal del hipotálamo (aunque parece nombre de animal, es una región del cerebro) y de la glándula pituitaria: juntos hacen que los hombres empiecen a producir testosterona y ahí empieza el rollo.

Los principales órganos sexuales del hombre son los testículos y el pene (posiblemente lo conoces como pilín, pajarito, pipí, pirrín, etcétera). Sólo existe algo que preocupa a los hombres más que el futbol, y es el tamaño del pene. El pene deja de crecer más o menos a los 18 años y la medida promedio de los latinos, cuando llega a su tamaño final, es de 13 centímetros, siempre y cuando no esté dormidito.

En las relaciones sexuales, un pene grande puede lastimar y uno muy chico puede casi no sentirse, pero es común que los chavos lo tengan tamaño estándar.

Los hombres son muy sexuales y muchas veces su principal interés contigo puede ser sexual, así que ponte muy buza. Quizá un chavo te haga sentir, o pienses tú, que no hay amor más sincero: te lleva flores, te escribe cartas súper profundas, te baja el cielo y las estrellas, pero en realidad, es muy posible que sólo esté tratando de enamorarte para llegar a otra cosa. También existen los hombres que de corazón se enamoran y respetan todas tus decisiones.

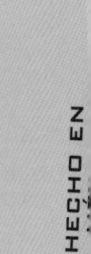

HECHO EN

Tamaño "Latino" estándar

A los 18

CON QUIÚBOLE LOS PAJARITOS

REGLA DE PAPEL BIEN EXACTA

Dormidito

Así como tú tienes algunas inquietudes en el rollo de la sexualidad, los hombres tienen las suyas; una de ellas es el tema de la erección (cuando la sangre se concentra y el pene se alarga y se pone duro para la penetración). El hombre tiene la erección cuando hay estimulación física o simplemente con pensamientos de tipo sexual, pero también puede ser así de repente y sin causa; o sea, puede tener una erección a cualquier hora por lo que puede despertar con el calzón como tienda de campaña.

Si te toca que a cierto amigo, hermano o primo tuyo se le despierta el amiguito, sé buena onda e ignóralo para que su amiguito se vuelva a dormir, y no empieces con preguntas como "¿Por qué no te sales de la alberca, vente ya todos se salieron?" O "Ya párate, no seas flojo; a ver, no me voy de aquí hasta que te levantes de la cama."

Relaciones sexuales

O lo que es lo mismo, "¿lo hago o no lo hago?"

Todos nos hemos planteado el punto de cuándo hacer el amor o no. Y neta, esta cuestión también dio vueltas en la cabeza de tus papás, tus abuelitos y hasta tu novio (aunque él diga casi casi que ilustró el Kamasutra).

Cada quien tiene distintas creencias, educación y teorías sobre tener o no tener relaciones sexuales. Hay que respetarlas. Recuerda que nunca debes sentirte presionada a hacer algo que no te late, no quieres, no estás segura o simplemente, te incomoda. TÚ decides.

Tener relaciones sexuales con amor y responsabilidad es la forma más cañona e intensa de comunicación, unión y amor que puede existir entre una pareja. Aquí se involucra todo: el cuerpo por supuesto, la cabeza, el alma y, ojo, el corazón.

Cuando se hace por presión, sólo por buscar placer o por puritita curiosidad, puede ser una experiencia insatis-factoria o hasta traumática, que puede tener repercusiones como sentirte usada o con un enorme sentimiento de vacío y soledad. Es súper importante que no te apresures: toma el tiempo suficiente para tomar una decisión, asegurarte de que tú y tu galán se quieran y se comprometan responsa-blemente antes de dar el paso.

Pero, ¡aguas!, piensa que a tu cuerpo lo puedes proteger para no embarazarte o no "ganarte" una infección de trans-misión sexual (ITS), o una enfermedad como el sida; pero a tu corazón y autoestima, ¿cómo los proteges?

Que no te pase

Muchos adolescentes confiesan haber empezado su vida sexual sin desearlo, llenos de dudas o presiones (como cuando el novio es mayor que tú y te presiona). Las razo-nes más frecuentes que escuchamos de las niñas son:

✖ No pude decir "no". Es importantísimo saber decir "no", so-bre todo cuando te presionan, así que si no sabes cómo negarte, checa la sección "No sé decir no (asertividad)".

✖ El alcohol. Cuando te tomas unos chupes tus sentidos se atontan y, como dicen las mamás: "Las cosas que al principio no te quedan, al ratito dan de sí," o sea, te puedes volver más cooperativa que una asociación al-truista, así que buza con los *drinks*. Ten en cuenta que a las mujeres se les sube mucho más rápido la misma

cantidad de alcohol que consumen los hombres. Además, el sexo puede ser muy divertido en el momento, pero no al día siguiente cuando tienes borrado el disco duro y no te acuerdas de lo que pasó. El remordimiento puede ser horrible; además ¡qué tal si te embarazas a la primera! ¡Porque claro que es posible!

✖ Temor. A veces, el miedo de lastimar a tu novio o a que te truene y se vaya con la niña guapa del otro salón, hace que aceptes tener sexo con él. ¡Ubícate! Recuerda que si eso es sólo lo que busca, cualquier niña se lo puede dar (la del salón de enfrente, la del salón de atrás, bueno hasta la chava de la tiendita). Tú eres alguien especial y diferente y él te debe querer por eso, por ti, por lo que eres, no por tu cuerpo. Si no es así, y tú te das cuenta, que le llegue a la que quiera. Recuerda que para los hombres una mujer que se da a respetar es ¡todo un reto! y mucho más interesante. Por eso los hombres clasifican a las mujeres en las que son para echar relajo y las que son para andar en serio.

✖ Presión. Otro rollo que te puede orillar a hacerlo es sentirte presionada o manipulada por tu novio, con la famosa "prueba de amor" (¡esto ya no debería pasar ni en las películas!). Es una forma de manipularte muy pasadita de moda. Si es tu caso, lo mejor es hablar netas con él, con amplias posibilidades de mandarlo a volar. Seguro estarás incómoda, pero será peor si te quedas callada. Recuerda que más vale sola que con ¡un pulpo de cuarta!

A veces las amigas que ya tuvieron relaciones te pueden presionar a que lo hagas, no de manera directa sino con comentarios como: "¡Es lo máximo!", "¡Tirarte a un niño es de pelos!", "¡No sabes lo que te pierdes!", "¡Todas lo hacen!", "¡Ya te tardaste!" Recuerda que la decisión es tuya y sólo tuya.

✖ **Desamor.** También es súper importante que sepas que algunas niñas que tienen relaciones sexuales lo hacen porque de alguna manera se sienten solas y desean sentirse queridas o aceptadas. Y al contrario, terminan sintiéndose más solas. Ser querida o aceptada se logra con menos complicaciones, como quererte y aceptarte por lo que eres, obvio, por lo que vales.

✖ **Los medios.** De una u otra manera el sexo está súper presente en los medios de comunicación. Nos lo ponen como algo fantástico, maravilloso y sale hasta en la sopa. La verdad es que las imágenes no son reales. En la mayoría de las escenas romanticonas de anuncios o películas, los modelos se acaban de conocer y son profesionales; por eso están tan guapos (si no, todo mundo tendría un galán de esos en su alacena) y, por supuesto, les pagan una buena lana por hacer su trabajo. Así que no te la creas; en la realización hay muchas repeticiones de tomas, ediciones, retoques, rellenos, bubis operadas y efectos especiales.

Algunos riesgos

○ Te puedes embarazar y hacer que tu vida dé un giro de 180 grados.

○ Si no existe comunicación honesta entre los dos, un amor verdadero, o la confianza ciega para ponerle, literalmente, el cuerpo en sus manos, puede ser una experiencia muy mala. Si existe todo lo anterior, el panorama es distinto.

○ Puedes contraer una ITS (Infección de Transmisión Sexual), o ser víctima del sida (Síndrome de Inmunodeficiencia Adquirida).

- ¿Sabías que, de acuerdo con estudios realizados por The Medical Institute for Sexual Health, es cuatro veces más probable que contraigas una ITS a que te embaraces?
- Se te puede hacer fama de "zorra". Puede ser que un niño quiera una niña bien y si sabe que te has acostado con muchos desista de salir contigo o quiera tu teléfono para la despedida de soltero de un amigo. Ya, en serio, vivimos en una sociedad que, nos guste o no, juzga muchísimo; acuérdate que la reputación es súper importante, cuando se daña es como si tiraras agua en la tierra, ¿cómo la recoges?
- Algunos hombres pueden llegar a ser peores que una revista quincenal de chismes: donde los encuentres tienen algo qué chismearte, así que pueden dañarte con sus comentarios.
- Puedes tener unos mega sentimientos de culpa, especialmente cuando lo has hecho por presión de tu novio o por intentar parecer cool con tus amigas.

¿Qué pasa si te esperas?

- Vas a sentirte súper tranquila, sin arrepentimientos por haberlo hecho sin estar preparada.
- Vas a estar tranquila porque no te embarazas, porque no te contagiaste y porque no le debes nada a nadie.
- Se ha comprobado que, entre más se espera la pareja, sienten más control sobre su vida.

- Recuerda que te quedan muchos años por delante para disfrutar de una vida sexual con quien elijas y cuando quieras.
- Cuando somos jóvenes creemos ser súper maduros; la verdad es que no, y en este rollo donde te juegas el corazón y muchas cosas más, es importantísimo estar preparada, así que entre más te esperas, más madura eres.
- Cuando te esperas, construyes tu relación con el respeto y el compromiso.

Pon tus límites

Si de repente sientes que tu noviecito súper mono se convirtió en un monstruo mano larga, o sea, que van rapidísimo y como que ya no te está gustando la cosa, tienes todo el derecho de detenerlo en cualquier punto y por cualquier razón. El niño te debe hacer caso inmediatamente.

Entre los hombres se maneja este dicho: "Los hombres llegan hasta donde las mujeres quieren", y es neto. Si insiste y no quieres, sé más firme y repítelo para que entienda. Si no capta, mándalo a volar. Un niño que vale la pena comprenderá y respetará tus decisiones. Por otro lado, el respeto debe ser de ambos. También puede suceder que el niño te dice que no y tú te lo quieres cenar completito. Respétalo. ¡Pobrecito!

Finalmente, creemos que en la actitud hacia la virginidad importan cosas como la educación, el ejemplo de tu familia, tus valores, amigos y creencias religiosas. Sin embargo, es algo que sólo tú puedes decidir. Lo importante es defender tu idea, sea cual sea, y respetar la forma de pensar de los demás.

¿Por qué se dice "hacer el amor"?

Realmente, se hace el amor cuando dos personas se aman, se respetan, esperan el momento adecuado y buscan darle placer al otro y a sí mismos.

Tener sexo por sexo es muy diferente, es un acto "físico-calenturiento" sin que necesariamente exista amor y respeto, en este caso el único fin es sentir placer.

La abstinencia

Aunque para algunas personas es casi casi una palabra prohibida, la abstinencia es hoy una opción para muchos jóvenes. Está tan denso el asunto de las ITS y de los embarazos no deseados, que hoy en día muchos chavos consideran la abstinencia en serio.

Entrevistamos a 30 niños de 17 y 18 años y nos encontramos con que siete habían optado por la abstinencia. Sí, leíste bien, hombres, del género de los calenturientos, prendidos y súper guerreros. Están tan

Yo, me aguanto

fuertes las broncas, los riesgos de contagio, las posibilidades de embarazo, que un buen porcentaje de jóvenes de ambos sexos prefiere llevársela leve.

El rollo es que la abstinencia no es algo del otro mundo. Si conoces a alguien que optó por ella, lejos de tacharlo como teto, ñoño, o *loser*, reconoce que es un mérito porque el cuate o la niña son igual de prendidos que tú. Cuando ellos ven a alguien que les gusta y traen dos chupes encima, también se les aloca la hormona, sin embargo deciden aguantarse y divertirse de otra manera. ¡Claro! de que se les antoja, se les antoja, y aunque no lo creas, los niños se clavan y respetan más a una niña que escoge esta opción.

La primera vez

Si lo haces, hazlo con responsabilidad

Hay un buen de cosas que pasan la primera vez que tienes una relación sexual. Lo más importante, como ya vimos, es que estés bien segura de tu decisión.

Si decides hacerlo, platica en serio con tu novio sobre el tema. Como no hay método cien por ciento seguro, pregúntale: "¿Qué significa para ti?, ¿cómo nos vamos a cuidar?, ¿qué haríamos en caso de embarazo?" (esta última pregunta te permite medir qué tan en serio te toma tu galán).

Muchos niños te bajan la luna y las estrellas pero, que te quede claro, si te embarazas se apanican, se hacen tontos y la mayoría desaparecen. Si eres clara y directa lo harás pensar para que sea más consciente y responsable. Asimismo, sería ideal ir al ginecólogo para que te haga un examen pélvico vaginal.

Las expectativas de hacer el amor

Generalmente lo has esperado y ¡te han dicho tanto! que juras que el lugar donde lo hagas se llenará de estrellas, la cama se elevará, tú sentirás lo más padre del mundo y brincarás de emoción. Y sí, vas a brincar, pero del susto cuando suene tu celular y descubras que es ¡tu papá!

El rollo es que la primera vez, generalmente, lejos de ser padre, es bastante rara, no es ni fantástico, ni mágico. De hecho, en las encuestas realizadas al respecto, los resultados no son nada favorables. Es lógico: existen un buen de pensamientos, dudas y sentimientos, a veces contradictorios, que flotan entre los dos. A veces, físicamente no sabes bien ni por dónde es el asunto por más que lo hayas visto en las clases de cuarto de primaria; lo cierto es que las veces futuras no se parecen en nada a la primera.

Lo más seguro es que cuando experimentes la primera penetración sientas dolor y tengas un leve sangrado. Esto sucede porque el himen puede no ser elástico y romperse al momento de la penetración.

Si estás tensa o nerviosa, tu vagina se reseca y se aprieta, por lo que puede doler. Esto es súper típico por ser la primera vez; conforme te relajas o tienes más relaciones, la vagina se dilata, se lubrica y el dolor disminuye hasta desaparecer por completo. Mientras, se puede usar un lubricante como Jalea K-Y, Soft Lube de Sico, Multi O, Benzal Gel, Wet, Extreme Lube de Sico, o un condón lubricado para reducir el dolor.

Aunque se te haga raro este rollo de la lubricada es básico, porque si están muy nerviosos les costará mucho trabajo. Recuerda que los condones de figuritas chistosas y musicales (aunque parezca broma, sí existen) son sólo para echar relajo, no te confíes.

Estoy embarazada

A continuación Mariana nos platica su experiencia:

¡Chin! ¿Cómo les voy a decir a mis papás? ¡Me van a matar! ¡Soy una imbécil! Y Joel, ¿qué va a decir? Yo siempre pensé: "A mí no me pasa." Se nos fue, carajo. Yo creo que el condón se rompió. ¡Tanto que critiqué a Susana que me dijo que se embarazó por una sola vez que lo hizo! Y le dije: "¡No manches!, ¿cómo crees?" Pues ahí va la bruta y me embarazo. ¿Qué voy a hacer? ¡No he terminado ni la prepa! Yo quería estudiar una carrera, irme de maestría a algún lado. ¿Y ahora? ¿Qué tal si a Joel le vale madres?

...Cuando hablé con Joel se sacó de onda durísimo, se puso todo nervioso, no quería que lo tuviera, me preguntó cómo lo íbamos a mantener, en dónde viviríamos, dijo que sólo teníamos 19 años...

Mientras Mariana, con su voz de niña, nos platica por teléfono sus primeras impresiones al descubrir que estaba embarazada, escucho también los ruiditos de la bebé, ya de tres meses.

...Cuando le di la noticia a mi mamá se quedó helada, no dijo nada y se soltó a llorar. A mi papá le tengo pavor, así que preferí escribirle una carta. No querían que la tuviera, así que discutí con ellos y decidí tenerla. Les ha costado mucho trabajo aceptar todo esto.

También me corrieron de la escuela; sentí horrible y tuve que terminar la prepa en la abierta. Pero estoy contenta por la decisión que tomé, aunque he perdido muchas cosas: ya no tengo tiempo para estar con mis amigos ni puedo salir de reventón los fines de semana. Vivo con mis papás, Joel viene a ver a la niña y aunque es cariñoso, se aburre y se pone triste. Para mí es difícil porque tengo que sacar adelante a la niña, y a él...

Le pregunto a Mariana qué consejo daría a las niñas de su edad.

Que se cuiden o se abstengan. A las que ya están embarazadas, que no crean que va a ser fácil: todo se descompone, te cambia la vida por completo. De todas formas, creo que vale la pena. El parto te aterra pero es lo de menos; pienso que ha de ser peor el remordimiento.

Síntomas de embarazo

- Cambios en el tamaño de las bubis y aumento de sensibilidad.
- Oscurecimiento de la zona que rodea el pezón (areola).
- Ausencia de menstruación.
- Náuseas por la mañana, al despertar.
- Cansancio.
- Muchas ganas de hacer pipí.
- Cambio en el color de la vulva.
- Aumento de secreción vaginal.
- Te pueden dar "antojos".
- Sabor metálico en la boca.
- Puedes sentir ligeros mareos.

Tus opciones

A veces te embarazas por descuido; otras para atraparlo, porque crees que así te amará toda la vida (es la mentira más grande del mundo). Fue una noche de jarra en la que te perdiste, no te cuidaste, te valieron los métodos anticonceptivos o creíste que no te iba a pasar. Pero a la hora de la hora sí te pasó, y ahora, ¿qué vas a hacer?

No hay salida fácil de un embarazo no planeado. Una vez confirmado tienes una situación muy seria por enfrentar y pocas opciones para decidir qué hacer.

Antes que nada, no tomes una decisión tú sola. Platícalo con el papá del bebé y con algún adulto que sepas que te quiere y puede comprender, alguien que te ayude a tomar la decisión que más te convenga. Piensa que cualquier elección será difícil y dolorosa, que cambiará tu vida por completo y que no habrá vuelta atrás.

Si decides tenerlo hay tres opciones: casarte, ser mamá soltera o darlo en adopción.

Casarte

Un hijo es una de las experiencias más maravillosas en la vida de una pareja. Pero la responsabilidad de traer un bebé al mundo es gruesísima. La naturaleza es sabia y nos da nueve meses para prepararnos lo mejor posible para este cambio tan drástico en la vida. ¿Van a vivir juntos? ¿Dónde? ¿Vas a trabajar? ¿Cómo se van a mantener? ¿Quién cuidará al bebé?

Si deciden no casarse, ¡tranquila!, debes saber que la mayoría de las madres solteras se sienten súper bien consigo mismas por su valor. Por supuesto no va a ser fácil, pero si quieres, puedes encontrar muchas formas de recibir ayuda.

Darlo en adopción

Se necesita mucha valentía para dar en adopción a tu hijo. Pero a veces, debido a las circunstancias, tú sabes que es lo mejor. Son muchas las parejas que no han podido concebir y desean muchísimo a ese bebé para hacerlo feliz. En nuestro país existen diversos centros donde se encargan de orientarte y buscar el mejor hogar para el bebé, para que viva rodeado de amor, reciba una buena educación y un buen ejemplo.

CENTROS DE ADOPCIÓN

SEDAC
Quinta Carmelita
01 (55) 55-68-83-72

Vida y Familia
01 (55) 53-93-74-05

Hogar y Futuro
01 (55) 58-10-29-51,
58-10-29-52

Desarrollo Integral
de la Familia (DIF)
www.dif.gob.mx

Yoliguani
01 (55) 52-51-85-86,
52-51-48-29,
www.yoliguani.com

Casa Cuna Amigo Daniel;
León, Guanajuato
01 (477) 776-04-04

Fundación Colosio
01 (55) 52-82-33-03

Tiempo Nuevo;
Guadalajara, Jalisco
VIFAC 01-800-36-22-07
nacional@vifac.org.mx,
www.vifac.org.mx

Filios; Monterrey,
Nuevo León
01 (81) 83-58-44-01

El aborto

El aborto fue ilegal en nuestro país, hasta el 26 de Abril del 2007, fecha en que se despenalizó únicamente en el Distrito Federal y sólo dentro de las primeras 12 semanas de gestación, según el artículo 144 del código penal. También puede practicarse si te embarazaste por causas de una violación, si el bebé tiene malformaciones congénitas o si el embarazo representa un grave riesgo para tu salud.

Datos de la OMS (Organización Mundial de la Salud) revelan que quienes mueren por la práctica de un aborto, legal o ilegal, son frecuentemente adolescentes que llegan al hospital con hemorragias o infecciones causadas por interrumpir la gestación cuando las jovencitas se encuentran muy desesperadas.

Físicamente, el aborto puede provocar infertilidad, perforación del útero y peritonitis; en casos extremos resulta necesario extraer la matriz. Psicológicamente, causa depresión, arrepentimiento y sentimiento de culpa que, según la opinión de algunas mujeres que se lo han practicado, puede durar muchos años, incluso toda la vida.

Por dichas razones, esta opción es la más dolorosa y difícil en la vida de cualquier mujer.

La realidad es que, aunque se despenalizó el aborto en el Distrito Federal, el tema aún es muy polémico y de mucha controversia. La mayoría de los doctores no lo practican por sus creencias o simplemente por el riesgo que puede existir hacia la paciente.

Si decides hacerlo, infórmate bien, no acudas a clínicas clandestinas ni con charlatanes o hierberos.

Hay quienes defienden el aborto diciendo que cada quien es libre de decidir sobre su cuerpo; sin embargo, no olvides que el cuerpo formándose dentro de ti no es el tuyo.

De todas las opciones anteriores lo mejor sería no tener que decidir. Sé inteligente, piensa muy bien las cosas y evita que la prendidez y el momento te ganen. Valórate, opta por la abstinencia o cuídate para que no te la juegues.

CENTRO DE APOYO

Instituto de Reconciliación para la Mujer que ha Abortado
01 (55) 52-60-72-73

Orientación sexual: heterosexuales, homosexuales, transexuales y bisexuales

Ya son tantos tipos y estilos que seguro te haces bolas.

Muy posiblemente conoces hombres y mujeres que se sienten atraídos por personas de su mismo sexo. Como sabes ellos se conocen como: **homosexuales, gays** o en el caso específico de las mujeres, **lesbianas**. Su atracción al mismo sexo es **física y emocional**.

Los heterosexuales son a quienes les atrae el sexo opuesto.

A quienes les atraen los dos sexos por igual, —o sea, que les da lo mismo— se les conoce como **bisexuales**. Y hay más: los *transexuales* son personas que sienten que nacieron con el sexo equivocado, porque lo que viven en su interior no corresponde con su cuerpo. Ven alguna parte de su cuerpo y dicen: "*Ah caray, esto no es mío.*" Muchos transexuales desde chicos, se comportan como si fueran del otro sexo. Esto sucede en una de cada 30,000 mujeres y en uno de cada 12,000 hombres. O sea que la probabilidad es más alta en los hombres que en las mujeres.

Se dice que un hombre es **travesti**, cuando le gusta vestirse de mujer, pero te tenemos una noticia que te va a sacar de onda: no necesariamente son homosexuales.

¿Naces o te haces?

Esta pregunta es como la del huevo y la gallina. Algunos expertos dicen que la homosexualidad es producto de la naturaleza. Muchas investigaciones se han enfocado en encontrar las posibles causas; hay quienes dicen que existe una diferencia física en el hipotálamo —un área específica

del cerebro que maneja la sexualidad entre otras cosas. Otros afirman que este rollo, se da por el origen genético, hormonal o que tiene que ver con algo durante la gestación o el nacimiento.

Lo que sí se sabe es que "No es algo que tu eliges", "Obviamente no es una enfermedad" y, esperamos que no se te ocurra ni pensarlo.

Otros expertos piensan que se debe a un tipo de educación, a un medio determinado, o algo que en tu vida te hace tomar la decisión de ser gay. El caso es que ninguna de las investigaciones es definitiva y hasta ahora no se ponen de acuerdo.

Popularidad

Ayyy, la odio...

- Tiene tanta ropa que... (estoy segura que su papá es dueño de Saks).
- Es tan guapa que... (he pensado que hasta a mí me gusta).
- La invitan a tantas fiesta que... (creo que hasta le pagan por ir).
- Se lleva tan bien con tanta gente que... (podría trabajar en la ONU).
- Tantos niños guapos mueren por ella que... (¡estoy segura que hace tratos con el diablo!).
- Tanta gente la conoce que... (aparece hasta en el mapa del GPS).

...Y la verdad es que... que... que... ¡¡Quiero ser ELLA!!

El rollo de la popularidad puede ser una pesadilla (y de esas en las que sueñas que hiciste pipí, y resulta pues que... sí te hiciste).

179

Ser popular es primo-hermano de ser aceptado y pues a todo mundo nos gusta la aprobación, es completamente natural. La bronca es que como este asunto ahora incluye el Kit Hollywood (dinero, belleza, mascota más mamila que su dueña, marcas, amigos, y hasta botox... ipara la mascota!) ya ha llegado a niveles súper cañones.

Claro que es normal querer verte guapa, vestirte padre y sentirte cool, y por supuesto que se vale, la bronca es que dejes de ser tú para convertirte en la híper-ultra-súper Abeja Reina de la escuela (aunque no estaría mal tener por ahí algunos obreros a tu servicio).

Muchas veces queremos ser aceptados porque nos sentimos rechazados o inseguros, como si la ley fuera "si soy popular, es porque valgo" y aquí es donde viene la bronca porque entre más busquemos ser populares, más riesgo tenemos de rechazo y si nuestra autoestima ya estaba en el suelo se puede ir enterrando hasta casi casi hacerte una mascarilla de lodo.

Lo más importante es que seas tu misma, buscar qué te gusta, cómo eres y ser exactamente así, no hay nada menos popular que una *wannabe*. (Bueno sí... dos *wannabes*.)

Cuando alguien hace esto es como un foco rojo gigante, porque todo mundo se da cuenta y la rechazan durísimo; de hecho, ya no sólo es CERO popular... ahora es cero popular y mentirosa.

La mayoría de las personas populares (aunque parezca lo contrario) no son tan felices como parecen, porque se la pasan tratando de agradar a todo mundo, no son reales consigo mismas. (Imagínate quererte ir a echar unos *nuggets* al McDonald's con tus pants despintados, bien fodonga y con los pelos de plumero y no poder porque... ¿qué va a decir la sociedad estudiantil?)

También aunque estén rodeados de tanta gente en realidad muchas veces se sienten muy solos porque sus amistades son más interesadas que sinceras.

Por otro lado hay gente que es popular porque verdaderamente le gusta vestirse de esa forma, ser de esa manera, tiene mucho dinero, es todo un *party animal*, es líder o simplemente tiene mucho *charm* con la gente. Pero eso es algo que no escogemos y que si no es nuestro caso, solamente estamos presionándonos a ser lo que de plano no somos y lastimándonos cada vez que nos mandan a la… a la… (o sea muy lejos).

Otra cosa muy importante de ubicar es que la popularidad es sólo en la escuela y por un rato. Cuando sales de la escuela eso se acabó. Finito. ¡Caput!

En el mundo real, más que gente popular, hay gente exitosa.

Hay genios de la computación muy respetados (que antes eran los Nerds), Cantantes famosísimas (que antes las veían medio freaks), Doctoras que salvan vidas (que antes eran las matadas), Grandes diseñadoras (que en la escuela sólo les preocupaba la ropa, y qué combinaba con qué), ecologistas con movimientos a nivel mundial (que antes la gente se reía de ellos), excelentes madres de familia –una de las cosas más difíciles de lograr– (que creían que no les gustaba hacer nada y resultaron haciendo lo más difícil)… En fin, todas esas personas son hoy lo que son porque decidieron ser ellas, porque hicieron lo que les gusta en lugar de tratar de ser algo que no son.

Así que para no hacer el cuento más largo, hay de dos sopas:

+ Tratar de agradar a todos, olvidándote de ti y enseñándole a todo mundo una versión pirata de ti misma.
+ Hacer lo que de verdad te gusta, tener amigas que les llama la atención lo mismo que a ti, no sufrir mintiendo acerca de ti y disfrutar la escuela al máximo.

Tú decides, y recuerda:

Que una sola persona, te quiera, te respete y sea incondicional con tu amistad, es la popularidad más grande y sincera que pueda existir

¿Seré gay o no?

"Estoy asustada, no sé si me gustan las mujeres o no. Tengo una amiga y me encanta estar con ella. Me gustan sus ojos, su cara y hasta sus manos. Pero no sé si es porque se arregla muy bonito, o porque soy gay. Me preocupa que cuando otra chava se le acerca y le platica mucho, me dan mas celos de lo normal y trato de alejarla. Siento como que estoy haciendo todo lo posible para convencerme de que no soy, pero en el fondo creo que me estoy engañando.

La mayoría de las veces que digo que un niño me gusta es mentira, lo hago porque todas dicen que es guapísimo; aunque sí hay un niño que me gusta. Estoy muy confundida.

Me da mucha pena qué pensarían mis papás, mis hermanos y todos los demás. Un día en una borrachera me pasó por la mente darle un beso a otra amiga, pero no sé si se me ocurrió por cool, como en los videos, o porque quería. Tengo miedo, ¿es normal eso, o no?"

Georgina
16 años

Algunos expertos opinan que hay jóvenes que, en un periodo de transición como la adolescencia, pueden pasar por algún tipo de experiencia homosexual. A veces puede ser algo breve, pasajero, sin importancia o bien, en un futuro, convertirse en una forma de vida.

Hablando de este periodo, es común que durante tu desarrollo y despertar sexual, tengas experiencias sexuales estimulantes con alguien del mismo género... ¡hasta fantasías con otra chava! Eso no tiene nada que ver con que seas o no homosexual. No sientas culpa; piensa, es lógico. La menstruación, tus bubis, el vello, ¡tus hormonas! están como locas trabajando por primera vez y hacen que estrenes sensaciones. Así que, si de casualidad tu amiga pasaba por ahí y sientes "chistosito", no necesariamente eres gay.

También es normal que tengas miles de dudas tipo: "¿Seré gay porque me gusta estar siempre con mi amiga?", "¿por qué le veo mucho el cuerpo?", "¿por qué me dan celos de que mi mejor amiga sea más amiga de otra?", "¿por qué me encanta cuando me abraza?"

Muchas veces, todo lo anterior pasa por la necesidad de sentirte segura, comprendida y apoyada. Quizás también porque admiras la forma de ser de tu amiga y quieres aprender de ella. Una vez más, nada que ver con ser lesbiana. También puede ser que no sientas ningún tipo de atracción por nadie ni por nada, o todavía no tengas claro quién te gusta. No te preocupes, este tipo de confusiones son de lo más normal en la adolescencia.

¿Hasta aquí vamos bien? (frase típica de profe de secundaria). Entonces seguimos: otros especialistas opinan que hay niñas y niños que desde la infancia se sienten y se saben diferentes, pero como la sociedad no lo entiende o no lo acepta, se quedan callados muchísimo tiempo o para siempre.

Sobre este tema hay mucha desinformación. No hay recetas de cuánto tiempo se debe tardar una persona con este tipo de dudas en reconocer su orientación sexual. Lo

más importante es que, si crees que es tu caso, te informes con personas, libros o sitios de internet confiables sobre el tema. Y, por supuesto, acuérdate de que la decisión es sólo tuya.

El día que estés segura podrás enfrentar tus miedos. Sólo tú vas a saber cuándo estás lista para dar los siguientes pasos. Es básico que sepas que cuando te crees o te sabes gay, te causa mucha angustia, sufrimiento y depresión; incluso puedes tener pensamientos de suicidio por no entenderte a ti misma y por el profundo miedo al rechazo. Puedes pensar que la homofobia (odio a los homosexuales) y todas las bromas que se hacen de los gays son muy crueles, y te angustia enfrentarte a "esa soy yo". Aunque no es algo fácil, debes tranquilizarte y pensar que, si estás segura, es algo que no decidiste, que no por ello vas a ser más o menos feliz que los demás, que hay muchísimas chavas en la misma situación y que llegará el momento de enfrentarlo.

Por lo pronto, si tienes dudas lo mejor es hablarlo con algún especialista que te pueda informar y orientar (puede ser cualquier sexólogo o psicólogo, particular o el de la escuela). Además, te recomendamos leer mucho sobre este rollo para que te informes más y te des cuenta de que no eres la única a la que le sucede.

Ch–k–t lo siguiente:

Según el informe del *Surgeon General's, Call to Action to Promote Sexual Health and Responsable Sexual Behavior* de 2001: "Ningún niño puede considerarse homosexual. En la mayoría de las personas se consolida la identidad homosexual durante la adolescencia y en la vida adulta".

Se dice "salir del clóset" para referirse al momento en que una persona está totalmente convencida de que es gay y decide no ocultarlo. Si es tu caso, debes estar preparada para enfrentar situaciones y problemas que la mayoría de la veces no son nada fáciles, entre los que se encuentran la aceptación...

De ti misma. Esto es lo básico de lo básico, el primer paso. Aceptarte de esa manera, entender que no estás haciendo nada malo y que, así como mucha gente tiene ciertas características, ésta te tocó a ti. Si todavía te deprimes con el tema, mejor no lo platiques aún. Debes tener la fuerza suficiente para enfrentar los prejuicios y reacciones de algunas personas. Infórmate mega bien sobre todo esto, ve con un sexólogo, con un terapeuta o checa libros confiables.

De la sociedad. Cuando se trata de diferencias sexuales, muchas personas se portan de manera distinta respecto de lo que consideran que está bien o no. Hay quienes no están de acuerdo y quienes no le ven ninguna bronca. En el caso de quienes no están de acuerdo con los sentimientos y formas de actuar de los homosexuales, es muy importante que sepas que pueden criticarte, ponerte apodos, marginarte o hasta discriminarte. A eso se le llama homofobia.

De tus amigas. La noticia puede sorprender a algunas y a otras no tanto. Sin embargo, tienes que ubicar que unas te pueden aceptar y otras rechazar, es normal. También es normal que tus amigas se saquen un poco de onda, porque no saben nada de esto, por eso debes explicarles que no las vas a seducir, atacar o tratar de convencer para que se vuelvan gays; que no tiene nada que ver con eso y que no es una decisión personal, mucho menos una enfermedad y, por lo tanto , no se puede curar con un doctor. Todo esto es el miedo típico de los amigos.

De tu familia. Ésta es quizá la más cañona de todas: enfrentar a la familia. Las reacciones de incomodidad, enojo y decepción de tus papás pueden ser súper fuertes, sobre todo porque choca de frente con las expectativas que ellos tenían. Igual y ellos te veían casada con un príncipe azul y con tres hijos, y de repente las cosas no son así. Para ellos es una sorpresa y un mega trancazo. Viven una gran pérdida. Ellos lo sienten como un fracaso. Sobre todo, se preguntan cosas como: "¿En qué fallamos?", y pueden, equivocadamente, sentir mucha culpa. ¡Entiéndelos! Al igual que tus amigas, hermanos y demás, no tienen información, y la mayoría todavía no saben ni por qué pasa esto. Escoge un momento apropiado para decirlo, no cuando estés jarra o enojada por otras broncas. Puedes encontrar a papás que inmediatamente te den todo su apoyo y que se porten súper cariñosos, otros que no sepan ni que decir, o algunos que te rechacen y te empiecen a repetir frases que te lastimen. Tienes que ser muy paciente y demostrarles que los quieres y los necesitas más que nunca. Entiende que lo que tú haz asimilado en varios años, a ellos les cae de golpe, y al igual que tú tienen miedo y no saben cómo actuar.

En el caso del rechazo, es importante que sepas que la mayoría de los papás, con el paso del tiempo lo llegan a entender o, al menos, a tolerar. Se necesita mucho valor y convencimiento absoluto de que eres gay para superar todos los obstáculos y encontrar tranquilidad y paz personal. Esto no puede detener tu vida; la existencia y el valor de una persona va mucho más allá de una preferencia sexual. No hay gente "normal" y "anormal", todos somos iguales y debemos respetar la sexualidad de los otros. Obviamente puedes ser tan feliz como tu quieras y recuerda que hoy en día, las diferentes orientaciones sexuales son protegidas por las leyes contra la discriminación.

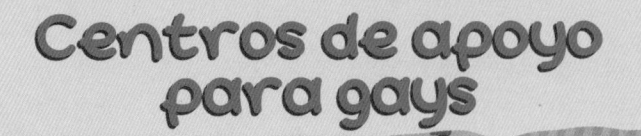

Centros de apoyo para gays

Si tienes alguna duda sobre tu forma de ser, o algo no te late respecto a cómo te sientes, no dudes en buscar consejo en los siguientes lugares:

El Armario Abierto
www.elarmarioabierto.com

. . . .

Fundación Triángulo por la Igualdad Social de Gays y Lesbianas
http://www.fundaciontriangulo.es/juventud/e__jovenes.htm

. . . .

Comisión de Derechos Humanos del Distrito Federal
www.cdhdf.org.mx

. . . .

Grupo de Madres y Padres por la diversidad sexual (Grupo Condesa)
Tel. (01 55) 52 11 82 50
http://mx.geocities.com/padresporladiversidad

. . . .

Telsida
01 55 52 07 40 77 y 01 800 712 08 86

. . . .

Nuestras Hijas y Nuestros Hijos
www.pflag.org

. . . .

Consejo Nacional para Prevenir la Discriminación
www.conapred.org.mx

. . . .

Comisión Nacional de los Derechos Humanos
www.cndh.org.mx

. . . .

Demysex. Red Democracia y Sexualidad
www.demysex.org.mx

Expertos EUA

Maestro Darío Sánchez Ma
Maestría Terapia Familiar
San Diego Ca.

Tel. 001 6192068744
mail4dario@yahoo.com

Niñas que ayudaron
Quiúbole inglés

Maria Angelica Villegas Gastelum, 17 años
Claudia Yanina Morales Morales, 18 años
Jocelyn Puente, 18 años
Danna Mirlet Melendez, 18 años
Dalia Archundia Gutierrez, 16 años
Ana Lilia Hernández Madrazo, 18 años
Valeria D. Labra Cortez, 16 años
Karla Ximena García, 15 años
Miriam Sarahi Lara, 18 años
Lucero Itzel López Patiño, 18 años
Manuella Mejía
Tania Ruiz Galindo

Sexo cuando no quieres

La música de la fiesta está a todo lo que da mientras Rodrigo y yo platicamos, nos besamos, fumamos y bailamos cañón. Él tiene 19 años y yo acabo de cumplir 16. Como a la una de la mañana siento que las cubas se me subieron y voy al baño. Rodrigo me sigue, entra detrás de mí y cierra la puerta, no digo nada. No protesto mientras él me besa.

Recargada contra la pared siento que su mano me desabrocha el pantalón. A pesar de la jarra que traigo me asusto porque nunca antes he tenido relaciones sexuales. Al mismo tiempo, una serie de pensamientos pasan por mi mente: "Si ya lo dejaste entrar aquí cómo le vas a decir que no. Ahora, ¿qué vas a hacer? No vas a perder tu virginidad en un baño. Estás hasta atrás."

En eso, Rodrigo me jala fuertemente para acostarme sobre el piso. Siento el peso de su cuerpo encima de mí. Yo lucho, forcejeo, quiero gritar y salirme de ese lugar. Él me lo impide, usa toda su fuerza hasta que, al fin, puedo sacar una pierna y logro empujarlo y salir corriendo...

Después de agradecerle a Martha, ahora de 27 años, su confianza para narrarnos su experiencia, le preguntamos:

¿Cómo te afectó lo sucedido?

Por un par de años lo bloqueé, me dañó mucho emocionalmente y, al mismo tiempo, estaba afectada por haberme mantenido en silencio. Sentía miedo y también culpa, me di cuenta de que no me había valorado y por mucho tiempo le tuve coraje a los hombres. Aprendí que era muy soberbio de mi parte creer que podía ligarme a quien quisiera y coquetear a mi antojo como si fuera un juego sin consecuencias.

¿Por qué crees que te pasó?

El alcohol tuvo mucho que ver, yo estaba jarrísima. Aprendí que el abuso sexual se da fácilmente cuando hay droga o alcohol de por medio.

¿Cuándo es abuso sexual?

El abuso sexual puede darse de diversas formas, hasta sin contacto físico de por medio. Por ejemplo: los comentarios que te incomoden, la forma en que te volteen a ver, muestras de exhibicionismo, que te obliguen a ver determinadas imágenes, algún tipo de contacto físico, toqueteo de tus partes, o simplemente ser chantajeada por alguien en posición de poder; por ejemplo, un maestro a cambio de buenas calificaciones, pasarte en un examen, etcétera.

Que no te pase

En general, cualquier tipo de abuso sexual no tiene que ver estrictamente con el sexo, sino que está más relacionado con un rollo grueso de poder. Ser víctima de una situación

así es de las cosas más humillantes que te pueden suceder, pues los sentimientos de culpa y vulnerabilidad te pegan durísimo. Por eso, es importante que sepas que:

- Alrededor de 80 por ciento de las violaciones definidas como penetración sexual no deseada, ocurren entre personas que se conocen. Puede suceder entre amigos, novios o parientes. Imagínate, ¡personas en quienes confías!

- El alcohol es un factor determinante en dos terceras partes de los casos de violación y abuso sexual. Éste, como otras drogas, puede nublar la razón o hacer perder la conciencia al grado de aceptar la violación o, lo que es lo mismo, no resistirse a ella.

- ¡Aguas! En muchos casos, la mujer está dispuesta a llegar sólo hasta un punto del acto sexual; pero sucede que cuando decide detenerse, al hombre le vale, la chantajea y la obliga a continuar. Por eso es importante decir de manera clara y fuerte: "No, no quiero," y repetirlo cuantas veces sea necesario, para que quede constancia de que lo dijiste en caso de que se proceda legalmente.

Encuesta de abuso sexual

La doctora Guillermina Mejía, directora general de Adolescentes A.C., realizó un estudio piloto con un grupo de 222 jóvenes estudiantes de entre 18 y 22 años, mediante una dinámica llamada "Cuéntame tu secreto". Los cuestionarios respondidos por escrito de manera anónima y espontánea, sin presión o inducción alguna, arrojaron los siguientes resultados: 57 por ciento de las niñas habían sido abusadas sexualmente. La edad promedio de la víctima fue 8.5 años, y la del abusador, 20.3 años.

191

El parentesco del abusador era:

- 27% tío
- 19% primo
- 16% un extraño*
- 14% amigo o conocido de la familia
- 11% no se menciona parentesco
- 9% hermano mayor
- 4% pareja
- 3% papá/padrastro
- 2% abuelo
- 1% sacerdote

¿Comunicaste a alguien del abuso?

NUNCA: 84%
Sí: 16%

* la mayoría en este rubro coincide con exhibicionismo

¿Cómo ubicar a los que quieren hacerte algo?

Es importante que estés consciente de lo frecuente que se da un abuso sexual o violación. Piensa bien con quién andas, con quién sales, con quién te sientes segura y por qué. Observa cómo te tratan; si el niño con el que sales o cualquier otra persona siempre insiste en ir a un lugar en donde tengan que estar solos, o notas que tiene cambios de personalidad y se comporta agresivamente: ¡ojo!

¿Cómo evitarlo?

¿A todas nos puede pasar? Sí, a cualquiera. ¿Lo puedes prevenir? También, o reducir las posibilidades de que suceda, especialmente cuando eres joven. Sólo es cuestión de tener algunas precauciones:

En la casa

- No permitas que nadie, ya sea tío, hermano mayor, primo, padrino, padrastro, vecino o lo que sea, toque tus partes íntimas cuando no quieres. De acuerdo con las estadísticas, 38 por ciento de los abusos ocurren en casa de la víctima y otro 38 por ciento en la de familiares o amigos.
- Ten en cuenta que si con los ojos cerrados, aunque sea una calaca te acaricia la piel, ¡vas a sentir bonito! Pues la piel está llena de terminaciones nerviosas. Así que cuando alguien abusa de ti, al principio quizá te sentiste bien, luego ya no quisiste que siguiera y al terminarse el abuso puedes sentirte culpable y hasta avergonzarte. No lo permitas. Tal vez estas circunstancias contribuyan a que te quedes callada: ¡JAMÁS!
- Se ha dicho que más que un abuso sexual, se le debería llamar seducción sexual. El abusador lo sabe y lo usará como herramienta para amenazarte. No lo permitas NUNCA.
- Por ningún motivo toques los genitales de un adulto (buza, porque para convencerte son capaces de hacer e inventar lo que sea).
- Si algo así ocurriera avisa de inmediato a un adulto de tu confianza, no te calles; entre más tiempo guardes el secreto más trabajo te costará decirlo. Por favor, habla de inmediato, te prometemos que te van a creer.

EN LA CALLE

- Muchas de las violaciones se cometen en medio de un parque público y durante el día. Si notas que te siguen, grita, corre, entra a una tiendita o a un lugar con gente.
- Evita caminar sola por lugares desconocidos, oscuros o poco transitados. Hay calles tan, pero tan solas que hasta parece que se llaman "Avenida Abuso Sexual": trata de no caminar por ahí.
- Si tienes que pasar por ahí, usa zapatos cómodos con los que puedas correr; camina con paso firme, derecha, muy segura y con la cabeza en alto. Que se note que sabes a dónde te diriges.
- De ser posible, lleva un celular en la mano con un teléfono premarcado para que, en caso de necesitarlo, sólo aprietes la tecla "llamar". (Incluso puedes fingir que estás hablando con alguien que supuestamente está muy cerca de donde tu estás.)
- Cuando camines por la calle evita pegarte a la pared al dar vuelta en la esquina; alguien podría estar esperándote del otro lado.
- Procura no subirte sola al elevador con un desconocido, o con un conocido que no te dé confianza.
- Si alguien en un coche te pide información responde de lejitos, no te acerques a él.
- Si manejas sola, mantén tus vidrios arriba y las puertas cerradas con seguro. Si sospechas que alguien te sigue, si otro coche te pega por atrás, o te ponen algún obstáculo en la calle, nunca te detengas ni te bajes del auto. Maneja hacia una área transitada y toca el cláxon constantemente hasta que alguien se acerque o el sospechoso se vaya; si traes celular llama inmediatamente al teléfono de emergencia (es recomendable guardarlo en la memoria). Por supuesto no le des *ride* a nadie.

- Si notas que algún hombre te mira con insistencia y te hace sentir incómoda, no lo pienses, cámbiate de lugar o vete.
- Ya que las drogas y el alcohol disminuyen tu posibilidad de defenderte, no bebas en exceso ni utilices otro tipo de sustancias.
- Confía en tus instintos. Si el niño con el que estás comienza a actuar raro o alguna situación o lugar no te late, vete, corre o, si es necesario, haz una escena para llamar la atención.
- Se sabe que cuando una niña está en un bar o en un antro y alguien quiere abusar sexualmente de ella, el violador puede introducir en la bebida de la mujer un sedante muy potente o sobornar al mesero para que lo haga. La niña se siente paralizada, se le nubla la vista, se marea y entra en un estado de somnolencia que afecta seriamente su memoria. Quienes han sido víctimas de esta situación, dicen que no se acuerdan de nada de lo que les pasó. Ten cuidado antes de aceptar bebidas de tipos desconocidos.
- Aunque un galán te haya invitado la mejor cena en un restaurante muy caro y te haya pedido la mejor botella en el antro de moda, eso no le da derecho a disponer de tu cuerpo.
- Evita regresarte sola en el coche de un cuate que acabas de conocer en la fiesta o el antro, aunque aparente ser el más buena onda.
- De ser posible toma clases de alguna disciplina relacionada con defensa personal, por ejemplo el judo te ayuda a hacerle llaves a una persona aun cuando está muy cerca de ti, como en el coche o abrazándote. También el karate es buena opción y no olvides que una buena patada en las partes nobles del abusador puede ser tu mejor arte marcial.

AHORA:
PONTE SÚPER BUZA PARA QUE NO TE VAYAN A DAR UNA DE LAS...

CHECA ESTO

Drogas de la violación

Estas drogas facilitan de manera impresionante los asaltos sexuales, en personas que obviamente no desean tenerlos. Los efectos que estas drogas producen hacen a las victimas (tus amigas o tú) más indefensas, incapaces de rehusarse y confundidas de lo que pasó o de plano no se acuerdan de nada.

KETAMINA

Muchos chavos (y no tan chavos) les dicen Special K, Vitamina K, Kit Kat, o Keta. Es un anestésico general, que casi no se usa para las cirugías con humanos, pero se usa mucho en la práctica veterinaria. Son legales para uso médico, pero ilegales para uso recreativo. La principal bronca es que se diluye súper fácil en las bebidas porque es insípida e incolora. Dentro de los efectos en las victimas está la reducción en la conciencia, se les olvidan los eventos inmediatos, causa sueño y se distorsiona lo que ven y lo que oyen.

Imagínate qué peligroso, la persona que te la da te tiene prácticamente con control remoto y sin preocupación de que te acuerdes de lo que pase.

Por eso el testimonio que la víctima ofrece a la hora de una declaración después de la violación es cero confiable. Algunos la combinan con cocaína y cristal para inhalarla, lo que se conoce como CK, o Calvin Klein.

GHB

También se conoce como Éxtasis líquido. Es un depresor del sistema nervioso central; produce sueño, amnesia y modifica tu voluntad; ¡imagínate qué grueso! También se diluye fácilmente en bebidas o se añade a la comida, produce deterioro del juicio y consumiéndolo percibes cosas y situaciones alteradas, distintas de cómo son en realidad.

¿Qué hacer?

- No pierdas de vista tu bebida.
- No aceptes bebidas que no hayan sido abiertas enfrente de ti o por ti.
- Asegúrate de que sea un envase cerrado.
- Ni por equivocación aceptes bebidas de extraños o de personas a quienes tienes poco tiempo de conocer.
- Al ir a fiestas o antros, ve en grupo y ponte de acuerdo con tus amigos y amigas para que todos cuiden las bebidas de los demás.
- Si llegas a una fiesta en grupo, sal con ese mismo grupo.
- Si piensas que has sido víctima de un asalto sexual, avísale a tus papás y a las autoridades inmediatamente.

Recuerda que hay muchos hombres que parecen ser buena onda y tienen pésimas intenciones, así que si estás en plena fiesta y te das cuenta de que te empiezas a sentir mal, de volada díselo a una amiga o a un amigo de confianza para que llamen a tus papás y te lleven a tu casa, antes de que sea demasiado tarde.

Que no te intimiden

Si de repente te encuentras en una situación donde un tipo te pide que tengas alguna relación con él de tipo sexual, a pesar de que tú no quieras, ¡no te dejes! Es muy probable que proteste, te asuste, te haga sentir culpable o trate de amenazarte con frases tipo: "¿Qué te pasa? No seas niña", "¡Qué ridícula!", "Mira cómo me pusiste, ¿crees que me puedo ir así?", "Todo el mundo va a enterarse de que eres una wila", o ¡qué sé yo! Quizá recurra a los chantajes más inimaginables. ¡No te la creas! ¡No te dejes intimidar! Lo hace para provocarte miedo, para que te calles y él logre lo que quiere.

Insistimos, denúncialo, no te quedes callada, platícalo con tu mamá, tu papá o con algún adulto al que le tengas confianza. Que no te dé pena. ¡Al contrario!, sentirás un gran alivio. No hay nada peor que sobrellevar en soledad esta humillación. Nadie tiene derecho a forzar a una mujer a tener relaciones sexuales si ella no quiere, ni aun estando casados.

Quienes abusan sexualmente de una niña o una mujer dependen del silencio de su víctima; en el momento en que hables eso se acaba. Por eso, denúncialo de inmediato, sin importar quién sea. ¡No te sientas culpable de nada! Si tomaste un poco, si permitiste que te besara o accediste a ir a un lugar solitario, eso no le da derecho a sobrepasar tus límites. No te calles. ¡Alza la voz!

En caso de que hayan logrado dañarte o violarte, te proporcionamos los datos de instituciones donde puedes encontrar ayuda.

Centros de atención a víctimas

▶ Agencias especializadas en delitos sexuales
Dan servicio en la ciudad de México las 24 horas, todos los días del año. Te atienden mujeres que además pueden informarte sobre los centros de servicio en tu localidad.

Agencia 5:	**01 (55) 53-45-56-56**
Agencia 47:	**01 (55) 52-00-93-84**

▶ Centro de Terapia de Apoyo a Víctimas de Delitos Sexuales

01 (55) 52-00-96-32 al 36

▶ Comisión Nacional de Derechos Humanos

01 (55) 56-81-81-25
54-90-74-00

▶ Asociación para la Defensa de la Mujer

01 (55) 55-74-85-47, 55-75-01-52

▶ Asociación para el Desarrollo Integral de Personas Violadas

01 (55) 56-82-79-69, 55-43-47-00

▶ Asociación Mexicana Contra la Violencia hacia las Mujeres COVAC

covac@laneta.apc.org

▶ Instituto Nacional de las Mujeres

www.inmujeres.gob.mx
contacto@inmujeres.gob.mx

¡Cuídate de las ITS!

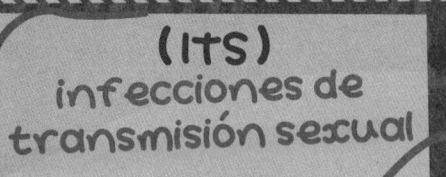

(ITS)
infecciones de transmisión sexual

No olvides que los hombres, por más decentes y lindos que se vean, son desconocidos, no conoces su curriculum completo. Tal vez ese niño que hoy parece príncipe de sangre azul, ayer en la noche estaba en un table dance y en lugar de príncipe era sapo.

El niño que jura estar sano y que no tiene "nada raro" puede meterte en una bronca gruesa porque no sabes en qué antros, ¡perdón!, "castillos", se ha metido. Si un niño tiene herpes genital o el virus del papiloma humano, ¿crees que te lo dirá?

Nadie habla de las Enfermedes (ETS) o infecciones de transmisión sexual (ITS) ni siquiera con su mejor amigo/a. Es un rollo penoso, incómodo y lamentablemente bastante común. Es difícil que escuches hablar de esto a alguien en reuniones, fiestas, en la escuela o a la hora del club. Bueno, incluso hay personas que ni al doctor van.

Queremos informarte sobre esto porque, estamos seguros, a la hora del chupe, el reventón y la calentura, es en lo último que piensas o lo que menos te interesa, así ya no cabe el rollo de: "No sabía", "si alguien me lo hubiera dicho", "de haberme informado".

Es fácil encontrar a alguien que se reconozca como persona en recuperación de drogas o anorexia, y esto es súper admirable. Sin embargo, es muy difícil, o casi imposible, encontrar a quien acepte o confiese que tiene o tuvo una ITS. ¿Te imaginas? "Hola, soy Luis y tengo verrugas genitales," o bien: "Oye, quiero contigo. ¡Ah! por cierto, tengo

herpes genital, es contagioso y si te embarazas es posible que tu bebé tenga broncas de salud pero, vamos, ¿no?"
Por lo general, tener alguna de estas enfermedades es un sufrimiento que se enfrenta a solas. Checa estos datos:

* ¿Sabías que en los años cincuenta del siglo pasado se conocían sólo cinco enfermedades de transmisión sexual y que ahora se conocen más de 50? (está cañón, ¿no?).
* ¿Que 25 de ellas son súper comunes entre los jóvenes y 30 por ciento incurables?
* ¡El 80 por ciento de las ITS no presentan síntomas! Así que, ¿cómo curar algo que no sabes que tienes?
* Contagias sin saber y, a largo plazo, te puede causar infertilidad, inflamación pélvica, cáncer y hasta ¡la muerte! La neta es que está densísimo.
* Una de las enfermedades más comunes actualmente es el virus de papiloma humano y, ¿sabías que hoy en día mueren más mujeres por broncas de papiloma que de sida? Y como ya dijimos, es cuatro veces más probable que contraigas una ITS a que te embaraces.

¿Cómo saber si te tienes que hacer una prueba de ITS?

Piensa: ¿has tenido relaciones sexuales con alguien que, a su vez, las haya tenido con alguien más? ¡Imagínate la cadenita que se puede hacer! Si la respuesta es sí, ¡hazte una prueba de ITS o de ETS! Ve al médico, sácate un análisis de sangre o hazte un cultivo en un laboratorio. De hecho, se recomienda que si eres sexualmente activa en una relación monógama (o sea, sólo con tu novio), te hagas una prueba cada seis meses.

Sobre todo, quítate de la mente los choros falsos de: "A mí no me va a pasar. Si no tengo síntomas, es que no estoy enferma de nada. Si no hay penetración, no existe riesgo de contagio." ¡Olvídalo! Estas enfermedades no sólo se transmiten por medio del esperma y fluidos vaginales, sino que algunas pueden ser por el simple contacto con los genitales; así, de piel a piel, en esos encuentros donde la ropa ya salió sobrando o a través de la saliva o de la sangre. Por eso los condones no son cien por ciento efectivos para protegerte. Así que si no te cuidas, con una sola vez que estés íntimamente con un chavo puedes contagiarte.

Mentiras y verdades de las ITS

→ ESTO ES SÚPER MEGA FALSO →

→ Sólo te contagias cuando practicas el acto sexual completo.

→ Si te lavas mucho, o después del acto sexual, no contraes ninguna de esas enfermedades o infecciones.

→ Si te contagias, lo descubres de volada porque te empieza a dar una comezón insoportable en todo el cuerpo.

→ La única enfermedad seria es el sida, las otras se quitan con pomadas que venden en las farmacias.

→ En cuanto deja de picarte ya no hace falta que te sigas tratando.

- ⊃ Son muy contagiosas.
- ⊃ La mejor manera de evitar el contagio es evitar las relaciones sexuales.
- ⊃ Los síntomas no son inmediatos y hay que conocerlos. Infórmate.
- ⊃ El único medio para combatirlas es un tratamiento prescrito por el médico.
- ⊃ Algunas enfermedades desaparecen un tiempo pero quedan latentes y reaparecen en una nueva fase.
- ⊃ De no atenderse, muchas pueden causar la muerte.

Infórmate y reflexiona sobre esto. Piensa: cualquiera puede tener relaciones sexuales, y eso no nos hace ni más mujeres ni más hombres. En cambio, la firmeza, la integridad, el respeto por ti y por los demás ¡sí te convierte en mejor persona! Además, no hay nada como entregarte a quien amas, sin broncas, sin miedos y sin preocupaciones.

¿De qué te puedes contagiar?

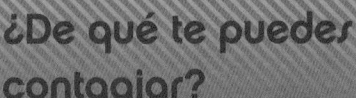

A continuación, te presentamos una lista que te explica, a grandes rasgos, cómo se adquieren estas enfermedades, los síntomas y el tratamiento médico adecuado.

Gonorrea

✱ ¿Qué es?

Una infección bacterial.

✱ ¿Cómo te da?

Por contacto vaginal, anal o sexo oral.

✱ Síntomas

Son más molestos para el hombre que para la mujer, quien a veces no presenta síntomas. Los hombres sufren dolor intenso al orinar o cuando el pene secreta. Las mujeres pueden tener secreciones e hincharse los labios vaginales.

✱ Prevención

Evita las relaciones sexuales hasta que la persona esté curada. El condón y los espermicidas reducen el riesgo pero no al 100 por ciento.

✱ Tratamiento

Antibióticos.

✱ Implicaciones a largo plazo

La gonorrea no tratada puede provocar enfermedades inflamatorias pélvicas y esterilidad.

Ladillas

✱ ¿Qué son?

Piojos que se instalan en el vello púbico y se alimentan de sangre. También pueden vivir en el cabello y en las axilas.

✱ ¿Cómo te dan?

A través del contacto cercano con una persona que las tenga. Compartiendo ropa interior, sábanas y ropa de cama. Las mascotas pueden traer consigo estos bichos.

✳ Síntomas

Mucha comezón. Posiblemente manchitas de sangre en la ropa interior por las mordidas. Si miras de cerca las podrás ver.

✳ Prevención

Evita contacto íntimo con personas que las tengan.

✳ Tratamiento

Medicamento prescrito por el médico. Lavar toda la ropa utilizada recientemente y los sitios o prendas donde pueda haber ladillas. Estos bichos pueden ser difíciles de quitar y tal vez necesites repetir el tratamiento varias veces.

✳ Implicaciones a largo plazo

Ninguna.

Herpes

✳ ¿Qué es?

Hay dos clases de virus de herpes. El herpes oral puede aparecer en forma de llagas o fuegos alrededor de la boca. Es extremadamente común pero no es considerada una ITS. El herpes genital es otra historia, definitivamente una ITS. Esta clase de herpes se caracteriza por dolor, comezón y llagas en la zona genital.

Lo que resulta confuso es que el herpes oral puede aparecer en los genitales y causar síntomas similares a los del herpes genital. El virus del herpes genital se aloja en la base de los nervios de la columna vertebral y vive ahí permanentemente.

Los síntomas pueden aparecer al contraerse el virus, o tiempo después, y regresar de manera esporádica. Algunos detonantes de estas reapariciones son la fatiga y el estrés.

✱ ¿Cómo te da?

A través de contacto oral, genital o anal con una persona con llagas activas de herpes; es decir, cuando la llaga está abierta y se dice que está derramando. Puedes contraerlo por contacto de piel a piel o mediante fluidos vaginales o esperma, que lo trasladan de la llaga a otra locación.

✱ Síntomas

La primera vez aparecen una o más llagas en la zona genital, que se pueden romper, sangrar o supurar, y dar comezón. Tardan en secarse entre siete y catorce días.

Algunas veces los brotes son seguidos por síntomas parecidos a los de la gripe (dolor de cabeza y cuerpo cortado, fiebre y fatiga), así como dificultad al orinar. Los síntomas pueden surgir después de varios meses del contagio. Los siguientes brotes usualmente son más leves y pueden confundirse con infecciones o alergias. Los brotes también aparecen sin presencia de síntomas.

✱ Prevención

Siempre utiliza condón, así como espermicidas. Hay riesgo de contagio aun cuando las llagas no sean visibles. Los condones para mujer son todavía mejores que los de hombre porque cubren más del área genital.

✱ Tratamiento

Las pomadas pueden reducir la molestia del herpes, disminuyen la comezón y aceleran el proceso de cicatrización. Son recomendables los baños de asiento. Las cremas anestésicas pueden disminuir la molestia; además, algunos medicamentos antivirales pueden reducir los brotes. Comer bien y dormir bien ayuda al tratamiento.

✱ Implicaciones a largo plazo

Una vez que contraes herpes tendrás que vivir con él toda la vida y necesitarás tener muchos cuidados. Lávate las

manos frecuentemente cuando tengas brotes, evita tocarte ojos y cara después de tener contacto con una llaga. El herpes en los ojos es peligroso y puede provocar ceguera. Si estás infectada es difícil dar a luz en parto natural, pues un brote podría tener graves consecuencias en el recién nacido. Si te embarazas dile a tu doctor que tienes herpes.

Virus del papiloma humano

✳ ¿Qué es?

Es un virus de transmisión sexual muy común, relacionado con el virus que causa verrugas en cualquier parte del cuerpo.

✳ ¿Cómo te da?

Se adquiere a través del contacto de la piel, contacto vaginal, anal o sexo oral con alguien que tenga el virus.

✳ Síntomas

Usualmente no causa dolor, algunas veces aparecen verrugas que dan comezón en alguna zona genital externa o interna.

Tienen una apariencia diferente dependiendo de si son más duras, blancas o cafés en los genitales externos, más suaves y rosadas en la parte interior del canal vaginal o en el cérvix. Pueden aparecer individualmente o en grupo.

✳ Prevención

Algunos métodos como los condones y los diafragmas ayudan a reducir el riesgo. Se puede transmitir de piel a piel aun con protección. Muchas personas tienen verrugas y no lo saben, otros tienen el virus y lo ignoran.

✳ Tratamiento

Una vez que el médico diagnostica, las verrugas pueden congelarse, quemarse, tratarse con láser o cortarse. El sis-

tema inmunológico del cuerpo parece que limpia el virus del cuerpo permanentemente o por un largo tiempo. Existen medicamentos para eliminarlo.

✳ Implicaciones a largo plazo

Algunas verrugas que no se han tratado pueden seguir creciendo, romperse y sangrar si son irritadas. Algunos efectos del virus que causan las verrugas se relacionan con el cáncer cervical y con condiciones precancerosas del cérvix, aunque el porcentaje de estos casos es bajo. El papanicolau es una forma confiable para detectar el cáncer cervical, que es fácil de tratar y curar en fases iniciales. Cada mujer necesita practicárselo una vez al año. Aquellas que han sido diagnosticadas con el VPH (virus del papiloma humano) deberán hacérselo cada seis meses.

NOTA:

Ya existe una vacuna preventiva que puede ayudar a que no te contagies de VPH.

Consulta con un médico.

Clamidia

✳ ¿Qué es?

Una infección bacterial en los genitales.

✳ ¿Cómo te da?

Se adquiere a través del contacto con la piel, el contacto vaginal o anal y el sexo oral.

✳ Síntomas

Sensación de quemazón al orinar y en los genitales. Cambio de olor y textura en el flujo. Posibles cólicos.

✳ Prevención

Asegúrate de que tú y tu novio no estén contaminados. Usen condones (para hombre o mujer) con espermicida al tener sexo oral, vaginal o anal.

✳ Tratamiento

Con antibióticos si es diagnosticada en las fases iniciales.

✳ Implicaciones a largo plazo

Sin diagnosticar y sin tratar puede causar daños en vías urinarias y órganos reproductores, enfermedades de inflamaciones pélvicas (EIP) en la mujer y esterilidad.

Hepatitis B

✳ ¿Qué es?

Un virus que daña al hígado.

✳ ¿Cómo te da?

Se transmite por medio de los fluidos corporales incluyendo la saliva. La puedes contraer al besar a una persona infectada, o al tener contacto sexual oral, anal o vaginal. También al compartir agujas usadas, navajas, cepillos de dientes, tijeras para uñas, o al utilizar instrumentos no esterilizados para hacer *piercings* o tatuajes.

✳ Síntomas

Sarpullido, fatiga, náuseas, vómito, dolor corporal, dolor abdominal, pérdida de apetito, tono amarillento en la piel. También hay quienes no presentan síntomas.

✳ Prevención

Existe una vacuna que se suministra en tres inyecciones. La hepatitis B es altamente contagiosa, así que debes evi-

tar el contacto íntimo con quienes la padezcan. Los condones femenino y masculino, utilizados con espermicidas, reducen el riesgo de contagio durante el sexo, pero seguirás expuesta aun si se besan.

✱ tratamiento

La vacuna es efectiva aun después de la exposición. También las inyecciones de inmunoglobina ayudan a fortalecer el sistema inmunológico para combatir el virus.

✱ Implicaciones a largo plazo

Si te cuidas bien, con descanso, una buena dieta, nada de alcohol y el tratamiento médico adecuado, esta enfermedad puede controlarse. Sin embargo, es crónica. Sin tratamiento y sin control puede dañar el hígado y causar la muerte.

Sífilis

✱ ¿Qué es?

Es una bacteria de transmisión sexual que entra en la corriente sanguínea y provoca úlceras, llagas y sarpullido.

✱ ¿Cómo te da?

Por sexo oral, anal o vaginal. Algunas veces por besos ya que las llagas pueden aparecer en el interior de la boca.

✱ Síntomas

Se manifiesta en diferentes etapas: primero aparece una llaga donde se dio el contacto, la llaga comienza a supurar y, posteriormente, se seca (la etapa de supuración es la más contagiosa).

Sin tratar, la bacteria avanza hasta provocar sarpullido, fiebre y dolores de cabeza. La llaga seca no implica curación: la enfermedad es latente y quien la padece se convierte en portador.

* Prevención

Los métodos como el condón masculino y femenino, utilizados con espermicida, reducen el riesgo. Claro, debes pensarlo muy bien antes de tener relaciones sexuales con alguien que la padece.

* Tratamiento

Antibióticos.

* Implicaciones a largo plazo

La sífilis sin tratar puede deteriorar órganos vitales, provocar daño cerebral y hasta la muerte.

Vaginosis bacteriana

* ¿Qué es?

La vaginosis bacteriana es el tipo más común de infección vaginal.

* ¿Cómo te da?

La causa de la vaginosis bacteriana (VB) no se conoce del todo. Tiene que ver con un desequilibrio en la cantidad de bacterias que por lo general están en la vagina. Normalmente, la mayoría de las bacterias en la vagina son "buenas", pero también hay unas cuantas bacterias que son "dañinas". La VB se presenta cuando hay un aumento del número de bacterias dañinas.

Algunas de las situaciones que pueden aumentar el riesgo de contraer la VB son:

* Tener una nueva pareja o múltiples parejas sexuales.
* Hacer lavados vaginales.

La relación de la actividad sexual en la aparición de la VB no es clara. Las mujeres no contraen la vaginosis bacteria-

na por el contacto con los baños, las pijamas, las albercas o por tocar los objetos que las rodean. Sin embargo, las mujeres que nunca han tenido relaciones sexuales también pueden padecer esta infección.

✳ Síntomas

Las mujeres con VB pueden tener un flujo vaginal anormal con un olor desagradable, u olor a pescado, sobre todo después de haber tenido relaciones sexuales. Cuando tienes VB, el flujo vaginal es generalmente de color blanco o gris y puede ser un poco espeso. También se puede sentir ardor al orinar o comezón en la parte externa de la vagina o de plano los dos síntomas. Debes tener cuidado, pues muchas mujeres sienten que estos síntomas son normales y no saben que tienen VB.

✳ Prevención

Dentro de los puntos que pueden ayudar a prevenirla, están el tener una buena higiene diaria, en especial cuando tienes tu menstruación; tener una sola pareja sexual, no darse lavados vaginales, ni ponerse desodorantes en aerosol que tapen tu olor vaginal.

✳ Tratamiento

Antibiótico, crema o gelatina que se inserta en la vagina con un aplicador. Es muy importante que si estás tomando algún otro medicamento, lo comentes con tu doctor.

✳ Implicaciones a largo plazo

En la mayoría de los casos, la vaginosis bacteriana no produce complicaciones; pero cuando la tienes puede aumentar la posibilidad de que te contagies de otra ITS.

A mí sólo me daban catarritos

Sida (Síndrome de inmunodeficiencia adquirida)

Es casi imposible que haya alguien que desconozca la existencia del sida, pero ¿qué es exactamente? Es una enfermedad que se transmite por un virus en la sangre, en los flujos vaginales o en el semen, llamado VIH, que ataca el sistema inmunológico; así, la persona es más vulnerable a enfermarse porque queda sin defensas ni protección.

Hasta ahora no se ha descubierto una cura contra el virus, aunque existen tratamientos súper caros que lo pueden más o menos controlar.

El virus hace un trabajo silencioso, va destruyendo células (linfocitos CD4) por lo que una persona puede tardarse años en descubrir que está enferma (a esto se le llama ser portador). Tener el virus no es lo mismo que tener sida, aunque un portador puede desarrollar la enfermedad con el tiempo.

Se puede transmitir al tener relaciones sexuales con una persona infectada, a través de la penetración oral, anal o vaginal. También al utilizar objetos como jeringas usadas, agujas de tatuaje, instrumental quirúrgico no esterilizado, navajas de rasurar, o de madre a hijo durante el embarazo o la lactancia.

Los síntomas

En las fases iniciales son imperceptibles. Después, se inflaman los ganglios linfáticos, hay una pérdida gruesísima de peso, sudoración por las noches, fiebre intermitente, diarrea, dolor de cabeza, infecciones frecuentes y cansancio.

Se puede prevenir usando el condón masculino o femenino, acompañado de espermicida (que mata a los espermatozoides) al tener relaciones sexuales.

Aguas con el sida, porque sí... da

Sobra decir que el sida es un asunto de vida o muerte. No le dedicamos tanto espacio por mera casualidad; mucha, pero mucha gente se está muriendo por esta enfermedad.

Cuando eres joven crees que tus decisiones no serán trascendentales: todo lo contrario, ¡son muy importantes! Como a esa edad se vive "la vida loca", puedes tener mucho más riesgo.

Como ya dijimos, la ciencia no ha encontrado la cura para el sida, así que no importa cuánto tomaste, cuánto te gusta el chavo o si es tu única oportunidad para estar con él: si no tienes condón, no te la juegues. Ni el momento más increíble del universo es suficiente para arriesgar tu vida.

NOTA:

Si algún día sospechas que te contagiaste de sida, espera a que pasen tres meses de la relación, hazte un análisis de sangre y acude al médico con los resultados. No hagas caso de remedios caseros, de curanderos o de brujos. Lo más importante entonces, es que dejes de tener relaciones sexuales para evitar que la enfermedad se propague.

CENTROS DE APOYO:

telsida
01 (55) 52-07-40-77
01-800-712-08-89
Diversitel
01 (55) 52-72-25-22

Sexo oral

Es la unión de la boca con los genitales. Es importante tener cuidado porque muchas enfermedades como el herpes y el sida se pueden transmitir de esta manera. Como los virus no son visibles y nunca sabes si tu pareja está contagiada, lo mejor es protegerte. Si decides practicarlo, recuerda que el uso del condón aminora el riesgo, pero aguas porque no es 100 por ciento seguro.

Sexo anal

Es la penetración del pene o los dedos en el ano. Ahí se encuentran muchas terminaciones nerviosas por lo que para muchos es una zona placentera. Sin embargo, el acto sexual puede ser doloroso y con riesgos pues es posible que las paredes del recto se desgarren y sangren, lo que lo convierte en lugar ideal para transmitir o adquirir una enfermedad sexual.

Esta situación empeora cuando el pene, posteriormente, se introduce en la vagina: si estuvo en contacto con el ano, se encuentra muy contaminado por materia fecal. ¡Evítalo!

Protección sexual

Wooowww ya le viste su "ESE"

Métodos anticonceptivos

Sí tú y tu galán van a compartir y a conocerse sus cositas, es fundamental que te informes sobre el tema.

Si eres sexualmente activa, no importa qué pastilla o qué método uses, siempre existe la posibilidad de que te embaraces o contraigas una ITS.

Una vez más, ¡sólo la abstinencia es 100 por ciento segura!

Puedes aumentar la protección al utilizar dos métodos anticonceptivos a la vez (como pastilla y condón), ¡siempre y cuando las pastillas no sean de menta!

Checa estos datos:

- Según un artículo publicado en el diario Reforma, en México, de acuerdo con la Universidad Nacional Autónoma de México, nacen anualmente más de 500 mil bebés de mamás menores de 20 años. Es decir, 1369 partos diarios. ¡Qué tal!

- De acuerdo con el Instituto Nacional de Estadística, Geografía e Informática (INEGI), sólo 45 por ciento de mujeres entre 15 y 19 años utilizan métodos anticonceptivos, cuando 96 por ciento de los jóvenes las conocen; o sea, que al otro 55 por ciento ¿que onda?

Cualquier método es mejor que ninguno. Hay diferentes y cada uno tiene sus ventajas y desventajas.

TABLA

DE MÉTODOS ANTICONCEPTIVOS Y PROTECCIÓN

Tipo de anticonceptivo	Efectividad contra las ITS	Efectividad contra embarazos
Condón.	Alta. A excepción de la abstinencia, el condón es el mejor método para no contraerlas.	88% (condón masculino) la efectividad aumenta si además se usa algún espermicida.
Diafragma con espermicida.	Baja. El espermicida te puede proteger contra el virus del papiloma humano y la gonorrea.	82%
Método natural, ritmo.	Ninguna.	Muy baja.
Óvulos, espuma o jaleas.	Baja. Puede proteger contra clamidia y gonorrea.	79%
Píldora anticonceptiva.	Ninguna.	99%
Coitus interruptus.	Ninguna.	38%
Preservativo femenino.	Buena. Cubre una superficie vaginal considerable.	90%
DIU: Dispositivo intrauterino.	Ninguna.	Entre 98 y 99%
Ligamiento de trompas.	Ninguna.	99%
Esponja.	Ningujna.	Entre 64 y 94%
Píldora anticonceptiva de emergencia.	Ninguna.	Entre 80 y 95% depende del tiempo en que se tomó después del coito.
Implante anticonceptivo	Ninguna.	99%
Anillo intravaginal	Ninguna.	99%

Existen mitos acerca de métodos anticonceptivos que no tienen nada que ver, o sea, no tienen fundamento:

✚ Tomar mucho limón. Sólo sirve para cuando tienes gripe.
✖ Hacerse lavados vaginales con vinagre.
✚ Tomar una pastilla anticonceptiva sólo el día que se tienen relaciones sexuales o llevar dietas especiales: estas creencias son como de película futurista.
✖ Brincar después de tener relaciones sexuales para que se salga el semen: no sirve de nada.
✖ Retirar el pene antes de la eyaculación.

Métodos anticonceptivos más comunes

La pastilla

Es recomendable que la recete un médico pues hay de diferentes tipos. Es una pequeña pastilla que contiene dosis mínimas de hormonas que impiden la ovulación. Existen diferentes marcas y las concentraciones hormonales varían de una a otra. Algunas deben tomarse el día que te baja; otras, a los siete días de haber terminado la menstruación; unas más, a partir del quinto día del inicio de la menstruación. El ginecólogo sabrá cuál es la mejor para

ti. Se pueden comprar en cualquier farmacia. Como método anticonceptivo es bastante seguro; además, los ciclos menstruales se hacen más regulares y el dolor disminuye. Puede tener efectos secundarios, especialmente durante los tres primeros meses de uso:

- Aumento de peso.
- Aumento de vello.
- Dolor en los pechos.
- Dolor de cabeza.
- Depresión.
- Náuseas.

Por último, está contraindicada a las fumadoras y cuando tienes algún problema en las bubis.

A pesar de todo, muchas mujeres la prefieren y es uno de los métodos anticonceptivos más utilizados.

Hay que recordar tomarla diario a la misma hora porque si no lo haces pierde su efectividad.

El dispositivo intrauterino

Es un aparato de plástico o cobre en forma de "T". El médico lo inserta en el útero y lo revisa cada seis meses para comprobar que esté bien colocado. Actúa como anticonceptivo al hacer que el útero sea inhabitable para un óvulo fecundado. Tiene una efectividad de 98 por ciento y puede durar de tres a cinco años sin necesidad de cambiarlo. Debido al dispositivo puedes tener más cólicos menstruales al comenzar a usarlo y notar un aumento de sangrado.

Manuel

el diafragma

Es como una copita de goma que se coloca en el cuello uterino. Mide entre cinco y diez centímetros de diámetro y es "quita-pon". Su función consiste en que el semen no pase por el cuello uterino. Dura dos años y tiene una efectividad de 90 por ciento. El doctor te dice cuál es el tamaño que necesitas. La mujer lo inserta en la vagina antes de la relación sexual y lo cubre con jalea espermicida dejándoselo puesto siete horas después de la relación para que el espermicida haga su trabajo. Antes de ponerlo hay que revisarlo para comprobar que no tenga algún agujerito. Se puede insertar en la vagina hasta cuatro horas antes de tener relaciones. Si está bien colocado no molesta. Al quitarlo debe lavarse bien y guardarse en su estuche.

el condón

Tus papás lo conocían como preservativo; es una funda de látex con la que se cubre el pene cuando está erecto para que, al eyacular, el semen quede atrapado en él y no pase al cuello uterino.

Hay diferentes tipos: lubricados, no lubricados, con figuritas, colores, sabores y hasta musicales.

Obviamente se pueden comprar sin receta médica y, como ya leíste, te protege de enfermedades de transmisión sexual incluyendo el sida. Tiene una efectividad de 88 por ciento. El porcentaje de protección aumenta si lo usas con anticonceptivos vaginales como óvulos o espuma.

LO QUE TE LÁTEX

Y LO QUE NO TE LÁTEX

- La sensación de usarlo no cambia mucho; el hombre siente 95 por ciento igual que si no lo usara, así que no dejes que tu galán se mal viaje.
- Se debe usar un preservativo nuevo en cada relación y no nos referimos a cada novio ieh!, sino a cada vez que hagan el amor.
- Te repetimos que los condones musicales, de figuritas chistosas y todos esos rollos cómicos no sirven, sólo se usan para jugar, nada más no se los prestes a tu hermanito menor.
- Se tiene que interrumpir "el romance" para que se lo ponga el galán, pero vale la pena. Nunca abran el paquetito de los condones con los dientes porque pueden perforar el condón y luego ni te das cuenta (si te sucede, no te preocupes: nueve meses después te enteras porque te enteras).
- Algunos hombres son alérgicos al látex y al espermicida.

¿Cómo se usan?

- Se coloca en el pene erecto antes del coito. La punta del condón debe apretarse con los dedos mientras lo desenrollas para evitar que se quede aire adentro y se

rompa. Debe evitarse que el pene toque la vagina antes de tener el condón puesto ya que los fluidos masculinos contienen espermatozoides.

- La punta del condón debe separarse un centímetro del pene para que allí se concentre el semen. Después de que el hombre eyacule y antes de que la erección desaparezca se debe apretar la base del condón contra el pene, al mismo tiempo que se retira de la vagina, se quita, se anuda y se tira a la basura. Es importante saber que si una pareja, después del orgasmo se quedan abrazados sin retirar el condón de la vagina, el pene pierde rigidez por lo que es posible que se salga del condón, con lo que el riesgo de embarazo sigue latente, ya que el condón se convierte en una bolsita llena de espermatozoides deseosos de salir: ¡Ten mucho cuidado!
- Evita usar un condón con vaselina porque provoca reacción en el látex del condón y lo hace frágil; tampoco se recomienda colocar dos condones pues se rozan entre ellos y se rompen. Ten cuidado con las uñas, no lo vayas a romper.

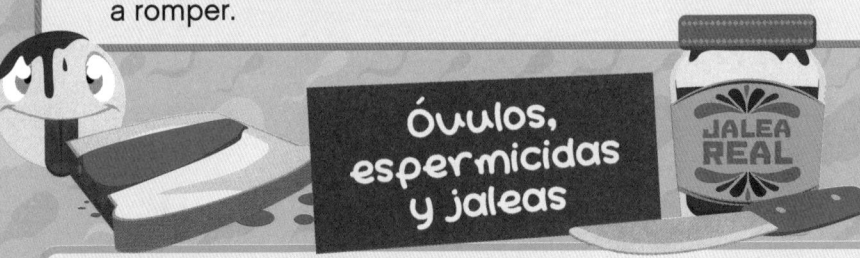

Óvulos, espermicidas y jaleas

Son sustancias químicas conocidas cómo espermicidas que se insertan hasta el fondo de la vagina antes de la relación sexual, que matan o inmovilizan a los espermatozoides sin dañar los órganos sexuales. La mayoría se introduce con los dedos o con un aplicador quince minutos antes del coito. Siempre encontrarás las instrucciones en el empaque. Después de una hora de su introducción pierden efectividad. Si se usan solos su protección es de 79 por ciento, pero aumenta si se acompaña de otros métodos como el condón o el diafragma.

Coitus interruptus

Significa que en el momento de la eyaculación el hombre retira el pene de la vagina para que el semen no quede dentro. Su efectividad es muy muy baja ya que durante el coito hay pre eyaculaciones que contienen esperma. Además, no evita el contagio de enfermedades de transmisión sexual. ¡Aguas!

El preservativo femenino

Es una membrana de látex con forma de tubo con un anillo en cada extremo que se introduce en la vagina (viene lubricado para facilitar su colocación). Sirve para evitar que el semen pase al cuello uterino y cubrir las paredes para evitar el contacto directo. Tú te lo pones y su efectividad se calcula en 90 por ciento. Quienes lo han usado dicen que se siente un poco raro pero es muy efectivo para evitar enfermedades porque cubre más superficie vaginal.

NOTA:

no es recomendable que la mujer lo utilice mientras el hombre usa también condón porque se pegan uno con otro.

implante anticonceptivo (implanon)

Algunas personas lo conocen como chip anticonceptivo. Es un implante con la forma de una varilla del tamaño de un cerillo, se pone debajo de la piel en la parte superior interna del brazo. No se puede ver pero sí se puede sentir.

Es altamente confiable para prevenir el embarazo y dura de 3 a 5 años aproximadamente. Después de la inserción —un procedimiento sencillo que obviamente debe hacer un doctor— la varilla libera lentamente una hormona sintética llamada la hormona progestogénica etonogestrel, que es uno de los componentes de la mayoría de las pastillas anticonceptivas más modernas.

El implante es fácil, rápido de poner y de quitar. Se puede dejar de utilizar en cualquier momento y una vez que te lo quitan, la ovulación regresa en aproximadamente 5 días. Ojo: el uso del implante debe ser consultado con un médico profesional.

Anillo intravaginal (nuvaring)

Es un anillo de plástico blando como del tamaño del aro de un condón, que te da protección por un mes. Es fácil introducirlo en tu vagina por ti misma, y una vez adentro puede mantenerse puesto en su lugar durante 3 semanas. Durante este tiempo libera ciertos componentes cada 24 horas, para inhibir la ovulación. Estas hormonas entran en el organismo a través de la pared vaginal.

Despues de tres semanas puedes quitarte el anillo fácilmente. Durante la semana siguiente, ya sin el anillo, muchas mujeres tienen un sangrado. Una semana después (exactamente) se debe poner un anillo nuevo. Tiene un nivel de efectividad del 99%. Debes de consultar su uso con un médico profesional.

El método natural

Se trata de tener relaciones sólo durante los días infértiles (cuando la mujer no ovula). Para conocer tus días fértiles puedes hacer lo siguiente:

Tomarte la temperatura. Hazlo antes de levantarte de la cama. Lo normal es que no supere los 37°C, pero justo después de la ovulación puede aumentar alrededor de 0.5°C. Así que tu periodo de fertilidad es tres días antes y después de la ovulación.

Observa el flujo vaginal. En los días fértiles, el flujo cambia, se hace transparente y gelatinoso como clara de huevo.

Ritmo. Esto significa no tener relaciones en los días fértiles: en un ciclo de 28 días, el día 13 y 14 serían los de más alto riesgo. Pero los días fértiles son del 10 al 17. Para que sea efectivo hay que llevar un control muy estricto. Su efectividad es muy baja. Además tienes que ser súper regular para que funcione.

Anticonceptivos de emergencia

ROMPER EN CASO DE SER SÚPER NECESARIO

Si a pesar de que te cuidaste tienes una situación inesperada, como el hecho de que el preservativo esté roto o que él no haya sacado el pene a tiempo, tu doctor te puede recetar la "píldora de emergencia". Esta pastilla contiene cierta cantidad de hormonas que alteran el endometrio (las paredes del útero) para que el óvulo no se instale; así, el embarazo no se produce y baja la menstruación.

Para que la píldora funcione, es muy importante tomarla dentro de las 72 horas siguientes al coito. Es un recurso extremo que sólo tu ginecólogo puede recomendar.

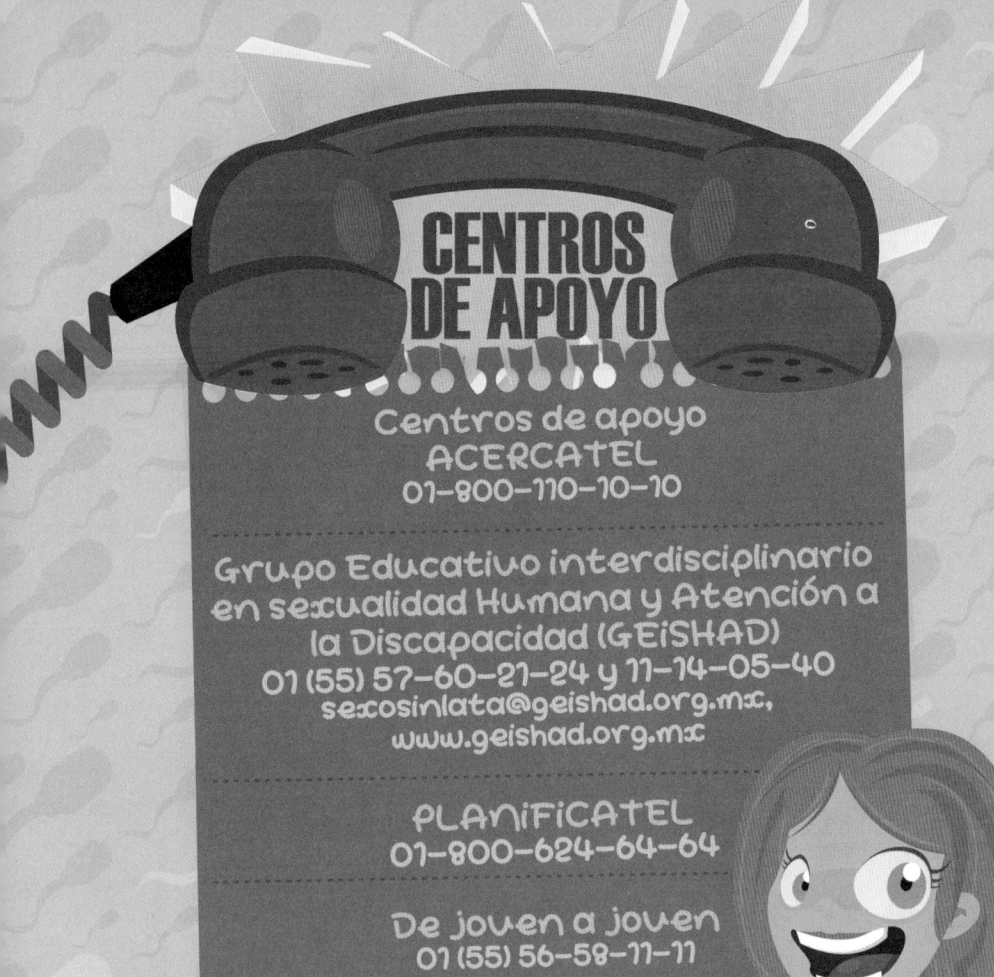

CENTROS DE APOYO

Centros de apoyo
ACERCATEL
01-800-110-10-10

Grupo Educativo interdisciplinario
en sexualidad Humana y Atención a
la Discapacidad (GEiSHAD)
01 (55) 57-60-21-24 y 11-14-05-40
sexosinlata@geishad.org.mx,
www.geishad.org.mx

PLANIFICATEL
01-800-624-64-64

De joven a joven
01 (55) 56-58-11-11

Como pudiste ver, el universo de la sexualidad tiene de todo. Está en tus manos, y sólo en tus manos, hacer que sea maravilloso o que se convierta en una pesadilla. Como siempre: ¡tú decides!

Capítulo 5
Quiúbole con...
mi mente
COMER O NO COMER
LAS EMOCIONES
LAS DROGAS
LA DEPRESIÓN
EL SUICIDIO
EL CHUPE

Si crees que los cambios en tu cuerpo son muchos, no creerás en los cambios que puedes tener en la mente. Seguro eres consciente de algunos: los de humor o los del estado de ánimo, los de la sensación de "pérdida de ti misma", que surge cuando no sabes quién eres, quién eras, a dónde vas y, mucho menos, de dónde vienes. En fin, un rollo donde las inseguridades, las dudas y las confusiones te llevan a descubrir que tienes muchos "yo" que desconocías (lo que NO significa que tus "yo" diferentes puedan tener varios novios o frees distintos).

Problemas emocionales

Las dudas existenciales se las han planteado los seres humanos desde la era de los cavernícolas, es decir SIEMPRE. Así que no te claves ni te sientas mal; de hecho, la mayoría de los adultos todavía no logran encontrar las respuestas. ¿Te pasa a veces que, cuando estás sola eres de una manera, y al estar en un grupo o con alguien más eres de otra forma? Digamos que, más que doble cara, de plano ite sientes triple cara! ¿Te pasa que un día eres tímida, otros te vale, eres cariñosa o de plano indiferente? ¿Una semana te vistes de una manera y a la siguiente te pones lo que antes te chocaba? ¿Ya sabes? Relájate, itodo eso es ser tú misma! Es de lo más normal. Tómalo con calma, piensa que pronto pasará y aplica con esta bronca lo mismo que con la gripe: déjala fluir.

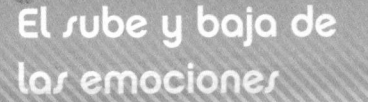

El sube y baja de las emociones

Hay muchas emociones padres, divertidas y disfrutables como las que surjen del amor, la satisfacción, la alegría y muchas más; pero hay otras que duelen y son más difíciles de manejar. Cada quien las vive y las maneja a su manera.

Las emociones son sentimientos, no acciones. Es cierto: muchas veces no puedes controlar lo que sientes (si te cuesta trabajo controlar a tus tortuguitas japonesas, imagínate esto). Lo que sí puedes controlar es lo que haces al respecto. Si llegas a sentir que es imposible manejar alguna emoción negativa y que te encuentras haciendo cosas que son destructivas para ti o los demás, pide ayuda.

me siento como dedo

Emociones que no nos gustan

Me siento sola

¿Te ha pasado que aunque estés con mucha gente te sientes como dedo? De hecho, puedes estar en tu mismísima fiesta de cumpleaños y sentir que no te mueve la cola ni el perro. No te preocupes, si has tenido este sentimiento de soledad, has llorado horas en tu cama o simplemente sientes que nadie te quiere, es importante que sepas que puede ser normal. Todos lo hemos sentido alguna vez.

Siento ansiedad y angustia

¿Has sentido un hoyo en el estómago que no es por hambre ni por un *piercing* en el ombligo? La ansiedad y la angustia son un estado como de inquietud y miedo a situaciones por venir donde no sabes qué va a pasar. Puede ser temor a algo específico o a algo que desconoces.

Si sientes angustia y ansiedad puedes tratar de distraerte con tus amigas, tomar clases de algo (nada más no se te ocurra tomar el curso: depresión 1 y depresión 2), hacer deporte o besuquearte con tu novio; de hecho, éste es uno de los pasatiempos más divertidos.

Por otro lado, si la angustia y la ansiedad afectan lo que haces todos los días lo mejor es que busques ayuda con un psicólogo o psiquiatra, cosa que no te debe asustar porque a mucha gente le pasa, es algo frecuente y con una pequeña terapia o medicamento es muy posible que pronto superes el problema.

Tengo depresión

Estar deprimida es nefasto, sin embargo a mucha gente le sucede. Puedes sentirte así porque tronaste con tu novio, por broncas en tu casa, por exceso de buenas calificaciones, porque tronaste con tu novio (no, no nos equivocamos, lo que pasa es que es la quinta vez que truenan y regresan) o por algo que no logras ubicar, pero te pasa.

La mejor manera de aliviarte es enfrentar la depresión y ubicar qué es lo que te tiene en el hoyo. Hay veces que con sólo abrirte de verdad y platicar lo que sientes con alguien querido, te puedes animar y salir adelante. Sin embargo, hay otras en las que de plano no puedes sola y necesitas la ayuda de un experto.

PRECAUCIÓN
LA VIDA EN EL HOYO

SI LA DEPRESIÓN DURA MÁS DE DOS SEMANAS Y...

- ► lloras casi todos los días,
- ► te sientes cansada, culpable o desesperanzada,
- ► te alejas de los demás,
- ► deja de emocionarte lo que antes te gustaba,
- ► estás más irritable y molesta (y no es sólo porque tengas el síndrome "ch"),
- ► adoptas conductas autodestructivas,
- ► hasta has pensado en el suicidio...

...es probable que tengas una depresión seria y lo mejor que puedes hacer es buscar terapia con un psicólogo o un psiquiatra. A veces, la terapia es suficiente; si no, la combinan con medicina. Existen casos especiales para los que hay tratamientos específicos.

Conductas autodestructivas

Una conducta autodestructiva es cuando te pones física o psicológicamente en peligro; es como querer lanzarte del bungee, pero sin cuerda. Esto puede pasar por diferentes factores, como una situación dolorosa en tu vida, para huir de un dolor o un riesgo futuro que te da miedo enfrentar o que no sabes cómo resolver.

Una conducta autodestructiva puede expresarse de un buen de maneras, desde dejar de esforzarte en conseguir algo, hasta lastimarte a propósito (esto sí es bajonearte en serio). Algunas conductas autodestructivas son peores que otras.

Suicidio

Aunque es difícil descubrirlo, existe un importante número de jóvenes que piensan en él y lamentablemente algunos lo realizan.

El suicidio es una de las cosas más difíciles que existen en este mundo. Cuando alguien se suicida no sólo se lastima a sí mismo, sino que provoca sufrimiento en toda la gente a su alrededor, dejándole sentimientos de culpabilidad, rabia, tristeza, impotencia y depresión.

Muchas veces puedes creer que sería imposible que tu vida esté peor, que tus problemas no tienen solución y que no vale la pena continuar. No es cierto, todos, absolutamente todos (aunque de momento pienses que en tu caso no es así), pueden resolver sus broncas o mejorar, desde:

➤ Jamás haber tenido novio, y que no le intereses a nadie.
➤ Tener un accidente y no moverte por el resto de tu vida.
➤ La muerte de alguien muy querido, inclusive de toda tu familia.
➤ Un divorcio.
➤ Tener una dependencia total a las drogas.
➤ Tronar con el único hombre que has amado y sentir un dolor imposible de explicar.
➤ Tener problemas serios con tus papás, al grado de no querer que esos padres sean tuyos.
➤ Tener una deuda impagable y recibir amenazas.
➤ Sentirte la persona menos importante de este planeta y con serias broncas de autoestima.
➤ Hasta el gran gran gran problema que estés viviendo en este momento y sientes que te rebasa.

Recuerda sólo una cosa: TODO PASA. Después del agobio y los momentos difíciles, las cosas SIEMPRE cambian y los sentimientos pasan. Aun los más negativos e intensos.

Aunque efectivamente algunos problemas son irremediables, lo mejor es aceptarlos y ver qué puedes aprender de la situación. Descubrir que creces mentalmente cuando los enfrentas, que maduras, y que a pesar del dolor y las terribles experiencias puedes volver a disfrutar tu vida.

Lo fuerte no es lo complicado del problema, sino que la persona se niegue a salir de él, y definitivamente un paso tan duro como buscar la muerte, no es la solución.

Si alguna vez pensaste en el suicidio como solución a tus problemas, es importantísimo que se lo cuentes a una amiga o adulto en quien confíes, a un médico, psicólogo o maestro que te caiga bien; también puedes llamar a una línea de ayuda telefónica.

Si has escuchado a una amiga o amigo hablar de suicidio, tómalo en serio, habla neto con él o ella y de inmediato busquen ayuda. Si de plano se rehúsa a ser ayudado, coméntalo urgentemente con algún adulto y llama tú misma a una línea de apoyo para saber qué puedes hacer en esta situación.

Mitos acerca del suicidio

m = mito
R = Realidad

Ocho de cada 10 personas que se suicidan, antes de hacerse daño, se lo comunican a alguien. Si te lo dicen a ti, no dejes de ayudarlo.

m. El índice de suicidios entre jóvenes ha disminuido.
R. En México, en los últimos años, ha aumentado del 15 al 21 por ciento. De hecho, es la segunda causa de muerte en los adolescentes, así que, ¡cuidado!

m. Sólo ciertas personas se suicidan.
R. Cualquier persona, sin distinción, hombres o mujeres; ricos y pobres; jóvenes y adultos; gente del campo, de la ciudad y de cualquier religión, se puede suicidar.

m. Cuando una persona hable sobre suicidio, cambia el tema y trata de quitárselo de la mente.

r. Al contrario, tómalo en serio. Escucha lo que dice. Dale la oportunidad de decir qué siente y hazle saber que te preocupa. Pide ayuda de volada.

m. La mayoría de las personas que se quieren suicidar, en verdad se quieren morir.

r. La mayoría de los que se quieren quitar la vida están confundidos. No saben si quieren morir o no. Casi siempre, el suicidio es un grito de alguien que pide ayuda.

LOS FOCOS ROJOS QUE INDICAN QUE ALGUIEN PUEDE LLEGAR A SUICIDARSE

- Habla constantemene sobre la muerte.
- Se olvida de sus cosas de valor o las regala.
- Tiene un plan para quitarse la vida.
- Guarda pastillas, una pistola u otra arma.
- Se ha lastimado.
- Sin explicación, ves a la persona súper tranquila después de haber pasado una depresión muy gruesa.
- Deja de ver a sus amigos, de estudiar y pierde interés en arreglarse.
- Se aisla de todo el mundo, o permanece con un grupo de amigos súper cerrado que siempre parecen misteriosos y nadie sabe nada de ellos.

CENTRO DE APOYO

SAPTEL
01 (55) 52-59-81-21
01-800-472-78-35

Las drogas

¿Qué son las drogas?

Churro, tacha, cristal, toque, LSD, piedra, ácido, coca o base; como quieras llamarlas, el rollo es el mismo.

Las drogas son sustancias naturales o sintéticas que causan efectos en tu cuerpo y mente. Dichos efectos pueden ser permanentes y provocar cambios en tu comportamiento y sentimientos.

¿Por qué la gente se mete drogas la primera vez?

Por curiosidad, "sólo por probar"; esto le pasa a muchos por la cabeza y lamentablemente también por la nariz, la boca y hasta las venas. La idea de "sólo por probar" es más peligrosa de lo que te imaginas, es muy fácil caer en la adicción. ¿Sabías que siete de cada 10 personas que prueban cualquier tipo de droga después la siguen consumiendo? Este dato es súper cañón. Lo que empieza como curiosidad puede terminar en un problema nefasto para tu vida.

A veces alguna de nuestras emociones está enferma y no lo sabemos porque se ubica en el inconsciente y sólo espera un pretexto para salir.

Por ejemplo, crees sentirte bien y no te das cuenta de que realmente estás triste porque tus papás se separaron

o se divorciaron; que van varios novios con los que truenas rápido y no sabes por qué o en el fondo te sientes menos que otras personas. Este tipo de momentos se vuelven el escenario ideal para que las drogas entren en acción. Por eso, por más que estés prendida, divertida o quedando bien con un galán, si llegas al punto en que debes decidir entre probar o no probar, de verdad no pienses: "No pasa nada", ¡porque sí pasa!

LAS NIÑAS CONSUMEN DROGAS...

- ...por experimentar, para saber qué se siente.
- ...por presión, para que sus amigos no la saquen del grupo y por miedo a sus burlas.
- ...por presión del galán que "supuestamente" las ama.
- ...por imitar a alguien y sentirse aceptada.
- ...para alejarse de su realidad y escapar de los problemas.
- ...y piensan que no pasa nada. "Tengo un grupo de amigas que llevan dos años metiéndose coca y están de pelos, no les pasa nada." Aunque cada organismo es distinto, las drogas conducen, tarde o temprano, al mismo punto. Algunas personas que se meten drogas en meses enfrentan problemas muy cañones, y otras se tardan más.

Si tuvieras rayos X en los ojos comprobarías cómo esas amigas o amigos cada día tienen más daños en el organismo y que su adicción crece diariamente. Muchas personas que "se ponen" con drogas hacen toda una carrera (por llamarlo de algún modo) de cinco a 10 años, o hasta menos, y finalmente, terminan en una clínica, reclusorio o muriéndose.

¿Las drogas te alivianan los problemas?

Cuando te ofrecen drogas generalmente se dicen cosas como:

Güey, te vas a pasar la mejor fiesta de tu vida.

no te la vas a acabar.

Deja de preocuparte, métete esto y bye a todas tus broncas.

nunca sentirás tan rico al hacer el amor, ¡pruébalo!

¿Es cierto? En la mayoría de los casos… SÍ.

- Puedes pasarte la mejor fiesta de tu vida, olvidarte de tus problemas y relajarte como nunca... el problema es: ¿por cuánto tiempo?
- Son el gancho perfecto. Cuando crees que no pasa nada sucede todo. Al principio (en la mayoría de los casos) funciona como te dijeron, pero en menos de lo que te imaginas los problemas que te quitaste regresan 100 veces más densos.
- La tranquilidad se transforma en ansiedad, angustia, miedo y soledad (además de que en tu primera vez te puede agarrar un mal viaje en el que te quieres morir).
- Dependiendo del tipo de droga, al principio con poca te alivianas; conforme la adicción crece necesitas dosis más altas. Te puedes meter droga todo el día y sentir tranquilidad sólo cinco minutos de cada hora; los otros 55 minutos vives un infierno. Así que ahora tienes dos problemas, el que tenías antes y la ansiedad, la angustia

y la soledad que te dan las drogas (bueno en realidad son muchos más, pues ahora por consumir tienes problemas extras con tus papás, tu novio, los amigos, la escuela, etcétera, y hasta broncas de lana para pagarlas).

- Así es el truco de la droga, es como un anzuelo para pescar. Primero se ve la carnada, que para el pez, obvio, es rica, pero en el momento en que la muerdes te enganchas, y lo peor de todo es que cuando quieres salir, el anzuelo tiene también un gancho por atrás que te atrapa y no te deja salir.
- Recuerda qué es la tolerancia: tu cuerpo se acostumbra a "x" sustancia y cada vez exige más para obtener el mismo efecto. Cuando menos te das cuenta ya estás consumiendo muchísimo y por si fuera poco, algunas personas hasta lo presumen, pues creen que "aguantan un buen"; lo que no tienen ni idea, es que su cuerpo adquiere una adicción que es para toda la vida.
- En pocas palabras buscas salir de tus problemas y lo único que logras es hundirte más profundo. Por eso, cuando la gente está ya muy dañada, dice: "No sabía en lo que me estaba metiendo."
- Al principio tus amigos te dicen: "Métete algo, no te la vas a acabar," y efectivamente, si le entras a las drogas, ¡no te la vas a acabar!

Una noticia buena y una mala

La mala es que mucha gente tiene problemas de adicción; la buena es que existen tratamientos para enfrentar las adicciones.

Ser adicto es estar enfermo. Así como algunas personas viven con "x" enfermedad, por alguna razón otras tienen la de la adicción.

¿Es fácil? No, no lo es. ¿Tiene solución? Claro que la tiene. Se necesita mucho esfuerzo, valor y constancia para salir; la bronca no es tener la adicción sino negarte a enfrentarla.

El primer paso es aceptar que tienes el problema. Si es así, ni modo, acéptalo y empieza a trabajar de volada. No dejes que pase ni un segundo más. Aplícate y recuerda que en las drogas, entre más lejos vas, más difícil es el regreso.

Si de plano no puedes dejarlo entonces necesitas asistir a un grupo de ayuda o clínica especializada. Pero recuerda: recuperarte de un rollo de drogas es un proceso largo y difícil, pero siempre es posible.

Drogas legales

EL ALCOHOL

Cuando estás en la adolescencia tienes curiosidad por saber qué se siente ponerte *happy* con unos chupes. Quizá has bebido algunos *drinks* a escondidas; o tus papás te dan permiso de tomar en ocasiones importantes, o tal vez has ido más allá y el alcohol es tu gasolina para estar en el reventón.

El asunto es que tomar es un arma de doble filo; si lo haces con responsabilidad puedes disfrutarlo y no tener ningún problema; sin embargo, si lo haces a lo loco puedes buscarte muchas broncas y hasta convertirte en adicta más rápido de lo que te imaginas.

Por eso, mejor échale un ojo a este capítulo antes de que te lleves mejor con las micheladas que con tus amigas.

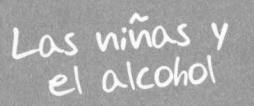

Las niñas y el alcohol

"No manches, ¡qué peda me puse anoche! Ja, ja, ja. ¿Viste a fulanita vomitando en el baño? Estaba jarrísima. ¡Pásame una chela que estoy súper cruda! Todavía sigo mareada."

Al tomar el sol en una playa de la Riviera Maya, mientras trato de concentrarme en el libro que leo, no puedo dejar de escuchar las frases anteriores que vienen de un grupito como de cinco niñas con bikinis muy modernos que, poniéndose bronceador, se instalan junto a nosotros. Volteo a verlas y no pasan de 15 o 16 años. Se ven bonitas y con clase, como si fueran educadas en un buen colegio; de no verlas, dudaría que los comentarios los hicieron ellas.

Antes, tomar unos *drinks* al grado de ponerse jarrísima era algo que por lo general veías entre los hombres. Ahora, cada día es más común que las niñas beban igual o más que los niños. Por eso decidimos incluir este capítulo, pues si estás informada tomarás una decisión responsable.

GABY

Nuevas sensaciones

Parte del rollo de crecer es enfrentarnos a la inevitable presencia del cigarro, el alcohol, las drogas y otras sustancias que alteran nuestra mente y nuestro estado de ánimo (las fiestas y los antros más bien parecen buffets de todo esto; los chefs serían los cantineros de la barra o los *dealers*).

Cuando eres adolescente experimentas un poco de libertad fuera de la casa y si estás lejos del cuidado de tus papás, quieres probar y probarte. La mayoría tomamos cerveza, le damos el golpe a un cigarro, ignoramos una orden o descubrimos el faje, un beso o el sexo. Experimentar nuevas y maravillosas sensaciones nos llama la atención. A muchos, que hoy somos adultos, también nos pasó y lo comprendemos. ¡Es lo más natural!

Algunos efectos del chupe

¡GRACIAS MÉXICO!

- A muchos, tomar un chupe los hace sentir a gusto, los estimula y les da confianza en sí mismos. (¿Quién no ha visto al típico borracho que se siente el artista famoso y baila hasta los pasos del cantante que le gusta?)
- En cinco o 10 minutos el alcohol pasa de tu intestino al torrente sanguíneo. Su efecto puede durar varias horas dependiendo de la cantidad, de lo rápido que lo ingieres y de tu tamaño corporal. Con frecuencia, sientes que te mareas y tus reacciones se entorpecen mientras el alcohol sale de tu cuerpo.
- Al día siguiente te levantas con dolor de cabeza, resaca, cruda o como le quieras decir; el asunto es que no te la acabas. De hecho, si no supieras que se trata de la cruda, le pedirías a tus papás que te llevaran ¡al hospital!

COSAS QUE HACEN QUE TE PONGAS MÁS JARRA

- Estómago vacío.
- Estar en tus días.
- Estar muy estresada o cansada.
- Tomar muy rápido (con popote es pésimo).
- Estar muy contenta o muy triste.
- Y por supuesto, que tu deporte favorito sea jugar a los "hidalgos".

¿CUÁNTO ALCOHOL TIENE LO QUE ME ESTOY TOMANDO?

Una cerveza	5%
Vino de mesa	12%
Tequila, whisky, vodka, ron y ginebra	40%
Frutsis, chaparritas, pau pau y boing	0%

RIESGOS

- Cuando tomas alcohol hasta perderte, además de que todo mundo te va a traer de bajada (incluyendo a los mismos que te pusieron jarra) y que puedes terminar cantando "Oaxaca" en el baño, puedes ponerte en peligro. Esto sucede cuando consumes un buen y muy rápido.
- Si alguna vez te toca ver que un amigo o amiga está inconsciente por haberse intoxicado con alcohol y no lo pueden despertar o tiene dificultad para respirar, pide ayuda de inmediato y acuéstalo de lado. Una persona inconsciente puede ahogarse con su propio vómito.

- Tomar en exceso traiciona la memoria (aguas, no le vayas a decir a tu novio el nombre de tu ex), la atención, la capacidad de solucionar problemas, la concentración, la coordinación y el equilibrio. Así que ni de broma se te ocurra manejar. Si eres de las que les da miedo el alcoholímetro que en algunas ciudades opera, espérate a que te digamos algo que te va a dar mucho más miedo: en México, la causa número uno de muerte en adolescentes, es por manejar en estado de ebriedad. ¡Imagínate lo cañón del asunto!, para que te des una idea, de cuatro a seis chupes en una adolescente promedio, aumenta 50 veces el riesgo de un accidente en el coche. Así que háblale a tus papás, pide un taxi, que te lleve un amigo conocido, o quédate a dormir en casa de una amiga, pero ni de broma manejes ebria.
- También tomar en exceso puede causar falta de apetito (a menos que sean los jochos a la salida del antro), falta de vitaminas, problemas estomacales y de la piel, impotencia sexual, daño al hígado, al páncreas, al corazón y al sistema nervioso central.
- Además, piensa: ¿quién va a querer algo en serio con una niña borracha?

EN LA MUJER

- El alcohol se le sube más rápido a las mujeres que a los hombres; después de tomar la misma cantidad (por más que bailes más que ellos, ése no es pretexto), tu nivel de alcohol puede ser de 25 a 30 por ciento más alto, así que ni intentes competir o seguirles el paso a esas bestias. Esto sucede, en parte, porque las mujeres son más pequeñas y producen menos enzimas de las que metabolizan el alcohol.
- Las mujeres son más vulnerables a los efectos negativos del alcohol en el corto y largo plazo. Después de tomar la misma cantidad de alcohol que un hombre, la habilidad de ella para determinar el riesgo de una situación como

"¿Puedo manejar?", "¿Me debo acostar con él?", "¿Debe usar condón?", también baja, y un buen.

- Piensa que entre más alcohol consume una mujer, lamentablemente aumentan más las posibilidades de que sea violentada sexualmente.

- ¿Sabías que tomar puede causar daños serios y permanentes en un bebé que aún no nace? Si sospechas que estás embarazada, ¡no tomes ni de broma!

EN LA ADOLESCENCIA

- Como tu cerebro no acaba de desarrollarse sino hasta los 20 años, ¡aguas!, éste puede ser más vulnerable a los daños del alcohol que un cerebro bien formado.

RIESGOS GENÉTICOS

- Si tienes un papá o una mamá alcohólica, el riesgo de caer en el alcoholismo es mayor que el de alguien que no tiene ese problema en su familia. Si tienes un pariente cercano alcohólico es muy importante que tomes decisiones inteligentes respecto al alcohol, por más que hagas como que no lo conoces.

- Aunque no lo creas, en el fondo todos respetan a una persona que se atreve a ser ella misma y no sigue como borrego lo que los demás hacen.

- Toma buenas decisiones, no dejes que tus amigas o amigos te presionen para que tomes. Cuando tomas no pareces más grande, más sexy ni más madura: al contrario; dejar de tomar cuando tú crees adecuado, demuestra que eres una mujer inteligente. Y de eso nunca te arrepentirás.

- Si tienes broncas más serias con el alcohol o conoces a alguien con este problema y quieres ayudarlo, consulta las secciones "Una noticia buena y una mala" y "Mi amigo es adicto, ¿qué hago?".

CENTROS DE APOYO

OFICINA GENERAL DE
SERVICIOS DE GRUPO
24 HORAS AA
01(55)57-61-59-26
01(55)57-61-56-28

GRUPO JOVENES 24 HORAS AA
01(55)57-61-59-26
01(55)57-61-56-28

CENTROS DE INTEGRACIÓN
JUVENIL
01(55)52-12-12-12
cij@cij.gob.mx
www.cij.gob.mx

Drogas ilegales

"Necesito 20 tachas de las más fuertes que tengas, porfis, porque me voy a Vallarta con mis amigos," le digo al *dealer* cuando voy a verlo a su casa.

Son las 10 de la noche y estamos cinco amigos y yo, cada uno con su tacha en la mano, listos para meternoslas y echarnos a la alberca. Me meto la tacha a la boca y la trago con un vodka. Pasa media hora y no me hace efecto. Después supe que era por el alcohol. Yo fui quien las compró así que tengo el control y, sin que los demás se den cuenta, me tomo otra a ver si así ya me hace algo porque ellos están "puestos" y yo no; la neta, me da coraje.

¡Uf! Ahora sí ya me está pegando, veo como si estuvieran cayendo estrellas del cielo, mis ojos se mueven a mil por hora, las luces se ven súper brillantes y chiquitas. De pronto, me invade una sensación de completo bienestar.

Todo es tan lento y armónico. Qué a gusto me siento, ¡no lo puedo creer! Amo el universo, se esfumaron las broncas, las preocupaciones y las deudas. No quiero que esto termine nunca.

Necesito otra, ya pasó hora y media y el efecto también; ahora me voy a tomar dos para lograr un efecto doble. Sólo pienso en eso, en el efecto, no me importa lo que me pueda pasar; dicen que las tachas fríen el cerebro pero estoy de vacaciones con mis amigos, ¿qué puede suceder? Nada, a mí nunca me pasa nada.

Las cuatro de la mañana, llevo seis tachas y dos churros, me duele horrible la cabeza y tengo miedo de salirme de la alberca, estoy angustiada, paranoica, veo sombras que caminan, mis amigos ya se quieren ir a dormir y yo sólo pienso en tomarme otras dos o tres tachas para ver si así se me quita el miedo; sin embargo, sé que el miedo será mayor. De todas maneras me las tomo.

La cruda es de terror, tiemblo, me da una depresión horrible, ataques de pánico, convulsiones, paranoia y hasta pienso en el suicidio. *LAURA*

Laura está ahora en rehabilitación y tiene 27 años. Desde los 16 años se hizo adicta a todo tipo de drogas. Con una honestidad que agradecemos, ofrece su testimonio para prevenir a otros jóvenes de caer en esa promesa de paraíso transformada en una gran pesadilla, y que puede desembocar en la muerte.

LAS TACHAS

¿QUÉ SON?

También conocidas como éxtasis; son pastillas de una sustancia llamada metilenedioximetanfetamina, pero como no es trabalenguas, mejor MDMA. Pueden encontrarse en forma de cápsula o polvo. Se distribuyen en las fiestas, *raves*,

antros, o donde sea que vaya un dealer a buscar clientes. Pueden tener nombres de marcas, películas, automóviles, etcétera. Los *dealers* suelen adulterarlas o mezclarlas con otras sustancias, haciéndolas más peligrosas.

EFECTOS

Pueden pasar entre 30 minutos y dos horas antes de que empiece el efecto. El "viaje" dura entre dos y seis horas; te quita la pena y todo lo ves como que no hay bronca. Como provocan la apertura de los sentidos, aumentan la capacidad de recepción de manifestaciones artísticas como la música (o sea que vas a oir cada sonidito de una rola como si fueran campanadas de la catedral). A veces produce temblores, movimientos involuntarios de los ojos (así como si uno de ellos se fuera de vacaciones), pérdida de apetito, náusea y vómito.

RIESGOS

A la experiencia del "viaje" sigue el "bajón", una caída súper fuerte del estado de ánimo. Como el regreso a la realidad puede parecer muy duro, los consumidores quieren repetir el "viaje" lo antes posible. Los síntomas del "bajón" pueden durar días y hasta semanas. Meterle mucho o constantemente a las tachas ocasiona ataques de ansiedad y vértigo.

EXTRAS

Muchas veces, los *dealers* te regalan la primera tacha para que te enganches. Ni siquiera ellos saben lo que contienen; en algunas se ha encontrado hasta raticida. Si después de leer todo esto usas tachas, ahora sí que "tache".

LA MARIHUANA

¿QUÉ ES?

Es una planta conocida también como Cannabis (*índica* o *sativa*). Sus flores pueden fumarse o comerse (ihay hasta

pasteles y brownies de marihuana!). Su primo hermano es el hachís, que también se fuma.

EFECTOS

Quienes la consumen se sienten relajados, olvidan sus problemas y sufren cambios en la percepción. Parece que el tiempo pasa más rápido o más lento según su estado de ánimo. En dosis altas puede alterar el sentido de la vista y producir alucinaciones.

RIESGOS

Baja la capacidad de concentración y memorización. Puede detonar enfermedades cardiacas y mentales en personas propensas. Ten mucho cuidado porque su consumo durante el embarazo aumenta el riesgo de dar a luz bebés de bajo peso.

EXTRAS

Hay quienes defienden a la marihuana más que a su mamá: "Es menos dañina que el alcohol", "Está comprobado que no es tan adictiva", "Es verde y el verde es vida". En fin, quien la consume va a decir cualquier cosa con tal de seguir haciéndolo. Pero aguas: un estudio sobre farmacodependencia realizado en México reveló que 36.4 por ciento de las personas que consumen drogas empezó con marihuana (y casi 100 por ciento con el alcohol).

LA COCAÍNA

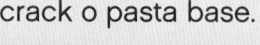

¿QUÉ ES?

Es un polvo blanco extraído de la planta de coca. Habitualmente se inhala, aunque se puede inyectar o fumar. En este último caso se utiliza un derivado de la coca llamado crack o pasta base.

EFECTOS

El "viaje" es muy breve: dura entre 20 y 40 minutos, y si se fuma, alrededor de 15 minutos. Por eso, muchos consumidores quieren de volada otro "pericazo". Las sensaciones que produce son bienestar, falta de apetito, excitación sexual y euforia.

RIESGOS

Uno de los principales es que es súper adictiva. Los que usan cocaína tienen muchos problemas para abandonarla. La que se vende en la calle suele ser impura y más peligrosa: si se inyecta puede causar la muerte. Su inhalación ocasiona padecimientos nasales, mientras que fumar crack origina problemas de respiración. Puede provocar aceleración del ritmo cardiaco, ansiedad, mareo, paranoia y náuseas, así como conductas violentas (o sea que te pones medio loco) y hasta males psiquiátricos irreversibles.

EXTRAS

Los estudios revelan que inhalar cocaína durante el embarazo aumenta el riesgo de aborto y de nacimiento prematuro. También que sus efectos pueden transmitirse al bebé durante la lactancia, lo que le provoca irritabilidad y falta de apetito.

LAS ANFETAMINAS

¿QUÉ SON?

Son estimulantes físicos y mentales que se utilizan en tratamientos médicos pero pueden conseguirse de manera ilegal. Suelen encontrarse en forma de tabletas y cápsulas, aunque líquidas pueden inyectarse (si ves a alguien tratando de inyectarse una tableta, ¡es porque trae muy mal viaje!).

A las anfetaminas, metanfetaminas y otros estimulantes de estructura química parecida se les conoce también como *speed*.

EFECTOS

Las anfetaminas son de las drogas más peligrosas. Te sientes bien por momentos, se te quita el hambre y el sueño, sientes reseca la garganta, se te dilatan las pupilas y pierdes coordinación. Otras reacciones negativas son: paranoia, dolor de cabeza, taquicardia, diarrea, vértigo, mareos, temblores, impotencia sexual. En dosis altas pueden provocar convulsiones.

RIESGOS

Su consumo frecuente puede provocar malnutrición severa y daños cerebrales irreparables que afectan la capacidad de hablar y pensar. Quienes la consumen necesitan poco a poco dosis más altas para obtener los efectos deseados.

EXTRAS

Es posible que los hijos de mamás que consumen anfetaminas nazcan con defectos cardiacos, paladar hendido y otros problemas. La sobredosis puede provocar estado de coma o muerte.

LAS METANFETAMINAS

¿QUÉ SON?

Son estimulantes sintéticos también conocidos como speed, cristal, etcétera. Al igual que las anfetaminas, se recetan para uso médico pero se consumen ilegalmente. Se encuentran en forma de polvo blanco de sabor amargo, en pastillas, cápsulas o "cristales". Habitualmente se inhalan, aunque a veces se comen, fuman o inyectan.

EFECTOS

El "viaje" de metanfetaminas es del tipo de las anfetaminas. Generan un estado de alerta y euforia, y a veces tienen efecto relajante. Incrementan la presión sanguínea y la temperatura de tu cuerpo, además provocan taquicardia.

RIESGOS

El consumo frecuente puede producir lo que se le conoce como "psicosis anfetamínica", o sea que puedes sufrir paranoia, alucinaciones visuales y auditivas, irritabilidad, falta de sueño y comportamiento errático y agresivo. Las metanfetaminas causan habituación psicológica y tolerancia; son súper peligrosas, ya que sus consumidores pueden tener ataques de ansiedad por falta de la droga y, al mismo tiempo, necesitar dosis más altas.

EXTRAS

Pueden afectar gruesísimo a personas con problemas cardiacos como hipertensión. Si se consumen durante el embarazo, el bebé puede nacer con problemas del corazón.

OTRAS DROGAS

Otras sustancias con las que debes tener cuidado son los opiáceos, derivados de la amapola. A diferencia de las anteriores, éstas son analgésicos y depresores del sistema nervioso. Entre ellas están la heroína y la morfina.

Nunca va a faltar gente que te ofrezca drogas ni oportunidades para tomarlas. La mejor forma de cuidarte es ponerte súper buza: el mejor escudo contra las drogas eres tú.

Mi amigo es adicto, ¿qué hago?

Hacer que un amigo/a acepte su adicción es uno de los pasos más importantes y difíciles (sobre todo si es mega necio). Muchas veces no están preparados para aceptarlo. Tristemente, deben tocar fondo y darse cuenta por sí mismos.

En este caso, lo mejor es que le hagas saber que estás súper consciente de su adicción. Lo más probable es que no quiera saber de ti, al grado de que hasta quiera borrarte de su celular; no te preocupes, es normal.

Algo que parece horrible pero tienes que hacer, es comentarle a su familia sobre su adicción. La familia tendrá que trabajar el problema y buscar ayuda.

Ayúdalo al no ayudarlo

En caso de que tu amiga o amigo no reconozca su adicción, la mejor ayuda que pueden darle tú y su familia es dejarlo vivir las consecuencias de sus actos sin intentar salvarlo con acciones que lo perjudican, como prestarle dinero, sacarlo de problemas legales, encubrirlo, permitir que duerma en tu casa cuando se encuentra mal o tiene problemas familiares y cosas por el estilo. Aunque esto no significa que te valga lo que hace.

Una vez que toque fondo y reconozca su enfermedad, probablemente aceptará su adicción. Éste será el momento perfecto para buscar apoyo en una clínica, grupo de ayuda mutua u organización especializada.

Muchas veces los familiares o amigos son coodependientes del adicto, o sea "adictos al adicto", lo que significa que por lástima o amor, inconscientemente, lo ayudan a que no enfrente sus problemas y siga en drogas. En este caso es importante que la familia asista a un grupo de ayuda para resolver este problema.

Por otro lado, muchas personas no enfrentan la enfermedad de sus amigos, por miedo a perderlos. Al contrario, tienes una oportunidad de oro, porque cuando tu amiga o amigo se recupere, va a saber que de todos los que consideraba sus amigos, tú eras la única verdadera, la que realmente lo ayudó y eso los unirá para siempre.

Recuerda que sacarle la vuelta a una bronca como ésta es lo más sencillo; aplicarse y ayudar a alguien que tenga este problema sólo lo hace una verdadera amiga.

CENTROS DE APOYO

MONTE FÉNIX
01(55)56-81-30-11

CLÍNICAS CLAIDER
01(55)56-82-45-00

LA QUINTA SANTA MARÍA
01(779) 79-60-506

CENTRO DE INTEGRACIÓN JUVENIL
01(55)52-12-12-12
cij@cij.gob.mx
www.cij.gob.mx

CONSEJO NACIONAL CONTRA LAS ADICCIONES (CONADIC)
01-800-911-20-00

HACIENDA DEL LAGO
01-800-713-7144

CLÍNICA LA ESPERANZA
01(477)77-26-100-02

CENTRO DE ATENCIÓN ESPECIALIZADO EN DROGODEPENDENCIA
01(55)56-74-91-12

FUNDACIÓN SAN JUAN
01(55)55-30-46-15
oficinacentral@drogadictosanonimos.org
secretarianacional@drogadictosanonimos.org

**DONDE LOS MONSTRUOS
MÁS HORRIBLES
DESCANSAN EN PAZ**

**Escribe los nombres de tus ex
con la fecha cuando comenzaron
y terminaron de andar**

SI QUIERES PONLES UN BREVE EPITAFIO

R.I.P.

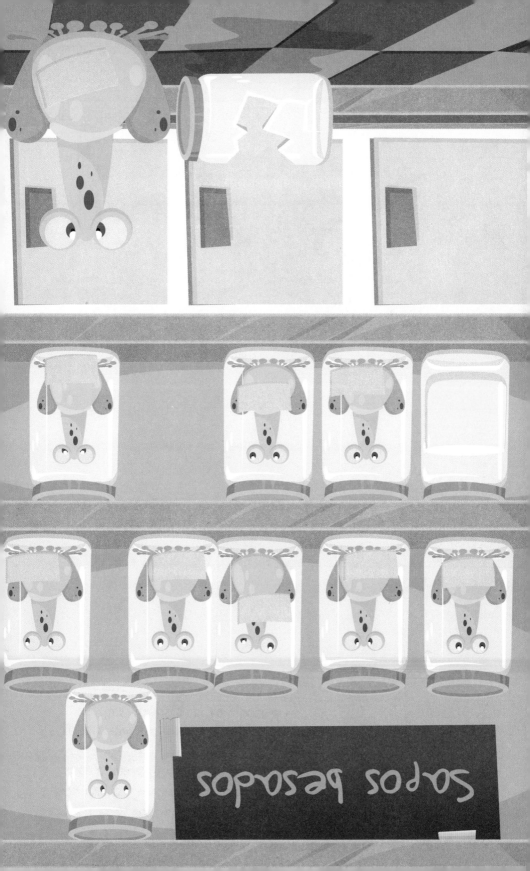

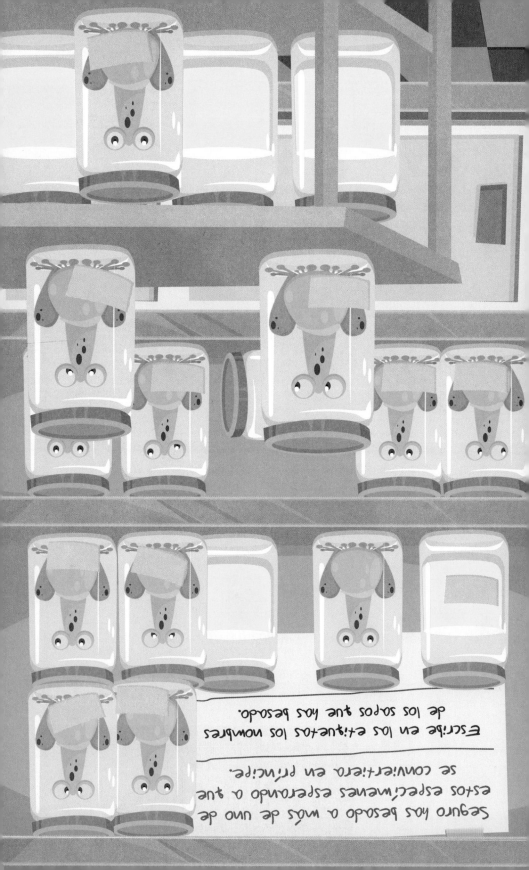

Seguro has pesado a más de uno de estos especímenes esperando a que se convirtiera en príncipe.

Escribe en los etiquetas los nombres de los sapos que has pesado.

CONCLUSIONES

Después de tantos *Quiúbole con...* tanto a ti como a nosotros nos queda súper claro que ser joven es muy divertido, pero no es tan fácil como mucha gente cree; son miles de cosas las que debes saber, decidir y enfrentar.

Esperamos que a lo largo de estas páginas te hayas reído, ligado a un galán (o mejor a varios), sentido más segura de ti misma, tronado al niño que no te late y que el descubrimiento de tu sexualidad haya sido una feliz y divertida experiencia.

Nuestro propósito es que *Quiúbole con...* sea un libro útil que te invite a analizar y discutir tus cambios físicos y emocionales. Sobre todo, debe ser tu cómplice, tu gran amigo que puedes consultar cuando lo desees.

Posiblemente no querías saber todo lo que leíste. Sin embargo, recuerda que un amigo que te quiere siempre te dice la verdad.

Lo que más deseamos es que con esta información disfrutes increíblemente esta etapa, que pasa más rápido de lo que crees y no se repetirá jamás en tu vida. Nadie más que tú puede decidir cómo será...

Así que, ¡goza, cuídate y disfruta al mil por ciento la vida!

Gaby y
Yordi

DEDICATORIA
GABY

Para Diego, Pablo, Toño,
Emilio, Nicolás, Pablito,
Valentina y Mateo:
gracias por enseñarme
a vivir y a disfrutar
el instante...

Gaby

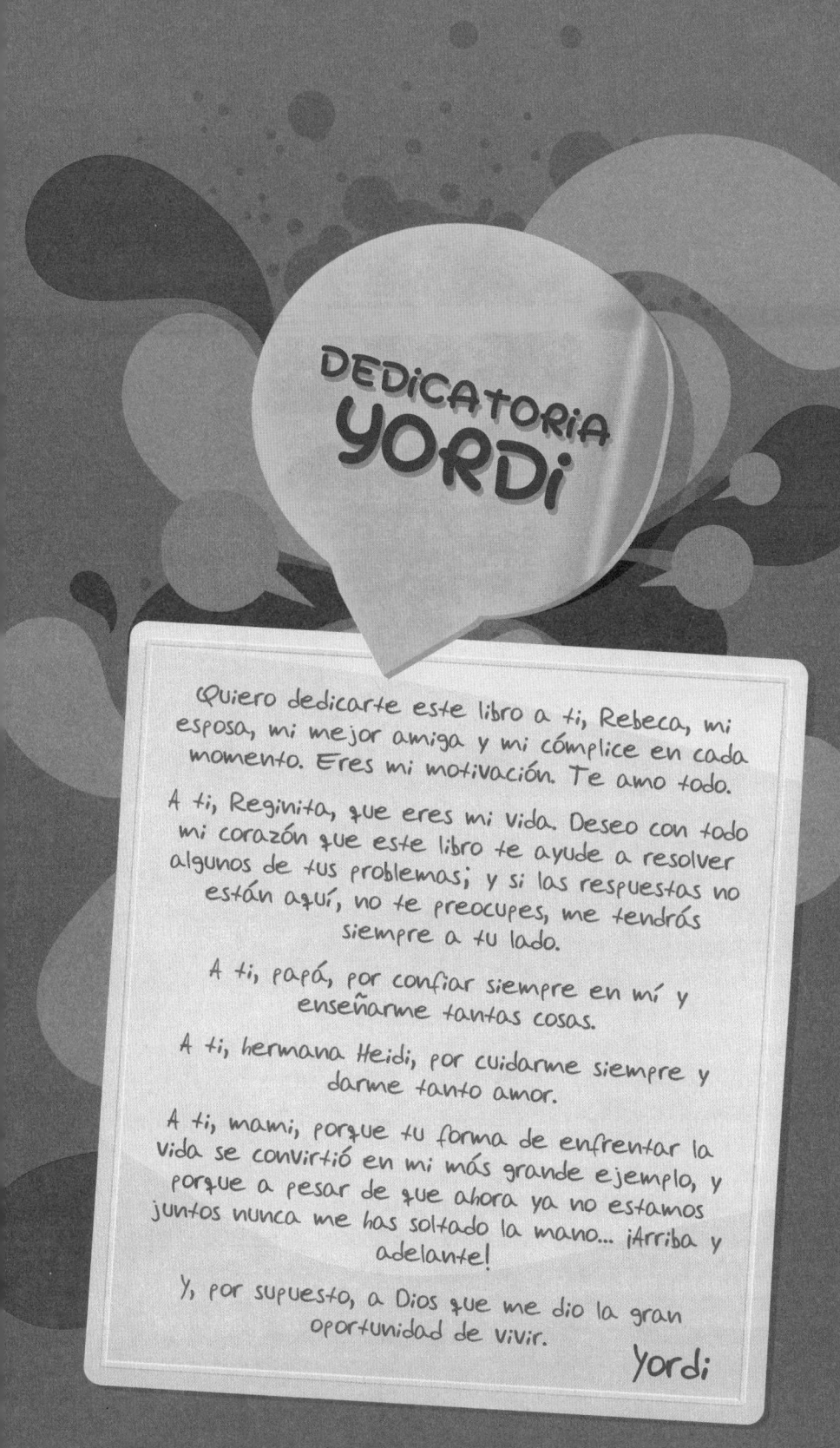

DEDICATORIA
YORDi

Quiero dedicarte este libro a ti, Rebeca, mi esposa, mi mejor amiga y mi cómplice en cada momento. Eres mi motivación. Te amo todo.

A ti, Reginita, que eres mi vida. Deseo con todo mi corazón que este libro te ayude a resolver algunos de tus problemas; y si las respuestas no están aquí, no te preocupes, me tendrás siempre a tu lado.

A ti, papá, por confiar siempre en mí y enseñarme tantas cosas.

A ti, hermana Heidi, por cuidarme siempre y darme tanto amor.

A ti, mami, porque tu forma de enfrentar la vida se convirtió en mi más grande ejemplo, y porque a pesar de que ahora ya no estamos juntos nunca me has soltado la mano... ¡Arriba y adelante!

Y, por supuesto, a Dios que me dio la gran oportunidad de vivir.

Yordi

GRACIAS

GRACIAS

GRACIAS A
NUESTROS EDITORES Y DISEÑADOR:

Fernando Esteves
Patricia Mazón
César Ramos
Diana Barreiro
Juan Carlos Valdivia
Adriana Beltrán
Orfa Alarcón
Dení Rico
Christian Michel
Infección Visual

No tenemos palabras para agradecerles todo su empeño, pasión y trabajo. Un millón de gracias por convertir lo que ya era GRANDE en algo GIGANTE.

A los expertos, por compartir sus conocimientos con nosotros:

Dr. Francisco R. de la Peña Olvera
Dr. Ramón Castro
Dr. Alfonso Castro
Dra. Julia Borbolla
Dr. Martín Tellich Vidal
Dra. María Esther Martínez Eroza
Dr. Luis Alfonso Reyes
Psic. Pilar del Olmo
Dr. Miguel Ortíz Monasterio
Dr. Gustavo Reyes Terán
Lic. Federico Cabrera
Dra. Adriana López García
Dr. Marco Antonio Pérez Cisneros
Dr. Manuel Sánchez Carmona
Dra. Kayros Vega
Dra. Connie Moreno
Dra. Laura Elliot R.
Dra. Guillermina Mejía
Francisco Ramos
Sra. Irma Miriam Jelinek de Anhalt
Luis Perelman
Lic. Alice Sutton
Psic. Pedro Sánchez
Luis Manuel Arellano
Gabriela Cámara
Patricia Moctezuma
Dra. Natalia Aguilar
Dr. Ramón Castro Vilchis
Dra. María Enriqueta Gómez
Dra. Atala Medina
Lic. Carlos M. Ochoa Sánchez
Dra. Marcela Ruelas
Dra. Perla Tavachnick
Lic. Irene Torices
Dr. Jorge Villavicencio
Andrea Vargas
Monte Fénix
FISAC
Eating Disorders México
Avalón

many, many, many thanks to:

Dr. Francisco R. de la Peña Olvera
Dr. Ramón Castro
Dr. Alfonso Castro
Dr. Julia Borbolla
Dr. Martín Tellich Vidal
Dr. María Esther Martínez Eroza
Dr. Luis Alfonso Reyes
Psic. Pilar del Olmo
Dr. Miguel Ortíz Monasterio
Dr. Gustavo Reyes Terán
Federico Cabrera
Dr. Adriana López García
Dr. Marco Antonio Pérez Cisneros
Dr. Manuel Sánchez Carmona
Dr. Kayros Vega
Dr. Connie Moreno
Dr. Laura Elliot R.
Dr. Guillermina Mejía
Francisco Ramos
Irma Miriam Jelinek de Anhalt
Luis Perelman
Alice Sutton
Psic. Pedro Sánchez
Luis Manuel Arellano
Gabriela Cámara
Patricia Moctezuma
Dr. Natalia Aguilar
Dr. Ramón Castro Vilchis
Dr. María Enriqueta Gómez
Dr. Atala Medina
Carlos M. Ochoa Sánchez
Dr. Marcela Ruelas
Dr. Perla Tavachnick
Irene Torices
Dr. Jorge Villavicencio
Andrea Vargas
Monte Fénix
FISAC
Eating Disorders México
Avalón

THANKS
THANKS
THANKS TO:

Fernando Esteves
Patricia Mazón
César Ramos
Diana Barreiro
Juan Carlos Valdivia
Adriana Beltrán
Orfa Alarcón
Dení Rico
Christian Michel
Infección Visual

There aren't enough words to thank you for all your drive, passion and hardwork. A million times "thank you", for turning something big into something extraordinary.

Dedication
YORDI

I want to dedicate this book to you, Rebeca, my wife, my best friend and my accomplice in each and every moment.

You are my motivation.

I love every bit of you.

To you, little Regina, you are my life. It is my deepest wish that this book helps you solve some of your problems, but, should the answers were not to be found in here, do not worry, you'll have me by your side.

To you, dad, for always trusting me and for teaching me so many things.

To Heidi, my sister, for always taking good care of me and for giving me so much love.

To you, mommy, because the way you face life became the greatest of examples. And even though we're not together anymore, you've never let me alone. Come on! Let's go!

And, of course, to God, who gave me the great opportunity to live.

Yordi

Dedication
GABY

To Diego, Pablo, Toño, Emilio, Nicolás, Pablito, Valentina and Mateo: thank you for teaching me how to live and enjoy every moment.

Gaby

Gaby Vargas is an entrepreneur, speaker, image consultant and author; she is also a wife and mother of three. She has sold more than two million copies of her self-help, image, protocol and well-being books—which include more than thirteen titles. She collaborates in more than thirty media in Mexico and Latin America.

CONCLUSION

After going through so many *What's up with...* in this book, both you and us can come to the conclusion that being young is a real joy. It's not as easy as lots of people would have us believe. There are thousands of things that you need to know before you can make intelligent decisions.

We hope that this book has made you laugh and feel more confident. We also hope you've had a chance to flirt with a guy —or lots of guys, to break up with the one you didn't like and to discover yourself in a fun, open and mature way as you read through these pages.

Our purpose when writing *What's up with...* was to create a useful book that inspires your own interest in analyzing and discussing the changes you're going through—both physically and emotionally. Moreover, we hope our book can be your accomplice: that good friend that you can consult whenever you wish.

Chances are this book contains some stuff you didn't really want to know. "Too Much Information!" But just remember that any friend who really cares for you is going to tell you the truth.

Most of all, we hope the information in this book will be helpful in making your teenage years as happy and invigorating as they should be—because you deserve it. It all goes by pretty quickly, and your teenage years won't ever happen again. No one except you can decide how they're going to end up.

So have fun, take care, and enjoy life 1000 percent!

Gaby &
Yordi